GENESIS

ALSO BY ROBERT ALTER

GENESIS

*TRANSLATION AND
COMMENTARY*

ROBERT
ALTER

W · W · *NORTON* & *COMPANY*

NEW YORK *LONDON*

Copyright © 1996 by Robert Alter

For information about permission to reproduce selections from this book,
write to Permissions, W. W. Norton & Company, Inc.,
500 Fifth Avenue, New York, NY 10110.

The text of this book is composed in 11/14.5 and 10/12 Fairfield LH Light
with the display set in Bodega Serif Light
Composition and manufacturing by the Maple-Vail Book Manufacturing Group.
Book design by Margaret M. Wagner

Library of Congress Cataloging-in-Publication Data
Bible. O.T. Genesis. English. Alter. 1996.
Genesis / translation and commentary by Robert Alter.
p.   cm.
Includes bibliographical references and index.
ISBN 0-393-03981-1
1. Bible O.T. Genesis—Commentaries.   I. Alter, Robert.
II. Title.
BS1233.A78   1996
222'.11077—dc20   96–4188
CIP

W. W. Norton & Company, Inc.
500 Fifth Avenue, New York, N.Y. 10110
http://web.wwnorton.com

W. W. Norton & Company Ltd.
10 Coptic Street, London WC1A 1PU

1 2 3 4 5 6 7 8 9 0

In Memory of Amos Funkenstein

$(1937–1995)$

a great scholar

a kind and generous friend

חבל על דאבדין ולא משתכחין

TO THE READER

I. THE BIBLE IN ENGLISH AND THE HERESY OF EXPLANATION

Why, after so many English versions, a new translation of Genesis? There is, as I shall explain in detail, something seriously wrong with all the familiar English translations, traditional and recent, of the Hebrew Bible. Broadly speaking, one may say that in the case of the modern versions, the problem is a shaky sense of English and in the case of the King James Version, a shaky sense of Hebrew. The present translation of Genesis is an experiment in re-presenting the Bible—and, above all, biblical narrative prose—in a language that conveys with some precision the semantic nuances and the lively orchestration of literary effects of the Hebrew and at the same time has stylistic and rhythmic integrity as literary English. I shall presently give a more specific account of the kind of English I have aimed for and of the features of the Hebrew that have prompted my choices, but I think it will be helpful for me to say something first about why English translations of the Bible have been problematic—more problematic, perhaps, than most readers may realize.

It is an old and in some ways unfair cliché to say that translation is always a betrayal, but modern English versions of the Bible provide unfortunately persuasive evidence for that uncompromising generalization. At first thought, it is rather puzzling that this should be the case. In purely quantitative terms, we live in a great age of Bible translation. Several integral translations of the Bible have been done since the middle of the twentieth century, and a spate of English versions of individual biblical books has appeared. This period, moreover, is one in which our understanding of ancient Hebrew has become considerably more nuanced and precise than it once was, thanks to comparative Semitic philology aided by archeology, and also thanks to the careful reanalysis of the formal structures—syntax, grammar, morphology, verb tenses—of biblical Hebrew. One might have expected that this recent flurry of translation activity, informed by the newly focused awareness of the meanings of biblical Hebrew, would have produced at least some English versions that would be both vividly precise and closer to the feel of the original than any of the older translations. Instead, the modern English versions—especially in their treatment of Hebrew narrative prose—have placed readers at a grotesque distance from the distinctive literary experience of the Bible in its original language. As a consequence, the King James Version, as Gerald Hammond, an eminent British authority on Bible translations, has convincingly argued, remains the closest approach for English readers to the original—despite its frequent and at times embarrassing inaccuracies, despite its archaisms, and despite its insistent substitution of Renaissance English tonalities and rhythms for biblical ones.

Some observers have sought to explain the inadequacy of modern Bible translations in terms of the general decline of the English language. It is certainly true that there are far fewer people these days with a cultivated sensitivity to the expressive resources of the language, the nuances of lexical values, the force of metaphor and rhythm; and one is certainly much less likely to find such people on a committee of ecclesiastical or scholarly experts than one would have in the first decade of the seventeenth century. There are, nevertheless, still some brilliant stylists among English prose writers; and if our age has been graced with remarkable translations of Homer, Sophocles, and Dante, why not of the Bible?

Part of the explanation, I suspect, is in the conjunction of philological scholarship and translation. I intend no churlish disrespect to philology. On the contrary, without it, our reading of the Bible, or indeed of any older text, is no better than walking through a great museum on a very gloomy day with all the lights turned out. To read the Bible over the shoulder of a great philological critic, like Abraham ibn Ezra (1092–1167), one of the earliest and still eminently worth studying, is to see many important things in fine focus for the first time. There is,

however, a crucial difference between philology as a tool for understanding literary texts and philology as an end in itself, for literature
and philology work with extremely different conceptions of what constitutes knowledge. To be fair to the broad enterprise of philology,
which has included some great literary critics, I use the term here as
shorthand for "biblical philology," a discipline that, especially in its
Anglo-American applications, has often come down to lexicography
and the analysis of grammar.

For the philologist, the great goal is the achievement of clarity. It is
scarcely necessary to say that in all sorts of important, but also
delimited, ways clarity is indispensable in a translator's wrestling with
the original text. The simplest case, but a pervasive one, consists of
getting a handle on the meaning of particular terms. It is truly helpful,
for example, to know that biblical *naḥal** most commonly indicates
not any sort of brook, creek, or stream but the kind of freshet, called
a *wadi* in both Arabic and modern Hebrew, that floods a dry desert
gulch during the rainy months and vanishes in the heat of the summer.
Suddenly, Job's "my brothers have betrayed like a *naḥal*" (6:14)
becomes a striking poetic image, where before it might have been a
minor puzzlement. But philological clarity in literary texts can quickly
turn into too much of a good thing. Literature in general, and the
narrative prose of the Hebrew Bible in particular, cultivates certain
profound and haunting enigmas, delights in leaving its audiences
guessing about motives and connections, and, above all, loves to set
ambiguities of word choice and image against one another in an end-
less interplay that resists neat resolution. In polar contrast, the
impulse of the philologist is—here a barbarous term nicely catches
the tenor of the activity—"to disambiguate" the terms of the text. The
general result when applied to translation is to reduce, simplify, and
denature the Bible. These unfortunate consequences are all the more
pronounced when the philologist, however acutely trained in that discipline, has an underdeveloped sense of literary diction, rhythm, and
the uses of figurative language; and that, alas, is often the case in an

---

*The symbol ḥ represents the Hebrew consonant *ḥet*, a light fricative that sounds something
like j in Spanish.

era in which literary culture is not widely disseminated even among the technically educated.

The unacknowledged heresy underlying most modern English versions of the Bible is the use of translation as a vehicle for *explaining* the Bible instead of representing it in another language, and in the most egregious instances this amounts to explaining away the Bible. This impulse may be attributed not only to a rather reduced sense of the philological enterprise but also to a feeling that the Bible, because of its canonical status, has to be made accessible—indeed, transparent—to all. (The one signal exception to all these generalizations is Everett Fox's 1995 American version of the Torah. Emulating the model of the German translation by Martin Buber and Franz Rosenzweig [begun in 1925, completed in 1961], which flaunts Hebrew etymologies, preserves nearly all repetitions of Hebrew terms, and invents German words, Fox goes to the opposite extreme: his English has the great virtue of reminding us verse after verse of the strangeness of the Hebrew original, but it does so at the cost of often being not quite English and consequently of becoming a text for study rather than a fluently readable version that conveys the stylistic poise and power of the Hebrew.) Modern translators, in their zeal to uncover the meanings of the biblical text for the instruction of a modern readership, frequently lose sight of how the text intimates its meanings—the distinctive, artfully deployed features of ancient Hebrew prose and poetry that are the instruments for the articulation of all meaning, message, insight, and vision.

One of the most salient characteristics of biblical Hebrew is its extraordinary concreteness, manifested especially in a fondness for images rooted in the human body. The general predisposition of modern translators is to convert most of this concrete language into more abstract terms that have the purported advantage of clarity but turn the pungency of the original into stale paraphrase. A good deal of this concrete biblical language based on the body is what a linguist would call lexicalized metaphor—imagery, here taken from body parts and bodily functions, that is made to stand for some general concept as a fixed item in the vocabulary of the language (as "eye" in English can be used to mean "perceptiveness" or "connoisseur's understanding").

Dead metaphors, however, are the one persuasive instance of the resurrection of the dead—for at least the ghosts of the old concrete meanings float over the supposedly abstract acceptations of the terms, and this is something the philologically driven translators do not appear to understand. "Many modern versions," Gerald Hammond tartly observes, "eschew anything which smacks of imagery or metaphor—based on the curious assumption, I guess, that modern English is an image-free language." The price paid for this avoidance of the metaphorical will become evident by considering two characteristic and recurrent Hebrew terms and the role they play in representing the world in the biblical story.

The Hebrew noun *zera*ʿ* has the general meaning of "seed," which can be applied either in the agricultural sense or to human beings, as the term for semen. By metaphorical extension, semen becomes the established designation for what it produces, progeny. Modern translators, evidently unwilling to trust the ability of adult readers to understand that "seed"—as regularly in the King James Version—may mean progeny, repeatedly render it as offspring, descendants, heirs, progeny, posterity. But I think there is convincing evidence in the texts themselves that the biblical writers never entirely forgot that their term for offspring also meant semen and had a precise equivalent in the vegetable world. To cite a distinctly physical example, when Onan "knew that the seed would not be his," that is, the progeny of his brother's widow should he impregnate her, "he would waste his seed on the ground, so to give no seed to his brother" (38:9). Modern translators, despite their discomfort with body terms, can scarcely avoid the wasted "seed" here because without it the representation of spilling semen on the ground in coitus interruptus becomes unintelligible. E. A. Speiser substitutes "offspring" for "seed" at the end of the verse, however, and the Revised English Bible goes him one better by putting "offspring" at the beginning as well ("Onan knew that the offspring would not count as his") and introducing "seed" in the middle as

---

* The symbol ʿ represents the Hebrew consonant ʿ*ayin*, a glottal stop that might sound something like the Cockney pronunciation of the middle consonant of "bottle," in which the dentalized *t* is replaced by a gulping sound produced from the larynx.

object of the verb "to spill" and scuttling back to the decorousness of "offspring" at the end—a prime instance of explanation under the guise of translation. But the biblical writer is referring to "seed" as much at the end of the verse as at the beginning. Onan adopts the strategem of coitus interruptus in order not to "give seed"—that is, semen—to Tamar, and, as a necessary consequence of this contraceptive act, he avoids providing her with offspring. The thematic point of this moment, anchored in sexual practice, law, and human interaction, is blunted by not preserving "seed" throughout.

Even in contexts not directly related to sexuality, the concreteness of this term often amplifies the meaning of the utterance. When, for example, at the end of the story of the binding of Isaac, God reiterates His promise to Abraham, the multiplication of seed is strongly linked with cosmic imagery—harking back to the Creation story—of heaven and earth: "I will greatly bless you and will greatly multiply your seed, as the stars in the heavens and as the sand on the shore of the sea" (22:17). If "seed" here is rendered as "offspring" or "descendants," what we get are two essentially mathematical similes of numerical increase. That is, in fact, the primary burden of the language God addresses to Abraham, but as figurative language it also imposes itself visually on the retina of the imagination, and so underlying the idea of a single lateborn son whose progeny will be countless millions is an image of human seed (perhaps reinforced by the shared white color of semen and stars) scattered across the vast expanses of the starry skies and through the innumerable particles of sand on the shore of the sea. To substitute offspring for seed here may not fundamentally alter the meaning but it diminishes the vividness of the statement, making it just a little harder for readers to sense why these ancient texts have been so compelling down through the ages.

The most metaphorically extended body part in biblical Hebrew is the hand, though head and foot are also abundantly represented in figurative senses. Now it is obvious enough, given the equivalent usages in modern Western languages, that "hand" can be employed figuratively to express such notions as power, control, responsibility, and trust—to which biblical Hebrew adds one meaning peculiar to itself, commemorative monument. But most modern translators substitute one or another of these abstract terms, introducing supposed clarity where things were perfectly clear to begin with and subverting the literary integrity of the story. In the two sequential episodes that end with Joseph's being cast into a pit—the first is a dry cistern, the second an Egyptian prison, but the two are explicitly linked by the use of the term *bor* for both—the recurrently invoked "hand" is a focusing device that both defines and complicates the moral themes of the story. Reuben, hearing his brothers' murderous intentions, seeks to rescue Joseph "from their hands." He implores his brothers, "Lay not a hand upon him," just as, in the other strand of the story, Judah says, "Let not our hand be against him." E. A. Speiser, faithful to the clarifying impulse of the modern Bible scholar's philological imagination, renders both these phrases as "do away with," explaining that it would be illogical to have Reuben, or Judah, say "Don't lay a hand on him," since in fact the counsel proffered involves seizing him, stripping him, and throwing him into the pit. But in fact this alleged illogic is the luminous logic of the writer's moral critique. Reuben pleads with his brothers not to lay a hand on Joseph, that is, not to shed his blood (this is the phrase he uses at the beginning of his speech), but neither his plea nor Judah's proposal is an entirely innocent one: although each urges that the brothers lay no hand on Joseph, there is a violent laying on of hands necessitated by the course of action each proposes. Even more pointedly, once Joseph is headed south with the caravan, those same fraternal hands will take his ornamented tunic (the King James Version's "coat of many colors"), slaughter a kid, dip the garment in the blood, and send it off to Jacob.

The image of hands holding a garment belonging to Joseph that is turned into false evidence brilliantly returns at the climactic moment of the next episode involving him, in chapter 39. When Joseph flees from the lust of his master's wife, "he left his garment in her hand" because she has virtually torn it off his back in trying to effect her reiterated "Lie with me" by seizing him. In her accusation of Joseph, she alters the narrator's twice-stated "in her hand" to "by me," implying that he disrobed deliberately before attempting to rape her. But the narrator's cunning deployment of repeated terms has conditioned us to zero in on these two pivotal words, *waya'azov beyad,* "he left in the hand of," for in the six initial framing verses of the story, "hand" appears four times, with the last, most significant occurrence being this summary of the comprehensiveness of Joseph's stewardship: "And he left all that he had in Joseph's hands" (39:6). (Hebrew idiom allows the writer to use "hand" in the singular, thus creating an exact phrasal identity between the figurative reference to the hand in which the trust of stewardship is left and the literal reference to the hand in which the garment belonging to the object of sexual desire is left.) The invocation of "hand" in chapters 37 and 39—the story of Judah and Tamar lies between them—forms an elegant A B A B pattern: in chapter 37 hands are laid on Joseph, an action carried forward in the resumptive repetition at the very beginning of chapter 39 when he is bought "from the hands of the Ishmaelites"; then we have the supremely competent hand, or hands, of Joseph, into which everything is placed, or left, and by which everything succeeds; then again a violent hand is laid on Joseph, involving the stripping of his garment, as in the episode with the brothers; and at the end of the chapter, Joseph in prison again has everything entrusted to his dependable hands, with this key term twice stated in the three and a half verses of the closing frame. A kind of dialectic is created in the thematic unfolding of the story between hand as the agency of violent impulse and hand as the instrument of scrupulous management. Although the concrete term is probably used with more formal precision in this particular sequence than is usually the case elsewhere, the hands of Joseph and the hands upon Joseph provide a fine object lesson about how biblical narrative is misrepresented when translators tamper with the purposeful and insistent physicality of its language, as here when "hand" is transmuted into "trust" or "care." Such substitutions offer explanations or interpretations instead of translations and thus betray the original.

There are, alas, more pervasive ways than the choice of terms in which nearly all the modern English versions commit the heresy of explanation. The most global of these is the prevalent modern strategy of repackaging biblical syntax for an audience whose reading experience is assumed to be limited to *Time, Newsweek,* and the *New York*

Times or the *Times* of London. Now, it is often asserted, with seemingly self-evident justice, that the fundamental difference between biblical syntax and modern English syntax is between a system in which parallel clauses linked by "and" predominate (what linguists call "parataxis") and one in which the use of subordinate clauses and complex sentences predominates (what linguists call "hypotaxis"). Modern English has a broad array of modal and temporal discriminations in its system of verbs and a whole armament of subordinate conjunctions to stipulate different relations among clauses. Biblical Hebrew, on the other hand, has only two aspects* (they are probably not tenses in our sense) of verbs, together with one indication of a jussive mode—when a verb is used to express a desire or exhortation to perform the action in question—and a modest number of subordinate conjunctions. Although there are certainly instances of significant syntactic subordination, the characteristic biblical syntax is additive, working with parallel clauses linked by "and"—which in the Hebrew is not even a separate word but rather a particle, *waw*† (it means "hook"), that is prefixed to the first word of the clause.

The assumption of most modern translators has been that this sort of syntax will be either unintelligible or at least alienating to modern readers, and so should be entirely rearranged as modern English. There are two basic problems with this procedure. First, it ignores the fact that parataxis is the essential literary vehicle of biblical narrative: it is the way the ancient Hebrew writers saw the world, linked events in it, artfully ordered it, and narrated it, and one gets a very different world if their syntax is jettisoned. Second, rejection of biblical parataxis presupposes a very simplistic notion of what constitutes modern literary English. The implicit model seems to be, as I have suggested, the popular press, as well as perhaps high-school textbooks, bureaucratic directives, and ordinary conversation. But serious writers almost

---

* Instead of a clear-cut expression of the temporal frame in which actions occur—past, present, future, past perfect, and so forth—aspects indicate chiefly whether the action has been completed or is to be completed.

† The modern Hebrew pronunciation is *vav,* with the vowel sounding like the short *a* in a French word like *bave,* with which it would rhyme.

never accept such leveling limitation to a bland norm of popular usage. If one thinks of the great English stylists among twentieth-century novelists—writers like Joyce, Nabokov, Faulkner, and Virginia Woolf— there is not one among them whose use of language, including the deployment of syntax, even vaguely resembles the workaday simplicity and patly consistent orderliness that recent translators of the Bible have posited as the norm of modern English. It is also well to keep in mind that literary style, like many other aspects of literature, is constantly self-recapitulative, invoking recollections of its near and distant literary antecedents, so that modernists like Joyce and Faulkner sometimes echo biblical language and cadences, and a mannered stylist like Hemingway, in making "and" his most prominent connective, surely has the King James Version of the Bible in mind. And in any event, the broad history of both Semitic and European languages and literatures evinces a strong differentiation in most periods between everyday language and the language of literature.

The assumption of biblical philologists that parallel syntax is alien to modern literary English is belied by the persistent presence of highly wrought paratactic prose even at the end of the twentieth century. A variety of self-conscious English stylists in the modern era, from Gertrude Stein to Cormac McCarthy, have exhibited a fondness for chains of parallel utterances linked by "and" in which the basic sentence-type is the same structurally as that used again and again in biblical prose. What such a style makes manifest in a narrative is a series of more or less discrete events, or micro-events, in a chain, not unlike the biblical names of begetters and begotten that are strung one after another in the chains of the genealogical lists. The biblical writers generally chose not to order these events in ramified networks of causal, conceptual, or temporal subordination, not because hypotaxis was an unavailable option, as the opening verses of the second Creation story (2:4–5) clearly demonstrate. The continuing appeal, moreover, for writers in our own age of this syntax dominated by "and," which highlights the discrete event, suggests that parallel syntax may still be a perfectly viable way to represent in English the studied parallelism of verbs and clauses of ancient Hebrew narrative.

Since a literary style is composed of very small elements as well as larger structural features, an English translator must confront the pesky question of whether the ubiquitous Hebrew particle that means "and" should be represented at all in translation. This is obviously not a problem when the *waw* simply connects two nouns—as in "the heavens and the earth"—but what of its constant use at the beginning of sentences and clauses prefixed to verbs? The argument against translating it in these cases is that the primary function of the *waw* appended to a verb is not to signify "and" but to indicate that the Hebrew prefix conjugation, which otherwise is used for actions yet to be completed, is reporting past events (hence its designation in the terminology of classical Hebrew grammar as "the *waw* of conversion"). It is far from clear, as modern Bible scholars tend to assume, that the fulfillment of one linguistic function by a particle of speech automatically excludes any others; on the contrary, it is entirely likely that for the ancient audience the *waw* appended to the verb both converted its temporal aspect and continued to signify "and." But, semantics aside, the general practice of modern English translators of suppressing the "and" when it is attached to a verb has the effect of changing the tempo, rhythm, and construction of events in biblical narrative. Let me illustrate by quoting a narrative sequence from Genesis 24 first in my own version, which reproduces every "and" and every element of parataxis, and then in the version of the Revised English Bible. The Revised English Bible is in general one of the most compulsive repackagers of biblical language, though in this instance the reordering of the Hebrew is relatively minor. Its rendering of these sentences is roughly interchangeable with any of the other modern versions— the Jerusalem Bible, the New Jewish Publication Society, Speiser— one might choose. I begin in the middle of verse 16, where Rebekah becomes the subject of a series of actions.

. . . and she came down to the spring and filled her jug and came back up. And the servant ran toward her and said, "Pray, let me sip a bit of water from your jug." And she said, "Drink, my lord," and she hurried and tipped down her jug on one hand and let him drink. And she let him drink his fill and said, "For your camels, too, I shall draw water until they drink their fill." And she hurried and emptied her jug into the trough, and she ran again to the well to draw water and drew water for all his camels.

And this is how the Revised English Bible, in keeping with the prevailing assumptions of most recent translations, renders these verses in what is presumed to be sensible modern English:

> She went down to the spring, filled her jar, and came up again. Abraham's servant hurried to meet her and said, "Will you give me a little water from your jar?" "Please drink, sir," she answered, and at once lowered her jar on her hand to let him drink. When she had finished giving him a drink, she said, "I shall draw water also for your camels until they have had enough." She quickly emptied her jar into the water trough, and then hurrying again to the well she drew water and watered all the camels.

There is, as one would expect, some modification of biblical parataxis, though it is not so extreme here as elsewhere in the Revised English Bible: "And she let him drink his fill" is converted into an introductory adverbial clause, "When she had finished giving him a drink" (actually in consonance with the otherwise paratactic King James Version): "and she hurried" is compressed into "quickly"; "and she ran again" becomes the participial "hurrying again." (Moves of this sort, it should be said, push translation to the verge of paraphrase—recasting and interpreting the original instead of representing it.) The most striking divergence between these two versions is that mine has fifteen "and's," corresponding precisely to fifteen occurrences of the particle *waw* in the Hebrew, whereas the Revised English Bible manages with just five. What difference does this make? To begin with, it should be observed that the *waw*, whatever is claimed about its linguistic function, is by no means an inaudible element in the phonetics of the Hebrew text: we must keep constantly in mind that these narratives were composed to be *heard*, not merely to be decoded by a reader's eye. The reiterated "and," then, plays an important role in creating the rhythm of the story, in phonetically punctuating the forward-driving movement of the prose. The elimination of the "and" in the

Revised English Bible and in all its modern cousins produces—certainly to my ear—an abrupt, awkward effect in the sound pattern of the language, or to put it more strictly, a kind of narrative arrhythmia.

More is at stake here than pleasing sounds, for the heroine of the repeated actions is in fact subtly but significantly reduced in all the rhythmically deficient versions. She of course performs roughly the same acts in the different versions—politely offering water to the stranger, lowering her jug so that he can drink, rapidly going back and forth to the spring to bring water for the camels. But in the compressions, syntactical reorderings, and stop-and-start movements of the modernizing version, the encounter at the well and Rebekah's actions are made to seem rather matter-of-fact, however exemplary her impulse of hospitality. This tends to obscure what the Hebrew highlights, which is that she is doing something quite extraordinary. Rebekah at the well presents one of the rare biblical instances of the performance of an act of "Homeric" heroism. The servant begins by asking modestly to "sip a bit of water," as though all he wanted were to wet his lips. But we need to remember, as the ancient audience surely did, that a camel after a long desert journey can drink as much as twenty-five gallons of water, and there are ten camels here whom Rebekah offers to water "until they drink their fill." The chain of verbs tightly linked by all the "and's" does an admirable job in conveying this sense of the young woman's hurling herself with prodigious speed into the sequence of required actions. Even her dialogue is scarcely a pause in the narrative momentum, but is integrated syntactically and rhythmically into the chain: "And she said, 'Drink, my lord,' and she hurried and tipped down her jug. . . . And she hurried and emptied her jug into the trough, and she ran again to the well to draw water and drew water for all his camels." The parallel syntax and the barrage of "and's," far from being the reflex of a "primitive" language, are as artfully effective in furthering the ends of the narrative as any device one could find in a sophisticated modern novelist.

Beyond these issues of syntax and local word choice lies a fundamental question that no modern translator I know of has really confronted: what level, or perhaps levels, of style is represented in biblical Hebrew? There is no reason, I believe, to be awestruck by the sheer antiquity of the text. If biblical Hebrew could be shown to reflect a pungent colloquial usage in the ancient setting, or a free commingling of colloquial and formal language, it would be only logical to render it with equivalent levels of diction in modern English. As a matter of fact, all the modern translators—from Speiser to Fox to the sundry ecclesiastical committees in both America and England—have shown a deaf ear to diction, acting as though the only important considerations in rendering a literary text were lexical values and grammatical structures, while the English terms chosen could be promiscuously borrowed from boardroom or bedroom or scholar's word hoard, with little regard to the tonality and connotation the words carried with them from their native linguistic habitat.

Whatever conclusions we may draw about the stylistic level of biblical Hebrew are a little precarious because we of course have no record of the ancient spoken language, and if, as seems likely, there were extracanonical varieties or genres of Hebrew writing in the ancient world, the vestiges have long since crumbled into dust. Did, for example, the citizens of Judea in the time of Jeremiah speak in a parallel syntax, using the *waw* consecutive, and employing roughly the same vocabulary that we find in his prophecies, or in Deuteronomy and Genesis? Although there is no proof, my guess is that vernacular syntax and grammar probably differed in some ways from their literary counterparts. In regard to vocabulary, there is evidence that what we see in the canonical books would not have been identical with everyday usage. First, there is the problem of the relative paucity of vocabulary in biblical literature. As the Spanish Hebrew scholar Angel Sáenz-Badillos has observed in his *History of the Hebrew Language* (1993), the biblical lexicon is so restricted that it is hard to believe it could have served all the purposes of quotidian existence in a highly developed society. The instance of the poetry of Job, with its unusual number of words not found elsewhere in Scripture, is instructive in this regard: the Job-poet in his powerful impulse to forge a poetic imagery that would represent humankind, God, and nature in a new and even startling light, draws on highly specific language from manufacturing processes, food preparation, commercial and legal institutions, which would never be used in biblical narrative. The plausible conclusion is that the Hebrew of the Bible is a conventionally delimited language, roughly analogous in this respect to the French of the neoclassical theater: it was understood by writers and their audiences, at least in the case of narrative, that only certain words were appropriate for the literary rendering of events.

There is evidence, moreover, that people in everyday life may have had different words for many of the basic concepts and entities that are mentioned in the Bible. This argument was persuasively made by the Israeli linguist Abba Ben-David in his still indispensable 1967 study, available only in Hebrew, *The Language of the Bible and the Language of the Sages.* Ben-David offers a fascinating explanation for one of the great mysteries of the Hebrew language—the emergence, toward the end of the pre-Christian era, of a new kind of Hebrew, which became the language of the early rabbis. Now, it is widely recognized that this new Hebrew reflected the influence of the Aramaic vernacular in morphology, in grammar, and in some of its vocabulary, and that, understandably, it also incorporated a vast number of Greek and Latin loanwords. But what is puzzling is that rabbinic Hebrew also uses a good many indigenous Hebrew terms that are absent from the biblical corpus, or reflected only in rare and marginal biblical cognates. The standard terms in rabbinical Hebrew for sun and moon, and some of its frequently used verbs like to look, to take, to enter, to clean, are entirely different from their biblical counterparts, without visible influence from any of the languages impinging on Hebrew. Where did these words come from? Ben-David, observing, as have others before him, that there are incipient signs of an emergent rabbinic Hebrew in late biblical books like Jonah and the Song of Songs, makes the bold and, to my mind, convincing proposal that rabbinic Hebrew was built upon an ancient vernacular that for the most part had been excluded from the literary language used for the canonical texts. This makes particular sense if one keeps in mind that the early rabbis were anxious to draw a line between their own "Oral Torah" and the written Torah they were expounding. For the purposes of legal and homiletic exegesis, they naturally would have used a vernacular Hebrew rather than the literary language, and when their discourse was first given written formulation in the Mishnah in the early third century C.E., that text would have recorded this vernacular, which probably had a long prehistory in the biblical period. It is distinctly possible that when a ninth-century B.C.E. Israelite farmer mopped his brow under the blazing sun, he did not point to it and say *shemesh*, as it is invariably called in biblical prose texts, but rather *ḥamah*, as it is regularly designated in the Mishnah.

There is, of course, no way of plotting a clear chronology of the evolution of rabbinic Hebrew from an older vernacular, no way of determining how far back into the biblical period various elements of rabbinic language may go. It is sufficient for our effort to gauge the level of style of the Bible's literary prose merely to grant the very high likelihood that the language of the canonical texts was not identical with the vernacular, that it reflected a specialized or elevated vocabulary, and perhaps even a distinct grammar and syntax. Let me cite a momentary exception to the rule of biblical usage that may give us a glimpse into this excluded vernacular background of a more formal literary language. It is well known that in biblical dialogue all the characters speak proper literary Hebrew, with no intimations of slang, dialect, or idiolect. The single striking exception is impatient Esau's first speech to Jacob in Genesis 25: "Let me gulp down some of this red red stuff." Inarticulate with hunger, he cannot come up with the ordinary Hebrew term for "stew," and so he makes do with *ha'adom ha'adom** *hazeh*—literally "this red red." But what is more interesting for our purpose is the verb Esau uses for "feeding," *hal'iteini*. This is the sole occurrence of this verb in the biblical corpus, but in the Talmud it is a commonly used term with the specific meaning of stuffing food into the mouth of an animal. One cannot be certain this was its precise meaning in the biblical period because words do, after all, undergo semantic shifts in a period of considerably more than a thousand years. But it seems safe to assume, minimally, that even a millennium before the rabbis *hal'it* would have been a cruder term for feeding than the standard biblical *ha'akhil*. What I think happened at this point in Genesis is that the author, in the writerly zest with which he

---

* The symbol ' designates the Hebrew letter *'aleph*, perhaps once a lightly aspirated sound but now a "silent" letter.

sought to characterize Esau's crudeness, allowed himself, quite exceptionally, to introduce a vernacular term for coarse eating or animal feeding into the dialogue that would jibe nicely with his phrase, "this red red stuff." After the close of the biblical era, this otherwise excluded term would surface in the legal pronouncements of the rabbis on animal husbandry, together with a host of vernacular words used in the ancient period but never permitted to enter the canonical texts.

All this strongly suggests that the language of biblical narrative in its own time was stylized, decorous, dignified, and readily identified by its audiences as a language of literature, in certain ways distinct from the language of quotidian reality. The tricky complication, however, is that in most respects it also was not a lofty style, and was certainly neither ornate nor euphemistic. If some of its vocabulary may have reflected a specialized literary lexicon, the language of biblical narrative also makes abundant use of ordinary Hebrew words that must have been in everyone's mouth from day to day. Just to mention the few recurrent terms on which I have commented, "hand," "house," "all," and "seed" are primary words in every phase of the history of Hebrew, and they continue to appear as such in the rabbinic language, where so much else is altered. Biblical prose, then, is a formal literary language but also, paradoxically, a plainspoken one, and, moreover, a language that evinces a strong commitment to using a limited set of terms again and again, making an aesthetic virtue out of the repetition. It should be added that the language of the Bible reflects not one level of diction but a certain range of dictions, as I shall explain presently.

What is the implication of this analysis for an appropriate modern English equivalent to ancient Hebrew style? The right direction, I think, was hit on by the King James Version, following the great model of Tyndale a century before it. There is no good reason to render biblical Hebrew as contemporary English, either lexically or syntactically. This is not to suggest that the Bible should be represented as fussily old-fashioned English, but a limited degree of archaizing coloration is entirely appropriate, employed with other strategies for creating a language that is stylized yet simple and direct, free of the overtones of contemporary colloquial usage but with a certain timeless homespun quality. An adequate English version should be able to indicate the small but significant modulations in diction in the biblical language—something the stylistically uniform King James Version, however, entirely fails to do. A suitable English version should avoid at all costs the modern abomination of elegant synonymous variation, for the literary prose of the Bible turns everywhere on significant repetition, not variation. Similarly, the translation of terms on the basis of immediate context—except when it becomes grotesque to do otherwise—is to be resisted as another instance of the heresy of explanation. Finally, the mesmerizing effect of these ancient stories will scarcely be conveyed if they are not rendered in cadenced English prose that at least in some ways corresponds to the powerful cadences of the Hebrew. Let me now comment more particularly on the distinctive biblical treatment of diction, word choice, syntax, and rhythm and what it implies for translation.

The biblical prose writers favor what we may think of as a primary vocabulary. They revel in repetition, sometimes of a stately, refrainlike sort, sometimes deployed in ingenious patterns through which different meanings of the same term are played against one another. Elegant synonymity is alien to biblical prose, and it is only rarely that a highly specialized term is used instead of the more general word. Here is a characteristic biblical way of putting things: "And God made the two great lights, the great light for dominion of day and the small light for dominion of night, and the stars" (1:16). In addition to the poised emphasis of the internal repetitions in the sentence, one should note that the primary term for a source of light—*ma'or,* transparently cognate with *'or,* the light that is divided from the darkness in 1:4—is placed in the foreground. In fact, there are half a dozen biblical synonyms for "light," suggesting a range roughly equivalent to English terms like "illumination," "effulgence," "brilliance," and "splendor," but these are all reserved for the more elaborate vocabulary of poetry, whereas in prose the writer sticks to the simplicity of *'or* and *ma'or,* and everywhere it behooves a translator to do the same with English equivalents.

Some biblical scholars might object that my example is skewed because it is taken from the so-called Priestly source (P), which has a stylistic predilection for high decorousness and cadenced repetitions. But the stylistic difference in this regard between P and the two other conjectured source documents of Genesis, designated J and E, is one of degree, not kind. Thus, when the second version of the Creation story, commonly identified as J's, begins in 2:4, we do get some greater degree of specification in the language, in keeping with the way creation is here imagined. Instead of the verbs "to create" (*bara'*) and "to make" (*'asah*) that accompany God's speaking the world into being in chapter 1 we are given the potter's term "to fashion" (*yatsar*) and the architectural term "to build" (*banah*). These remain, however, within the limits of a primary vocabulary. The nuanced and specialized lexicon of manufacturing processes one encounters in the poetry of Job and of Deutero-Isaiah is firmly excluded from the stylistic horizon of this narrative prose, though the subject might have invited it.

The translator's task, then, is to mirror the repetitions as much as is feasible. Let me cite one small example, where I learned from my own mistake. When Joseph's brothers recount to Jacob what happened on their first trip to Egypt, they say, in the English of my first draft, "The man who is lord of the land spoke harshly to us and accused us of being spies in the land" (42:30). (The verb "accused" is also used in the New Jewish Publication Society translation.) On rereading, I realized that I had violated the cardinal principle, not to translate according to context. The Hebrew says, very literally, "gave us as spies," "give" in biblical usage being one of those all-purpose verbs that variously means "to set," "to place," "to grant," "to deem." I hastened to change the last clause to "made us out to be spies" because "to make," with or without an accompanying preposition, is precisely such a primary term that serves many purposes and so is very much in keeping with biblical stylistic practice.

What is surprising about the biblical writers' use of this deliberately limited vocabulary is that it can be so precise and even nuanced. Our own cultural preconceptions of writers scrupulously devoted to finding exactly the right word are associated with figures like Flaubert and Joyce, who meticulously choose the terms of their narratives from a large repertory of finely discriminated lexical items. Biblical prose often exhibits an analogous precision within the severe limits of its primary vocabulary. There are, for example, two paired terms, masculine and feminine, in biblical Hebrew to designate young people: *naʿar* / *naʿarah* (in this translation, "lad" and "young woman") and *yeled* / *yaldah* (in this translation, "child" and "girl"). The first pair is somewhat assymetrical because *naʿar* often also means "servant" or anyone in a subaltern position, and sometimes means "elite soldier," whereas *naʿarah* usually refers to a nubile young woman, and only occasionally to a servant girl. Though there are rare biblical occurrences of *yeled* in the sense of "young man," it generally designates someone younger than a *naʿar*—etymologically, it means "the one who is born," reflecting a development parallel to the French *enfant*.

With this little to work with, it is remarkable how much the biblical writers accomplish in their deployment of the terms. In the first part of the story of the banishment of Hagar and Ishmael (chapter 21), Ishmael is referred to consistently as "the child," as was his infant half brother Isaac at the beginning of this chapter. The grief-stricken mother in the wilderness says to herself, "Let me not see when the child dies." From the moment God speaks in the story (verse 17), Ishmael is invariably referred to as "the lad"—evidently with an intimation of tenderness but also with the suggestion that he is a young man, *naʿar,* who will go on to have a future. In the elaborately parallel episode in the next chapter that features Abraham and Isaac in the wilderness, Isaac is referred to by man and God as "the lad," and the term is played off against "the lads" who are Abraham's servants accompanying him on his journey, and not his flesh and blood ("And Abraham said to his lads, 'Sit you here with the donkey and let me and the lad walk ahead.' ").

In the story of the rape of Dinah (chapter 34), she is first referred to as "Leah's daughter"—and not Jacob's daughter, for it is Leah's sons, Simeon and Levi, who will exact vengeance for her. The initial designation of daughter aligns her with both "the daughters of the land" among whom she goes out to see, and Shechem, Hamor's son, ("son" and "daughter" are cognates in Hebrew), who sees her, takes her, and rapes her. After the act of violation, Shechem is overcome with love for Dinah, and he implores his father, "Take me this girl [*yaldah*] as wife." Speaking to his father, then, he identifies—tenderly?—the victim of his own lust as a girl-child. When he parlays with Dinah's brothers, asking permission to marry her, he says, "Give me the young woman [*na'arah*] as wife," now using the term for a nubile woman that is strictly appropriate to betrothal negotiations. After the brothers stipulate their surgical precondition for the betrothal, the narrator reports, "and the lad [*na'ar*] lost no time in doing the thing, for he wanted Jacob's daughter." Suddenly, as the catastrophe of this gruesome tale becomes imminent, we learn that the sexually impulsive man is only a lad, probably an adolescent like Dinah—a discovery that is bound to complicate our task of moral judgment. And now Dinah is called Jacob's daughter, not Leah's, probably because that is how Shechem sees her, not realizing that the significant relationship is through her mother to her two full brothers who are plotting a terrible retribution for her violation.

It should be clear from all this that a translation that respects the literary precision of the biblical story must strive to reproduce its nice discrimination of terms, and cannot be free to translate a word here one way and there another, for the sake of variety or for the sake of context. It must be admitted, however, that some compromises are inevitable because modern English clearly does not coincide semantically with ancient Hebrew in many respects. The stuff from which the first human is fashioned, for example, *'adamah,* manifestly means "soil," and it continues to have that meaning as it recurs at crucial junctures in the story of the Garden and the primordial banishment. But, alas, *'adamah* also means "land," "farmland," "country," and even "earth," and to translate it invariably as "soil" for the sake of terminological consistency (as Everett Fox does) leads to local confusions and conspicuous peculiarities. To take a more extreme example, a term that has no semantic analogue in English, the Hebrew *nefesh,* which the King James Version, following the Vulgate, often translates as "soul," refers to the breath of life in the nostrils of a living creature and, by extension, "lifeblood" or simply "life," and by another slide of association, "person"; and it is also used as an intensifying form of the personal pronoun, having roughly the sense of "very self." In the face of this bewildering diversity of meaning, one is compelled to abandon the admirable principle of lexical consistency and to translate, regretfully, according to immediate context.

Finally, though many recurring biblical terms have serviceable English equivalents (like "lad" for *na'ar*), there are instances in which a translation must make another kind of compromise because, given the differences between modern and biblical culture, the social, moral, and ideological connotations of terms in the two languages do not adequately correspond. Consider the tricky case of verbs for sexual intercourse. In English, these tend to be either clinical and technical, or rude, or bawdy, or euphemistic, and absolutely none of this is true of the verbs used for sex in the Bible. In Genesis, three different terms occur: "to know," "to lie with," and "to come into." "To know," with one striking antithetical exception, indicates sexual possession by a man of his legitimate spouse. Modern solutions such as "to be intimate with," "to cohabit with," "to sleep with," are all egregiously wrong in tone and implication. Fortunately the King James Version has established a strong precedent in English by translating the verb literally, and "carnal knowledge" is part of our language, so it is feasible to preserve the literal Hebrew usage in translation. (There is, I think, a good deal to be said for the general procedure of Tyndale and the King James Version in imitating many Hebrew idioms and thus giving the English a certain Hebraic coloration.) "Lie with" is a literal equivalent of the Hebrew, though in English it is vaguely euphemistic, whereas in Hebrew it is a more brutally direct or carnally explicit idiom for sexual intercourse, without, however, any suggestion of obscenity. The most intractable of the three expressions is "to come into" or "to enter." In nonsexual contexts, this is the ordinary biblical verb for entering, or arriving. "To enter," or "to come into," however, is a misleading translation because the term clearly refers not merely to sexual penetration but to the whole act of sexual consummation. It is used with great precision—not registered by biblical scholarship—to indicate a man's having intercourse with a woman he has not yet had as a sexual partner, whether she is his wife, his concubine, or a whore. The underlying spatial imagery of the term, I think, is of the man's entering the woman's sphere for the first time through a series of concentric circles:

her tent or chamber, her bed, her body. A translator, then, ought not surrender the image of coming into, but "come into" by itself doesn't quite do it. My own solution, in keeping with the slight strangeness of Hebraizing idioms of the translation as a whole, was to stretch an English idiom to cover the biblical usage: this translation consistently renders the Hebrew expression in question as "come to bed with," an idiom that in accepted usage a woman could plausibly use to a man referring to herself ("come to bed with me") but that in my translation is extended to a woman's reference to another woman ("come to bed with my slavegirl") and to a reference in the third person by the narrator or a male character to sexual consummation ("Give me my wife," Jacob says to Laban, "and let me come to bed with her.")

Biblical syntax, beyond the basic pattern of parallel clauses, provides another occasion for what I have called a slight strangeness. The word order in biblical narrative is very often as finely expressive as the lexical choices. In many instances, the significant sequence of terms can be reproduced effortlessly and idiomatically in English, and it is a testament to the literary insensitivity of modern translators that they so often neglect to do so. Here, for example, is how the narrator reports Abimelech's discovery of the conjugal connection between Isaac and the woman Isaac had claimed was his sister: "Abimelech . . . looked out the window and saw—and there was Isaac playing with Rebekah his wife" (26:8). The move into the character's point of view after the verbs of seeing is signaled by the so-called presentative, *wehineh* (rather like *voici* in French), which in this case I have represented by "there" but usually render as "look" (following the King James Version's "behold" and so deliberately coining an English idiom because the biblical term is so crucial for indicating shifts in narrative perspective). What follows "and there" is the precise sequence of Abimelech's perception as he looks out through the window: first Isaac, then the act of sexual play or fondling, then the identity of the female partner in the dalliance, and at the very end, the conclusion that Rebekah must be Isaac's wife. All this is perfectly fluent as English, and modern translations like the Revised English Bible, the New Jewish Publication Society, and Speiser that place "wife" before Rebekah spoil a nice narrative effect in the original.

But biblical syntax is also more flexible than modern English syntax, and there are hundreds of instances in Genesis of significant syntactical inversions and, especially, emphatic first positioning of weighted terms. Syntactical inversion, however, is familiar enough in the more traditional strata of literary English, and if one adopts a general norm of decorous stylization for the prose of the translation, as I have done on the grounds I explained earlier, it becomes feasible to reproduce most of the Hebrew reconfigurations of syntax, preserving the thematic or psychological emphases they are meant to convey. The present translation does this, I think, to a greater degree than all previous English versions.

God repeatedly promises the patriarchs, "To your seed I will give this land" (e.g., 12:7), pointedly putting "your seed" at the beginning of the statement. Less rhetorically, more dramatically, when Hagar is asked by the divine messenger in the wilderness where she is going, she responds, "From Sarai my mistress I am fleeing" (16:8), placing Sarai, the implacable source of her misery, at the beginning of the sentence. Still more strikingly, when Jacob is told by his sons that Simeon has been detained as a hostage in Egypt and that the Egyptian regent insists Benjamin be brought down to him, the old man begins his lament by saying, "Me you have bereaved" (42:36). It is profoundly revelatory of Jacob's psychological posture that he should place himself as the object of suffering at the very beginning of his utterance (and again at the end, in a little formal symmetry). Normally, biblical Hebrew indicates a pronominal object of a verb by attaching a suffix to the verb itself. Here, however, instead of the usual accusative suffix we get an accusative first-person pronoun—*'oti*—placed before the verb, a procedure that beautifully expresses Jacob's self-dramatization as anguished and resentful father continually at the mercy of his sons. The "me" urgently needs to be thrust into the ear of the listener. Many translations simply suppress the inversion, but to put it decorously as "It is I" (Everett Fox) or paraphrastically as "It is always me" (New Jewish Publication Society) is to dilute the dramatic force of the original.

The sharpness and vividness of biblical style are also diluted when it is represented in English, as virtually all the versions do, by a single, indifferent level of diction. As I noted earlier, there seems to be nothing genuinely colloquial in the prose used by the narrator; but there is a palpable variation between passages that are more cadenced, more inclined to balanced structures of terms and elevated language, like the narrative of the Flood, and looser, more stylistically flexible passages. There are many instances, moreover, of single word choices that pointedly break with the stylistic decorum of the surrounding narrative, and for the most part these are fudged by the sundry English translations. When Hagar and Ishmael use up their supply of water in the wilderness, the despairing mother "flung the child under one of the bushes" (21:15). The verb here, *hishlikh*, always means "to throw," usually abruptly or violently. This is somewhat softened by the King James Version and Fox, who use "cast." The Revised English Bible is uncomfortable with the idea of throwing a child and so translates "thrust." Speiser and the New Jewish Publication Society Bible altogether disapprove of spasmodic maternal gestures and hence dissolve "flung" into a gentler "left." In all such manipulation, the violence of Hagar's action and feelings disappears. When Laban berates Jacob for running off with his daughters, he says, "What have you done, . . . driving my daughters like captives of the sword?" (31:26). All the English versions represent the verb here as "carrying away" or some approximation thereof, but *nahag* is a term for driving animals, and is used precisely in that sense earlier in this very chapter (verse 18). To translate it otherwise is to lose the edge of brutal exaggeration in Laban's angry words. In the throes of the great famine, the destitute Egyptians say to Joseph, "Nothing is left for our lord but our carcasses and our farmland" (47:18). Most English versions use "bodies" instead of "carcasses," with a couple of modern translations flattening the language even more by rendering the term as "persons." But the Hebrew *gewiyah,* with the sole exception of one famous mythopoeic text in Ezekiel, invariably means "corpse" or "carcass." What the miserable Egyptians are saying to their great overlord is that they have been reduced to little more than walking corpses, and he might as well have those. This sort of pungency can be conveyed if the translator recognizes that the Hebrew does not operate at a single bland level and that literary expression is not inevitably bound to decorous "logic."

These last two examples were taken from dialogue, and it is chiefly in dialogue that we get small but vivid intimations of the colloquial. Again, these are eliminated in the flat regularity of conventional Bible translation. When God rebukes Abimelech for taking Sarah into his harem, the king vehemently protests that he has acted in good conscience: "Did not he say to me, 'She is my sister'? and she, she, too, said, 'He is my brother'" (20:5). The repetition of "she, she, too" is a stammer or splutter of indignation clearly indicated in the Hebrew. In some English versions, it disappears altogether. The King James Version turns it into a rhetorical flourish: "she, even she herself." Everett Fox, because of his commitment to literalism, comes closer but without quite the requisite feeling of colloquial mimesis: "and also she, she said." The seventeen-year-old Joseph reports the first of his dreams to his brothers in the following manner: "And, look, we were binding sheaves in the field, and, look, my sheaf arose and actually [wegam] stood up, and, look, your sheaves drew round and bowed to my sheaf." (37:7). The language here is surely crafted mimetically to capture the gee-gosh wonderment of this naïve adolescent who blithely assumes his brothers will share his sense of amazement at his dream. The presentative hineh ("look") is the conventional term dreamers use to report the visual images of their dreams, perhaps partly because it readily introduces a surprising new perception, but here Joseph repeats the term three times in one breathless sentence, and the effect of naïve astonishment is equally expressed in his redundant "arose and actually stood up" (the Hebrew adverb gam most often means "also" but fairly frequently serves as well as a term of emphasis or intensification). The point is that the adolescent Joseph speaking to his brothers does not at all sound like the adult Joseph addressing Pharaoh, and a translation should not reduce either dialogue or narrator's language to a single dead level.

In the range of diction of the biblical text, the complementary opposite to these moments of colloquial mimesis occurs in the poetic insets. Most of these in Genesis are only a line or two of verse, though the book concludes with a relatively long poem, conventionally referred to as Jacob's Testament. Now, it has long been recognized by scholarship that biblical poetry reflects a stratum of Hebrew older than biblical prose: some of the grammatical forms are different, and there is a distinctive poetic vocabulary, a good deal of it archaic. No previous English translation has made a serious effort to represent the elevated and archaic nature of the poetic language in contradistinction to the prose, though that is clearly part of the intended literary effect of biblical narrative. The present translation tries to suggest this contrast in levels of style—through a more liberal use of syntactic inversion in the poetry, through a selective invocation of slightly archaic terms, and through the occasional deployment of rhetorical gestures broadly associated with older English poetry (like the ejaculation "O"). I wish I could have gone farther in this direction, but there is a manifest danger in sounding merely quaint instead of eloquently archaic, and so the stylistic baggage of "anent" and "forsooth" had to be firmly excluded.

Two minute examples will illustrate how these discriminations of stylistic level are made in the Hebrew and how they might be conveyed in English. The enigmatic notice about the Nephilim, the human-divine hybrids of the primeval age, concludes with these words: "They are the heroes of yore, the men of renown" (6:4). This line could conceivably be a fragment from an old mythological poem; more probably, it reads in the original as a kind of stylistic citation of the epic genre. The clearest clue to this in the Hebrew is the word "they," which here is *hemah* rather than the standard *hem*. This variant with the extra syllable is in all likelihood an older form: it occurs four times more often in poetry than in prose, and even in prose is often reserved for rather ceremonial gestures. There is no English variant of "they" that is similarly marked as poetic diction, and my translation compensates by using "of yore" instead of the phrase "of old" adopted by the King James Version and by most later English versions. In the next chapter, the unleashing of the Deluge is reported in this line of verse, with emphatic semantic parallelism and four Hebrew accents against three in the two halves of the line: "All the wellsprings of the great deep burst, / and the casements of the heavens opened" (7:11). In order to convey a sense that this is poetry, beyond the mechanics of typography, a translator of course has to create a good deal of rhythmic regularity, but there remains a problem of diction. The Hebrew word represented by "casements" is *'arubot*. It is a rare term, occurring only twice elsewhere in the Bible, and it clearly means window or windowlike niche. The decision of several different modern translators to render it as "sluices" or "floodgates" has no philological warrant and is a conspicuous instance of translation by context. "Windows" in the King James Version is on target semantically but not stylistically. The occurrence of a cognate of *'arubot* in Ugaritic poetry, several centuries before the composition of Genesis, is further indication that the term is poetic and probably somewhat archaic for the later Hebrew audience. "Casements," with its echoes of Keats and of Shakespeare behind Keats, seemed like a happy solution to the problem of diction. Though not all shifts in stylistic level in the Hebrew can be so readily represented by English equivalents, a translation that tries to do justice to the richness of the Hebrew must aim for some approximation of the nuances of diction in the original.

The most pervasive aspect of the magic of biblical style that has been neglected by English translators is its beautiful rhythms. An important reason for the magnetic appeal of these stories when you read them in the Hebrew is the rhythmic power of the words that convey the story. The British critic A. Alvarez has aptly described the crucial role of rhythm in all literary art: "the rhythm—the way the sounds move, combine, separate, recombine—is the vehicle for the feeling. . . . And without that inner movement or disturbance, the words, no matter how fetching, remain inert. In this way at least, the dynamics of poetry—and probably of all the arts—are the same as the dynamics of dreaming." I know of no modern English translation of the Bible that is not blotted by constant patches of arrhythmia, and the result is precisely the sense of inertness of which Alvarez speaks. The King James Version, of course, has its grand rhythmic movements—cultivated people around 1611 clearly had a much firmer sense of expressive sound in language than has been true of recent generations. But these rhythms are more orotund, less powerfully compact, than those of the Hebrew, and in fact there are far more local lapses in rhythm than nostalgic readers of the King James Version may recall.

The final arbiter of rhythmic effectiveness must be the inner ear of the sensitive reader, but I would like to show that there is a vital dimension of biblical prose that translation has to engage by quoting a couple of verses in transliteration and then in three English versions, together with my own. In regard to the transliteration, it should be kept in mind that we have an approximate notion, not an exact one, of how biblical Hebrew was originally pronounced. There is some question about vowels in particular because vowel points were added to the consonantal texts by the Masoretes—the Hebrew scholars of sixth- to tenth-century Tiberias who fixed the text of the Bible, with full punctuation, standard since then—more than a millennium after the texts were composed. There was, however, a continuous tradition for recitation of the texts on which the Masoretes drew, and anyone who has listened to the Masoretic Text read out loud can attest to its strong rhythmic integrity, which argues that its system of pronunciation was by no means an arbitrary imposition. Here is the narrative report of Noah's entering the ark as the Deluge is unleashed (7:13–14). (Acute accents are used to indicate accented syllables. *W* is used for the letter *waw* (pronounced as *v* in modern Hebrew but as *w* in biblical times), especially to distinguish it from *bet* without *dagesh,* pronounced as *v*. Ḥ indicates a light fricative (something like Spanish *j*); *kh* represents a heavier fricative, like the German *ch* in Bach.)

13. Be'étsem hayóm hazéh b'a nóaḥ weshém-weḥám wayéfet benei-nóaḥ we'éshet nóaḥ ushlóshet neshéi-vanáw 'itám 'el hateváh. 14. Hémah wekhol-haḥayáh lemináh wekhol-hebehemáh lemináh wekhol-harémes haromés 'al-ha'árets leminéhu wekhol-ha'óf leminéhu kól tsipór kol-kanáf.

The Hebrew rhythm unfolds in groupings of three or four words marked by three of four stresses, usually with no more than one or two unstressed syllables between the stressed ones, and the sense of the words invites a slight pause between one grouping and the next. The overall effect is that of a grand solemn sweep, a sort of epic march, and that effect is reinforced in the diction by the use of *hemah* instead of *hem* for "they" at the beginning of the second verse.

Here is the King James Version:

13. In the selfsame day entered Noah, and Shem, and Ham, and Japheth, the sons of Noah, and Noah's wife, and the three wives of his sons with them, into the ark; 14. They, and every beast after its kind, and all the cattle after their kind, and every creeping thing that creepeth upon the earth after his kind, and every fowl after his kind, every bird of every sort.

The first of the two verses (up to "into the ark") is nearly perfect. I envy the freedom of the King James Version to follow the Hebrew syntax and write "entered Noah," an inversion feasible at the beginning of the seventeenth century but a little too odd, I am afraid, at the end of the twentieth. But in the second verse rhythmic difficulties emerge. The repeated "after its kind," with its sequencing of a trochee and an iamb and its two stresses, is an ungainly equivalent of the Hebrew *leminâh;* "every creeping thing that creepeth upon the earth" is a whole mouthful of syllables in exchange for the compactness of the Hebrew; and "every bird of every sort" falls flat as a final cadence (apart from being inaccurate as a translation).

Here is E. A. Speiser's version of these two verses—a version, to be sure, intended to be accompanied by a philological commentary, but one which helped set a norm for recent Bible translations:

13. On the aforesaid day, Noah and his sons, Shem, Ham, and Japheth, Noah's wife, and the three wives of his sons had entered the ark—14. they as well as every kind of beast, every kind of creature that creeps on earth, and every kind of bird, every winged thing.

The initial phrase, "on the aforesaid day," is an ill-starred beginning in regard to diction as well as to rhythm. Something as mechanical as the list of the passengers of the ark is divided up in a way that undercuts its rhythmic momentum: at best, one can say that this version has intermittent moments of escape into rhythm.

Everett Fox, the most boldly literal of modern Bible translators, does a little better, but his attention to rhythm is by no means unflagging.

13. On that very day came Noah, and Shem, Ham, and Yefet, Noah's sons, Noah's wife and his three sons' wives with them, into the Ark, 14. they

and all wildlife after their kind, all herd-animals after their kind, all crawling things that crawl upon the earth after their kind, all fowl after their kind, all chirping-things, all winged-things.

The first short clause, with the courageous inversion of verb and subject, rings nicely in the ear. But the simple deletion of the "and" between Shem and Ham collapses the rhythm, and Fox's grouping of the list is not much better rhythmically than Speiser's. As in the King James Version, the decision to use "after" four times introduces a series of unwelcome extra syllables, and rhythm is virtually lost in "all herd-animals after their kind, all crawling things that crawl upon the earth after their kind."

Here is my own version, far from perfect, but meant to preserve more of the phonetic compactness of the Hebrew and to avoid such glaring lapses into arrythmia:

13. That very day, Noah and Shem and Ham and Japheth, the sons of Noah, and Noah's wife, and the three wives of his sons together with them, came into the ark, 14. they as well as beasts of each kind and cattle of each kind and each kind of crawling thing that crawls on the earth and each kind of bird, each winged thing.

Biblical Hebrew, in sum, has a distinctive music, a lovely precision of lexical choice, a meaningful concreteness, and a suppleness of expressive syntax, that by and large have been given short shrift by translators with their eyes on other goals. The present translation, whatever its imperfections, seeks to do fuller justice to all these aspects of biblical style in the hope of making the rich literary experience of the Hebrew more accessible to readers of English.

2. GENESIS AS A BOOK

All that I have said about the style of Genesis, as well as most of what I have to say in my commentary about the details of the narrative, presupposes that Genesis is a coherent book, what we moderns would think of as a work of literature. But, as many readers may be aware, two centuries of biblical scholarship have generally assumed that Genesis—and indeed most biblical texts—is not strictly speaking a book but rather an accretion of sundry traditions, shot through with disjunctions and contradictions, and accumulated in an uneven editorial process over several centuries. There are knotty issues of the dating and the evolution of the text that have been debated by generations of scholars and that I shall not pretend to resolve, but I do think that the historical and textual criticism of the Bible is not so damaging to a literary reading of the text as is often assumed.

The biblical conception of a book was clearly far more open-ended than any notion current in our own culture, with its assumptions of known authorship and legal copyright. The very difference in the technology of bookmaking is emblematic. For us, a book is a printed object boxed in between two covers, with title and author emblazoned on the front cover and the year of publication indicated on the copyright page. The biblical term that comes closest to "book" is *sefer*. Etymologically, it means "something recounted," but its primary sense is "scroll," and it can refer to anything written on a scroll—a letter, a relatively brief unit within a longer composition, or a book more or less in our sense. A scroll is not a text shut in between covers, and additional swathes of scroll can be stitched onto it, which seems to have been a very common biblical practice. A book in the biblical sphere was assumed to be a product of anonymous tradition. The only ones in the biblical corpus that stipulate the names of their authors, in superscriptions at the beginning, are the prophetic books, but even in this case, later prophecies by different prophet-poets could be tacked onto the earlier scrolls, and the earlier scrolls perhaps might even be edited to fit better into a continuous book with the later accretions.

Let me say just a few words about the different strands that are detectable in Genesis, and then I shall explain why I make very little of them in my commentary. Since well back into the nineteenth century, it has been the consensus of biblical scholarship that Genesis, together with the next three books of the Pentateuch, is woven together from three distinct literary sources or "documents"—The Yahwistic document (spelled with an initial capital J in German and hence designated J), the Elohistic document (E), and the Priestly document (P). Most scholars have concluded that J and E are considerably earlier than P, which could be as late as the sixth or fifth century B.C.E. (the period after the return from the Babylonian exile). According to one view, J would be a product of the tenth century B.C.E. (early in the Davidic dynasty) and E perhaps a century later; another common position is that J and E are roughly contemporary, the latter having been composed in the northern kingdom, Israel, the former in the southern kingdom, Judea. Scholars identify the different sources on the basis of different names used for the deity (emblematically, YHWH in J and Elohim in E), on the basis of certain stylistic features, and by virtue of what are claimed to be different ideological and historical assumptions. It is generally thought that the three sources were redacted into a single text quite early in the period of the Return to Zion, perhaps in Priestly circles.

This rapid summary may make matters sound pat, but in fact all the details of the Documentary Hypothesis are continually, and often quite vehemently, debated. There are strong differences of opinion about the dating of the various sources, especially J and E. Serious questions have been raised as to whether either J or E is the work of a single writer or school, and various scholars have contended that in fact there is a J^1, J^2, J^3, and so forth. Enormous energy has been invested in discriminating the precise boundaries between one document and the next, but disagreement on minute identifications continues to abound: one scholar will break down a particular text into an alternation between J and E, with an occasional conflation of the two and perhaps a brief intrusion from P, seeking to refine the documentary categories phrase by phrase, while another will call the whole passage "an authentic production of J." (I should add that efforts to distinguish between J and E on stylistic grounds have been quite unconvincing.) It is small wonder that the Documentary Hypothesis, whatever its general validity, has begun to look as though it has reached a point of diminishing returns, and many younger scholars, showing signs of restlessness with source criticism, have been exploring other approaches—literary, anthropological, sociological, and so forth—to the Bible.

The informing assumption of my translation and commentary is that the edited version of Genesis—the so-called redacted text—which has come down to us, though not without certain limited contradictions and disparate elements, has powerful coherence as a literary work, and that this coherence is above all what we need to address as readers. One need not claim that Genesis is a unitary artwork, like, say, a novel by Henry James, in order to grant it integrity as a book. There are other instances of works of art that evolve over the centuries, like the cathedrals of medieval Europe, and are the product of many hands, involving an elaborate process of editing, like some of the greatest Hollywood films. From where we stand, it is difficult to know to what extent the biblical redactors felt free to modify or reshape their inherited sources and to what extent they felt obliged to reproduce them integrally, permitting themselves only an occasional editorial bridge or brief gloss. What seems quite clear, however, is that the redactors had a strong and often subtle sense of thematic and narrative purposefulness in the way they wove together the inherited literary strands, and the notion of some scholars that they were actuated by a mechanical compulsion to incorporate old traditions at all costs is not sustained by a scrutiny of the text, with only a few marginal exceptions.

It is quite apparent that a concept of composite artistry, of literary composition through a collage of textual materials, was generally assumed to be normal procedure in ancient Israelite culture. The technique of collage could come into play at two stages. A writer in the first instance might feel free to introduce into his own narrative, as an integral textual unit, a genealogy, an etiological tale, an ethnographic table, or a vestige of a mythological story, or perhaps to recreate one of the aforementioned without an explicit textual source. Then the redactor, in shaping the final version of the text, could place disparate textual materials at junctures that would give the completed text the thematic definition or the large formal punctuation he sought. I am deeply convinced that conventional biblical scholarship has been trigger-happy in using the arsenal of text-critical categories, proclaiming contradiction wherever there is the slightest internal tension in the text, seeing every repetition as evidence of a duplication of sources, everywhere tuning in to the static of transmission, not to the complex music of the redacted story.

The reader will consequently discover that this commentary refers only occasionally and obliquely to the source analysis of Genesis. For even where such analysis may be convincing, it seems to me a good deal less interesting than the subtle workings of the literary whole represented by the redacted text. As an attentive reader of other works of narrative literature, I have kept in mind that there are many kinds of ambiguity and contradiction, and abundant varieties of repetition, that are entirely purposeful, and that are essential features of the distinctive vehicle of literary experience. I have constantly sought, in both the translation and the commentary, to make this biblical text accessible as a book to be read, which is surely what was intended by its authors and redactors. To that end, I discovered that some of the medieval Hebrew commentators were often more helpful than nearly all the modern ones, with their predominantly text-critical and historical concerns. Rashi (acronym for Rabbi Shlomo Itsḥaqi, 1080–1174, France) and Abraham ibn Ezra (1092–1167, migrated from Spain to Italy, France, and England) are the most often cited here; they are two of the great readers of the Middle Ages, and there is still much we can learn from them.

A few brief remarks about the structure of Genesis as a book are in order. Genesis comprises two large literary units—the Primeval History (chapters 1–11) and the Patriarchal Tales (chapters 12–50). The two differ not only in subject but to some extent in style and perspective. The approach to the history of Israel and Israel's relationship with God that will be the material of the rest of the Hebrew Bible is undertaken through gradually narrowing concentric circles: first an account of the origins of the world, of the vegetable and animal kingdom and of humankind, then a narrative explanation of the origins of all the known peoples, from Greece to Africa to Mesopotamia and Asia Minor, and of the primary institutions of civilization, including the memorable fable about the source of linguistic division. The Mesopotamian family of Terah is introduced at the end of this universal history in chapter 11, and then when God calls Abraham out of Ur of the Chaldees at the beginning of chapter 12 we move on to the story of the beginnings of the Israelite nation, though the national focus of the narrative is given moral depth because the universal perspective of the first part of Genesis is never really forgotten. Some critics have plausibly imagined this whole large process of biblical literature as a divine experiment with the quirky and unpredictable stuff of human freedom, an experiment plagued by repeated failure and dedicated to renewed attempts: first Adam and Eve, then the generation of Noah, then the builders of the Tower of Babel, and finally Abraham and his seed.

Although the Creation story with which the Primeval History begins does look forward to the proliferation of humanity and the human conquest of the natural world, by and large the first eleven chapters of Genesis are concerned with origins, not eventualities—with the past, not the future: "he was the first of all who play on the lyre and pipe" (4:21), the narrator says of Jubal, one of the antedeluvians. The literal phrasing of the Hebrew here, as in a series of analogous verses, is "he was the father of. . . ." That idiom is emblematic of the Primeval History, which is really a record of the archetypal fathers, a genealogy of human institutions and of ethnic and linguistic identity. Although the Patriarchal Tales are in one obvious way also the story of a chain of fathers—Abraham, Isaac, and Jacob—the horizon these tales constantly invoke is the future, not the past. God repeatedly tells Abraham what He intends to do with and for the offspring of Abraham in time to come, both in the impending near future of Egyptian enslavement and in the long-term future of national greatness. It is perfectly apt that the Patriarchal Tales should conclude with Jacob's deathbed poem envisaging the destiny of the future tribes of Israel, which he prefaces with the words, "Gather round, that I may tell you what shall befall you in the days to come" (49:1).

The Primeval History, in contrast to what follows in Genesis, cultivates a kind of narrative that is fablelike or legendary, and sometimes residually mythic. The human actors in these stories are kept at a certain distance, and seem more generalized types than individual characters with distinctive personal histories. The style tends much more than that of the Patriarchal Tales to formal symmetries, refrainlike repetitions, parallelisms, and other rhetorical devices of a prose that often aspires to the dignity of poetry, or that invites us to hear the echo of epic poetry in its cadences. As everywhere in biblical narrative, dialogue is an important vehicle, but in the Primeval History it does not have the central role it will play later, and one finds few of the touches of vivid mimesis that make dialogue in the Patriarchal Tales so brilliant an instrument for the representation of human—and human and divine—interactions. In sum, this rapid report of the distant early stages of the human story adopts something of a distancing procedure in the style and the narrative modes with which it tells the story.

God's very first words to Abraham at the beginning of chapter 12 enjoin him to abandon land, birthplace, and father's house. These very terms, or at least this very sphere, will become the arena of the narrative to the end of Genesis. The human creature is now to be represented not against the background of the heavens and the earth and civilization as such but rather within the tense and constricted theater of the paternal domain, in tent and wheatfield and sheepfold, in the minute rhythms of quotidian existence, working out all hopes of grand destiny in the coil of familial relationships, the internecine, sometimes deadly, warring of brothers and fathers and sons and wives. In keeping with this major shift in focus from the Primeval History to the Patriarchal Tales, style and narrative mode shift as well. The studied formality of the first eleven chapters—epitomized in the symmetries and the intricate repetition of word and sound in the story of the Tower of Babel—gives way to a more flexible and varied prose. Dialogue is accorded more prominence and embodies a more lively realism. When, for example, Sarai gives Abram her slavegirl Hagar as a concubine, and the proudly pregnant Hagar then treats her with disdain, the matriarch berates her husband in the following fashion: "This outrage against me is because of you! I myself put my slavegirl in your embrace and when she saw she had conceived, I became slight in her eyes" (16:5). Sarai's first sentence here has an explosive compactness in the Hebrew, being only two words, *ḥamasi ʿalekha*, that resists translation. In any case, these lines smoldering with the fires of female resentment

convey a sense of living speech and complexity of feeling and relationship one does not encounter before the Patriarchal Tales: the frustrated long-barren wife at cross-purposes with herself and with her
husband, first aspiring to maternity through the surrogate of her slavegirl, then after the fact of her new co-wife's pregnancy, tasting a new
humiliation, indignant at the slave's presumption, ready to blame her
husband, who has been only the instrument of her will. Such vivid
immediacy in the representation of the densely problematic nature
of individual lives in everyday settings is an innovation not only in
comparison with the Primeval History but also in comparison with
virtually all of ancient literature.

What nevertheless strongly binds the two large units of the Book of
Genesis is both outlook and theme. The unfolding history of the family
that is to become the people of Israel is seen, as I have suggested, as
the crucial focus of a larger, universal history. The very peregrinations
of the family back and forth between Mesopotamia and Canaan and
down to Egypt intimate that its scope involves not just the land Israel
has been promised but the wider reach of known cultures. National
existence, moreover, is emphatically imagined as a strenuous effort to
renew the act of creation. The Creation story repeatedly highlights the
injunction to be fruitful and multiply, while the Patriarchal Tales, in
the very process of frequently echoing this language of fertility from
the opening chapters, make clear that procreation, far from being an
automatic biological process, is fraught with dangers, is constantly
under the threat of being deflected or cut off. Abraham must live long
years with the seeming mockery of a divine promise of numberless
offspring as he and his wife advance childless into hoary old age. Near
the end of the book, Jacob's whole family fears it may perish in the
great famine, and Joseph must assure his brothers that God has sent
him ahead of them to Egypt in order to sustain life. Genesis begins
with the making of heaven and earth and all life, and ends with the
image of a mummy—Joseph's—in a coffin. But implicit in the end is
a promise of more life to come, of irrepressible procreation, and that
renewal of creation will be manifested, even under the weight of
oppression, at the beginning of Exodus. Genesis, then, works with
disparate materials, puts together its story with two large and very

different building blocks, but nevertheless achieves the cohesiveness, the continuity of theme and motif, and the sense of completion of an archetectonically conceived book. Although it looks forward to its sequel, it stands as a book, inviting our attention as an audience that follows the tale from beginning to end.

ABOUT THE COMMENTARY

My original intention had been simply to provide brief translator's notes. Puns, wordplay in the sundry naming-speeches, and other untranslatable maneuvers of the Hebrew needed to be glossed. The reader also had to be informed, I felt, of the occasional junctures where I adopted a reading that varied from the Masoretic Text, the received Hebrew text of the Bible. Similarly, it seemed proper to offer some explanation for translation choices that were likely to surprise either the general reader or the scholarly reader, or both. In some instances, such a choice reflects a proposed new solution to a crux in the Hebrew text. More often, it is an effort to represent a more precise understanding of the Hebrew than previous translations have shown (e.g., the tree of knowledge is "lovely to look at," not "lovely to impart wisdom"; Pharaoh puts a "golden collar" around Joseph's neck, not a "gold chain"). And most pervasively, the little surprises in the translation are attempts to find English equivalents for the nuances of implication and the significant changes of diction in the Hebrew that have not been much regarded by previous translators. Finally, since this translation is, within the limits of readable English style, quite literal—not out of fundamentalist principle but in an effort to reproduce some of the distinctive literary effects of the original—when the interests of English intelligibility compelled me to diverge from a literal translation, I have alerted readers to the divergence and given the literal sense of the Hebrew words in a note. And beyond all such considerations of word choice and level of style, I thought it necessary to offer succinct explanations of some of the ancient Near Eastern cultural practices and social institutions that are presupposed by the narratives, for without an understanding of them it is sometimes hard to see exactly what is going on in the story.

This last category of explanation is, of course, standard fare in modern Bible commentaries, and is admittedly intended here as an aid for the relatively uninitiated. But as I got caught up once again in this endlessly fascinating text, it struck me that there were important features of Genesis that by and large had been given short shrift in the modern commentaries. In fact, a good many of my observations on stylistic choices already shaded into a discussion of the literary vehicle of the biblical narratives, and this was the point at which the tightly cinched annotation began to loosen its bonds and reach out to commentary. There were whole orders of questions, it seemed to me, that had been neglected or addressed only intermittently and impressionistically by the modern commentators. Where are there detectible shifts of stylistic level in the Hebrew, and why do they occur? What are the reasons for the small poetic insets in the prose narratives? What are the principles on which dialogue is organized, and how are the speakers differentiated? Where and why are there shifts from the narrator's point of view to that of one of the characters? What are the devices of analogy, recurrent motifs, and key words, that invite us to link and contrast one episode with another? And does Genesis, granted its composite origins, exhibit overarching thematic and structural unities or lines of development?

On all these challenging questions I have surely not said the last word. Rather I have aspired to say some helpful first words in a commentary that I have sought to hold to modest proportions. Clearly, there is no way of separating a literary illumination of the biblical text from a confrontation with philological issues, on the one side, and, perhaps more indirectly, with historical issues, on the other. In any case, the exploration of Genesis as literary expression is the central focus of this commentary, and I would hope it would be of interest to everyone, from reader at large to scholar, who is drawn to the imaginative liveliness, the complexities, and the sheer narrative inventiveness of these splendid ancient stories.

ACKNOWLEDGMENTS

For an undertaking as audacious as a new translation of Genesis I felt particularly dependent on the counsel and encouragement of the friends who read my drafts. Thomas G. Rosenmeyer and Leonard Nathan looked at sections of the manuscript and raised some astute questions. The translation and commentary in their entirety were read by three people. Michael Bernstein's enthusiasm, coming from a reader with so discriminating a sense of English style, did a great deal to allay my own early doubts about the conception of Bible translation I was trying to carry out. Stanley Burnshaw, with an editorial eye that is virtually legendary in American publishing, ferreted out misusages, clunky clauses, and logical gaps in the commentary, and also compelled me to reconsider some of my local choices in the translation. My greatest debt is owed to Amos Funkenstein, whose presence I will continue to miss sorely, and to whose memory this book is dedicated. Amos, a great historian and also a brilliant Hebraist, brought to the scrutiny of philological and exegetical problems the same rare lucidity and the same ability to think out old issues in entirely fresh ways that he evinced in his far-ranging studies in intellectual history. When he disagreed with me, he did so vigorously, sometimes vehemently, but also in a spirit of friendly intellectual exchange, and with a reiterated admiration for what I was doing that means more to me than I can say.

Secretarial and research costs were covered by income from the Class of 1937 Chair of Hebrew and Comparative Literature at the University of California at Berkeley. I am grateful to Janet Livingstone for her patient devotion to the arduous task of transfering my handwritten drafts to a computer.

GENESIS

CHAPTER 1

When God began to create heaven and earth, and the earth then was [1,2] welter and waste and darkness over the deep and God's breath hovering over the waters, God said, "Let there be light." And there was [3] light. And God saw the light, that it was good, and God divided the [4] light from the darkness. And God called the light Day, and the dark- [5] ness He called Night. And it was evening and it was morning, first day. And God said, "Let there be a vault in the midst of the waters, [6] and let it divide water from water." And God made the vault and it [7] divided the water beneath the vault from the water above the vault, and so it was. And God called the vault Heavens, and it was evening [8] and it was morning, second day. And God said, "Let the waters under [9] the heavens be gathered in one place so that the dry land will appear,"

---

2. *welter and waste.* The Hebrew *tohu wabohu* occurs only here and in two later biblical texts that are clearly alluding to this one. The second word of the pair looks like a nonce term coined to rhyme with the first and to reinforce it, an effect I have tried to approximate in English by alliteration. *Tohu* by itself means emptiness or futility, and in some contexts is associated with the trackless vacancy of the desert.

hovering. The verb attached to God's breath-wind-spirit *(ruaḥ)* elsewhere describes an eagle fluttering over its young and so might have a connotation of parturition or nurture as well as rapid back-and-forth movement.

5. *first day.* Unusually, the Hebrew uses a cardinal, not ordinal, number. As with all the six days except the sixth, the expected definite article is omitted.

6. *vault.* The Hebrew *rakiʿa* suggests a hammered-out slab, not necessarily arched, but the English architectural term with its celestial associations created by poetic tradition is otherwise appropriate.

10 and so it was. And God called the dry land Earth and the gathering of
11 waters He called Seas, and God saw that it was good. And God said,
"Let the earth grow grass, plants yielding seed of each kind and trees
bearing fruit of each kind, that has its seed within it." And so it was.
12 And the earth put forth grass, plants yielding seed of each kind, and
trees bearing fruit that has its seed within it of each kind, and God
13 saw that it was good. And it was evening and it was morning, third
14 day. And God said, "Let there be lights in the vault of the heavens to
divide the day from the night, and they shall be signs for the fixed
15 times and for days and years, and they shall be lights in the vault of
16 the heavens to light up the earth." And so it was. And God made the
two great lights, the great light for dominion of day and the small light
17 for dominion of night, and the stars. And God placed them in the
18 vault of the heavens to light up the earth and to have dominion over
day and night and to divide the light from the darkness. And God saw
19 that it was good. And it was evening and it was morning, fourth day.
20 And God said, "Let the waters swarm with the swarm of living creatures and let fowl fly over the earth across the vault of the heavens."
21 And God created the great sea monsters and every living creature that
crawls, which the water had swarmed forth of each kind, and the
22 winged fowl of each kind, and God saw that it was good. And God
blessed them, saying, "Be fruitful and multiply and fill the water in
23 the seas and let the fowl multiply in the earth." And it was evening
24 and it was morning, fifth day. And God said, "Let the earth bring forth
living creatures of each kind, cattle and crawling things and wild
25 beasts of each kind. And so it was. And God made wild beasts of each
kind and cattle of every kind and crawling things on the ground of
each kind, and God saw that it was good.

---

24. *wild beasts.* Literally, the phrase would mean "beast of the earth," but the
archaic construct form for "beasts of," *ḥayto,* elsewhere regularly occurs in
collocations that denote wild beasts. In verse 25, the archaic form is not used,
but given the close proximity of *ḥayat haʾarets* there to *ḥayto ʾerets* here, it
seems likely that the meaning is the same.

And God said, "Let us make a human in our image, by our likeness,   26
to hold sway over the fish of the sea and the fowl of the heavens and
the cattle and the wild beasts and all the crawling things that crawl
upon the earth.

> And God created the human in his image,   27
>   in the image of God He created him,
>   male and female He created them.

And God blessed them, and God said to them, "Be fruitful and multi-   28
ply and fill the earth and conquer it, and hold sway over the fish of
the sea and the fowl of the heavens and every beast that crawls upon
the earth." And God said, "Look, I have given you every seed-bearing   29
plant on the face of all the earth and every tree that has fruit bearing
seed, yours they will be for food. And to all the beasts of the earth and   30

---

26. *a human.* The term *'adam,* afterward consistently with a definite article,
which is used both here and in the second account of the origins of
humankind, is a generic term for human beings, not a proper noun. It also
does not automatically suggest maleness, especially not without the prefix
ben, "son of," and so the traditional rendering "man" is misleading, and an
exclusively male *'adam* would make nonsense of the last clause of verse 27.

    hold sway. The verb *radah* is not the normal Hebrew verb for "rule" (the
latter is reflected in "dominion" of verse 16), and in most of the contexts in
which it occurs it seems to suggest an absolute or even fierce exercise of
mastery.

    the wild beasts. The Masoretic Text reads "all the earth," *bekhol ha'arets,*
but since the term occurs in the middle of a catalog of living creatures over
which humanity will hold sway, the reading of the Syriac Version, *ḥayat
ha'arets,* "wild beasts," seems preferable.

27. In the middle clause of this verse, "him," as in the Hebrew, is grammatically but not anatomically masculine. Feminist critics have raised the question as to whether here and in the second account of human origins, in
chapter 2, *'adam* is to be imagined as sexually undifferentiated until the fashioning of woman, though that proposal leads to certain dizzying paradoxes in
following the story.

to all the fowl of the heavens and to all that crawls on the earth, which has the breath of life within it, the green plants for food." And so it 31 was. And God saw all that He had done, and, look, it was very good. And it was evening and it was morning, the sixth day.

CHAPTER 2

T‌hen the heavens and the earth were completed, and all their array. 1
And God completed on the seventh day the work He had done, and 2
He ceased on the seventh day from all the work He had done. And 3
God blessed the seventh day and hallowed it, for on it He had ceased
from all His work that He had done. This is the tale of the heavens 4
and the earth when they were created.

On the day the LORD God made earth and heavens, no shrub of the 5
field being yet on the earth and no plant of the field yet sprouted, for
the LORD God had not caused rain to fall on the earth and there was
no human to till the soil, and wetness would well from the earth to 6

---

4. As many modern commentators have noted, the first Creation account
concludes with the summarizing phrase in the first half of this verse: "This is
the tale [literally, these are the begettings] of the heavens and the earth when
they were created," these two paired terms, heavens and earth, taking us back
in an envelope structure to the paired terms of the very first verse of the
Creation story. Now, after the grand choreography of resonant parallel utterances of the cosmogony, the style changes sharply. Instead of the symmetry
of parataxis, hypotaxis is initially prominent: the second account begins with
elaborate syntactical subordination in a long complex sentence that uncoils
all the way from the second part of verse 4 to the end of verse 7. In this more
vividly anthropomorphic account, God, now called *YHWH 'Elohim* instead
of *'Elohim* as in the first version, does not summon things into being from a
lofty distance through the mere agency of divine speech, but works as a
craftsman, fashioning (*yatsar* instead of *bar'a,* "create"), blowing life breath
into nostrils, building a woman from a rib. Whatever the disparate historical
origins of the two accounts, the redaction gives us first a harmonious cosmic
overview of creation and then a plunge into the technological nitty-gritty and
moral ambiguities of human origins.

---

7 water all the surface of the soil, then the LORD God fashioned the human, humus from the soil, and blew into his nostrils the breath of
8 life, and the human became a living creature. And the LORD God planted a garden in Eden, to the east, and He placed there the human
9 He had fashioned. And the LORD God caused to sprout from the soil every tree lovely to look at and good for food, and the tree of life was in the midst of the garden, and the tree of knowledge, good and evil.
10 Now a river runs out of Eden to water the garden and from there splits
11 off into four streams. The name of the first is Pishon, the one that
12 winds through the whole land of Havilah, where there is gold. And
13 the gold of that land is goodly, bdellium is there, and lapis lazuli. And the name of the second river is Gihon, the one that winds through all
14 the land of Cush. And the name of the third river is Tigris, the one
15 that goes to the east of Ashur. And the fourth river is Euphrates. And the LORD God took the human and set him down in the garden of
16 Eden to till it and watch it. And the LORD God commanded the human, saying, "From every fruit of the garden you may surely eat.
17 But from the tree of knowledge, good and evil, you shall not eat, for on the day you eat from it, you are doomed to die."

---

7. *the human, humus.* The Hebrew etymological pun is *'adam,* "human," from the soil, *'adamah.*

16.–17. *surely eat . . . doomed to die.* The form of the Hebrew in both instances is what grammarians call the infinitive absolute: the infinitive immediately followed by a conjugated form of the same verb. The general effect of this repetition is to add emphasis to the verb, but because in the case of the verb "to die" it is the pattern regularly used in the Bible for the issuing of death sentences, "doomed to die" is an appropriate equivalent.

And the LORD God said, "It is not good for the human to be alone, I 18
shall make him a sustainer beside him." And the LORD God fashioned 19
from the soil each beast of the field and each fowl of the heavens and
brought each to the human to see what he would call it, and whatever
the human called a living creature, that was its name. And the human 20
called names to all the cattle and to the fowl of the heavens and to all
the beasts of the field, but for the human no sustainer beside him was
found. And the LORD God cast a deep slumber on the human, and he 21
slept, and He took one of his ribs and closed over the flesh where it
had been, and the LORD God built the rib He had taken from the 22
human into a woman and He brought her to the human. And the 23
human said:

---

18. *sustainer beside him.* The Hebrew *'ezer kenegdo* (King James Version "help
meet") is notoriously difficult to translate. The second term means alongside
him, opposite him, a counterpart to him. "Help" is too weak because it suggests a merely auxiliary function, whereas *'ezer* elsewhere connotes active
intervention on behalf of someone, especially in military contexts, as often in
Psalms.

22. *built.* Though this may seem an odd term for the creation of woman, it
complements the potter's term, *fashion,* used for the creation of first human,
and is more appropriate because the LORD is now working with hard material,
not soft clay. As Nahum Sarna has observed, the Hebrew for "rib," *tsel'a,* is
also used elsewhere to designate an architectural element.

23. The first human is given reported speech for the first time only when
there is another human to whom to respond. The speech takes the form of
verse, a naming-poem, in which each of the two lines begins with the feminine indicative pronoun, z'*ot,* "this one," which is also the last Hebrew word
of the poem, cinching it in a tight envelope structure.

This one at last, bone of my bones
and flesh of my flesh,
This one shall be called Woman,
for from man was this one taken.

24 Therefore does a man leave his father and his mother and cling to his
25 wife and they become one flesh. And the two of them were naked,
the human and his woman, and they were not ashamed.

---

24. *Therefore.* This term, ʿ*al-ken,* is the formula for introducing an etiological
explanation: here, why it is that man separates from his parents and is drawn
to join bodily, and otherwise, to a woman.

25. *And the two of them.* But characteristically, the narrative immediately
unsettles the neatness of the etiological certainty, for the first couple are two,
not one flesh, and their obliviousness to their nakedness is darkened by the
foreshadow of the moment about to be narrated in which their innocence
will be lost.

CHAPTER 3

Now the serpent was most cunning of all the beasts of the field that the 1
LORD God had made. And he said to the woman, "Though God said, 2
you shall not eat from any tree of the garden—" And the woman said 3
to the serpent, "From the fruit of the garden's trees we may eat, but
from the fruit of the tree in the midst of the garden God has said, 'You
shall not eat from it and you shall not touch it, lest you die.'" And the 4
serpent said to the woman, "You shall not be doomed to die." For God 5
knows that on the day you eat of it your eyes will be opened and you

---

1. *cunning*. In the kind of pun in which the ancient Hebrew writers delighted,
ʿ*arum*, "cunning," plays against ʿ*arumim*, "naked," of the previous verse.

2. As E. A. Speiser has noted, the subordinate conjunction that introduces
the serpent's first utterance does not have the sense of "truly" that most translators assign it, and is better construed as the beginning of a (false) statement
that is cut off in midsentence by Eve's objection that the ban is not on *all*
the trees of the Garden.

3. But, as many commentators have observed, Eve enlarges the divine prohibition in another direction, adding a ban on touching to the one on eating,
and so perhaps setting herself up for transgression: having touched the fruit,
and seeing no ill effect, she may proceed to eat.

6   will become as gods knowing good and evil." And the woman saw that
the tree was good for eating and that it was lust to the eyes and the
tree was lovely to look at, and she took of its fruit and ate, and she
7   also gave to her man, and he ate. And the eyes of the two were opened,
and they knew they were naked, and they sewed fig leaves and made
themselves loincloths.

8   And they heard the sound of the LORD God walking about in the
garden in the evening breeze, and the human and his woman hid from
9   the LORD God in the midst of the trees of the garden. And the LORD
10   God called to the human and said to him, "Where are you?" And he
said, "I heard your sound in the garden and I was afraid, for I was
11   naked, and I hid." And He said, "Who told you that you were naked?
12   From the tree I commanded you not to eat have you eaten?" And the

---

6. *lust to the eyes.* There is a long tradition of rendering the first term here,
ta'awah, according to English idiom and local biblical context, as "delight" or
something similar. But *ta'awah* means that which is intensely desired, appetite, and sometimes specifically lust. Eyes have just been mentioned in the
serpent's promise that they will be wondrously opened; now they are linked
to intense desire. In the event, they will be opened chiefly to see nakedness.
Ta'awah is semantically bracketed with the next term attached to the tree,
"lovely," *nehmad,* which literally means "that which is desired."
    to look at. A venerable tradition renders this verb, *lehaskil,* as "to make one
wise." But Amos Funkenstein has astutely observed to me that there is an
internal parallelism in the verse, "lust to the eyes . . . lovely to look at."
Though the usual sense of *lehaskil* in the *hiphi'l* conjugation does involve the
exercise of wisdom, Funkenstein's suggestion leans on the meaning of the
same root in the *hitpa'el* conjugation in postbiblical Hebrew and Aramaic,
"to look." And in fact, the Aramaic Targums of both Onkelos and Yonatan
ben Uziel render this as *le'istakala beih,* "to look at." At least one other biblical
occurrence is almost certainly in the sense of look, the beginning of Psalm
41: "Happy is he who *maskil* to the poor man"—surely, who looks at, has
regard for, the poor man. A correlation between verbs of seeing and verbs of
knowledge or understanding is common to many languages.

human said, "The woman whom you gave by me, she gave me from the tree, and I ate." And the LORD God said to the woman, "What is 13 this you have done?" And the woman said, "The serpent beguiled me and I ate." And the LORD God said to the serpent, "Because you have 14 done this,

> Cursed be you
> > of all cattle and all beasts of the field.
> On your belly shall you go
> > and dust shall you eat all the days of your life.
> Enmity will I set between you and the woman, 15
> > between your seed and hers.
> He will boot your head
> > and you will bite his heel."

To the woman He said, 16

> "I will terribly sharpen your birth pangs,
> > in pain shall you bear children.
> And for your man shall be your longing,
> > and he shall rule over you."

---

12. *gave by me, she gave me*. The repeated verb nicely catches the way the first man passes the buck, not only blaming the woman for giving him the fruit but virtually blaming God for giving him the woman. She in turn of course blames the serpent. God's curse, framed in verse, follows the reverse order, from serpent to woman to man.

15. *Enmity*. Although the serpent is by no means "satanic," as in the lens of later Judeo-Christian traditions, the curse records a primal horror of humankind before this slithering, viscous-looking, and poisonous representative of the animal realm. It is the first moment in which a split between man and the rest of the animal kingdom is recorded. Behind it may stand, at a long distance of cultural mediation, Canaanite myths of a primordial sea serpent.

    boot . . . bite. The Hebrew uses what appear to be homonyms, the first verb meaning "to trample," the second, identical in form, probably referring to the hissing sound of the snake just before it bites.

17 And to the human he said, "Because you listened to the voice of your
wife and ate from the tree that I commanded you, 'You shall not eat
from it,'

> Cursed be the soil for your sake,
>> with pangs shall you eat from it all the days of your life.

18 Thorn and thistle shall it sprout for you
>> and you shall eat the plants of the field.

19 By the sweat of your brow shall you eat bread
>> till you return to the soil,
>>> for from there were you taken,
> for dust you are
>> and to dust shall you return."

---

17. *to the human.* The Masoretic Text vocalizes *le'adam* without the definite
article, which would make it mean "to Adam." But since Eve in the parallel
curse is still called "the woman," it seems better to assume the definite article
here.

  with pangs shall you eat. The noun *'itsavon* is the same used for the woman's birth pangs, confirming the lot of painful labor that is to be shared by
man and woman.

18. The vista of thorn and thistle is diametrically opposed to the luscious
vegetation of the garden and already intimates the verdict of banishment that
will be carried out in verses 23–24.

And the human called his woman's name Eve, for she was the mother   20
of all that lives. And the LORD God made skin coats for the human   21
and his woman, and He clothed them. And the LORD God said, "Now   22
that the human has become like one of us, knowing good and evil, he
may reach out and take as well from the tree of life and live forever."
And the LORD God sent him from the garden of Eden to till the soil   23
from which he had been taken. And he drove out the human and set   24
up east of the garden of Eden the cherubim and the flame of the
whirling sword to guard the way to the tree of life.

---

20. *Eve . . . all that lives.* Like most of the explanations of names in Genesis,
this is probably based on folk etymology or an imaginative playing with sound.
The most searching explanation of these poetic etymologies in the Bible has
been offered by Herbert Marks, who observes, "In a verisimilar narrative,
naming establishes and fixes identity as something tautologically itself; etymology, by returning it to the trials of language, compromises it, complicates
it, renders it potentially mobile." In the Hebrew here, the phonetic similarity
is between *ḥawah,* "Eve," and the verbal root *ḥayah,* "to live." It has been
proposed that Eve's name conceals very different origins, for it sounds suspiciously like the Aramaic word for "serpent." Could she have been given the
name by the contagious contiguity with her wily interlocutor, or, on the contrary, might there lurk behind the name a very different evaluation of the
serpent as a creature associated with the origins of life?

23. *the soil from which he had been taken.* This reminder of the first man's
clayey creatureliness occurs as a kind of refrain in this chapter, first in the
act of God's fashioning man, then in God's curse, and now in the banishment.
It is a mere thing shaped from clay that has aspired to be like a god.

24. The cherubim, a common feature of ancient Near Eastern mythology, are
not to be confused with the round-cheeked darlings of Renaissance iconogra-
phy. The root of the term either means "hybrid" or, by an inversion of consonants, "mount," "steed," and they are the winged beasts, probably of awesome
aspect, on which the sky god of the old Canaanite myths and of the poetry
of Psalms goes riding through the air. The fiery sword, not mentioned elsewhere but referred to with the definite article as though it were a familiar
image, is a suitable weapon to set alongside the formidable cherubim.

CHAPTER 4

₁ And the human knew Eve his woman and she conceived and bore Cain,
₂ and she said, "I have got me a man with the LORD." And she bore as
well his brother, Abel, and Abel became a herder of sheep while Cain
₃ was a tiller of the soil. And it happened in the course of time that
₄ Cain brought from the fruit of the soil an offering to the LORD. And
Abel too had brought from the choice firstlings of his flock, and the
₅ LORD regarded Abel and his offering but He did not regard Cain and

---

1. *knew.* The Hebrew verb suggests intimate knowledge and hence sexual
possession. Amos Funkenstein notes that it is the one term for sexual intercourse associated with legitimate possession—and in a few antithetical
instances, with perverse violation of legitimate possession. Given the clumsi-
ness of modern English equivalents like "had experience of," "cohabited
with," "was intimate with," and, given the familiarity of the King James Version's literal rendering, "to know" remains the least objectionable English
solution.

I have got me a man with the LORD. Eve's naming-speech puns on the verb
qanah, "to get," "acquire," or perhaps, "to make," and *qayin,* "Cain." His name
actually means "smith," an etymology that will be reflected in his linear
descendant Tubal-cain, the legendary first metalworker. ("Tubal" also means
"smith" in Sumerian and Akkadian.) Eve, upon bringing forth the third
human being, imagines herself as a kind of partner of God in man-making.

2. *Abel.* No etymology is given, but it has been proposed that the Hebrew
hevel, "vapor" or "puff of air," may be associated with his fleeting life span.

4.–5. The widespread culture-founding story of rivalry between herdsman and
farmer is recast in a pattern that will dominate Genesis—the displacement
of the firstborn by the younger son. If there is any other reason intimated as
to why God would favor Abel's offering and not Cain's, it would be in the
narrator's stipulation that Abel brings the very best of his flock to God.

his offering, and Cain was very incensed, and his face fell. And the   6
Lord said to Cain.

> "Why are you incensed,
>> and why is your face fallen?
> For whether you offer well,   7
>> or whether you do not,
> at the tent flap sin crouches
>> and for you is its longing
>>> but you will rule over it."

And Cain said to Abel his brother, "Let us go out to the field." And   8
when they were in the field, Cain rose against Abel his brother and

---

6.–7. This is the first of two enigmatic and probably quite archaic poems in the chapter. God's initial words pick up the two locutions for dejection of the immediately preceding narrative report and turn them into the parallel utterances of formal verse. The first clause of verse 7 is particularly elliptic in the Hebrew, and thus any construal is no more than an educated guess. The narrative context of sacrifices may suggest that the cryptic *s'eit* (elsewhere, "preeminence") might be related to *mas'eit,* a gift or cultic offering.

8. *Let us go out to the field.* This sentence is missing in the Masoretic Text but supplied in the Greek, Syriac, and Aramaic versions.
   his brother. In keeping with the biblical practice of using thematically fraught relational epithets, the victim of the first murder is twice called "his brother" here, and God will repeatedly refer to Abel in accusing Cain as "your brother."

9   killed him. And the Lord said to Cain, "Where is Abel your brother?"
10 And he said, "I do not know. Am I my brother's keeper?" And He said,
    "What have you done? Listen! your brother's blood cries out to me
11 from the soil. And so, cursed shall you be by the soil that gaped with
12 its mouth to take your brother's blood from your hand. If you till the
    soil, it will no longer give you its strength. A restless wanderer shall
13 you be on the earth." And Cain said to the Lord, "My punishment is
14 too great to bear. Now that You have driven me this day from the soil
    and I must hide from Your presence, I shall be a restless wanderer on
15 the earth and whoever finds me will kill me." And the Lord said to
    him, "Therefore whoever kills Cain shall suffer sevenfold vengeance."
    And the Lord set a mark upon Cain so that whoever found him would
    not slay him.

9.–12. There are several verbal echoes of Adam's interrogation by God and
Adam's curse, setting up a general biblical pattern in which history is seen as
a cycle of approximate and significant recurrences. Adam's being driven from
the garden to till a landscape of thorn and thistle is replayed here in God's
insistence that Cain is cursed by—the preposition also could mean "of" or
"from"—the soil (*'adamah*) that had hitherto yielded its bounty to him. The
biblical imagination is equally preoccupied with the theme of exile (this is
already the second expulsion) and with the arduousness or precariousness of
agriculture, a blessing that easily turns into blight.

11. *that gaped with its mouth to take your brother's blood from your hand.* The
image is strongly physical: a gaping *mouth* taking in *blood* from the murderer's
hand.

14. *whoever finds me.* This, and the subsequent report of Cain with a wife in
the land of Nod, are a famous inconsistency. Either the writer was assuming
knowledge of some other account of human origins involving more than a
single founding family, or, because the schematic simplicity of the single
nuclear-family plot impeded narrative development after Cain's banishment,
he decided not to bother with consistency.

15. *a mark.* It is of course a mark of protection, not a stigma as the English
idiom, "mark of Cain," suggests.

And Cain went out from the Lord's presence and dwelled in the land   16
of Nod east of Eden. And Cain knew his wife and she conceived and   17
bore Enoch. Then he became the builder of a city and called the name
of the city, like his son's name, Enoch. And Irad was born to Enoch,   18
and Irad begot Mehujael and Muhujael begot Methusael and Methusael begot Lamech. And Lamech took him two wives, the name of the   19
one was Adah and the name of the other was Zillah. And Adah bore   20
Jabal: he was the first of tent dwellers with livestock. And his brother's   21
name was Jubal: he was the first of all who play on the lyre and pipe.
As for Zillah, she bore Tubal-cain, who forged every tool of copper and   22

---

16. *the land of Nod.* Nod in Hebrew is cognate with "wanderer" in verse 12.

17. *the builder of a city.* The first recorded founder of a city is also the first
murderer, a possible reflection of the antiurban bias in Genesis.

20. *he was the first.* The Hebrew says literally "father of," in keeping with the
predisposition of the language and culture to imagine historical concatenation genealogically.

23 iron. And the sister of Tubal-cain was Naamah. And Lamech said to his wives,

> "Adah and Zillah, O hearken my voice,
>   You wives of Lamech, give ear to my speech.
> For a man have I slain for my wound,
>   a boy for my bruising.

24
> For sevenfold Cain is avenged,
>   and Lamech seventy and seven."

25 And Adam again knew his wife and she bore a son and called his name Seth, as to say, "God has granted me other seed in place of Abel,

---

22. *Naamah.* One might expect an identification that would align Naamah with her siblings as a founder of some basic activity of human culture, but if such an identification was part of the original epic role call, it has been either lost or deleted. The Midrash recognized that the root of her name can refer to song: perhaps Naamah is meant to be associated with her half brother Jubal, the founder of instrumental music—he as accompanist, she as singer.

23.–24. The narrative context of this poem is long lost, but it looks like a warrior's triumphal song, cast as a boast to his wives. Unlike the looser form of the earlier poetic insets, this poem follows the parallelistic pattern of biblical verse with exemplary rigor. Every term in each initial verset has its semantic counterpart in the second verset. In the Hebrew, the first pair of versets has four accented syllables in each; every subsequent verset has three accented syllables. The last pair of versets, with its numbers, provides a paradigm case for poetic parallelism in the Bible: when a number occurs in the first half of the line, it must be increased—by one, by a decimal, or by a decimal added to the original number, as here, in the second half of the line. In the same way, there is a pronounced tendency in the poetry to intensify semantic material as it is repeated in approximate synonymity. Perhaps, then, what Lamech is saying (quite barbarically) is that not only has he killed a man for wounding him, he has not hesitated to kill a mere boy for hurting him.

25. *Seth . . . granted me.* The naming pun plays on the similarity of sound between "Seth," *shet,* and "granted," *shat.*

for Cain has killed him." As for Seth, to him, too, a son was born, and   26
he called his name Enosh. It was then that the name of the LORD was
first invoked.

---

26. *Enosh.* The name is also a common noun in Hebrew meaning "man," and
that conceivably might explain why, from the universalist perspective of the
writer, the name YHWH began to be invoked in this generation. In any case,
the narrative unit that begins with one general term for human being, *'adam,*
in verse 1, here concludes with another, *'enosh,* and those two words elsewhere are bracketed together in poetic parallelism.

the name of the LORD was first invoked. That is, the distinctive Israelite
designation for the deity, YHWH, represented in this translation, according
to precedent in the King James Version, as the LORD. The existence of primordial monotheism is an odd biblical notion that seeks to reinforce the
universalism of the monotheistic idea. The enigmatic claim, made here with
an atypical and vague passive form of the verb, is contradicted by the report
in Exodus that only with Moses was the name YHWH revealed to man.

CHAPTER 5

1 This is the book of the lineage of Adam: On the day God created the
2 human, in the image of God He created him. Male and female He
created them, and He blessed them and called their name humankind
3 on the day they were created. And Adam lived a hundred and thirty
years and he begot in his likeness by his image and called his name
4 Seth. And the days of Adam after he begot Seth were eight hundred
5 years, and he begot sons and daughters. And all the days Adam lived
6 were nine hundred and thirty years. Then he died. And Seth lived a
7 hundred and five years and he begot Enosh. And Seth lived after he
8 begot Enosh eight hundred and seven years. Then he died. And all
the days of Seth were nine hundred and twelve years. Then he died.
9,10 And Enosh lived ninety years and he begot Kenan. And Enosh lived
after he begot Kenan eight hundred and fifteen years, and he begot
11 sons and daughters. And all the days of Enosh were nine hundred and
12 five years. Then he died. And Kenan lived seventy years and he begot
13 Mahalalel. And Kenan lived after he begot Mahalalel eight hundred
14 and forty years, and he begot sons and daughters. And all the days of
15 Kenan were nine hundred and ten years. Then he died. And Mahalalel
16 lived sixty-five years and he begot Jared. And Mahalalel lived after he
begot Jared eight hundred and thirty years, and he begot sons and

---

Nothing reveals the difference of the biblical conception of literature from later Western ones more strikingly than the biblical use of genealogies as an intrinsic element of literary structure. As J. P. Fokkelman (1987) has noted, the genealogical lists or "begats" (*toledot*) in Genesis are carefully placed compositional units that mark off one large narrative segment from another: here, the story of Creation and the antediluvian founding figures from the Deluge story. As Fokkelman also observes, the begettings of the genealogical lists are linked thematically with the initial injunction to be fruitful and multiply and with all the subsequent stories of a threatened or thwarted procreative drive.

Repetition of formula dominates the genealogical list stylistically. Here the procreative act and life span of each figure are conveyed in identical language, and when there is a divergence from the formula, in the case of Enoch, it is very significant. Formulaic numbers as well are characteristically used by the biblical writer to give order and coherence to the narrated world. The seven generations from Adam to Noah of chapter 4 are here displaced by a different formulaic number, ten. (Some critics have argued that the two lists reflect competing versions that deploy the same group of fathers and sons in different patterns: some of the names are identical in both lists, others—like Cain-Kenan, Irad-Jared—may well be variants of each other.) This list incorporates both of the formulaic numbers: Lamech, the last of the antediluvians before Noah, lives 777 years; Noah, unlike his predecessors, becomes a begetter at the age of 500, halfway through a round millennium, which is the ten of the ten generations with two decimal places added. A millennium is the age most of the antedeluvians come close to but never attain, as befits their mortality.

Surely part of the intention in using the genealogy is to give the history the look of authentically archaic documentation. If, as many assume, Priestly circles in the Second Temple period were ultimately responsible for the list here, they did not hesitate to include the fabulous ages of the antediluvians, which must have had their origins in hoary Semitic antiquity (as the old Mesopotamian parallels suggest), as well as the strange, evidently mythic fragment about Enoch, which could scarcely have been a late invention.

1. *This is the book.* The Hebrew *sefer,* which some render as "record," is anything written down, presumably in the form of a scroll. In any case, the introductory formula clearly announces this as a separate document.

Adam. The lack of a definite article would seem to indicate that the term is being used as a proper name. But the two subsequent occurrences of *'adam,* here and in the next verse, equally lack the definite article and yet clearly refer to "the human creature" or "humankind." God's calling "them" by the name *'adam* (verse 2) is also an explicit indication that the term is not exclusively masculine, and so it is misleading to render it as "man."

1.–2. *in the image of God . . . male and female He created them.* The pointed citation of the account in chapter 1 ties in the genealogical list with the initial story of human origins: creation is recapitulated, and continues.

3. *in his likeness by his image.* Adam, then, replicates God's making of the human being (with the order of "likeness" and "image" reversed) in his own act of procreation.

17 daughters. And all the days of Mahalalel were eight hundred and
18 ninety-five years. Then he died. And Jared lived a hundred and sixty-
19 two years and he begot Enoch. And Jared lived after he begot Enoch
20 eight hundred years, and he begot sons and daughters. And all the
days of Jared were nine hundred and sixty-two years. Then he died.
21,22 And Enoch lived sixty-five years and he begot Methuselah. And Enoch
walked with God after he begot Methuselah three hundred years, and
23 he begot sons and daughters. And all the days of Enoch were three
24 hundred and sixty-five years. And Enoch walked with God and he was
25 no more, for God took him. And Methuselah lived a hundred and
26 eighty-seven years and he begot Lamech. And Methuselah lived after
he begot Lamech seven hundred and eighty-two years, and he begot
27 sons and daughters. And all the days of Methuselah were nine hun-
28 dred and sixty-nine years. Then he died. And Lamech lived a hundred

---

22. *And Enoch walked with God.* This cryptic verse has generated mountains
of speculative commentary, not to speak of two whole books of the Apocrypha. The reflexive form of the verb "to walk" that occurs here is the same
form used for God's walking about in the garden. Instead of the flat report of
death, as in the case of the other antediluvians, the euphemism "was no
more" (literally "was not"), which is also applied to Joseph, merely supposed
by his brothers to be dead, is used. "Walked with" surely implies some sort
of special intimate relationship with God, but what that might be is anyone's
guess. This is one of several instances in the early chapters of Genesis of a
teasing vestige of a tradition for which the context is lost. Enoch is the seventh generation from Adam, and some scholars have seen an instructive analogy in a Mesopotamian list of kings before the Deluge, in which the seventh
antediluvian king, a certain Enmeduranki, is taken up to sit before the gods
Shamash and Adad, and is granted preternatural wisdom. Shamash is the sun
god, and the biblical Enoch lives as many years as the days of the solar year.

and eighty-two years and he begot a son. And he called his name   29
Noah, as to say, "This one will console us for the pain of our hands'
work from the soil which the LORD cursed." And Lamech lived after   30
he begot Noah five hundred and ninety-five years, and he begot sons
and daughters. And all the days of Lamech were seven hundred and   31
seventy-seven years. Then he died. And Noah was five hundred years   32
old and he begot Shem, Ham, and Japheth.

---

29. *This one will console us.* As usual, the sound-play on the name Noah,
which lacks the final *mem* of the word for "console," *naḥem*, is loose phonetic
association. What the nature of the consolation might be is a cloudier issue.
Rashi's proposal that Noah was the inventor of the plow has scant support in
the subsequent text. Others, more plausibly, have linked the consolation with
Noah's role as the first cultivator of the vine. The idea that wine provides the
poor man respite from his drudgery (see Proverbs 31:6–7) is common enough
in the biblical world. Wine, then, might have been thought of as a palliative
to the curse of hard labor, which is also the curse of the soil: the language of
3:17–18 is explicitly echoed here.

    the pain of our hands' work. Most translations render this as "our toil, our
work," or something equivalent. But the second term *'itsavon*, does not mean
"labor" but rather "pain," and is the crucial word at the heart of Adam's curse,
and Eve's. Given that allusion, the two terms in the Hebrew—which reads
literally, "our work and the pain of our hands"—are surely to be construed as
a hendiadys, a pair of terms for a single concept indicating "painful labor." It
should be noted that the "work of our hands" is a common biblical collocation
while "pain of our hands" occurs only here, evidently under the gravitational
pull of "work" with which it is paired as a compound idiom. Equally noteworthy is that the word *'itsavon* appears only three times in the Bible (other
nominal forms of the root being relatively common)—first for Eve, then for
Adam, and now for Noah.

CHAPTER 6

1 And it happened as humankind began to multiply over the earth and
2 daughters were born to them, that the sons of God saw that the daughters of man were comely, and they took themselves wives howsoever
3 they chose. And the LORD said, "My breath shall not abide in the human forever, for he is but flesh. Let his days be a hundred and twenty years."

---

2. *man*. Here it seems better to render the generic *ha'adam* as "man" both because in the patrilineal imagination (compare the immediately preceding genealogy) males are seen as the begetters of daughters and sons, and because the term "daughters of man" is played against "sons of God."

1.–4. This whole passage is obviously archaic and mythological. The idea of male gods coupling with mortal women whose beauty ignites their desire is a commonplace of Greek myth, and E. A. Speiser has proposed that both the Greek and the Semitic stories may have a common source in the Hittite traditions of Asia Minor. The entourage of celestial beings obscurely implied in God's use of the first person plural in the Garden story (compare 3:22) here produces, however fleetingly, active agents in the narrative. As with the prospect that man and woman might eat from the tree of life, God sees this intermingling of human and divine as the crossing of a necessary line of human limitation, and He responds by setting a new retracted limit (three times the formulaic forty) to human life span. Once more human mortality is confirmed, this time in quantitative terms.

2. *comely*. The Hebrew also means "good" but it very often occurs in the sense of goodly appearance, and is sometimes explicitly paired with the word for "beautiful." The same term is used for Eve's perception of the tree of knowledge (3:6).

3. *abide . . . is but*. Both pertinent Hebrew terms are cryptic, and the translation is somewhat speculative.

The Nephilim were then on the earth, and afterward as well, the sons 4
of God having come to bed with the daughters of man who bore
them children: they are the heroes of yore, the men of renown.

---

4. *Nephilim.* The only obvious meaning of this Hebrew term is "fallen
ones"—perhaps, those who have come down from the realm of the gods; but
then the word might conceivably reflect an entirely different, un-Hebraic
background. In any case, the notion of semidivine, heroic figures—in Numbers the Nephilim are thought of as giants who are offspring of miscegenation
between gods and women—again touches on common ground with Greek
and other mythologies.

come to bed with. The Hebrew idiom is literally "come into," that is,
"entered." It involves a more direct reference to the mechanics of the sexual
act than "to know" and thus has a more carnal coloration, but at the same
time it seems to be perfectly decorous. The English "entered" would be too
clinical, and, in any case, the Hebrew idiom refers to the whole act of intercourse, not merely to penetration. Of the three expressions used for sexual
intercourse in Genesis—the other two are "to know" and "to lie with"—this
one is reserved for sexual intimacy with a woman with whom the man has
not previously had carnal relations, whether or not she is his legitimate wife.
The spatial imagery of the idiom of "coming into" appears to envisage entering
concentric circles—the woman's private sphere, her bed, her body.

heroes of yore. The Hebrew style of this entire clause reflects a certain epic
heightening, hence the archaizing turn in the translation. One suspects that
these words are either a citation of an old heroic poem or a stylistic allusion
to the epic genre.

5 And the LORD saw that the evil of the human creature was great
on the earth and that every scheme of his heart's devising was only
6 perpetually evil. And the LORD regretted having made the human on
7 earth and was grieved to the heart. And the LORD said, "I will wipe
out the human race I created from the face of the earth, from human
to cattle to crawling thing to the fowl of the heavens, for I regret that
8 I have made them." But Noah found favor in the eyes of the LORD.
9 This is the lineage of Noah—Noah was a righteous man, he was
10 blameless in his time, Noah walked with God—and Noah begot three
11 sons, Shem and Ham and Japheth. And the earth was corrupt before
12 God and the earth was filled with outrage. And God saw the earth
and, look, it was corrupt, for all flesh had corrupted its ways on the

---

5. *was great*. With a minor change in vocalization, this adjective could be read
as a verb, "multiplied": in any case, the whole phrase echoes the "multiply
over the earth" of verse 1. The nature of the evil, distinct from the preceding
tale of human-divine miscegenation, is not specified, and God's subsequent
indictment uses only general terms ("corruption" and "outrage"/"law-
lessness"). It is noteworthy that the sundry Mesopotamian Flood stories, on
which this account draws heavily, present the Deluge as the gods' response
to overpopulation or as an arbitrary act whereas here it is evil, not humankind,
that multiplies and fills the earth.

heart's devising. In the Bible the heart is usually thought of as the seat of
intelligence, only occasionally as the seat of emotion; thus many modern
translators use "mind" here. But man's evil heart is pointedly meant to stand
in contrast to God's grieving heart (the same Hebrew word) in the next verse.

6. *grieved*. The same verbal root, '-ts-b, is reflected in Eve's pangs, Adam's
pain, and "the pain of our hands' work."

9. *lineage*. The listing of Noah's three sons in the next verse supports this
sense of *toledot*, but it might also mean "story."

11. *filled with outrage*. Humankind had been enjoined to multiply and fill the
earth, but the proliferation of human population leads to a proliferation of
lawless behavior. This is one of several verbal echoes of the Creation story,
suggesting, first, a perversion of creation by man and, then, a reversal of
creation by God.

earth. And God said to Noah, "The end of all flesh is come before me, 13
for the earth is filled with outrage by them, and I am now about to
destroy them, with the earth. Make yourself an ark of cypress wood, 14
with cells you shall make the ark, and caulk it inside and out with
pitch. This is how you shall make it: three hundred cubits, the ark's 15
length; fifty cubits, its width; thirty cubits, its height. Make a skylight 16
in the ark, within a cubit of the top you shall finish it, and put an
entrance in the ark on one side. With lower and middle and upper
decks you shall make it. As for me, I am about to bring the Flood, 17
water upon the earth, to destroy all flesh that has within it the breath
of life from under the heavens, everything on the earth shall perish.
And I will set up my covenant with you, and you shall enter the ark, 18
you and your sons and your wife and the wives of your sons, with you.
And from all that lives, from all flesh, two of each thing you shall bring 19
to the ark to keep alive with you, male and female they shall be. From 20
the fowl of each kind and from the cattle of each kind and from all
that crawls on the earth of each kind, two of each thing shall come to
you to be kept alive. As for you, take you from every food that is eaten 21
and store it by you, to serve for you and for them as food." And this 22
Noah did; as all that God commanded him, so he did.

---

13. *destroy.* The Hebrew verb is identical with the one used three times above
in the sense of "corrupt" and so inscribes a pattern of measure for measure.

13.–21. God's pronouncement of imminent doom and His instructions about
the ark are the longest continuous speech up to this point in Genesis, considerably exceeding the triple curse in chapter 3. Most of the length is dictated
by the necessity to provide specifications for the construction of the ark and
the arrangements for the animals. But the writer also uses the speech as a
vehicle for realizing God's awesome presence in the story: the language is not
arranged in actual verse but it sounds a drum roll of grand formal cadences,
stressing repeated terms and phrases that are rhythmically or semantically
parallel.

CHAPTER 7

¹ And the LORD said to Noah, "Come into the ark, you and all your house-
hold, for it is you I have seen righteous before me in this generation.
² Of every clean animal take you seven pairs, each with its mate, and of
³ every animal that is not clean, one pair, each with its mate. Of the

---

1. *for it is you I have seen righteous before me in this generation.* God's words
here reflect a frequently used technique of biblical narrative, in which the
narrator's report or evaluation is confirmed by a near-verbatim repetition in
dialogue, or vice versa. The judgment that Noah is "righteous in this generation" explicitly echoes the narrator's declaration in 6:9 that Noah is "a righteous man . . . blameless in his time" (the Hebrew for "time" is literally
"generations").

2. *Of every clean animal take you seven pairs.* Clean and unclean evidently
refer to fitness for sacrificial use, not for eating, as in the later dietary prohibi-
tions. As scholarship has often noted, two versions of the Flood story, the
Priestly and the Yahwistic, are intertwined in a somewhat confusing fashion.
According to the former, two of each species are to be brought into the ark
and no distinction is made between clean and unclean. According to the
latter, seven pairs of clean animals and one pair of the unclean are to be
saved. Abraham ibn Ezra and other medieval exegetes rescue consistency by
proposing that when God directed attention to the clean-unclean distinction,
He had to add the difference in numbers because more animals were needed
to be sacrificed. (Noah, like his counterpart in the Mesopotamian Flood stories, does in fact offer a thanksgiving sacrifice after the waters recede.) But
the tensions between the two versions, including how they record the time
span of the Flood, persist, and there are some indications that the editor
himself struggled to harmonize them.

fowl of the heavens as well seven pairs, male and female, to keep seed
alive over all the earth. For in seven days' time I will make it rain on   4
the earth forty days and forty nights and I will wipe out from the face
of the earth all existing things that I have made." And Noah did all   5
that the Lord commanded him.

Noah was six hundred years old when the Flood came, water over the   6
earth. And Noah and his sons and his wife and his sons' wives came   7
into the ark because of the waters of the Flood. Of the clean animals   8
and of the animals that were not clean and of the fowl and of all that
crawls upon the ground two each came to Noah into the ark, male   9
and female, as God had commanded Noah. And it happened after   10
seven days, that the waters of the Flood were over the earth. In the

---

3. *seed.* The Hebrew term means both semen and the offspring that is its
product. It is a very concrete way of conceiving propagation and the survival
of a line, and seems worth preserving in a literal English rendering.

4. *I will make it rain.* The Hebrew uses a participial form indicating action
virtually on the point of beginning, but in English the introductory temporal
clause requires a simple future.

7. *because of.* The Hebrew also means "in the face of" and may have the
implied sense here of fleeing from the rising waters, as ibn Ezra observes.

11   six hundredth year of Noah's life, in the second month, on the seventeenth day of the month, on that day,

> All the wellsprings of the great deep burst
>   and the casements of the heavens were opened.

12,13   And the rain was over the earth forty days and forty nights. That very
day, Noah and Shem and Ham and Japheth, the sons of Noah, and
Noah's wife, and the three wives of his sons together with them, came
14   into the ark, they as well as beasts of each kind and cattle of each
kind and each kind of crawling thing that crawls on the earth and each
15   kind of bird, each winged thing. They came to Noah into the ark, two
16   by two of all flesh that has the breath of life within it. And those that
came in, male and female of all flesh they came, as God had com-

---

11. *In the six hundredth year.* The precise indications of age and date give the
report of the inception of the Flood a certain epic solemnity.

All the wellsprings of the great deep burst. This line of poetry has been cited
by Umberto Cassuto and others as a fragment from an old epic poem on the
Flood. This is by no means a necessary assumption, however, because it is a
regular practice of biblical narrative to introduce insets of verse at moments
of high importance, and in many instances the composition of verse and
prose may be by the same hand. The grand flourish of this line of poetry is
perfectly consonant with the resonant repetitions and measured cadences of
the surrounding prose. The surge of waters from the great deep below and
from the heavens above is, of course, a striking reversal of the second day of
creation, when a vault was erected to divide the waters above from the waters
below. The biblical imagination, having conceived creation as an orderly
series of divisions imposed on primordial chaos, frequently conjures with the
possibility of a reversal of this process (see, for example, Jeremiah 4:23–26):
biblical cosmogony and apocalypse are reverse sides of the same coin. The
Flood story as a whole abounds in verbal echoes of the Creation story (the
crawling things, the cattle and beasts of each kind, and so forth) as what was
made on the six days is wiped out in these forty.

manded him, and the LORD shut him in. And the Flood was forty days 17
over the earth, and the waters multiplied and bore the ark upward and
it rose above the earth. And the waters surged and multiplied mightily 18
over the earth, and the ark went on the surface of the water. And the 19
waters surged most mightily over the earth, and all the high mountains
under the heavens were covered. Fifteen cubits above them the waters 20
surged as the mountains were covered. And all flesh that stirs on the 21
earth perished, the fowl and the cattle and the beasts and all swarming
things that swarm upon the earth, and all humankind. All that had the 22
quickening breath of life in its nostrils, of all that was on dry land,
died. And He wiped out all existing things from the face of the earth, 23
from humans to cattle to crawling things to the fowl of the heavens,
they were wiped out from the earth. And Noah alone remained, and
those with him in the ark. And the waters surged over the earth one 24
hundred and fifty days.

---

17. *and the waters multiplied.* The very verb of proliferation employed in the
Creation story for living creatures is here attached to the instrument of their
destruction.

22. *the quickening breath of life.* The Hebrew, *nishmat ruaḥ ḥayim,* is unusual,
the first two terms in a way doubling each other ("the breath of the breath of
life"). Some recent scholars construe this as a minimizing idiom that implies
something like "the faintest breath of life." But the one other occurrence of
the phrase *nishmat ruaḥ,* in David's victory psalm (2 Samuel 22:16), is part of
an anthropomorphic vision of God breathing fire on the battlefield ("From
the LORD's roaring, / the blast of his nostril's breath"); and so it is more plausible that the doubled terms are intensifiers, underlining the physical exhala-
tion of breath from the nostrils that is the sign of life.

CHAPTER 8

¹ And God remembered Noah and all the beasts and all the cattle that were with him in the ark. And God sent a wind over the earth and the ² waters subsided. And the wellsprings of the deep were dammed up, and the casements of the heavens, the rain from the heavens held ³ back. And the waters receded from the earth little by little, and the ⁴ waters ebbed. At the end of a hundred and fifty days the ark came to rest, on the seventeenth day of the seventh month, on the mountains ⁵ of Ararat. The waters continued to ebb, until the tenth month, on ⁶ the first day of the tenth month, the mountaintops appeared. And it happened, at the end of forty days, that Noah opened the window of ⁷ the ark he had made. And he let out the raven and it went forth to ⁸ and fro until the waters should dry up from the earth. And he let out the dove to see whether the waters had abated from the surface of the ⁹ ground. But the dove found no resting place for its foot and it returned to him to the ark, for the waters were over all the earth. And he ¹⁰ reached out and took it and brought it back to him into the ark. Then

---

2. *the wellsprings of the deep . . . , and the casements of the heavens, the rain.* In keeping with the stately symmetry that governs the style of the whole Flood narrative, the ending of the Flood precisely echoes the terms in which its beginning was represented, in the same order: the poetic inset of 7:11 immediately followed by "rain" at the beginning of 7:12.

5. *the mountaintops appeared.* There is an echo here of "that the dry land will appear" of 1:9.

6. *at the end of forty days.* After the ark comes to rest, not the forty days of deluge.

he waited another seven days and again let the dove out of the ark.
And the dove came back to him at eventide and, look, a plucked olive   11
leaf was in its bill, and Noah knew that the waters had abated from
the earth. Then he waited still another seven days and let out the   12
dove, and it did not return to him again. And it happened in the six   13
hundred and first year, in the first month, on the first day of the month,
the waters dried up from the earth, and Noah took off the covering of
the ark and he saw and, look, the surface of the ground was dry. And   14
in the second month, on the twenty-seventh day of the month, the
earth was completely dry. And God spoke to Noah, saying, "Go out of   15,16
the ark, you and your wife and your sons and your sons' wives, with
you. All the animals that are with you of all flesh, fowl and cattle and   17
every crawling thing that crawls on the earth, take out with you, and
let them swarm through the earth and be fruitful and multiply on the
earth." And Noah went out, his sons and his wife and his sons' wives   18
with him. Every beast, every crawling thing, and every fowl, everything   19

---

13. *in the six hundred and first year.* Of Noah's life. The Septuagint adds these
words, though whether that reflects a gloss or a more reliable text at this
point is unclear.

   ground. The Hebrew is *'adamah,* the word that also means "soil" and that
figures importantly in the Garden story and its immediate aftermath. It recurs
again in verse 21 in God's vow not to destroy the earth again.

14. *completely dry.* There is no "completely" in the Hebrew but that may be
implied by the verb used. The verb for "was dry" in the preceding verse is
ḥarev; the verb here is *yavesh.* The two are occasionally paired in poetic parallelism (e.g., Hosea 13:15), but they also occur twice in what looks like a temporal sequence (Isaiah 19:5 and Job 14:11): first a water source dries up
(*ḥarev*), then it is in a state of complete dryness (*yavesh*).

19. The verb *ramas* and the noun *remes* usually refer to crawling life-forms,
but there are a few contexts in which they appear to designate any kind of
moving creature. (The meaning of the root is probably linked with minute
movement, shuffling, or trampling.) In 9:3, *remes* must indicate all kinds of
animals because Noah's diet is surely not restricted to reptiles and insects.
Here, the initial *romes* seems to mean "crawling things," because it stands in
contradistinction to "every beast," whereas *romes* in the next clause summa-
rizes the catalogue that precedes it, which includes birds.

20   that stirs on the earth, by families, came out of the ark. And Noah
built an altar to the LORD and he took from every clean cattle and
21   every clean fowl and offered burnt offerings on the altar. And the
LORD smelled the fragrant odor and the LORD said in His heart, "I will
not again damn the soil on humankind's score. For the devisings of
the human heart are evil from youth. And I will not again strike down
22   all living things as I did. As long as all the days of the earth—

> seedtime and harvest
> and cold and heat
> and summer and winter
> and day and night
> shall not cease."

---

21. *And the* LORD *smelled the fragrant odor.* Noah has followed in the literary
footsteps of the hero of the Mesopotamian Flood stories in offering thanksgiving sacrifice after the waters recede. The frankly anthropomorphic imagination that informs Genesis has no difficulty in conceiving God enjoying the
aroma of the burnt offerings. What is rigorously excluded from the monotheistic version of the story is any suggestion that God eats the sacrifice—in the
Mesopotamian traditions, the gods are thought to be dependent on the food
men provide them through the sacrifices, and they swoop down on the postdiluvian offering "like flies." The word for "fragrance" (or perhaps, something
pleasing or soothing), *nihoah,* is always attached to "odor" as a technical term
linked with sacrifices, and it probably puns here on the name Noah.

    The thanksgiving sacrifice is evidently a requisite narrative motif taken
from the Mesopotamian antecedents, but the Hebrew writer's attitude
toward it may be more complicated than meets the eye. The first reported
animal sacrifice, though equally pleasing to God, led to the murder of the
sacrificer. Noah is about to be warned about the mortal danger of bloodguilt,
and he himself will become the victim of an act of violation, though not as a
consequence of his sacrifice. In any case, divine acceptance of ritual offerings
does nothing to mitigate man's dangerous impulses.

    and the LORD *said in His heart.* The idiom means "said to himself" but it
is important to preserve the literal wording because it pointedly echoes 6:6,
"and was grieved to the heart," just as "the devisings of the human heart are
evil" explicitly echoes 6:5. The Flood story is thus enclosed by mutually mir-
roring reports of God's musing on human nature. Whether the addition here

of "from youth" means, as some commentators claim, that God now has a more qualified view of the human potential for evil, is questionable. But after the Flood, God, once more recognizing the evil of which man is capable, concludes that, given what man is all too likely disposed to do, it is scarcely worth destroying the whole world again on his account.

damn. The Hebrew verb, from a root associated with the idea of lack of importance, or contemptibility, may occasionally mean "to curse," as in the Balaam story, but its usual meaning is to denigrate or vilify. Perhaps both senses are intimated here.

I will not again. The repetition of this phrase may reflect, as Rashi suggests, a formal oath, the solemnity of which would then be capped by the poetic inset at the end (which uses an unconventional short-line form, with only two accents in each verset). What is peculiar is that this is a pledge that God makes to Himself, not out loud to Noah. The complementary promise to Noah, in the next chapter, will be accompanied by the external sign of the rainbow. The silent promise in God's interior monologue invokes no external signs, only the seamless cycle of the seasons that will continue as long as the earth.

CHAPTER 9

1 **A**nd God blessed Noah and his sons and He said to them, "Be fruitful
2 and multiply and fill the earth. And the dread and fear of you shall be
upon all the beasts of the field and all the fowl of the heavens, in all
that crawls on the ground and in all the fish of the sea. In your hand
3 they are given. All stirring things that are alive, yours shall be for food,
4 like the green plants, I have given all to you. But flesh with its lifeblood
5 still in it you shall not eat. And just so, your lifeblood I will requite,
from every beast I will requite it, and from humankind, from every
man's brother, I will requite human life.

6   He who sheds human blood
           by humans his blood shall be shed,

1.–7. God's first postdiluvian speech to Noah affirms man's solidarity with
the rest of the animal kingdom—the covenant He goes on to spell out is,
emphatically, with all flesh, not just with humankind—but also modifies the
arrangement stipulated in the Creation story. Vegetarian man of the Garden
is now allowed a carnivore's diet (this might conceivably be intended as an
outlet for his violent impulses), and in consonance with that change, man
does not merely rule over the animal kingdom but inspires it with fear.

6. *He who sheds human blood / by humans his blood shall be shed.* "by humans"
might alternately mean "on account of the human." In either case, a system
of retributive justice is suggested. As many analysts of the Hebrew have
noted, there is an emphatic play on *dam,* "blood," and *'adam,* "human," and
the chiastic word order of the Hebrew formally mirrors the idea of measure
for measure: *shofekh* [spills] *dam* [blood] *ha'adam* [of the human], *ba'adam*
[by the human] *damo* [his blood] *yishafekh* [will be spilled] (=A B C C' B'
A'). Perhaps the ban on bloodshed at this point suggests that murder was the
endemic vice of the antediluvians.

for in the image of God
   He made humankind.
As for you, be fruitful and multiply,   7
   swarm through the earth, and hold sway over it."

And God said to Noah and to his sons with him, "And I, I am about   8,9
to establish My covenant with you and with your seed after you, and   10
with every living creature that is with you, the fowl and the cattle and
every beast of the earth with you, all that have come out of the ark,
every beast of the earth. And I will establish My covenant with you,   11
that never again shall all flesh be cut off by the waters of the Flood,
and never again shall there be a Flood to destroy the earth." And God   12
said, "This is the sign of the covenant that I set between Me and you
and every living creature that is with you, for everlasting generations:
My bow I have set in the clouds to be a sign of the covenant between   13
Me and the earth, and so, when I send clouds over the earth, the bow   14
will appear in the cloud. Then I will remember My covenant, between   15

---

7. *hold sway.* The translation here follows some versions of the Septuagint, which read *uredu,* "and hold sway," instead of *urevu,* "and multiply," as in the Masoretic Text. The latter reading looks suspiciously like a scribal transposition of *urevu* from the end of the first clause. The entire line, of course, picks up the language of 1:28 as the process of human history is resumed after the Flood.

12. *And God said.* This is the first instance of a common convention of biblical narrative: when a speaker addresses someone and the formula for introducing speech is repeated with no intervening response from the interlocutor, it generally indicates some sort of significant silence—a failure to comprehend, a resistance to the speaker's words, and so forth. (Compare Judges 8:23–24. First Gideon declares to his men that he will not rule over them. Seeing their evident resistance, he proposes a concrete alternative they can understand, the collection of gold ornaments to make an ephod.) Here, God first flatly states His promise never to destroy the world again. The flood-battered Noah evidently needs further assurance, so God goes on, with a second formula for introducing speech, to offer the rainbow as outward token of His covenant. The third occurrence of the *wayomer* formula, at the beginning of verse 17, introduces a confirming summary of the rainbow as sign of the covenant.

Me and you and every living creature of all flesh, and the waters will
16   no more become a Flood to destroy all flesh. And the bow shall be in
the cloud and I will see it, to remember the everlasting covenant
between God and all living creatures, all flesh that is on the earth."
17   And God said to Noah, "This is the sign of the covenant I have established between Me and all flesh that is on the earth."

18   And the sons of Noah who came out from the ark were Shem and
19   Ham and Japheth, and Ham was the father of Canaan. These three
were the sons of Noah, and from these the whole earth spread out.
20,21   And Noah, a man of the soil, was the first to plant a vineyard. And he
drank of the wine and became drunk, and exposed himself within his
22   tent. And Ham the father of Canaan saw his father's nakedness and
23   told his two brothers outside. And Shem and Japheth took a cloak and
put it over both their shoulders and walked backward and covered
their father's nakedness, their faces turned backward so they did not
24   see their father's nakedness. And Noah woke from his wine and he
25   knew what his youngest son had done to him. And he said,

---

20.–27. Like the story of the Nephilim, this episode alludes cryptically to
narrative material that may have been familiar to the ancient audience but
must have seemed to the monotheistic writer dangerous to spell out. The big
difference is that, for the first time in Genesis, the horizon of the story is the
national history of Israel: Ham, the perpetrator of the act of violation, is
mysteriously displaced in the curse by his son Canaan, and thus the whole
story is made to justify the—merely hoped-for—subject status of the Canaanites in relation to the descendents of Shem, the Israelites. (Ham also now
figures as the youngest son, not the middle one.) No one has ever figured out
exactly what it is that Ham does to Noah. Some, as early as the classical
Midrash, have glimpsed here a Zeus-Chronos story in which the son castrates
the father or, alternately, penetrates him sexually. The latter possibility is reinforced by the fact that "to see the nakedness of" frequently means "to copu-
late with," and it is noteworthy that the Hebrews associated the Canaanites
with lasciviousness (see, for example, the rape of Dinah, Genesis 34). Lot's
daughters, of course, take advantage of his drunkenness to have sex with him.
But it is entirely possible that the mere seeing of a father's nakedness was
thought of as a terrible taboo, so that Ham's failure to avert his eyes would
itself have earned him the curse.

"Cursed be Canaan,
    the lowliest slave shall he be
        to his brothers."

And he said,   26

"Blessed be the LORD
    the God of Shem,
        unto them shall Canaan be slave.
May God enlarge Japheth,   27
    may he dwell in the tents of Shem,
        unto them shall Canaan be slave."

And Noah lived after the Flood three hundred and fifty years. And all   28,29
the days of Noah were nine hundred and fifty years. Then he died.

28.–29. These verses resume the precise verbal formulas of the antediluvian genealogy in chapter 5. The story of Noah is given formal closure with this recording of his age, and the stage is set for the Table of Nations of the next chapter, which will constitute a historical divider between the tale of the Flood and the next narrative episode, the Tower of Babel.

CHAPTER 10

1   And this is the lineage of the sons of Noah, Shem, Ham, and Japheth.
2   Sons were born to them after the Flood. The sons of Japheth: Gomer and Magog and Madai and Javan and Tubal and Meshech and Tiras.
3,4   And the sons of Gomer: Ashkenaz and Riphath and Torgamah. And the sons of Javan: Elishah and Tarshish, the Kittites and the Dodanites.

As elsewhere, genealogy is adopted as a means of schematizing complex historical evolution, and thus the terms "father of" and "begot" are essentially metaphors for historical concatenation. The total number of figures in the Table of Nations (excluding Nimrod) comes to seventy, the biblical formulaic number for a sizeable and complete contingent of any sort. It should be observed that representing the origins of nations as a genealogical scheme preserves a thematic continuity with the divine injunction after Creation to be fruitful and multiply and sets the stage for the history of the one people whose propagation is repeatedly promised but continually threatened.

In keeping with the universalist perspective of Genesis, the Table of Nations is a serious attempt, unprecedented in the ancient Near East, to sketch a panorama of all known human cultures—from Greece and Crete in the west through Asia Minor and Iran and down through Mesopotamia and the Arabian Peninsula to northwestern Africa. This chapter has been a happy hunting ground for scholars armed with the tools of archeology, and in fact an impressive proportion of these names have analogues in inscriptions and tablets in other ancient Near Eastern cultures. The Table mingles geographic, ethnic, and linguistic criteria for defining nations, and the list intersperses place-names and gentilic designations (the latter appearing first in plural forms and beginning with verse 16 in singular forms). Some analysts have argued for a splicing together of two different lists of nations. One may infer that the Table assumes a natural evolutionary explanation for the multiplicity of languages that does not involve an act of divine intervention of the sort that will be narrated in the next episode, the Tower of Babel.

From these the Sea Peoples branched out. [These are the sons of   5
Japheth,] in their lands, each with his own tongue, according to their
clans in their nations. And the sons of Ham: Cush and Mizraim and   6
Put and Canaan. And the sons of Cush: Seba and Havilah and Raa-   7
mah and Sabteca. And the sons of Raamah: Sheba and Dedan. And   8
Cush begot Nimrod. He was the first mighty man on earth. He was a   9
mighty hunter before the LORD. Therefore is it said: Like Nimrod, a
mighty hunter before the LORD. The start of his kingdom was Babylon   10
and Erech and Accad, all of them in the land of Shinar. From that land   11
Ashur emerged, and he built Nineveh and Rehoboth-ir and Calah,
and Resen, between Nineveh and Calah, which is the great city. And   12,13
Mizraim begot the Ludites and the Anamites and the Lehubites and
the Naphtuhites, and the Pathrusites and the Casluhites, and the   14
Caphtorites, from whom the Philistines emerged. And Canaan begot   15

---

5. *the Sea Peoples*. The probable reference is to the migrants from the Greek
islands ("Javan" is Ion, or Greece) who established a foothold in the coastal
region of Palestine during the eleventh century.

These are the sons of Japheth. These words do not occur in the Masoretic
Text, but the scholarly consensus is that there is a scribal omission here, as
this is part of the formula used in verse 20 and verse 31 to summarize the list
of the descendants of each of Noah's other two sons.

8. *He was the first mighty man on earth*. The Hebrew, which says literally, "he
began to be a mighty man," uses the same idiom that is invoked for Noah's
planting a vineyard. The implication, then, is that Nimrod, too, was the
founder of an archetypal human occupation. The next verse suggests that
this occupation is that of hunter, with his founding of a great Mesopotamian
empire then introduced in verses 10–12 as an ancillary fact. Perhaps his prowess as hunter is put forth as evidence of the martial prowess that enabled
him to conquer kingdoms, since the two skills are often associated in the
ruling classes of older civilizations. Numerous Neo-Assyrian bas-reliefs
depict royal lion hunts or royal bull hunts. Nimrod has been conjecturally
identified with the thirteenth-century Tukulti-Ninurta I, the first Assyrian
conqueror of Babylonia.

10. *all of them*. This translation adopts a commonly accepted emendation
wekhulanah, instead of the Masoretic Text's *wekhalneh*, "and Calneh."

16 Sidon, his firstborn, and Heth and the Jebusite and the Amorite and
17,18 the Girgashite and the Hivite and the Archite and the Sinite and the
Arvadite and the Zemarite and the Hamatite. Afterward the clans of
19 the Canaanite spread out. And the border of the Canaanite was from
Sidon till you come to Gerar, as far as Gaza, till you come to Sodom
20 and Gomorrah and Admah and Zeboyim, as far as Lasha. These are
the sons of Ham according to their clans and their tongues, in their
21 lands and their nations. Sons were born, too, to Shem, the father of
22 all the sons of Eber, the older brother of Japheth. The sons of Shem:
23 Elam and Asshur and Arpachshad and Lud and Aram. And the sons
24 of Aram: Uz and Hul and Gether and Mash. And Arpachshad begot
25 Shelah and Shelah begot Eber. And to Eber two sons were born. The
name of one was Peleg for in his days the earth was split apart; and
26 his brother's name was Joktan. And Joktan begot Almodad and Shel-
27 eph and Hazarmaveth and Jerah and Hadoram and Uzal and Diklah
28,29 and Obal and Abimael and Sheba and Ophir and Havilah and Jobab.
30 All these were the sons of Joktan. And their settlements were from

---

24. *Eber.* He is the eponymous father of the Hebrews, *'ibrim.* Whatever the actual original meanings of the names, there is a clear tendency in the Table to intimate exemplary meanings in the names of these mythic founders: else-where, "Eber" is explicitly linked with the term that means "from the other side" (of the river).

25. *Peleg . . . in his days the earth split apart.* The three consonants of the name Peleg, which as a common noun means "brook," form the verbal root that means "to split." It is a stronger verb than "divide," the term used by most English translators. Rabbinic tradition construes the splitting here as a reference to the Tower of Babel, but it is at least as plausible to see it as an allusion to an entirely different epochal event of "division," such as a cataclys-mic earthquake.

Mesha till you come to Sephar, in the eastern highlands. These are   31
the sons of Shem according to their clans and tongues, in their lands
and their nations. These are the clans of the sons of Noah according   32
to their lineage in their nations. And from these the nations branched
out on the earth after the Flood.

---

32. *branched out.* Literally, the Hebrew verb means "separated." The whole
Table of Nations is devised to explain how the many separate nations came
into being. The immediately following verse, which begins the tale of the
Tower of Babel, announces a primeval unity of all people on earth. This seeming flat contradiction might reflect a characteristically biblical way of playing
dialectically with alternative possibilities: humankind is many and divided, as
a consequence of natural history; and, alternately, humankind was once one,
as a consequence of having been made by the same Creator, but this God-
given oneness was lost through man's presumption in trying to overreach his
place in the divine scheme.

CHAPTER 11

1,2   And all the earth was one language, one set of words. And it happened as they journeyed from the east that they found a valley in the land of
3   Shinar and settled there. And they said to each other, "Come, let us bake bricks and burn them hard." And the brick served them as stone,
4   and bitumen served them as mortar. And they said, "Come, let us build us a city and a tower with its top in the heavens, that we may
5   make us a name, lest we be scattered over all the earth." And the LORD came down to see the city and the tower that the human creatures had
6   built. And the LORD said, "As one people with one language for all, if this is what they have begun to do, nothing they plot will elude them.
7   Come, let us go down and baffle their language there so that they will
8   not understand each other's language." And the LORD scattered them
9   from there over all the earth and they left off building the city. Therefore it is called Babel, for there the LORD made the language of all the earth babble. And from there the LORD scattered them over all the earth.

1.–9. The story of the Tower of Babel transforms the Mesopotamian ziggurat, built with bricks (in contrast to Canaanite stone structures) and one of the wonders of ancient technology, into a monotheistic fable. Although there is a long exegetical tradition that imagines the building of the Tower as an attempt to scale the heights of heaven, the text does not really suggest that. "Its top in the heavens" is a hyperbole found in Mesopotamian inscriptions for celebrating high towers, and to make or leave a "name" for oneself by erecting a lasting monument is a recurrent notion in ancient Hebrew culture.

The polemic thrust of the story is against urbanism and the overweening confidence of humanity in the feats of technology. This polemic, in turn, is lined up with the stories of the tree of life and the Nephilim in which humankind is seen aspiring to transcend the limits of its creaturely condition. As in those earlier moments, one glimpses here the vestiges of a mythological background in which God addresses an unspecified celestial entourage in the first-person plural as He considers how to respond to man's presumption.

2. *a valley in the land of Shinar*. The Hebrew for "valley" might also mean "plain," as was recognized as long ago as ibn Ezra in the twelfth century. That would fit the Mesopotamian setting better.

3. *Come, let us*. As many commentators have noted, the story exhibits an intricate antithetical symmetry that embodies the idea of "man proposes, God disposes." The builders say, "Come, let us bake bricks," God says, "Come, let us go down"; they are concerned "lest we be scattered," and God responds by scattering them. The story is an extreme example of the stylistic predisposition of biblical narrative to exploit interechoing words and to work with a deliberately restricted vocabulary. The word "language" occurs five times in this brief text as does the phrase "all the earth" (and the "land" of Shinar is the same Hebrew word as that for earth). The prose turns language itself into a game of mirrors.

    bake bricks and burn them hard. A literal rendering of the Hebrew would be something like "brick bricks and burn for a burning." This fusion of words reflects the striking tendency of the story as a whole to make words flow into each other. "Bitumen," *ḥeimar*, becomes *ḥomer*, "mortar." The reiterated "there," *sham*, is the first syllable of *shamayim*, "heavens," as well as an odd echo of *shem*, "name." Meaning in language, as the biblical writer realized long before the influential Swiss linguist, Ferdinand de Saussure, is made possible through differences between terms in the linguistic system. Here difference is subverted in the very style of the story, with the blurring of lexical boundaries culminating in God's confounding of tongues. The Hebrew *balal*, to mix or confuse, represented in this translation by "baffle" and "babble," is a polemic pun on the Akkadian "Babel," which might actually mean "gate of the god." As for the phonetic kinship of babble and *balal*, *Webster's New World Dictionary of the American Language* (1966) notes that a word like "babble" occurs in a wide spectrum of languages from Greek, Latin, and Sanskrit to Norwegian, and prudently concludes, "of echoic origin; probably not of continuous derivation but recoined from common experience."

10 This is the lineage of Shem: Shem was a hundred years old when he
11 begot Arpachshad two years after the Flood. And Shem lived after
begetting Arpachshad five hundred years and he begot sons and
12 daughters. And Arpachshad lived thirty-five years and he begot
13 Shelah. And Arpachshad lived after begetting Shelah four hundred
14 and three years and he begot sons and daughters. And Shelah lived
15 thirty years and he begot Eber. And Shelah lived after begetting Eber
16 four hundred and three years and he begot sons and daughters. And
17 Eber lived thirty-four years and he begot Peleg. And Eber lived after
begetting Peleg four hundred and thirty years and he begot sons and
18,19 daughters. And Peleg lived thirty years and he begot Reu. And Peleg
lived after begetting Reu two hundred and nine years and he begot
20 sons and daughters. And Reu lived thirty-two years and he begot
21 Serug. And Reu lived after begetting Serug two hundred and seven
22 years and he begot sons and daughters. And Serug lived thirty years
23 and he begot Nahor. And Serug lived after begetting Nahor two hun-
24 dred years and he begot sons and daughters. And Nahor lived twenty-
25 nine years and he begot Terah. And Nahor lived after begetting Terah
one hundred and nineteen years and he begot sons and daughters.
26 And Terah lived seventy years and he begot Abram, Nahor, and Haran.

10.–26. There are ten generations from Shem to Abraham (as the universal
history begins to focus down to a national history) as there are ten from Adam
to Noah. In another formal symmetry, the ten antediluvian generations end
with a father who begets three sons, just as this series of ten will end with
Terah begetting Abram, Nahor, and Haran. This genealogy, which constitutes
the bridge from the Flood to the beginning of the Patriarchal Tales, uses
formulas identical with those of the antediluvian genealogy in chapter 5,
omitting the summarizing indication of life span and the report of death of
each begetter. Longevity now is cut in half, and then halved again in the
latter part of the list, as we approach Abram. From this point, men will have
merely the extraordinary life spans of modern Caucasian mountain dwellers
and not legendary life spans. The narrative in this way is preparing to enter
recognizable human time and family life. There is one hidden number-game
here, as the Israeli Bible scholar Moshe Weinfeld has observed: the number
of years from the birth of Shem's son to Abram's migration to Canaan is
exactly a solar 365.

And this is the lineage of Terah: Terah begot Abram, Nahor, and   27
Haran, and Haran begot Lot. And Haran died in the lifetime of Terah   28
his father in the land of his birth, Ur of the Chaldees. And Abram and   29
Nahor took themselves wives. The name of Abram's wife was Sarai
and the name of Nahor's wife was Milcah daughter of Haran, the
father of Milcah and the father of Iscah. And Sarai was barren, she   30
had no child. And Terah took Abram his son and Lot son of Haran,   31
his grandson, and Sarai his daughter-in-law, the wife of his son Abram,
and he set out with them from Ur of the Chaldees toward the land of
Canaan, and they came to Haran and settled there. And the days of   32
Terah were two hundred and five years, and Terah died in Haran.

27.–32. This is a second genealogical document, using different language, and
zeroing in on Abram's immediate family and its migrations.

31. *he set out with them.* Two small changes in the vocalization of the two
Hebrew words here yield "he took them out with him." This is the reading of
the Septuagint and the Samaritan Version.

   Haran. In the Hebrew there is no confusion with the name of Abram's
deceased brother, because the latter begins with an aspirated *heh,* the former
with a fricative *ḥet.*

CHAPTER 12

And the Lord said to Abram, "Go forth from your land and your birthplace and your father's house to the land I will show you. And I will make you a great nation and I will bless you and make your name great, and you shall be a blessing. And I will bless those who bless

---

1. *Go forth from your land . . . to the land I will show you.* Abram, a mere figure in a notation of genealogy and migration in the preceding passage, becomes an individual character, and begins the Patriarchal narratives, when he is here addressed by God, though he himself as yet says nothing, responding only by obedience. The name Canaan is never mentioned, and the divine imperative to head out for an unspecified place resembles, as Rashi observes, God's terrible call to Abraham in chapter 22 to sacrifice his son on a mountain God will show him. Rashi also draws a shrewd connection between the triplet here—"your land and your birthplace and your father's house"—with the triplet in chapter 22—"your son, your only one, whom you love." The series in each case focuses the utterance more specifically from one term to the next. Thus the Hebrew *moledet* almost certainly has its usual sense of "birthplace" and not its occasional sense of "kinfolk," which would turn it into a loose synonym of "father's house" (*bet 'av,* a fixed term for the family social unit). In 11:28 *moledet* appears as part of a genetive construction, *'erets moladeto,* "land of his birth." Here those two terms are broken out from each other to yield the focusing sequence: land–birthplace–father's house.

2. *you shall be a blessing.* The verb here as vocalized in the Masoretic Text literally means, "Be you a blessing," which makes the Hebrew syntax somewhat problematic. A change in vocalization would yield, "and it [your name] will be a blessing." The Israeli biblical scholar Moshe Weinfeld has aptly noted that after the string of curses that begins with Adam and Eve, human history reaches a turning point with Abraham, as blessings instead of curses are emphatically promised.

you, and those who damn you I will curse, and all the clans of the
earth through you shall be blessed." And Abram went forth as the 4
LORD had spoken to him and Lot went forth with him, Abram being
seventy-five years old when he left Haran. And Abram took Sarai his 5
wife and Lot his nephew and all the goods they had gotten and the
folk they had bought in Haran, and they set out on the way to the land
of Canaan, and they came to the land of Canaan. And Abram crossed 6
through the land to the site of Shechem, to the Terebinth of the Oracle. The Canaanite was then in the land. And the LORD appeared to 7
Abram and said, "To your seed I will give this land." And he built an
altar to the LORD who had appeared to him. And he pulled up his 8
stakes from there for the high country east of Bethel and pitched his
tent with Bethel to the west and Ai to the east, and he built there an
altar to the LORD, and he invoked the name of the LORD. And Abram 9
journeyed onward by stages to the Negeb.

---

3. *those who damn you*. The Masoretic Text uses a singular form, but the
plural, attested in several manuscripts and ancient versions, makes better
sense as parallelism. The balanced formulation of this and the preceding
verse are almost scannable as poetry.

5. *the folk they had bought in Haran*. Slavery was a common institution
throughout the ancient Near East. As subsequent stories in Genesis make
clear, this was not the sort of chattel slavery later practiced in North America.
These slaves had certain limited rights, could be given great responsibility,
and were not thought to lose their personhood.

6. *The Canaanite was then in the land*. Ibn Ezra famously detected a hint here
that at the time of writing this was no longer the case. In any event, the point
of the notation, as Gerhard von Rad has seen, is to introduce a certain tension
with the immediately following promise that the land will be given to Abram's
offspring.

8. *And he pulled up his stakes*. The Hebrew vocabulary (here, the verb *waya'-
teq*) in this sequence is meticulous in reflecting the procedures of nomadic
life. The verb for "journey" in verse 9 also derives from another term for the
pulling up of tent stakes, and the progressive form in which it is cast is a
precise indication of movement through successive encampments.

10 And there was a famine in the land and Abram went down to Egypt
11 to sojourn there, for the famine was grave in the land. And it happened
as he drew near to the border of Egypt that he said to Sarai his wife,
12 "Look, I know you are a beautiful woman, and so when the Egyptians
see you and say, 'She's his wife,' they will kill me while you they will
13 let live. Say, please, that you are my sister, so that it will go well with
14 me on your count and I shall stay alive because of you." And it happened when Abram came into Egypt that the Egyptians saw the
15 woman was very beautiful. And Pharaoh's courtiers saw her and
praised her to Pharaoh, and the woman was taken into Pharaoh's
16 house. And it went well with Abram on her count, and he had sheep
and cattle and donkeys and male and female slaves and she-asses and

---

10. *And there was a famine in the land.* The puzzling story of the sister-wife
occurs three times (here, chapter 20, and chapter 26:1–12). It is the first
instance of type-scene in biblical narrative, in which the writer invokes a
fixed sequence of narrative motifs, familiar as a convention to his audience,
while pointedly modifying them in keeping with the needs of the immediate
narrative context. The Midrash recognized that the tale of going down to
Egypt at a time of famine was a foreshadowing of the sojourn in Egypt ("the
actions of the fathers are a sign for the sons"). But in contrast to the versions
in chapters 20 and 26, here, at the beginning of the whole Patriarchal cycle,
the writer goes out of his way to heighten the connections with the Exodus
story. Only here is the land of sojourn Egypt and only here is the foreign
potentate Pharaoh. Only here does the narrator speak explicitly of "plagues"
(though a different term is used in Exodus). Only here is the danger of the
husband's death set off by the phrase "you they will let live" attached to the
wife, a pointed echo of Exodus 1:22, "Every boy that is born you shall cast
into the Nile and every girl you shall let live." This is also the most compact,
and the most archetypal, of the three versions; the other two will elaborate
and complicate the basic scheme, each in its own way.

11. *I know.* This is the construal of *yada'ti* according to normative Hebrew
grammar. But the *ti* ending could be an archaic second-person singular feminine, and "you know" would make better conversational sense here.

13. *my sister.* Chapter 20 reveals that Sarah is actually Abraham's half sister.
It is not clear whether the writer means to endorse the peculiar strategem of
the patriarch in any of these three stories.

camels. And the LORD afflicted Pharaoh and his household with terri- 17
ble plagues because of Sarai the wife of Abram. And Pharaoh sum- 18
moned Abram and said, "What is this you have done to me? Why did 19
you not tell me she was your wife? Why did you say, 'She's my sister,'
so that I took her to me as wife? Now, here is your wife. Take her and
get out!" And Pharaoh appointed men over him and they sent him out, 20
with his wife and all he had.

---

17. *plagues.* The nature of the afflictions is not spelled out. Rashi's inference
of a genital disorder preventing intercourse is not unreasonable. In that case,
one might imagine a tense exchange between Pharoah and Sarai ending in a
confession by Sarai of her status as Abram's wife. In the laconic narrative art
of the Hebrew writer, this is left as a gap for us to fill in by an indeterminate
compound of careful deduction and imaginative reconstruction.

19. *Take her and get out!* "Her" is merely implied in the Hebrew, which gives
us three abrupt syllables, two of them accented: *qákh walékh.* There may be
an intended counterpoint between the impatient brusqueness of this imperative, *lekh,* and the same imperative, softened by an ethical dative, *lekh lekha,*
"go forth" (literally, "go you"), in God's words to Abram that inaugurate the
Patriarchal cycle.

CHAPTER 13

1 And Abram came up from Egypt, he and his wife and all he had, and
2 Lot together with him, to the Negeb. And Abram was heavily laden
3 with cattle, with silver and gold. And he went on by stages from the
Negeb up to Bethel, to the place where his tent had been before,
4 between Bethel and Ai, to the place of the altar he had made the first
time, and Abram invoked there the name of the LORD.

5 And Lot, too, who came along with Abram, had flocks and herds and
6 tents. And the land could not support their dwelling together, for their
7 substance was great and they could not dwell together. And there was
strife between the herdsmen of Abram's flocks and the herdsmen of
Lot's flocks. The Canaanite and the Perizite were then dwelling in the
8 land. And Abram said to Lot, "Pray, let there be no contention
between you and me, between your herdsmen and mine, for we are

---

7. *The Canaanite and the Perizite.* This second notation of the indigenous
population of Canaan, at the moment of friction between the two immigrants
from Mesopotamia, suggests that they can scarcely afford such divisiveness
when they are surrounded by potential enemies. (In the next episode, Abram
will be compelled to bring military aid to his nephew.) There may also be a
hint of irony in their dividing up a land here that already has inhabitants.

8.–9. This is only the second report of direct speech of Abram. The first, his
address to Sarai as they are about to enter Egypt, reveals a man fearful about
his own survival. Here we get a very different image of Abram as the reasonable peacemaker and as a man conscious of family bonds in alien surround-
ings. The language in which he addresses Lot is clear, firm, and polite.

kinsmen. Is not all the land before you? Pray, let us part company. If   9
you take the left hand, then I shall go right, and if you take the right
hand, I shall go left." And Lot raised his eyes and saw the whole plain   10
of the Jordan, saw that all of it was well-watered, before the LORD's
destruction of Sodom and Gomorrah, like the garden of the LORD, like
the land of Egypt, till you come to Zoar. And Lot chose for himself   11
the whole plain of the Jordan, and Lot journeyed eastward, and they
parted: Abram dwelled in the land of Canaan and Lot dwelled in the   12
cities of the plain, and he set up his tent near Sodom.

---

9. *Pray, let us part company.* The Hebrew is cast in the form of a polite imperative, literally: "Kindly part from me."

10. *saw that all of it was well-watered.* There is no repetition of "saw" in the
Hebrew; Hebrew grammar allows the single verb to govern simultaneously
the direct object ("the whole plain of the Jordan") and the relative clause that
modifies the direct object. What is significant thematically is that the point
of view of the entire clause is Lot's. The writer may well have drawn on a
tradition that the whole plain of the Jordan down to the Dead Sea, before
some remembered cataclysm, was abundantly fertile, but it is Lot who sees
the plain in hyperbolic terms, likening it to "the garden of the LORD"—presumably, Eden, far to the east—and to the fabulously irrigated Egypt to the
south. (Archeologists have in fact discovered traces of an ancient irrigation
system in the plain of the Jordan.)

12. *dwelled in the cities . . . set up his tent.* At least in this first phase of his
habitation of the plain, Lot is represented ambiguously either living in a town
or camping near one. From the writer's perspective, abandoning the seminomadic life for urban existence can only spell trouble. The verb *'ahal* derived
from the noun "tent" is relatively rare, and seems to mean both to set up a
tent and (verse 18) to fold up a tent in preparation for moving on.

13 Now the people of Sodom were very evil offenders against the LORD.
14 And the LORD had said to Abram after Lot parted from him, "Raise
    your eyes and look out from the place where you are to the north and
15 the south and the east and the west, for all the land you see, to you I
16 will give it and to your seed forever. And I will make your seed like

---

13. *Now the people of Sodom.* This brief observation, as many commentators
have noted, suggests that Lot has made a very bad choice. The consequences
will become manifest in chapter 19.

14. *And the* LORD *had said to Abram.* Although all previous translations treat
this as a simple past, the word order—subject before verb—and the use of
the suffix conjugation instead of the prefix conjugation that is ordinarily
employed for past actions indicate a pluperfect. The definition of temporal
frame is pointed and precise: once Lot actually parts from Abram, heading
down to his fatal involvement in the cities of the plain, God proceeds to
address His promise of the land to Abram. The utterance of the promise is
already an accomplished fact as Lot takes up settlement in the plain to the
east.
    Raise your eyes and look. The location between Bethel and Ai is in fact a
spectacular lookout point, and the already implicit contrast between Abram
and Lot is extended—Abram on the heights, Lot down in the sunken plain.

the dust of the earth—could a man count the dust of the earth, so
too, your seed might be counted. Rise, walk about the land through   17
its length and its breadth, for to you I will give it." And Abram took   18
up his tent and came to dwell by the Terebinths of Mamre, which are
in Hebron, and he built there an altar to the LORD.

---

16. *could a man count the dust of the earth.* Unusually for the use of simile in
the Bible, the meaning of the simile is spelled out after the image is introduced. Perhaps this reflects the high didactic solemnity of the moment of
promise, though the comparison with dust might also raise negative associations that would have to be excluded. (The great Yiddish poet Yakov Glatstein
wrote a bitter poem after the Nazi genocide which proposes that indeed the
seed of Abraham has become like the dust of the earth.)

17. *walk about the land through its length and its breadth.* Walking around the
perimeter of a piece of property was a common legal ritual in the ancient
Near East for taking final possession, and the formula "I have given it to so-
and-so and to his sons forever" is a well-attested legal formula in the region
for conveyance of property going back as far as the Ugaritic texts, composed
in the fourteenth and thirteenth centuries, B.C.E.

CHAPTER 14

¹ And it happened in the days of Amraphel king of Shinar, Arioch king of ² Ellasar, Chedarlaomer king of Elam, and Tidal king of Goiim. They made war on Bora king of Sodom and Birsha king of Gomorrah, on Shinab king of Admah and Shemeber king of Zeboiim and the king of

---

1. *And it happened in the days of.* This introductory formula (just two words in the Hebrew, *wayehi biymey*) signals a drastic stylistic shift to an annalistic narrative. Because verse 2 has no explicit subject, E. A. Speiser, followed by later scholars, has conjectured that the first two Hebrew words of the text are a somewhat awkward Hebrew translation of an Akkadian idiom used at the beginning of literary narratives that simply means "when." This solution is a little strained, and would compromise the effect of introducing the audience to a historical account that is conveyed by the formula, "And it happened in the days of such-and-such a king, or kings." Scholarship is virtually unanimous in identifying this chapter as the product of a different literary source from the three principal strands out of which Genesis is woven. The whole episode is in fact a prime instance of the technique of literary collage that is characteristic of biblical narrative. Abram, having been promised national tenure in the land in the immediately preceding episode, is now placed at the center of a different kind of narrative that makes him a figure on the international historical scene, doing battle with monarchs from the far-flung corners of Mesopotamia and treating with the king of Jerusalem (Salem), one of the principal cities of Canaan. The dating of the narrative is in dispute, but there are good arguments for its relative antiquity: at least four of the five invading kings have authentic Akkadian, Elamite, or Hittite names; and the repeated glossing of place-names ("Bela, that is, Zoar") suggests an old document that invoked certain names which usage had replaced by the time this text was woven into the larger Abraham narrative.

Bela, that is, Zoar. All of them joined forces in the Valley of Siddim,   3
that is, the Dead Sea. Twelve years they had been subject to Chedar-   4
laomer and in the thirteenth year they rebelled. And in the fourteenth   5
year Chedarlaomer and the kings who were with him came and struck
down the Rephaim at Ashteroth-karnaim and the Zuzim at Ham and
the Emim at Shaveh-kiriathaim, and the Horite in the high country of   6
Seir as far as El-paran which is by the wilderness. And they swung   7
back and came to En-mishpat, that is, Kadesh, and they struck all the
territory of the Amalekite and also the Amorite who dwelt in Hazazon-
tamar. And the king of Sodom and the king of Gomorrah and the king   8
of Admah and the king of Zeboiim and the king of Bela, that is, Zoar,
went forth and joined battle with them in the Valley of Siddim, with   9
Chedarlaomer king of Elam and Tidal king of Goiim and Amraphael
king of Shinar and Arioch king of Ellasar—four kings against the five.
And the Valley of Siddim was riddled with bitumen pits, and the kings   10
of Sodom and Gomorrah fled there and leaped into them, while the
rest fled to the high country. And the four kings took all the substance   11
of Sodom and Gomorrah and all their food, and went off. And they   12

---

3. *joined forces.* The verb is a technical military term and initiates a whole
chain of military or political terms not evident in the surrounding Patriarchal
narratives: "had been subject," "rebelled" (verse 4), "joined battle" (verse 8),
"marshaled his retainers" (verse 14), "fanned out against them" (verse 15). The
narrative perspective is geostrategic, and there is no dramatic engagement
of characters in dialogue until the rather ceremonial and didactic exchange
between Melchizedek and Abram at the end.

11. *the four kings.* The subject is supplied for clarity by the translation: the
Hebrew simply says "they." A similar employment of a verb without a stipulated subject, not uncommon in biblical usage, occurs at the end of verse 20,
where the Hebrew does not state what the context implies, that it is Abram
who gives the tithe.

took Lot, Abram's nephew, and all his substance, and went off, for he
was then dwelling in Sodom.

13 And a fugitive came and told Abram the Hebrew, for he was then
encamped at the Terebinths of Mamre the Amorite, kinsman of Esh-
14 kol and Aner, who were Abram's confederates. And Abram heard that
his kinsman was taken captive and he marshaled his retainers, natives
of his household, three hundred and eighteen of them, and gave chase
15 up to Dan. And he and his servants with him fanned out against them
by night and he struck them and pursued them up to Hobah, which
16 is north of Damascus. And he brought back all the substance, and
also Lot his kinsman and his substance he brought back, and the
17 women and the other people as well. And the king of Sodom went
forth to meet him after he came back from striking down Chedarlaomer and the kings that were with him, to the Valley of Shaveh, that

---

13. *Abram the Hebrew.* Only here is he given this designation. Although scholars have argued whether "Hebrew" is an ethnic or social term or even the
name for a warrior class, it is clear that it is invoked only in contexts when
Abraham and his descendants stand in relation to members of other national
groups.

14. *he marshaled his retainers.* The noun and the verb in this particular sense
occur only here. The former may derive from a root that means to train,
and thus might imply "trained fighters." The latter is applied elsewhere to
unsheathing a sword, and thus may be metaphorically extended to the
"unsheathing" of warriors.

   three hundred and eighteen. This number sounds quite realistic, whereas
the geographical origins and the huge sweeping itinerary of the four kings,
coming hundreds of miles to subdue five petty princelets in eastern Canaan,
sound legendary.

is, the Valley of the King. And Melchizedek king of Salem brought out   18
bread and wine, for he was priest to El Elyon. And he blessed him,   19
and he said,

> "Blessed be Abram to El Elyon,
> > possessor of heaven and earth,
> and blessed be El Elyon   20
> > who delivered your foes into your hand."

And Abram gave him a tithe of everything. And the king of Sodom   21
said to Abram, "Give me the folk, and the substance take for yourself."
And Abram said to the king of Sodom, "I raise my hand in oath to the   22
LORD, the Most High God, possessor of heaven and earth, that I will   23
take not a single thread or sandal strap, lest you say, 'I have made

---

18. *Melchizedek.* The name means "righteous king," which has suggested to many commentators a Davidide agenda in this tale of the founder of the people of Israel in ceremonial encounter with a priest-king of Jerusalem.

19. *possessor.* Although conventional Semitic lexicography claims that the original meaning of this verb, *qanah,* is "to make," the overwhelming majority of biblical occurrences reflect the meaning "to buy," "to acquire," "to gain possession," which is the standard acceptation of the word in post-biblical Hebrew.

19.–20. *El Elyon.* El is the proper name of the sky god in the Canaanite pantheon, and Elyon is evidently a distinct, associated deity, though here the two appear as a compound name. But the two terms are also plain Hebrew words that mean "God the Most High," and elsewhere are used separately or (once) together as designations of the God of Israel. Whatever Melchizedek's theology, Abram elegantly co-opts him for monotheism by using *El Elyon* in its orthodox Israelite sense (verse 22) when he addresses the king of Sodom.

24   Abram rich.' Nothing for me but what the lads have consumed. And
as for the share of the men who came with me, Aner, Eshkol, and
Mamre, let them take their share."

---

24. *lads.* The primary meaning of the word is "lads" but it also has a technical
military sense of picked fighters. Its use here makes a neat contrast with "the
men," who do not belong to Abram's household and are entitled to a share of
the booty.

    In all this, it is a little surprising that Abram should figure as a military
hero, and some scholars (most forcefully, Yochanan Muffs) have seen this
story as an Israelite adaptation of an old Akkadian literary form, the *naru,* a
historical romance meant to glorify kings. One should note, however, that the
military exploit—apparently, a surprise attack by night—is dispatched very
quickly while the main emphasis is placed on the victorious Abram's mag-
naminity and disinterestedness. Thus the idea of the patriarch's maintaining
fair and proper relations with the peoples of the land, already intimated in
his dealings with Lot in the previous chapter, comes to displace the image of
mere martial prowess.

CHAPTER 15

After these things the word of the LORD came to Abram in a vision,   1
saying, "Fear not, Abram, I am your shield. Your reward shall be very
great." And Abram said, "O my Master, LORD, what can You give me   2
when I am going to my end childless, and the steward of my household
is Dammesek Eliezer?" And Abram said, "Look, to me you have given   3
no seed, and here a member of my household is to be my heir." And   4

---

1. *the word of the* LORD *came to Abram.* This is a formula for revelation characteristic of the prophetic books, not of the Patriarchal Tales. It is noteworthy
that in Genesis 20 God refers to Abraham as a "prophet." The night-vision
(*maḥazeh*) invoked here is also a prophetic mode of experience.

2. *And Abram said.* Until this point, all of Abram's responses to God have
been silent obedience. His first actual dialogue with God—in this, too, Prophetic precedents may be relevant—expresses doubt that God's promise can
be realized: this first speech to God reveals a hitherto unglimpsed human
dimension of Abram.
    I am going to my end. The Hebrew says simply "I am going," but elsewhere
"to go" is sometimes used as a euphemism for dying, and, as several analysts
have argued, the context here makes that a likely meaning.
    steward. The translation follows a traditional conjecture about the anoma-
lous Hebrew *mesheq,* but the meaning is uncertain. The word might be a
scribal repetition of the last three consonants in "Dammesek," or, alternately,
it could be a deliberate play on words (Dammesek and *mesheq,* "household
maintenance"). The enigma is compounded by the fact that only here is Abraham's majordomo named as Eliezer—a West Semitic name, moreover, that
would be surprising in someone from Damascus.

3. *And Abram said.* God remains impassively silent in the face of Abram's
brief initial complaint, forcing him to continue and spell out the reason for
his skepticism about the divine promise.

now the word of the Lord came to him, saying, "This one will not be

5   your heir, but he who issues from your loins will be your heir." And
He took him outside and He said, "Look up to the heavens and count
the stars, if you can count them." And He said, "So shall be your

6   seed." And he trusted in the Lord, and He reckoned it to his merit.

7   And He said to him, "I am the Lord who brought you out of Ur of

8   the Chaldees to give you this land to inherit." And he said, "O my

---

5. *count the stars*. This is a complementary image to that of the numberless
dust in chapter 13 but, literally and figuratively, loftier, and presented to Abraham in the grand solemnity of a didactic display, not merely as a verbal trope
to be explained.

6. *And he trusted*. After his initial skepticism, Abram is reassured by the
imposing character of God's reiterated promise under the night sky, which
for the first time stresses the concrete idea of Abram's biological propagation,
"he who issues from your loins."

7.–21. Since this covenant is sealed at sunset, it can scarcely be a direct continuation of the nocturnal scene just narrated. The two scenes are an orchestration of complementary covenantal themes. In the first, God grandly
promises and Abram trusts; in the second, the two enter into a mutually
binding pact, cast in terms of a legal ritual. In the first scene, progeny is
promised; in the second, the possession of the land, together with the dark
prospect of enslavement in Egypt before the full realization of the promise.
The first scene highlights dialogue and the rhetorical power of the divine
assurance; the second scene evokes mystery, magic, the troubling enigma of
the future.

7. *I am the Lord who brought you out*. This formula—the initial words of self-
identification are a commonplace of ancient Near Eastern royal decrees—
used here for the first time, looks forward to "who brought you out of the
land of Egypt" of the Decalogue and other texts. Compositionally, it also picks
up "He took him outside" (the same verb in the Hebrew) at the end of the
preceding scene.

Master, LORD, how shall I know that I shall inherit it?" And He said   9
to him, "Take Me a three-year-old heifer and a three-year-old she-goat
and a three-year-old ram and a turtledove and a young pigeon." And   10
he took all of these and clove them through the middle, and each set
his part opposite the other, but the birds he did not cleave. And carrion   11
birds came down on the carcasses and Abram drove them off. And as   12
the sun was about to set, a deep slumber fell upon Abram and now a
great dark dread came falling upon him. And He said to Abram, "Know   13
well that your seed shall be strangers in a land not theirs and they shall
be enslaved and afflicted four hundred years. But upon the nation for   14
whom they slave I will bring judgment, and afterward they shall come
forth with great substance. As for you, you shall go to your fathers in   15

---

8. *how shall I know that I shall inherit it?* In this instance, Abram's doubt is
to be assuaged by a formal pact. Covenants in which the two parties step
between cloven animal parts are attested in various places in the ancient
Near East as well as in Greece. The idea is that if either party violates the
covenant, his fate will be like that of the cloven animals. The Hebrew idiom
karat berit, literally, "to cut a covenant" (as in verse 18), may derive from this
legal ritual.

10. *each set his part.* Existing translations fudge the vivid anthropomorphism
of the Hebrew here: *'ish,* literally, "man," means "each" but is a word applied
to animate beings, not to things, so it must refer to the two parties to the
covenant facing each other, not to the animal parts.

11. *carrion birds.* Unaccountably, most English translators render this collective noun as "birds of prey," though their action clearly indicates they belong
to the category of vultures, not hawks and eagles.

12. *deep slumber.* This is the same Hebrew word, *tardemah,* used for Adam's
sleep when God fashions Eve.

16 peace, you shall be buried in ripe old age. And in the fourth generation
they shall return here, for the iniquity of the Amorites is not yet full."

17 And just as the sun had set, there was a thick gloom and, look, a
smoking brazier with a flaming torch that passed between those parts.

18 On that day the LORD made a covenant with Abram, saying, "To your
seed I have given this land from the river of Egypt to the great river,

19 the river Euphrates: the Kenite and the Kenizite and the Kadmonite

20,21 and the Hittite and the Perizite and the Rephaim and the Amorite and
the Canaanite and the Girgashite and the Jebusite."

---

16. *the fourth generation.* This would seem to be an obvious contradiction of
the previously stated four hundred years. Some scholars have argued that the
Hebrew *dor* does not invariably mean "generation" and may here refer to "life
span" or "time span."

17. *a smoking brazier with a flaming torch.* All this is mystifying and is surely
meant to be so, in keeping with the haunting mystery of the covenantal
moment. It seems unwise to "translate" the images into any neat symbolism
(and the same is true of the ominous carrion birds Abram drives off). There
may be some general association of smoke and fire with the biblical deity
(Nahmanides notes a link with the Sinai epiphany), and the pillars of fire and
cloud in Exodus also come to mind, but the disembodied brazier (or furnace)
and torch are wonderfully peculiar to this scene. The firelight in this preternatural after-sunset darkness is a piquant antithesis to the starstudded heavens of the previous scene.

18. *To your seed I have given.* Moshe Weinfeld shrewdly observes that for the
first time the divine promise—compare 12:1–3, 12:7, 13:14–17, 15:4–5—is
stated with a perfective, not an imperfective, verb—that is, as an action that
can be considered already completed. This small grammatical maneuver
catches up a large narrative pattern in the Abraham stories: the promise
becomes more and more definite as it seems progressively more implausible
to the aged patriarch, until Isaac is born.

CHAPTER 16

Now Sarai Abram's wife had born him no children, and she had an [1]
Egyptian slavegirl named Hagar. And Sarai said to Abram, "Look, pray, [2]
the LORD has kept me from bearing children. Pray, come to bed with
my slavegirl. Perhaps I shall be built up through her." And Abram

---

1. *Slavegirl.* Hebrew *shifhah.* The tradition of English versions that render
this as "maid" or "handmaiden" imposes a misleading sense of European gen-
tility on the sociology of the story. The point is that Hagar belongs to Sarai as
property, and the ensuing complications of their relationship build on that
fundamental fact. Later on, Hagar will also be referred to as *'amah.* The two
terms designate precisely the same social status. The only evident difference
is that *'amah,* the more international of the two terms, is often used in administrative lists whereas *shifhah* occurs in contexts that are more narrative and
popular in character.

2. *And Sarai said.* Sarai-Sarah's first reported speech, like that of Rachel later
on in the cycle, is a complaint about her childlessness. The institution of
surrogate maternity to which she resorts is by no means her invention, being
well attested in ancient Near Eastern legal documents. Living with the
human consequences of the institution could be quite another matter, as the
writer shrewdly understands: Sarai's first two-sided dialogue with her husband (verses 5–6) vividly represents the first domestic squabble—her bitterness and her resentment against the husband who, after all, has only
complied with her request; his willingness to buy conjugal peace at almost
any price.
be built up through her. The Hebrew *'ibaneh* puns on *ben,* "son," and so
also means, "I will be sonned through her."

3 heeded the voice of Sarai. And Sarai Abram's wife took Hagar the Egyptian her slavegirl after Abram had dwelt ten years in the land of
4 Canaan, and she gave her to Abram her husband as a wife. And he came to bed with Hagar and she conceived and she saw that she had
5 conceived and her mistress seemed slight in her eyes. And Sarai said to Abram, "This outrage against me is because of you! I myself put my slavegirl in your embrace and when she saw she had conceived, I became slight in her eyes. Let the LORD judge between you and me!"
6 And Abram said to Sarai, "Look, your slavegirl is in your hands. Do to her whatever you think right." And Sarai harassed her and she fled

---

3. *as a wife.* Most English versions, following the logic of the context, render this as "concubine." The word used, however, is not *pilegesh* but *'ishah,* the same term that identifies Sarai at the beginning of the verse. The terminological equation of the two women is surely intended, and sets up an ironic backdrop for Sarai's abuse of Hagar.

4. *in her eyes.* It is best to leave the Hebrew idiom literally in place in English because Hagar's sight will again be at issue in her naming of the divinity after the epiphany in the wilderness.

5. *your embrace.* Literally, "your lap," often a euphemism for the genital area. The emphasis is pointedly sexual.

from her. And the LORD's messenger found her by a spring of water in 7
the wilderness, by the spring on the way to Shur. And he said, "Hagar, 8
slavegirl of Sarai! Where have you come from and where are you
going?" And she said, "From Sarai my mistress I am fleeing." And 9
the LORD's messenger said to her, "Return to your mistress and suffer

---

7. *the LORD's messenger.* This is the first occurrence of an "angel" (Hebrew,
mal'akh, Greek, *angelos*) in Genesis, though "the sons of God," the members
of the divine entourage, are mentioned in chapter 6. "Messenger," or one who
carries out a designated task, is the primary meaning of the Hebrew term, and
there are abundant biblical instances of *mal'akhim* who are strictly human
emissaries. One assumes that the divine messenger in these stories is supposed to look just like a human being, and all postbiblical associations with
wings, halos, and glorious raiment must be firmly excluded. One should note
that the divine speaker here begins as an angel but ends up (verse 13) being
referred to as though he were God Himself. Gerhard von Rad and others
have proposed that the angel as intermediary was superimposed on the earliest biblical tradition in order to mitigate what may have seemed an exces-
sively anthropomorphic representation of the deity. But it is anyone's guess
how the Hebrew imagination conceived agents of the LORD three thousand
years ago, and it is certainly possible that the original traditions had a blurry
notion of differentiation between God's own interventions in human life and
those of His emissaries. Richard Elliott Friedman has actually proposed that
the angels are entities split off, or emanated, from God, and that no clear-cut
distinction between God and angel is intended.

in the wilderness, . . . on the way to Shur. Hagar is in the Negeb, headed
south, evidently back toward her native Egypt. Shur means "wall" in Hebrew,
and scholars have linked the name with the line of fortifications the Egyptians built on their northern border. But the same word could also be construed as a verb that occurs in poetic texts, "to see" (or perhaps, more loftily,
"to espy"), and may relate to the thematics of seeing in Hagar's story.

10 harassment at her hand." And the LORD's messenger said to her, "I will
11 surely multiply your seed and it will be beyond all counting." And the
LORD's messenger said to her:

> "Look, you have conceived and will bear a son
> and you will call his name Ishmael.
>   for the LORD has heeded your suffering.

---

10. *surely multiply.* The repetition of the verb in an infinitive absolute could
refer either to the certainty of multiplication or to the scale of multiplication
("I will mightily multiply").

11. *and the LORD's messenger said to her.* The formula for introducing speech
is repeated as Hagar stands in baffled silence in response to the command
that she return to suffer abuse at Sarai's hand. Even the promise of progeny
does not suffice to allay her doubts, so, with still another repetition of the
introductory formula, the messenger proceeds (verse 11) to spell out the
promise in a poetic oracle.

 Ishmael. The name means "God has heard," as the messenger proceeds to
explain. The previous occurrence of hearing in the story is Abram's "heeding"
(*sham'a*, the same verb) Sarai's voice. God's hearing is then complemented
by His and Hagar's seeing (verse 13).

 your suffering. The noun derives from the same root as the verb of harassment (or, abuse, harsh handling, humiliation) used for Sarai's mistreatment
of Hagar.

And he will be a wild ass of a man—   12
    his hand against all, the hand of all against him,
      he will encamp in despite of all his kin."

And she called the name of the LORD who had addressed her, "El-roi,"   13
for she said, "Did not I go on seeing here after He saw me?" Therefore   14
is the well called Beer-lahai-roi, which is between Kadesh and Bered.
And Hagar bore a son to Abram, and Abram called his son whom   15
Hagar had born Ishmael. And Abram was eighty-six years old when   16
Hagar bore Ishmael to Abram.

---

12. *his hand against all.* Although this may be a somewhat ambiguous blessing, it does celebrate the untamed power—also intimated in the image of the
wild ass or onager—of the future Ishmaelites to thrive under the bellicose
conditions of their nomadic existence.

    in despite of. The Hebrew idiom suggests defiance, as E. A. Speiser has
persuasively shown.

13. *El-roi.* The most evident meaning of the Hebrew name would be "God
Who sees me." Hagar's words in explanation of the name are rather cryptic
in the Hebrew. The translation reflects a scholarly consensus that what is at
issue is a general Israelite terror that no one can survive having seen God.
Hagar, then, would be expressing grateful relief that she has survived her
epiphany. Though this might well be a somewhat garbled etiological tale to
account for the place-name Beer-lahai-roi (understood by the writer to mean,
"Well of the Living One Who Sees Me"), it is made to serve the larger thematic ends of Hagar's story: the outcast slavegirl is vouchsafed a revelation
which she survives, and is assured that, as Abram's wife, she will be progenitrix of a great people.

CHAPTER 17

¹ A nd Abram was ninety-nine years old and the LORD appeared to Abram
and said to him, "I am El Shaddai. Walk with Me and be blameless,
² and I will grant My covenant between Me and you and I will multiply
³ you very greatly." And Abram flung himself on his face, and God spoke
⁴ to him, saying, "As for Me, this is My covenant with you: you shall be

---

1. *El Shaddai.* The first term, as in El Elyon (chapter 14), means God. Scholarship has been unable to determine the origins or precise meaning of the
second term—tenuous associations have been proposed with a Semitic word
meaning "mountain" and with fertility. What is clear (compare Exodus 6:3) is
that the biblical writers considered it an archaic name of God.

Walk with Me. The Hebrew is literally "before me." In verse 18, the same
preposition manifestly has the idiomatic sense of "in Your favor," and that
may be true here as well. The verb is the same used for Enoch's walking with
God, but there the Hebrew preposition is actually "with."

2. *My covenant.* The articulation of the covenant in this chapter is organized
in three distinct units—first the promise of progeny and land, then the com-
mandment of circumcision as sign of the covenant, then the promise of Sarah's maternity. The politics of the promise is now brought to the foreground
as for the first time it is stipulated that both Abraham and Sarah will be
progenitors of kings. Source critics have observed that this second covenantal
episode, attributed to Priestly circles, abandons the sense of an almost equal
pact between two parties of chapter 15 and gives us an Abraham who is
merely a silent listener, flinging himself to the ground in fear and trembling
as God makes His rather lengthy pronouncements. But Abraham's emphatic
skepticism in verses 17–18 suggests that there is more complexity in his characterization here than such readings allow.

father to a multitude of nations. And no longer shall your name be   5
called Abram but your name shall be Abraham, for I have made you
father to a multitude of nations. And I will make you most abundantly   6
fruitful and turn you into nations, and kings shall come forth from
you. And I will establish My covenant between Me and you and your   7
seed after you through their generations as an everlasting covenant to
be God to you and to your seed after you. And I will give unto you   8
and your seed after you the land in which you sojourn, the whole land
of Canaan, as an everlasting holding, and I will be their God."

And God said to Abraham, "As for you, you shall keep My command-   9
ment, you and your seed after you through their generations. This is   10
My covenant which you shall keep, between Me and you and your
seed after you: every male among you must be circumcised. You shall   11

---

5. *Abram . . . Abraham.* The meaning of both versions of the name is something like "exalted father." The longer form is evidently no more than a dialec-
tical variant of the shorter one. The real point is that Abraham should
undergo a name change—like a king assuming the throne, it has been proposed—as he undertakes the full burden of the covenant. Similarly in verse
15, the only difference between Sarai and Sarah is that the former reflects an
archaic feminine suffix, the latter, the normative feminine suffix: both versions of the name mean "princess."

10. *every male among you must be circumcised.* Circumcision was practiced
among several of the West Semitic peoples and at least in the priestly class
in Egypt, as a bas-relief at Karnach makes clear in surgical detail. To Abraham
the immigrant from Mesopotamia, E. A. Speiser notes, it would have been a
new procedure to adopt, as this episode indicates. The stipulation of circumcision on the eighth day after birth dissociates it from its common function
elsewhere as a puberty rite, and the notion of its use as an apotropaic measure (compare Exodus 4) is not intimated here. A covenant sealed on the
organ of generation may connect circumcision with fertility—and the threat
against fertility—which is repeatedly stressed in the immediately preceding
and following passages. The contractual cutting up of animals in chapter 15
is now followed by a cutting of human flesh.

circumcise the flesh of your foreskin and it shall be the sign of the
12   covenant between Me and you. Eight days old every male among you
shall be circumcised through your generations, even slaves born in the
household and those purchased with silver from any foreigner who is
13   not of your seed. Those born in your household and those purchased
with silver must be circumcised, and My covenant in your flesh shall
14   be an everlasting covenant. And a male with a foreskin, who has not
circumcised the flesh of his foreskin, that person shall be cut off from
15   his folk. My covenant he has broken." And God said to Abraham,
"Sarai your wife shall no longer call her name Sarai, for Sarah is her
16   name." And I will bless her and I will also give you from her a son and
I will bless him, and she shall become nations, kings of peoples shall

---

13. *silver.* If the language of the text reflects the realia of the Patriarchal
period, the term would refer to silver weights. If it reflects the writer's period,
it would refer to money, since by then coins had been introduced. The
weighing-out of silver by Abraham in Chapter 23 argues for the likelihood of
the former possibility.

16. *and I will bless him.* The Masoretic Text has "bless her," evidently to make
the verb agree with the following clause, but this looks like a redundance in
light of the beginning of the verse, and several ancient versions plausibly read
here "bless him."

issue from her." And Abraham flung himself on his face and he   17
laughed, saying to himself,

> "To a hundred-year-old will a child be born,
>   will ninety-year-old Sarah give birth?"

And Abraham said to God, "Would that Ishmael might live in Your   18
favor!" And God said, "Yet Sarah your wife is to bear you a son and   19
you shall call his name Isaac and I will establish My covenant with
him as an everlasting covenant, for his seed after him. As for Ishmael,   20

---

17. *and he laughed.* The verb *yitshaq* is identical with the Hebrew form of the
name Isaac that will be introduced in verse 19. The laughter here—hardly
the expected response of a man flinging himself on his face—is in disbelief,
perhaps edged with bitterness. In the subsequent chapters, the narrative will
ring the changes on this Hebrew verb, the meanings of which include joyous
laughter, bitter laughter, mockery, and sexual dalliance.

To a hundred-year-old. Abraham's interior monologue is represented as a
line of verse that neatly illustrates the pattern of heightening or intensification from first to second verset characteristic of biblical poetry: here, unusually (but in accord with the narrative data), the numbers go down from first
to second verset, but the point is that, as incredible as it would be for a
hundred-year-old to father a child, it would be even more incredible for a
ninety-year-old woman, decades past menopause, to become a mother. The
Abraham who has been overpowered by two successive epiphanies in this
chapter is now seen as someone living within a human horizon of expecta-
tions. In the very moment of prostration, he laughs, wondering whether God
is not playing a cruel joke on him in these repeated promises of fertility as
time passes and he and his wife approach fabulous old age. He would be
content, he goes on to say, to have Ishmael carry on his line with God's
blessing.

20. *As for Ishmael, I have heard you.* Once again, the etymology of the name
is highlighted. These seven English words reflect just two Hebrew words in
immediate sequence, *uleyishmaʿel shemaʿtikha,* with the root *sh-m-ʿ* evident
in both.

I have heard you. Look, I will bless him and make him fruitful and will multiply him most abundantly, twelve chieftains he shall beget,

21 and I will make him a great nation. But My covenant I will establish

22 with Isaac whom Sarah will bear you by this season next year." And He finished speaking with him, and God ascended from Abraham.

23 And Abraham took Ishmael his son and all the slaves born in his household and those purchased with silver, every male among the people of Abraham's household, and he circumcised the flesh of their

24 foreskin on that very day as God had spoken to him. And Abraham was ninety-nine years old when the flesh of his foreskin was circum-

25 cised. And Ishmael was thirteen years old when the flesh of his fore-

26 skin was circumcised. On that very day Abraham was circumcised,

27 and Ishmael his son, and all the men of his household, those born in the household and those purchased with silver from the foreigners, were circumcised with him.

CHAPTER 18

And the LORD appeared to him in the Terebinths of Mamre when he
was sitting by the tent flap in the heat of the day. And he raised his
eyes and saw, and, look, three men were standing before him. He saw,
and he ran toward them from the tent flap and bowed to the ground.
And he said, "My lord, if I have found favor in your eyes, please do

1. *And the* LORD *appeared.* The narrator at once apprises us of the divine
character of Abraham's guests, but when Abraham peers out through the
shimmering heat waves of the desert noon (verse 2), what he sees from his
human perspective is three "men." The whole scene seems to be a monotheistic adaptation to the seminomadic early Hebrew setting of an episode from
the Ugaritic *Tale of Aqhat* (tablet V: 6–7) in which the childless Dan'el is
visited by the craftsman-god Kothar. As Moshe Weinfeld has observed, there
are several verbal links between the two texts: Dan'el also is sitting by an
entrance, overshadowed by a tree; he also "lifts up his eyes" to behold the
divine visitor; and similarly enjoins his wife to prepare a meal from the choice
of the flock.

3. *My lord.* The Masoretic Text vocalizes this term of courtly address (*not*
YHWH) to read "my lords," in consonance with the appearance of three visitors. But the vocative terms that follow in this verse are in the singular, and
it is only in verse 4 that Abraham switches to plural verbs. Rashi, plausibly,
suggests that Abraham initially addresses himself to "the greatest" of the
three. As verses 10 and 13–15 make clear, that greatest one is God Himself,
who will tarry to speak with Abraham while the two human-seeming angels
of destruction who accompany Him head down to the cities of the plain.

4   not go on past your servant. Let a little water be fetched and bathe
5   your feet and stretch out under the tree, and let me fetch a morsel of
    bread, and refresh yourselves. Then you may go on, for have you not
6   come by your servant?" And they said, "Do as you have spoken." And
    Abraham hurried to the tent to Sarah and he said, "Hurry! Knead three
7   *seahs* of choice flour and make loaves." And to the herd Abraham ran
    and fetched a tender and goodly calf and gave it to the lad, who hur-
8   ried to prepare it. And he fetched curds and milk and the calf that
    had been prepared and he set these before them, he standing over
    them under the tree, and they ate. And they said to him, "Where is
9
10 Sarah your wife?" And he said, "There, in the tent." And he said, "I
    will surely return to you at this very season and, look, a son shall Sarah

---

4. *Let a little water be fetched.* With good reason, the Jewish exegetical tradition makes Abraham figure as the exemplary dispenser of hospitality.
Extending hospitality, as the subsequent contrasting episode in Sodom indicates, is the primary act of civilized intercourse. The early Midrash (*Abot di
Rabbi Nathan*) aptly noted that Abraham promises modestly, a little water
and a morsel of bread, while hastening to prepare a sumptuous feast. "Fetch"
appears four times in rapid succession, "hurry" three times, as indices of the
flurry of hospitable activity.

9. *Where is Sarah?* The fact that the visitors know her name without prompt-
ing is the first indication to Abraham (unless one assumes a narrative ellipsis)
that they are not ordinary humans.

10. *he said.* Evidently, one of the three visitors, unless the text reflects a fusion
of two traditions, one in which there were three visitors, another in which
there was one (which would then explain the switch from singular to plural
early in the story).
    at this very season. This phrase, or its equivalent, recurs in the various
annunciation type-scenes, of which this is the first instance. The narrative
motifs of the annunciation type-scene, in sequence, are: the fact of barrenness, the promise of a son by God or angel or holy man, and the fulfillment
of the promise in conception and birth. But only here is the emphatically
matriarchal annunciation displaced from wife to husband, with the woman
merely eavesdropping on the promise; only here is the barren woman actually
postmenopausal; and only here is there a long postponement, filled in with
seemingly unrelated episodes, until the fulfillment of the promise (chapter
21). Thus the patriarch takes over the center-stage location of the matriarch,

your wife have," and Sarah was listening at the tent flap, which was behind him. And Abraham and Sarah were old, advanced in years, Sarah no longer had her woman's flow. And Sarah laughed inwardly, 11 saying, "After being shriveled, shall I have pleasure, and my husband 12 is old?" And the LORD said to Abraham, "Why is it that Sarah laughed, saying, 'Shall I really give birth, old as I am?' Is anything beyond the 13 LORD? In due time I will return to you, at this very season, and Sarah 14 shall have a son." And Sarah dissembled, saying, "I did not laugh," for she was afraid. And He said, "Yes, you did laugh." 15

---

and the difficult—indeed, miraculous—nature of the fulfillment is underscored.

11.–13. This sequence of three utterances is a brilliant example of how much fine definition of position and character can be achieved in biblical narrative through variation in repetition. First the narrator informs us, objectively and neutrally, of Abraham's and Sarah's advanced age, stating the fact, repeating it with the emphasis of a synonym, and reserving for last Sarah's postmenopausal condition, which would appear to make conception a biological impossibility. When Sarah repeats this information in her interior monologue, it is given new meaning from her bodily perspective as an old and barren woman: her flesh is shriveled, she cannot imagine having pleasure again (the term 'ednah is cognate with Eden and probably suggests sexual pleasure, or perhaps even sexual moistness), and besides—her husband is old. The dangling third clause hangs on the verge of a conjugal complaint: how could she expect pleasure, or a child, when her husband is so old? Then the LORD, having exercised the divine faculty of listening to Sarah's unspoken words, her silent laughter of disbelief, reports them to Abraham, tactfully editing out (as Rashi saw) the reference to the patriarch's old age and also suppressing both the narrator's mention of the vanished menses and Sarah's allusion to her withered flesh—after all, nothing anaphrodisiac is to be communicated to old Abraham at a moment when he is expected to cohabit with his wife in order at last to beget a son.

15. *I did not laugh . . . Yes, you did laugh.* Sarah's fearful denial and God's rejection of it afford an opportunity to foreground the verb of laughter, *tsaḥaq,* already stressed through Abraham's laughter in chapter 17, which will become the name of her son. After the birth, Sarah will laugh again, not in bitter disbelief but in joy, though perhaps not simply in joy, as we shall have occasion to see in chapter 21.

16 And the men arose from there and looked out over Sodom, Abraham
17 walking along with them to see them off. And the LORD had thought,
18 "Shall I conceal from Abraham what I am about to do? For Abraham
will surely be a great and mighty nation, and all the nations of the
19 earth will be blessed through him. For I have embraced him so that
he will charge his sons and his household after him to keep the way
of the LORD to do righteousness and justice, that the LORD may bring
20 upon Abraham all that He spoke concerning him." And the LORD said,

"The outcry of Sodom and Gomorrah, how great!
Their offense is very grave.

---

17. *And the* LORD *had thought.* The verb '*amar,* "say," is sometimes used elliptically for '*amar belibo,* "said to himself," and that seems clearly the case here.
With the two divine messengers about to be sent off on their mission of
destruction, God will be left alone with Abraham, and before addressing him,
He reflects for a moment on the nature of His covenantal relationship with
the patriarch and what that dictates as to revealing divine intention to a
human partner. Abraham is in this fashion thrust into the role of prophet,
and God will so designate him in chapter 20.

19. *to do righteousness and justice.* This is the first time that the fulfillment of
the covenantal promise is explicitly made contingent on moral performance.
The two crucial Hebrew nouns, *tsedeq* and *mishpat,* will continue to reverber-
ate literally and in cognate forms through Abraham's pleas to God on behalf
of the doomed cities, through the Sodom story itself, and through the story
of Abraham and Abimelech that follows it.

20. *outcry.* The Hebrew noun, or the verb from which it is derived, *tsa'aq* or
za'aq, is often associated in the Prophets and Psalms with the shrieks of
torment of the oppressed.

Let Me go down and see whether as the outcry that has come to me   21
they have dealt destruction, and if not, I shall know." And the men   22
turned from there and went on toward Sodom while the LORD was
still standing before Abraham. And Abraham stepped forward and   23
said, "Will you really wipe out the innocent with the guilty? Perhaps   24
there may be fifty innocent within the city. Will you really really wipe
out the place and not spare it for the sake of the fifty innocent within
it? Far be it from You to do such a thing, to put to death the innocent   25

---

21. *Let Me go down.* The locution indicating God's descent from on high echoes the one in the story of the Tower of Babel.

dealt destruction. Some construe the Hebrew noun as an adverb and render this as "done altogether." But the verb "to do" (*'asah*) with the noun *kalah* as direct object occurs a number of times in the Prophets in the clear sense of "deal destruction."

22. *while the LORD was still standing before Abraham.* The Masoretic Text has Abraham standing before the LORD, but this reading is avowedly a scribal euphemism, what the Talmud calls a *tiqun sofrim,* introduced because the original formulation smacked of *lèse-majesté.*

23. *And Abraham stepped forward.* The verb, often used for someone about to deliver a legal plea, introduces an Abraham who is surprisingly audacious in the cause of justice, a stance that could scarcely have been predicted from the obedient and pious Abraham of the preceding episodes.

the innocent. The term *tsadiq* has a legal usage—the party judged not guilty in a court of law, though it also has the moral meaning of "righteous." Similarly, the term here for guilty, *rashaʿ,* also means "wicked." *Tsadiq* is derived from the same root as *tsedaqah,* "righteousness," the very term God has just used in His interior monologue reflecting on what it is the people of Abraham must do.

with the guilty, making innocent and guilty the same. Far be it from
26   You! Will not the Judge of all the earth do justice?" And the LORD said,
"Should I find in Sodom fifty innocent within the city, I will forgive
27   the whole place for their sake." And Abraham spoke up and said,
"Here, pray, I have presumed to speak to my Lord when I am but dust
28   and ashes. Perhaps the fifty innocent will lack five. Would you destroy
the whole city for the five?" And He said, "I will not destroy if I find
29   there forty-five." And he spoke to Him still again and he said, "Perhaps
there will be found forty." And He said, "I will not do it on account of
30   the forty." And he said, "Please, let not my Lord be incensed and let
me speak, perhaps there will be found thirty." And He said, "I will not
31   do it if I find there thirty." And he said, "Here, pray, I have presumed
to speak to my Lord. Perhaps there will be found twenty." And He
32   said, "I will not destroy for the sake of the twenty." And he said,

---

25. *the Judge of all the earth.* The term for "judge," *shofet,* is derived from
the same root as *mishpat,* "justice," which equally occurs in God's interior
monologue about the ethical legacy of the seed of Abraham.

27. *Here, pray, I have presumed to speak to my Lord when I am but dust and
ashes.* Like the previous verbal exchange with the three divine visitors, this
whole scene is a remarkable instance of the use of contrastive dialogue in
biblical narrative. In the preceding scene, Abraham is voluble in his protestations of hospitable intention, whereas the three visitors only answer impassively and tersely, "Do as you have spoken." Here, Abraham, aware that he is
walking a dangerous tight rope in reminding the Judge of all the earth of the
necessity to exercise justice, deploys a whole panoply of the abundant rhetorical devices of ancient Hebrew for expressing self-abasement before a powerful figure. At each turn of the dialogue, God responds only by stating flatly
that He will not destroy for the sake of the number of innocent just stipulated. The dialogue is cast very much as a bargaining exchange—it is not the
last time we shall see Abraham bargaining. After Abraham's second bid of 45,
each time he ratchets down the number he holds back the new, smaller
number, in good bargaining fashion, to the very end of this statement.

"Please, let not my Lord be incensed and let me speak just this time. Perhaps there will be found ten." And He said, "I will not destroy for the sake of the ten." And the LORD went off when He finished speaking with Abraham, and Abraham returned to his place.   33

---

32. *just this time . . . ten.* Abraham realizes he dare not go any lower than ten, the minimal administrative unit for communal organization in later Israelite life. In the event, Lot's family, less than the requisite ten, will be the only innocent souls in Sodom.

33. *and Abraham returned to his place.* The report of a character's returning to his place or home is a formal convention for marking the end of an episode in biblical narrative. But this minimal indication has a thematic implication here—the contrast between Abraham's "place" in the nomadic, uncorrupted existence in the land of promise and Lot's location in one of the doomed cities of the plain.

CHAPTER 19

1 And the two messengers came into Sodom at evening, when Lot was sitting in the gate of Sodom. And Lot saw, and he rose to greet them 2 and bowed, with his face to the ground. And he said, "O please, my lords, turn aside to your servant's house to spend the night, and bathe your feet, and you can set off early on your way." And they said, "No.

---

1. *came into Sodom at evening, when Lot was sitting in the gate.* The whole episode is framed in an elegant series of parallels and antitheses to Abraham's hospitality scene at the beginning of chapter 18. Both men are sitting at an entrance—the identical participial clause with the same verb—when the visitors appear. Lot's entrance is the city gate: he can sit "in" it because Canaanite cities had what amounted to a large chamber at the gateway; here people gathered to gossip, to do business, and above all, to conduct justice; the gate would have given on the town square, the area referred to by the messengers in verse 2. There is an antipodal thematic distance from tent flap to city gate, as the narrative quickly makes clear. Abraham's visitors, moreover, arrive at midday, whereas Lot's visitors come as darkness falls—a time when it is as dangerous to be out in the streets of Sodom as in those of any modern inner city.

2. *turn aside.* Lot resembles his uncle in the gesture of hospitality. He uses the verb "turn aside" (*sur*) instead of Abraham's "come by" (*'avar*) because, unlike the solitary tent in the desert, there are many habitations here, in addition to the public space of the square.

set off early. This may merely be to emphasize that he will not delay them unduly, but it could hint that they can depart at daybreak before running into trouble with any of the townsfolk.

We will spend the night in the square." And he pressed them hard, 3
and they turned aside to him and came into his house, and he prepared them a feast and baked flat bread, and they ate. They had not 4
yet lain down when the men of the city, the men of Sodom, surrounded the house, from lads to elders, every last man of them. And 5
they called out to Lot and said, "Where are the men who came to you
tonight? Bring them out to us so that we may know them!" And Lot 6
went out to them at the entrance, closing the door behind him, and 7
he said, "Please, my brothers, do no harm. Look, I have two daughters 8
who have known no man. Let me bring them out to you and do to

---

3. *a feast . . . flat bread.* Perhaps an ellipsis is to be inferred, but this is a
scanty-looking "feast." In contrast to Abraham's sumptuous menu, the only
item mentioned is the lowly unleavened bread (*matsot*) of everyday fare, not
even the loaves from fine flour that Sarah prepares.

4.–5. *the men of the city, the men of Sodom. . . . Where are the men?* Throughout this sequence there is an ironic interplay between the "men" of Sodom,
whose manliness is expressed in the universal impulse to homosexual gang
rape, and the divine visitors who only seem to be "men."

7. *brothers,* or "kinsmen," an appellation the Sodomites will vehemently reject
in verse 9.

8. *I have two daughters who have known no man.* Lot's shocking offer, about
which the narrator, characteristically, makes no explicit judgment, is too patly
explained as the reflex of an ancient Near Eastern code in which the sacred-
ness of the host–guest bond took precedence over all other obligations. Lot
surely is inciting the lust of the would-be rapists in using the same verb of
sexual "knowledge" they had applied to the visitors in order to proffer the
virginity of his daughters for their pleasure. The concluding episode of this
chapter, in which the drunken Lot unwittingly takes the virginity of both his
daughters, suggests measure-for-measure justice meted out for his rash offer.

them whatever you want. Only to these men do nothing, for have they
9 not come under the shadow of my roof-beam?" And they said, "Step
aside." And they said, "This person came as a sojourner and he sets
himself up to judge! Now we'll do more harm to you than to them,"
and they pressed hard against the man Lot and moved forward to
10 break down the door. And the men reached out their hands and drew
11 Lot to them into the house and closed the door. And the men at the
entrance of the house they struck with blinding light, from the small-
12 est to the biggest, and they could not find the entrance. And the men
said to Lot, "Whom do you still have here? Your sons and your daugh-
13 ters and whomever you have in the city take out of the place. For we
are about to destroy this place because the outcry against them has
grown great before the LORD and the LORD has sent us to destroy it."

---

for have they not come under the shadow of my roof-beam? This looks like a
proverbial expression for entering into someone's home and so into the bonds
of the host–guest relationship. But "roof-beam" implies a fixed structure and
so accords with the urban setting of Lot's effort at hospitality; Abraham, living
in a tent, in the parallel expression in his hospitality scene, merely says, "for
have you not come by your servant?"

9. *came as a sojourner . . . sets himself up to judge.* The verb "to sojourn" is the
one technically used for resident aliens. "Judge," emphatically repeated in an
infinitive absolute *(wayishpot shafot)*, picks up the thematic words of judge
and just from God's monologue and His dialogue with Abraham in chapter
18.

12. *Your sons and your daughters.* The Masoretic Text prefaces these words
with "son-in-law" (in the singular); but as numerous critics have observed,
this makes no grammatical sense, and this particular term would not belong
at the head of the list, before sons and daughters. It seems quite likely that
the word was erroneously transcribed from verse 14 and was not part of the
original text.

13. *the outcry.* This term is a pointed repetition of the word God uses twice
in His initial speech about Sodom.

And Lot went out and spoke to his sons-in-law who had married his   14
daughters and he said, "Rise, get out of this place, for the LORD is
about to destroy the city." And he seemed to be joking to his sons-in-
law. And as dawn was breaking the messengers urged Lot, saying,   15
"Rise, take your wife and your two daughters who remain with you,
lest you be wiped out in the punishment of the city." And he lingered,   16
and the men seized his hand and his wife's hand and the hands of his
two daughters in the LORD's compassion for him and led them outside
the city. And as they were bringing them out, he said, "Flee for your   17
life. Don't look behind you and don't stop anywhere on the plain. Flee
to the high country lest you be wiped out." And Lot said to them, "Oh,   18
no, my lord. Look, pray, your servant has found favor in your eyes, and   19
you have shown such great kindness in what you have done for me in
saving my life, but I cannot flee to the high country, lest evil overtake

---

14. *his sons-in-law who had married his daughters.* Especially because of the
reference to the two virgin daughters in the next verse as ones "who remain
with you" (literally, "are found with you"), it appears that Lot had other daughters already married, and not that the two in the house were betrothed but
still unmarried.

   he seemed to be joking to his sons-in-law. The verb, though in a different
conjugation, is the same as the one used for Sarah's and Abraham's "laughter."
It is, of course, a wry echo—the laughter of disbelief of those about to be
divinely blessed, the false perception of mocking laughter by those about to
be destroyed. The common denominator in the antithetical usages is skepticism about divine intentions, for good and for evil.

17. *he said.* The reader is meant to infer: one of the two of them.

19. *I cannot flee to the high country.* Lot seems a weak character—he has to
be led out by the hand from the city—and his zigzagging determinations of
flight make psychological sense. Accustomed to an urban setting, he is terri-
fied at the idea of trying to survive in the forbidding landscape of cliffs and
caves to the south and east of the Dead Sea. But once having settled in the
little town of Zoar (verse 30), he has understandable premonitions of another
cataclysm and so decides that, after all, the rocky wilderness is the lesser of
two evils.

20   me and I die. Here, pray, this town is nearby to escape there, and it is
     a small place. Let me flee there, for it is but a small place, and my life
21   will be saved." And he said, "I grant you a favor in this matter as well,
22   and I will not overthrow the town of which you spoke. Hurry, flee
     there, for I can do nothing before you arrive there." Thus is the name
23   of the town called Zoar. The sun had just come out over the earth
24   when Lot arrived at Zoar. And the Lord rained upon Sodom and
25   Gomorrah brimstone and fire from the Lord from the heavens. And
     He overthrew all those cities and all the plain and all the inhabitants

---

20. *a small place.* The Hebrew *miz'ar* plays on the name Zoar and for once
this could be a correct etymology. Lot's point is that it is, after all, only a
piddling town and so it would not be asking a great deal to spare it from
destruction.

21. *overthrow.* This is the physical image presented by the Hebrew verb,
though the obvious sense of the word throughout the story (and in later biblical references to Sodom) is something like "destroy by sudden cataclysm."

24. *rained . . . brimstone and fire from the Lord from the heavens.* The slightly
awkward repetition of "from the Lord" with the added phrase "from the heavens," taken together with the verb "to rain" *(himtir),* underscores the connection with the Deluge story: the first time the Flood, the fire next time. Moshe
Weinfeld has aptly observed a whole series of parallels between the two stories. In each case, God wipes out a whole population because of epidemic
moral perversion, marking one family for survival. In each case, the idiom "to
keep alive seed" is used for survival. In each case, the male survivor becomes
drunk and is somehow sexually violated by his offspring, though only Lot is
unambiguously represented as the object of an incestuous advance. One
might add that the phrase used by the elder sister, "there is no man on earth
[or, 'in the land,' *ba'arets*] to come to bed with us," equally reinforces the
connection with the global cataclysm of the Flood story: she looks out upon
the desolate landscape after the destruction of the cities of the plain and
imagines that she, her sister, and their father are the sole survivors of
humankind.

of the cities and what grew in the soil. And his wife looked back and   26
she became a pillar of salt. And Abraham hastened early in the morn-   27
ing to the place where he had stood in the presence of the LORD. And
he looked out over Sodom and Gomorrah and over all the land of the   28
plain, and he saw and, look, smoke was rising like the smoke from a
kiln.

And it happened when God destroyed the cities of the plain that God   29
remembered Abraham and sent Lot out of the upheaval as the cities

---

26. *And his wife looked back and she became a pillar of salt.* As has often been
observed, this tale looks doubly archaic, incorporating both an etiological
story about a gynemorphic rock formation in the Dead Sea region and an old
mythic motif (as in the story of Orpheus and Euridyce) of a taboo against
looking back in fleeing from a place of doom. But the blighted looking of
Lot's wife is antithetically integrated with the "looking out" (a different verb)
of Abraham in the next two verses over the scene of destruction from his safe
vantage on the heights of Hebron.

27. *early in the morning.* There is a nice temporal dovetailing of the two
scenes. Down in the plain, just as the sun rises, the LORD rains brimstone
and fire. A few minutes later, still early in the morning, Abraham hurries to
take in the awful panorama.

28. *he saw and, look, smoke was rising.* The visual setup also represents the
tight closing of an envelope structure. The Sodom episode began with Abraham's dialogue with God on the heights of Hebron. Now at the end, in a
definition of visual perspective unusual for biblical narrative, Abraham,
standing in the same place, makes out from a distance of forty or more miles
the cloud of smoke rising from the incinerated cities.

30 in which Lot dwelled were overthrown. And Lot came up from Zoar
and settled in the high country, his two daughters together with him,
for he was afraid to dwell in Zoar, and he dwelt in a certain cave, he
31 and his two daughters. And the elder said to the younger, "Our father
is old, and there is no man on earth to come to bed with us like the
32 way of all the earth. Come, let us give our father wine to drink and let
33 us lie with him, so that we may keep alive seed from our father." And
they gave their father wine to drink that night, and the elder came and
lay with her father, and he knew not when she lay down or when she
34 arose. And on the next day the elder said to the younger, "Look, last
night I lay with my father. Let us give him wine to drink tonight as
well, and come, lie with him, so that we may keep alive seed from our
35 father." And on that night as well they gave their father wine to drink,
and the younger arose and lay with him, and he knew not when she

---

30.–38. The narrator witholds all comment on the incestuous enterprise of
the two virgin sisters. Perhaps the story may draw on old—pre-Israelite?—
traditions in which the supposed origins of these two peoples in incest were
understood as evidence of their purity, or their vitality. (One recalls that
Tamar, the progenitrix of the future kings of Judea, became pregnant by her
father-in-law through pretending to be a whore.) But from the Israelite perspective, this story might well have cast a shadow of ambiguity over these
two enemy peoples. Both names are etymologized to refer to incest: Moab
(which probably means "desired place") is construed as me-'ab, "from the
father," and Ben-ammi (yielding the gentilic benei-'ammon) is construed as
"my own kinsman's son."

32. *let us lie with him.* Although "lie with" is a somewhat euphemistic reference to coitus in English, its uses in Scripture suggest it is a rather coarse
(though not obscene) verb for sexual intercourse in biblical Hebrew. Two
linked sexual assailants, the Egyptian woman in Genesis 39 and Amnon in 2
Samuel 13, use it in urging the object of their lust to submit to them. When
the verb is followed by a direct object in sexual contexts, the meaning seems
close to "rape." Ironically, the more decorous verb "to know" is used twice
here asexually (verses 33 and 35) to indicate the drunken Lot's unconscious
state as he deflowers each of his daughters.

lay down or when she arose. And the two daughters of Lot conceived   36
by their father. And the elder bore a son and called his name Moab;   37
he is the father of the Moab of our days. And the younger as well bore   38
a son and called his name Ben-ammi; he is the father of the Ammo-
nites of our days.

CHAPTER 20

1 And Abraham journeyed onward from there to the Negeb region and
2 dwelt between Kadesh and Shur, and he sojourned in Gerar. And
Abraham said of Sarah his wife, "She is my sister." And Abimelech the
3 king of Gerar sent and took Sarah. And God came to Abimelech in a
night-dream and said to him, "You are a dead man because of the

---

1. *And Abraham journeyed onward from there to the Negeb region.* This second
instance of the sister-wife type-scene is in several ways fashioned to fit the
particular narrative context in which it is inserted. The emphatic foreshadowing of the Sojourn in Egypt of the episode in chapter 12 is deleted. Here there
is no mention of a famine as the cause of the patriarch's migration, and the
place he comes to is not Egypt but Gerar, a Canaanite city-state in the western Negeb.

3. *And God came to Abimelech.* This potentate is immediately given a higher
moral status than Pharaoh in chapter 12: to Pharaoh God speaks only through
plagues, whereas Abimelech is vouchsafed direct address from God in a
night-vision.

You are a dead man. Or, "you are about to die." Abimelech's distressed
response to this peremptory death sentence is understandable, and leads
back to the preceding episodes in the narrative chain.

woman you took, as she is another's wife." But Abimelech had not   4
come near her, and he said, "My Lord, will you slay a nation even if
innocent? Did not he say to me, 'She is my sister'? and she, she, too,   5
said, 'He is my brother.' With a pure heart and with clean hands I have
done this." And God said to him in the dream, "Indeed, I know that   6
with a pure heart you have done this, and I on My part have kept you
from offending against Me, and so I have not allowed you to touch
her. Now, send back the man's wife, for he is a prophet, and he will   7
intercede for you, and you may live. And if you do not send her back,
know that you are doomed to die, you and all that belongs to you."

And Abimelech rose early in the morning and called to all his servants,   8
and he spoke these things in their hearing, and the men were terribly

---

4. *will you slay a nation even if innocent?* This phrase, which might also be
construed "slay a nation even with the innocent," sounds as peculiar in the
Hebrew as in translation, and has led some critics to see the word "nation"
(*goy*) as a scribal error. But the apparent deformation of idiom has a sharp
thematic point. "Innocent" (*tsadiq*) is the very term Abraham insisted on in
questioning God as to whether He would really slay the innocent together
with the guilty in destroying the entire nation of Sodom. If the king of Gerar
chooses, oddly, to refer to himself as "nation," leaning on the traditional identification of monarch with people, it is because he is, in effect, repeating
Abraham's question to God: will not the Judge of all the earth do justice?

5. *and, she, she, too.* This repetitive splutter of indignation is vividly registered
in the Hebrew, though the existing translations smooth it over.

6. *I have not allowed you to touch her.* The means by which consummation is
prevented is intimated, cannily, only at the very end of the story.

9   afraid. And Abimelech called to Abraham and said to him, "What have you done to us, and how have I offended you, that you should bring upon me and my kingdom so great an offense? Things that should not

10   be done you have done to me." And Abimelech said to Abraham,

11   "What did you imagine when you did this thing?" And Abraham said, "For I thought, there is surely no fear of God in this place and they

12   will kill me because of my wife. And, in point of fact, she is my sister,

---

9.–10. *And Abimelech . . . said . . . and Abimelech said.* The repetition of the formula for introducing direct speech, with no intervening response from Abraham, is pointedly expressive. Abimelech vehemently castigates Abraham (with good reason), and Abraham stands silent, not knowing what to say. And so Abimelech repeats his upbraiding, in shorter form (verse 10).

11.–12. When Abraham finally speaks up, his words have the ring of a speaker floundering for self-justification. Introducing the explanation of Sarah's half sister status—there might be a Mesopotamian legal background to such a semi-incestuous marriage—he uses a windy argumentative locution, *wegam 'omnah,* "and, in point of fact," that may hint at a note of special pleading.

and they will kill me because of my wife. What Abraham fears is that Gerar, without "fear of God," will prove to be another Sodom. In Sodom, two strangers came into town and immediately became objects of sexual assault for the whole male population. Here again, two strangers come into town, one male and one female, and Abraham assumes the latter will be an object of sexual appropriation, the former the target of murder. In the event, he is entirely wrong: Abimelech is a decent, even noble, man; and the category of "Sodom" is not to be projected onto everything that is not the seed of Abraham. On the contrary, later biblical writers will suggest how easily Israel turns itself into Sodom.

my father's daughter, though not my mother's daughter, and she became my wife. And it happened, when the gods made me a wan- 13 derer from my father's house, that I told her, 'This is the kindness you can do for me: in every place to which we come, say of me, he is my brother.' " And Abimelech took sheep and cattle and male and female 14 slaves and gave them to Abraham, and he sent back to him Sarah his wife. And Abimelech said, "Look, my land is before you. Settle wher- 15 ever you want." And to Sarah he said, "Look, I have given a thousand 16

---

13. *the gods made me a wanderer.* The word *'elohim,* which normally takes a singular verb (though it has a plural suffix) when it refers to God, as every- where else in this episode, is here linked with a plural verb. Conventional translation procedure renders this as "God," or "Heaven," but Abraham, after all, is addressing a pagan who knows nothing of this strange new idea of monotheism, and it is perfectly appropriate that he should choose his words accordingly, settling on a designation of the deity that ambiguously straddles polytheism and monotheism. It is also noteworthy that Abraham, far from suggesting that God has directed him to a promised land, stresses to the native king that the gods have imposed upon him a destiny of wandering.

in every place to which we come. The writer, quite aware that this episode approximately repeats the one in chapter 12, introduces into Abraham's dia- logue a motivation for the repetition: this is what we must do (whatever the problematic consequences) in order to survive wherever we go.

14. *And Abimelech took sheep and cattle.* Unlike Pharoah in chapter 12, who bestows gifts on Abraham as a kind of bride-price, the noble Abimelech offers all this bounty *after* Sarah leaves his harem, as an act of restitution.

pieces of silver to your brother. Let it hereby serve you as a shield against censorious eyes for everyone who is with you, and you are now publicly vindicated." And Abraham interceded with God, and God healed Abimelech and his wife and his slave-women and they gave birth. For the LORD had shut fast every womb in the house of Abimelech because of Sarah, Abraham's wife.

17

18

---

16. *to your brother.* Surely there is an edge of irony in Abimelech's use of this term.

a shield against censorious eyes. The Hebrew, which has long puzzled scholars, is literally "a covering of the eyes." That phrase may mean "mask," but its idiomatic thrust seems to be: something that will ward off public disapproval.

18. *For the LORD had shut fast every womb.* Contrary to some textual critics who conjecture that this verse was inadvertently displaced from an earlier point in the story, it is a lovely piece of delayed narrative exposition. Shutting up the womb is a standard idiom for infertility, which ancient Hebrew culture, at least on the proverbial level, attributes to the woman, not to the man. But given the earlier reference to Abimelech's having been prevented from touching Sarah, this looks suspiciously like an epidemic of impotence that has struck Abimelech and his people—an idea not devoid of comic implications—from which the Gerarite women would then suffer as the languishing partners of the deflected sexual unions. (Nahmanides sees an allusion to impotence here.) It is noteworthy that only in this version of the sister-wife story is the motif of infertility introduced. Its presence nicely aligns the Abimelech episode with what precedes and what follows. That is, first we have the implausible promise of a son to the aged Sarah; then a whole people is wiped out; then the desperate act of procreation by Lot's daughters in a world seemingly emptied of men; and now an entire kingdom blighted with an interruption of procreation. The very next words of the story—one must remember that there were no chapter breaks in the original Hebrew text, for both chapter and verse divisions were introduced only in the late Middle Ages—are the fulfillment of the promise of progeny to Sarah: "And the LORD singled out Sarah as He had said." As several medieval Hebrew commentators note, the plague of infertility also guarantees that Abimelech cannot be imagined as the begetter of Isaac.

CHAPTER 21

nd the LORD singled out Sarah as He had said, and the LORD did for   1
Sarah as He had spoken. And Sarah conceived and bore a son to   2
Abraham in his old age at the set time that God had spoken to him.
And Abraham called the name of his son who was born to him, whom   3
Sarah bore him, Isaac. And Abraham circumcised Isaac his son when   4
he was eight days old, as God had commanded him. And Abraham   5
was a hundred years old when Isaac his son was born to him. And   6
Sarah said,

> "Laughter has God made me,
>   Whoever hears will laugh at me."

---

6. *Laughter has God made me.* The ambiguity of both the noun *tsehoq* ("laughter") and the accompanying preposition *li* ("to" or "for" or "with" or "at me") is wonderfully suited to the complexity of the moment. It may be laughter, triumphant joy, that Sarah experiences and that is the name of the child Isaac ("he-who-laughs"). But in her very exultation, she could well feel the absurdity (as Kafka noted in one of his parables) of a nonagenarian becoming a mother. *Tsehoq* also means "mockery," and perhaps God is doing something *to* her as well as for her. (In poetry, *tsahaq* is often linked in parallelism with *la'ag,* to scorn or mock, and it should be noted that *la'ag* is invariably followed by the preposition *l^e*, as *tsahaq* is here.) All who hear of it may laugh, rejoice, with Sarah, but the hint that they might also laugh at her is evident in her language.

7   And she said,

> "Who would have uttered to Abraham—
>   'Sarah is suckling sons!'
>   For I have born a son in his old age."

8   And the child grew and was weaned, and Abraham made a great feast
9   on the day Isaac was weaned. And Sarah saw the son of Hagar the
10 Egyptian, whom she had born to Abraham, laughing. And she said to

---

7. *uttered.* Hebrew *milel* is a term that occurs only in poetic texts and is presumably high diction, perhaps archaic.

for I have born a son in his old age. In a symmetrical reversal of God's report in chapter 18 of Sarah's interior monologue, where Abraham's advanced age was suppressed, Sarah's postpartem poem, like the narrator's report that precedes it, mentions only *his* old age. Hers is implied by her marveling reference to herself as an old woman suckling infants, a pointed reversal of her own allusion in chapter 18 to her shrivelled body.

9. *laughing.* Hebrew *metsaheq.* The same verb that meant "mocking" or "joking" in Lot's encounter with his sons-in-law and that elsewhere in the Patriarchal narratives refers to sexual dalliance. It also means "to play." (Although the conjugation here is *pi'el* and Sarah's use of the same root in verse 6 is in the *qal* conjugation, attempts to establish a firm semantic differentiation between the deployment of the root in the two different conjugations do not stand up under analysis.) Some medieval Hebrew exegetes, trying to find a justification for Sarah's harsh response, construe the verb as a reference to homosexual advances, though that seems far-fetched. Mocking laughter would surely suffice to trigger her outrage. Given the fact, moreover, that she is concerned lest Ishmael encroach on her son's inheritance, and given the inscription of her son's name in this crucial verb, we may also be invited to construe it as "Isaac-ing-it"—that is, Sarah sees Ishmael presuming to play the role of Isaac, child of laughter, presuming to be the legitimate heir.

Abraham, "Drive out this slavegirl and her son, for the slavegirl's son
shall not inherit with my son, with Isaac." And the thing seemed evil   11
in Abraham's eyes because of his son. And God said to Abraham, "Let   12
it not seem evil in your eyes on account of the lad and on account of
your slavegirl. Whatever Sarah says to you, listen to her voice, for
through Isaac shall your seed be acclaimed. But the slavegirl's son,   13
too, I will make a nation, for he is your seed."

And Abraham rose early in the morning and took bread and a skin of   14
water and gave them to Hagar, placing them on her shoulder, and he
gave her the child, and sent her away, and she went wandering through
the wilderness of Beersheba. And when the water in the skin was   15

---

10. *Drive out this slavegirl.* In language that nicely catches the indignation of
the legitimate wife, Sarah refers to neither Hagar nor Ishmael by name, but
instead insists on the designation of low social status.

12. *listen to her voice.* The Hebrew idiom has the obvious meaning, "to obey,"
but the literal presence of hearing a voice is important because it resonates
with the occurrence of the same verb and object at the heart of the wilderness scene that immediately follows.
   acclaimed. The literal meaning of the Hebrew is "called."

14. *rose early in the morning.* This is precisely echoed in the story of the binding of Isaac (22:3), as part of an intricate network of correspondences
between the two stories.
   and he gave her the child. The Hebrew has only "the child," with an accusative prefix. This has led many commentators to imagine that Abraham is
putting Ishmael on Hagar's shoulders together with the bread and water—a
most unlikely act, since the boy would be about sixteen. But biblical syntax
permits the use of a transitive verb ("gave [them] to Hagar") interrupted by a
participial clause ("placing [them] on her shoulder"), which then controls a
second object ("the child"). The only way to convey this in English is by
repeating the verb.

16 gone, she flung the child under one of the bushes and went off and
    sat down at a distance, a bowshot away, for she thought, "Let me not
    see when the child dies." And she sat at a distance and raised her
17 voice and wept. And God heard the voice of the lad and God's messen-
    ger called out from the heavens and said to her, "What troubles you,
    Hagar? Fear not, for God has heard the lad's voice where he is.

18   Rise, lift up the lad
                and hold him by the hand,
                    for a great nation will I make him."

19 And God opened her eyes and she saw a well of water, and she went
20 and filled the skin with water and gave to the lad to drink. And God
    was with the lad, and he grew up and dwelled in the wilderness, and

---

16. *a bowshot away.* This particular indication of distance is carefully chosen,
for it adumbrates the boy's vocation as bowman spelled out at the end of the
story.

when the child dies. Like the narrator in verses 14 and 15, Hagar refers to
her son as *yeled,* "child" (the etymology—"the one who is born"—is the same
as *enfant* in French). This is the same term that is used for Isaac at the
beginning of verse 8. From the moment the angel speaks in verse 17, Ishmael
is consistently referred to as *na'ar,* "lad"—a more realistic indication of his
adolescent status and also a term of tenderness, as in the story of the binding
of Isaac in the next chapter.

17. *And God heard the voice of the lad.* The narrator had reported only Hagar's
weeping. Now we learn that the boy has been weeping or crying out, and it
is his anguish that elicits God's saving response. In the earlier version of the
banishment of Hagar (chapter 16), the naming of her future son Ishmael
stands at the center of the story. Here, as though the writer were ironically
conspiring with Sarah's refusal to name the boy, Ishmael's name is suppressed
to the very end. But the ghost of its etymology—"God will hear"—hovers at
the center of the story.

he became a seasoned bowman. And he dwelled in the wilderness of   21
Paran and his mother took him a wife from the land of Egypt.

And it happened at that time that Abimelech, and Phicol captain of   22
his troops with him, said to Abraham, "God is with you in whatever
you do. Therefore swear to me by God that you will not deal falsely   23
with me, with my kith and kin. Like the kindness I have done you, so
you shall do for me, and for the land in which you have sojourned."
And Abraham said, "I indeed will swear it." But Abraham upbraided   24,25
Abimelech concerning the well of water that Abimelech's servants had
seized. And Abimelech said, "I do not know who has done this thing,   26
and you, too, have not told me, and I myself never heard of it till this
day." And Abraham took sheep and cattle and gave them to Abime-   27
lech, and the two of them sealed a pact. And Abraham set apart seven   28
ewes of the flock, and Abimelech said to Abraham, "What are these   29
seven ewes that you set apart?" And he said, "Now, the seven ewes   30
you shall take from my hand, so that they may serve me as witness

---

20. *a seasoned bowman.* There is an odd doubling of the professional designation in the Hebrew (literally "archer-bowman"), which I construe as an indication of his confirmed dedication to this hunter's calling, or his skill in
performing it.

22. This episode is clearly a continuation of the Abimelech story in chapter
20, interrupted by the linked episodes of the birth of Isaac and the expulsion
of Ishmael. Abimelech had offered Abraham the right of settlement in his
territories ("Look, my land is before you"). Now, as Abraham manifestly prospers ("God is with you in whatever you do"), Abimelech proposes a treaty
which will insure that the Hebrew sojourner does not unduly encroach on
him or his land.

25. *concerning the well.* The particular instance of the clash between Abimelech's retainers and Abraham links this story with the immediately preceding
one, in which Ishmael is rescued by the discovery of a well in the wilderness.

31 that I have dug this well." Therefore did he call the name of that place
32 Beer-sheba, for there did the two of them swear. And they sealed a
pact in Beer-sheba, and Abimelech arose, and Phicol captain of his
33 troops with him, and they returned to the land of the Philistines. And
Abraham planted a tamarisk at Beer-sheba, and he invoked there the
34 name of the LORD, everlasting God. And Abraham sojourned in the
land of the Philistines many days.

---

31. *the name of that place Beer-sheba*. The Hebrew makes a transparent etymological pun. *Be'er* means "well." *Sheb'a* can be construed as "oath" but it
is also the number seven, ritually embodied here in the seven ewes Abraham
sets apart. A second etymology may be intimated, not for the place-name
Beersheba but for the term *shev'uah*, "oath," which seems to be derived by
the writer from the sacred number seven, made part of the oath-taking.

32. *the land of the Philistines*. This is an often-noted anachronism, the incur-
sion of the Philistines from Crete to the coastal area of Canaan postdating
the Patriarchal period by more than four centuries. The writer may mean
merely to refer casually to this region in geographical terms familiar to his
audience; it is not clear that Abimelech with his Semitic name is meant to
be thought of as a "Philistine" king.

33. *at Beer-sheba*. The cultic tree is planted at rather than in Beer-sheba
because it is evident that the site of the oath is a well in the wilderness, not
a built-up town.

CHAPTER 22

And it happened after these things that God tested Abraham. And He   1
said to him, "Abraham!" and he said, "Here I am." And He said, "Take,   2
pray, your son, your only one, whom you love, Isaac, and go forth to
the land of Moriah and offer him up as a burnt offering on one of the

---

1. The abrupt beginning and stark, emotion-fraught development of this troubling story have led many critics to celebrate it as one of the peaks of ancient
narrative. Among modern commentators, Gerhard von Rad, Claus Westermann, and E. A. Speiser have all offered sensitive observations on the
details of the story, and the luminous first chapter of Erich Auerbach's *Mimesis*, which compares this passage with one from the Odyssey, remains a land-
mark of twentieth-century criticism.

2. *your son, your only one, whom you love, Isaac.* The Hebrew syntactic chain
is exquisitely forged to carry a dramatic burden, and the sundry attempts of
English translators from the King James Version to the present to rearrange
it are misguided. The classical Midrash, followed by Rashi, beautifully
catches the resonance of the order of terms. Rashi's concise version is as
follows: *"Your son.* He said to Him, 'I have two sons.' He said to him, '*Your
only one.*' He said, 'This one is an only one to his mother and this one is an
only one to his mother.' He said to him, '*Whom you love.*' He said to him, 'I
love both of them.' He said to him, '*Isaac.*'" Although the human object of
God's terrible imperative does not actually speak in the biblical text, this
midrashic dialogue demonstrates a fine responsiveness to how the tense
stance of the addressee is intimated through the words of the addresser in a
one-sided dialogue.
    your only one. Some scholars, bothered by the technical inaccuracy of the
term, have followed an ancient reading of *yadid*, "favored one," instead of the
Masoretic *yaḥid*. This seriously misses the point that in regard to Abraham's
feelings, Isaac, this sole son by his legitimate wife, is his only one. The phrase

3 mountains which I shall say to you." And Abraham rose early in the
   morning and saddled his donkey and took his two lads with him, and
   Isaac his son, and he split wood for the offering, and rose and went to
4 the place that God had said to him. On the third day Abraham raised
5 his eyes and saw the place from afar. And Abraham said to his lads,
   "Sit you here with the donkey and let me and the lad walk ahead and
6 let us worship and return to you." And Abraham took the wood for the
   offering and put it on Isaac his son and he took in his hand the fire

---

"your son, your only one," will return as a thematic refrain at the end of the
story (verses 12, 16).

   Moriah. Though traditional exegesis, supported by the reference to the
Mount of the LORD at the end of the tale, identifies this with Jerusalem, the
actual location remains in doubt. In any case, there is an assonance between
"Moriah" and *yir'eh,* "he sees," the thematic key word of the resolution of the
story.

3. *and Isaac his son.* The crucial item is left to the very end. The narrator does
not miss a chance in the story to refer to Isaac as "his son" and Abraham as
"his father," thus sharpening the edge of anguish that runs through the tale.

   and he split wood. In a narrative famous for its rigorous economy in
reporting physical details, this act of Abraham, wielding an axe and cutting
things apart is ominously singled out for attention.

5. *said to his lads . . . let me and the lad.* An identity of terms, an ironic divergence of meanings—the young men who are his servants—in fact, his
slaves—and the boy to whom he fondly refers, whom he thinks he is going
to kill.

   let me. The Hebrew uses a jussive form for the three verbs, a gentler mode
of speech than a flat declarative about future actions.

and the cleaver, and the two of them went together. And Isaac said to   7
Abraham his father, "Father!" and he said, "Here I am, my son." And
he said, "Here is the fire and the wood but where is the sheep for the
offering?" And Abraham said, "God will see to the sheep for the offer-   8
ing, my son." And the two of them went together. And they came to   9
the place that God had said to him, and Abraham built there an altar
and laid out the wood and bound Isaac his son and placed him on the
altar on top of the wood. And Abraham reached out his hand and took   10

---

6. *the cleaver.* E. A. Speiser notes, quite rightly, that the Hebrew term here is
not the usual biblical term for knife, and makes a good argument that it is a
cleaver. Other terms from butchering, rather than sacrifice, are used: to
slaughter (verse 10) and to bind (verse 9—a verb occurring only here but used
in rabbinic Hebrew for binding the legs of animals).

7. *Father.* The Hebrew is literally "My father," but that noun with the possessive ending is the form of intimate address in biblical Hebrew, like *Abba* in
postbiblical Hebrew.

   the fire and the wood. A moment earlier, we saw the boy loaded with the
firewood, the father carrying the fire and the butcher knife. As Gerhard von
Rad aptly remarks, "He himself carries the dangerous objects with which the
boy could hurt himself, the torch and the knife." But now, as Isaac questions
his father, he passes in silence over the one object that would have seemed
scariest to him, however unwitting he may have been of his father's intention—the sharp-edged butcher knife.

8. *God will see to.* Literally, "see for himself." The idiomatic force is "provide,"
but God's seeing lines up with Abraham's seeing the place from afar, his
seeing the ram, and the seeing on the Mount of the LORD. Beyond the tunnel
vision of a trajectory toward child slaughter is a promise of true vision.

   And the two of them went together. The impassive economy of this
refrainlike repeated clause is haunting: two people, father and son, together
for what threatens to be the last time, together "in one purpose" (Rashi), the
father to sacrifice the son.

9.–10. In contrast to the breathless pace of the narrative as a whole, this
sequence inscribes a kind of slow motion: building the altar, laying out the
wood, binding the child on top of the wood, reaching out the hand with the
butcher knife—until the voice calls out from the heavens.

11 the cleaver to slaughter his son. And the LORD's messenger called out
to him from the heavens and said, "Abraham, Abraham!" and he said,
12 "Here I am." And he said, "Do not reach out your hand against the
lad, and do nothing to him, for now I know that you fear God and you
13 have not held back your son, your only one, from Me." And Abraham
raised his eyes and saw and, look, a ram was caught in the thicket by
its horns, and Abraham went and took the ram and offered him up as
14 a burnt offering instead of his son. And Abraham called the name of
that place YHWH-yireh, as is said to this day, "On the mount of the
15 LORD there is sight." And the LORD's messenger called out to Abraham

---

11. *and the LORD's messenger called out to him from the heavens.* This is nearly
identical with the calling-out to Hagar in 21:17. In fact, a whole configuration
of parallels between the two stories is invoked. Each of Abraham's sons is
threatened with death in the wilderness, one in the presence of his mother,
the other in the presence (and by the hand) of his father. In each case the
angel intervenes at the critical moment, referring to the son fondly as *na'ar,*
"lad." At the center of the story, Abraham's hand holds the knife, Hagar is
enjoined to "hold her hand" (the literal meaning of the Hebrew) on the lad.
In the end, each of the sons is promised to become progenitor of a great
people, the threat to Abraham's continuity having been averted.

Here I am. The third time Abraham pronounces this word—*hineni*—of
readiness: first to God, then to Isaac, now to the divine messenger.

13. *a ram.* The Masoretic Text reads "a ram behind [*aḥar*]," but scholarship is
virtually unanimous in following numerous ancient versions in reading *eḥad,*
"one," a very similar grapheme in the Hebrew.

14. *sight.* The place-name means "the LORD sees." The phrase at the end
means literally either "he sees" or "he will be seen," depending on how the
verb is vocalized, and this translation uses a noun instead to preserve the
ambiguity. It is also not clear whether it is God or the person who comes to
the Mount who sees / is seen.

once again from the heavens, and He said, "By my own Self I swear,   16
declares the LORD, that because you have done this thing and have
not held back your son, your only one, I will greatly bless you and will   17
greatly multiply your seed, as the stars in the heavens and as the sand
on the shore of the sea, and your seed shall take hold of its enemies'
gate. And all the nations of the earth will be blessed through your seed   18
because you have listened to my voice." And Abraham returned to his   19
lads, and they rose and went together to Beer-sheba, and Abraham
dwelled in Beer-sheba.

And it happened after these things that it was told to Abraham, "Look,   20
Milcah, too, has born sons to Nahor your brother. Uz, his firstborn,   21
and Buz his brother, and Kemuel the father of Aram. And Chesed   22
and Hazo and Pildash and Jidlaph, and Bethuel. And Bethuel begot   23
Rebekah. These eight Milcah bore to Nahor, Abraham's brother. And   24
his concubine, whose name was Reumah, she, too, gave birth—to
Tebah, and to Gaham, and to Tahash, and to Maacah."

---

16. *because you have done this thing.* The LORD's invocation of causation thick-
ens the ambiguities of the story. Abraham has already been promised an innumerable posterity (chapters 15, 17). Perhaps now he has proved himself fully
worthy of the promise. One might note that here for the first time a future of
military triumph is added to the promise.

20.–24. The genealogical list inserted here, which reflects a Mesopotamian
confederation of twelve tribes akin to the twelve tribes of Abraham's descendants, is directed toward the introduction of Rebekah (verse 23), soon to join
the Patriarchal narrative as a principal figure. The genealogy marks a kind of
boundary in the larger narrative. Abraham has accomplished his chief
actions; all that is really left to him is to acquire a suitable burial plot for
Sarah, which will be his final gesture in laying claim to the land. At that
point, even before Abraham's death, the concerns of the next generation will
take center stage (chapter 24).

CHAPTER 23

A nd Sarah's life was a hundred and twenty-seven years, the years of Sar-
2 ah's life. And Sarah died in Kiriath-arba, which is Hebron, in the land
of Canaan, and Abraham came to mourn Sarah and to keen for her.
3 And Abraham rose from before his dead and he spoke to the Hittites,

---

1. *years, the years.* The Hebrew is still more extravagant in its use of repetition, unusually repeating "year" after a hundred, after twenty, and after seven. The same device of stylistic emphasis is used in the obituary notices of Abraham and Ishmael.

2. *Kiriath-arba,* which is Hebron. The older name of the town means "city of four," perhaps a reference to its being a federation (a possible meaning of "Hebron") of four townlets. (Alternately, the name might refer to "four hills.") But some scholars think the earlier name is a Hebraization of a non-Semitic place-name, which would have been given to the town by its "Hittite" inhabitants.

3. *Hittites.* Whether these are actually Hittites who have migrated from Anatolia into Canaan or a loose Hebrew designation for non-Semitic Canaanites is unclear.

saying: "I am a sojourning settler with you. Grant me a burial hold-   4
ing with you, and let me bury my dead now before me." And the   5
Hittites answered Abraham, saying: "Pray, hear us, my lord. You are a   6
prince of God among us! In the pick of our graves bury your dead. No
man among us will deny you his grave for burying your dead." And   7
Abraham rose and bowed to the folk of the land, to the Hittites. And   8
he spoke with them, saying, "If you have it in your hearts that I should

---

4. *sojourning settler . . . Grant me a burial holding.* The Hebrew, which reads
literally, "sojourner and settler," is a legal term that means "resident alien,"
but the bureaucratic coloration of that English equivalent misrepresents the
stylistic decorum of the Hebrew. At the very beginning of Abraham's speech,
he announces his vulnerable legal status, a hard fact of institutional reality
that stands in ironic tension with his inward consciousness that the whole
land has been promised to him and his seed. "Grant"—literally "give"—is
pointedly ambiguous both here and in the subsequent exchange with Ephron.
Abraham avoids the frank term "sell," yet speaks of acquiring a "holding"
(*ahuzah*), a word that clearly indicates permanent legal possession.

6. *Pray.* This translation follows E. A. Speiser, as well as the ancient Aramaic
version of Yonatan ben Uziel, in reading *lu* for *lo* ("to him") and moving the
monosyllabic term from the end of verse 5 to the beginning of verse 6. The
identical emendation is made at the end of verse 14 moving into the beginning of verse 15. Though one critic, Meir Sternberg (1991), has made an ingenious attempt to rescue the Masoretic Text at these two points, there is a
simple compelling argument against it: the formula for introducing direct
speech, *le'mor*, "saying," is always immediately followed by the direct speech,
not by a preposition "to him" (*lo*). And the repetition of the optative particle
lu, "pray," is just right for beginning each round of this elaborately polite
bargaining.
　You are a prince of God among us! In the pick of our graves bury your dead.
On the surface, this is a courtly gesture of extravagant generosity. But as Meir
Sternberg (1991), who provides an acute reading of the sinuous turns of the
subsurface bargaining, nicely shows, there is ambiguity of intention here: a
certain exaggeration in calling Abraham a prince of God—which could simply
mean "preeminent dignitary"—"among us" (*he* had claimed to be only "with"
them); and a pointed deletion of any reference to a "holding" or to transfer of
property.

bury my dead now before me, hear me, entreat for me Ephron son of
9   Zohar, and let him grant me the cave of Machpelah that belongs to
him, which is at the far end of his field. At the full price let him grant
10   it to me in your midst as a burial-holding." And Ephron was sitting in
the midst of the Hittites, and Ephron the Hittite answered Abraham
in the hearing of the Hittites, all the assembled in the gate of his town,
11   saying: "Pray, my lord, hear me. The field I grant you and the cave that

---

9. *at the far end of his field.* In settling on this particular location for a burial
cave, Abraham wants to make it clear that he will not need to pass through
or encroach on the rest of the Hittite property. "Field," *sadeh,* a flexible term
for territory that stretches from field to steppe, could mean something like
"land" or "property" in context, but rendering it as "field" preserves the distinction from *'erets,* "land," as in the repeated phrase, "folk of the land."

At the full price. At this point Abraham makes it altogether unambiguous
that the "grant" he has been mentioning means a sale. The Hebrew is literally
"with full silver," and the phrase in verse 16, "the silver that he spoke of,"
refers back to this speech.

10. *in the hearing of the Hittites, all the assembled in the gate of his town.* Legal
business was conducted in the gateway: the men assembled there constitute,
as E. A. Speiser proposes, a kind of town council; and these two phrases in
apposition are a legal formula. Scholarship has abundantly observed that the
actual language used by Ephron and Abraham and the narrator bristles with
set terms familiar from other ancient Near Eastern documents for the conveyance of property.

11. *Pray, my lord, hear me.* Reading here *lu* for the Masoretic *l'o* ("no"). This
polite formula for initiating speech is not the sort of repetition that allows
significant variation.

The field. As Meir Sternberg shrewdly notes, Abraham had wanted to buy
only the cave at the far end of the field, and so Ephron's seeming generosity
in throwing the unrequested field into the bargain is a ploy for demanding an
exorbitant price.

I grant you . . . I grant it . . . I grant it. This is a performative speech-act, the
repetition indicating that Ephron is formally conveying the plot to Abraham.
Ephron, of course, knows that what Abraham really wants is to be able to
buy the land and thus acquire inalienable right to it, and so this "bestowal" is
really a maneuver to elicit an offer from Abraham.

is in it. I grant it to you in full view of my kinfolk. I grant it to you. Bury your dead." And Abraham bowed before the folk of the land, and 12,13
he spoke to Ephron in the hearing of the folk of the land, saying: "If you would but hear me—I give the price of the field, take it from me, and let me bury my dead there." And Ephron answered Abraham, 14
saying: "Pray, my lord, hear me. Land for four hundred silver shekels 15
between me and you, what does it come to? Go bury your dead." And 16
Abraham listened to Ephron and Abraham weighed out to Ephron the silver that he spoke of in the hearing of the Hittites, four hundred

---

14. *Land for four hundred silver shekels.* A comparison with the prices stipu-lated for the purchase of property elsewhere in the Bible suggests that this pittance is actually a king's ransom. Abraham, having twice declared his readiness to pay "the full price," is in no position to object to the extortionate rate. In fact, his only real bargaining aim has been to make a legitimate pur-chase, and he is unwilling to haggle over the price, just as he refused to accept booty from the king of Salem. Perhaps Ephron refers to the property as "land" (*'erets*) instead of *sadeh* in order to provide rhetorical mitigation for the huge sum, intimating, by way of a term that also means "country," that Abraham is free to imagine he is getting more than a field with a burial cave for his money.

16. *listened to.* That is, agreed. But it is the same verb, "to hear" (*sham'a*), repeatedly used at the beginning of the bargaining speeches.
   weighed out . . . four hundred silver shekels. The transaction antedates the use of coins, and the silver is divided into weights (the literal meaning of shekel).

17   silver shekels at the merchants' tried weight. And Ephron's field at
Machpelah by Mamre, the field and the cave that was in it and every
18   tree in the field, within its boundaries all around, passed over to Abraham as a possession, in the full view of the Hittites, all the assembled
19   in the gate of his town. And then Abraham buried Sarah his wife in
the cave of the Machpelah field by Mamre, which is Hebron, in the
20   land of Canaan. And the field and the cave that was in it passed over
to Abraham as a burial-holding from the Hittites.

17.–20. The language of these concluding verses is emphatically legalistic,
recapitulating the phraseology that would appear in a contract for the conveyance of property. The verbal stem, *qanah,* "to buy," which was studiously
avoided in the bargaining, finally surfaces in the term for "possession" (*miq-
nah*). Many interpreters view this whole episode as a final gesture of the aged
Abraham toward laying future claim to possession of the land. Meir Sternberg, on the other hand, reads it as thematically coordinated with the previous episode of the binding of Isaac: first the promise of seed seems
threatened in the command to sacrifice Isaac; then the promise of the land
seems to be mocked in Abraham's need to bargain with these sharp-dealing
Hittites for a mere gravesite.

CHAPTER 24

nd Abraham was old, advanced in years, and the LORD had blessed 1
Abraham in all things. And Abraham said to his servant, elder of his 2
household, who ruled over all things that were his, "Put your hand,
pray, under my thigh, that I may make you swear by the LORD, God of 3
the heavens and God of the earth, that you shall not take a wife for
my son from the daughters of Canaanite in whose midst I dwell. But 4
to my land and to my birthplace you shall go, and you shall take a wife
for my son, for Isaac." And the servant said to him, "Perhaps the 5
woman will not want to come after me to this land. Shall I indeed
bring your son back to the land you left?" And Abraham said to him, 6
"Watch yourself, lest you bring my son back there. The LORD God of 7

---

2. *Put your hand . . . under my thigh.* Holding the genitals, or placing a hand
next to the genitals, during the act of solemn oath-taking is attested in several
ancient societies (a fact already noted by ibn Ezra in the twelfth century),
though here it may have the special purpose of invoking the place of procreation as the servant is to seek a bride for the only son Isaac.

4. *to my land and to my birthplace you shall go.* These words are still another
echo of the first words God speaks to Abraham at the beginning of chapter
12 sending him forth from his native land.

7. Abraham's language explicitly echoes the reiterated covenantal promises he
has received. Later in the story, when the servant gives the family a seemingly
verbatim report of this initial dialogue with his master, he discreetly edits out
this covenantal language.

the heavens, Who took me from my father's house and from the land
of my birthplace, and Who spoke to me and Who swore to me saying,
'To your seed will I give this land,' He shall send His messenger before
8   you and you shall take a wife for my son from there. And if the woman
should not want to go after you, you shall be clear of this vow of mine;
9   only my son you must not bring back there." And the servant put his
hand under Abraham's thigh and he swore to him concerning this
10 thing. And the servant took ten camels from his master's camels, with
all the bounty of his master in his hand, and he rose and went to
Aram-naharaim, to the city of Nahor.

---

10. *camels.* The camels here and elsewhere in Genesis are a problem. Archeological and extrabiblical literary evidence indicates that camels were not
adopted as beasts of burden until several centuries after the Patriarchal
period, and so their introduction in the story would have to be anachronistic.
What is puzzling is that the narrative reflects careful attention to other details
of historic authenticity: horses, which also were domesticated centuries later,
are scrupulously excluded from the Patriarchal Tales, and when Abraham
buys a gravesite, he deals in weights of silver, not in coins, as in the later
Israelite period. The details of betrothal negotiation, with the brother acting
as principal agent for the family, the bestowal of a dowry on the bride and
bethrothal gifts on the family, are equally accurate for the middle of the second millennium B.C.E. Perhaps the camels are an inadvertant anachronism
because they had become so deeply associated in the minds of later writers
and audiences with desert travel. There remains a possibility that camels may
have already had some restricted use in the earlier period for long desert
journeys, even though they were not yet generally employed. In any case the
camels here are more than a prop, for their needs and treatment are turned
into a pivot of the plot.

And he made the camels kneel outside the city by the well of water at   11
eventide, the hour when the water-drawing women come out. And he   12
said, "LORD, God of my master Abraham, pray, grant me good speed
this day and do kindness with my master, Abraham. Here, I am poised   13
by the spring of water, and the daughters of the men of the town are
coming out to draw water. Let it be that the young woman to whom I   14
say, 'Pray, tip down your jug that I may drink,' if she says, 'Drink, and
your camels, too, I shall water,' she it is whom You have marked for
your servant, for Isaac, and by this I shall know that You have done
kindness with my master." He had barely finished speaking when,   15
look, Rebekah was coming out, who was born to Bethuel son of Milcah, the wife of Nahor, Abraham's brother, with her jug on her shoulder. And the young woman was very comely to look at, a virgin, no   16
man had known her. And she came down to the spring and filled her
jug and came back up. And the servant ran toward her and said, "Pray,   17

---

11. *by the well of water at eventide, the hour when the water-drawing women
came out.* This is the first occurrence of the betrothal type-scene. The conventionally fixed sequence of motifs of this type-scene is: travel to a foreign
land, encounter there with the future bride (almost always referred to as
na'arah, "girl") at a well, drawing of water, "hurrying" or "running" to bring
the news of the stranger's arrival, a feast at which a betrothal agreement is
concluded. As a social institution, the well was probably a plausible place to
encounter nubile maidens, though the well in a foreign land also has an
archetypal look, suggesting fertility and the nuptial encounter with the otherness of the female. This version is the most elaborate and leisurely of the
betrothal type-scenes, rich in detail, full of stately repetition. It is also the
only version in which the bridegroom himself is not present but rather a
surrogate, and in which the young woman, not the man, draws the water,
with the verb of hurrying that is linked with the bringing of the news amply
describing her actions at the well. There is surely some intimation in all this
of the subsequent course of the marriage of Isaac and Rebekah—he in most
respects the most passive of all the patriarchs, she forceful and enterprising.

17. *Pray, let me sip a bit of water.* With perfect politeness, the parched desert
traveler speaks as though he wanted no more than to wet his lips. In the
event, prodigious quantities of water will have to be drawn.

18   let me sip a bit of water from your jug." And she said, "Drink, my
lord," and she hurried and lowered her jug onto her hand and let him
19   drink. And she let him drink his fill and said, "For your camels, too, I
20   shall draw water until they drink their fill." And she hurried and emptied her jug into the trough and she ran again to the well to draw water
21   and drew water for all his camels. And the man was staring at her,
keeping silent, to know whether the LORD had granted success to his
22   journey. And it happened, when the camels had drunk their fill, that
the man took a gold nose ring, a *beqʿa* in weight, and two bracelets for
23   her arms, ten gold shekels in weight. And he said, "Whose daughter
are you? Tell me, pray. Is there room in your father's house for us to
24   spend the night?" And she said to him, "I am the daughter of Bethuel

---

18.–19. *Drink, my lord . . . and let him drink. And she let him drink his fill.*
As Meir Sternberg (1985) acutely observes, this long delay before she finally
produces the requisite offer to water the camels, is a heart-stopper, enough
to leave the servant in grave momentary doubt as to whether God has
answered his prayer.

    onto her hand. The motion, as Rashi notes, is lowering the jug from her
shoulder to her hand, so that she can pour water out.

20. *and drew water for all his camels.* This is the closest anyone comes in
Genesis to a feat of "Homeric" heroism (though the success of Rebekah's son
Jacob in *his* betrothal scene in rolling off the huge stone from the well invites
comparison). A camel after a long desert journey drinks many gallons of
water, and there are ten camels here to water, so Rebekah hurrying down the
steps of the well would have had to be a nonstop blur of motion in order to
carry up all this water in her single jug.

22. *beqʿa.* The term is derived from a verb that means "to split" and so may
refer to half a shekel, the standard weight, though that is not certain.

the son of Milcah whom she bore to Nahor." And she said to him,   25
"We have abundance of bran and feed as well and room to spend the
night." And the man did obeisance and bowed to the LORD, and he   26
said, "Blessed be the LORD, God of my master Abraham, Who has not   27
left off His steadfast kindness toward my master—me on this journey
the LORD led to the house of my master's kinsmen."

And the young woman ran and told her mother's household about   28
these things. And Rebekah had a brother named Laban, and Laban   29
ran out to the man by the spring. And it happened, when he saw the   30
nose ring, and the bracelets on his sister's arms, and when he heard
the words of Rebekah his sister, saying, "Thus the man spoke to me,"
he came up to the man and, look, he was standing over the camels by

---

25. *bran.* The Hebrew *teven* appears to have two different meanings in the
Bible. In the brickmaking process mentioned in Exodus, and in several other
occurrences, it means "straw," and this becomes its only meaning in later
Hebrew. But there are several texts in which *teven* is clearly edible (Isaiah
11:7, 65:25; 1 Kings 5:8), and despite the preponderance of English versions,
both Renaissance and modern, that opt for "straw" here, edible grain makes
more sense.

30. *when he saw the nose ring, and the bracelets.* A brilliant moment of exposition of character. The narrator makes no comment about what kind of person
Laban may be. His sharp eye on the precious gifts surely invites us to wonder
about him—though for the moment, we might conclude that he simply sees
here evidence that Isaac comes of good family. Hovering suspicions about
Laban's rapacity will be confirmed many decades later in narrated time in the
course of his slippery dealings with Jacob. In contrast to the marriage so
easily arranged for Isaac, Jacob will face immense difficulties, created by
Laban, in working out the terms of his betrothal.

31 the spring. And he said, "Come in, blessed of the LORD, why should
you stand outside, when I have readied the house and a place for the
32 camels?" And the man came into the house and unharnassed the camels; and he gave bran and feed to the camels and water to bathe his
33 feet and the feet of the men who were with him. And food was set
before him. But he said, "I will not eat until I have spoken my word,"
34,35 and he said, "Speak." And he said, "I am Abraham's servant. The LORD
has blessed my master abundantly, and he has grown great. He has
given him sheep and cattle and silver and gold and male and female
36 slaves and camels and donkeys. And Sarah, my master's wife, bore a
son to my master after she had grown old, and he has given him all
37 that he has. And my master made me swear, saying, 'You shall not take
a wife for my son from the daughters of the Canaanite in whose land
38 I dwell, but to my father's house you shall go and to my clan, and you
39 shall take a wife for my son.' And I said to my master, 'Perhaps the

---

31. *Come in, blessed of the* LORD. Laban's gesture of hospitality stands in a
direct sequence with Abraham's and Lot's. The language is courtly, the hospitality "Oriental," but we are not meant to forget his just noted observation of
the nose ring and bracelets.

32. *the men who were with him.* The servant would of course have had men
with him and his ten camels, but in keeping with the rigorous economy of
biblical narrative, these are not mentioned until now, when they become
requisite participants in the hospitality scene. Before this, they are only fleetingly intimated in the "us" of verse 23.

35. The servant's speech, in keeping with the biblical technique of near-verbatim repetition, echoes in detail the language first of the narrator and then
of his own dialogue with Abraham at the beginning of the chapter. But as
several modern commentators have noted, he makes numerous adjustments
of the language he is quoting because of the practical and diplomatic requirements of addressing this particular audience. Thus, the narrator simply said
that "the LORD had blessed Abraham in all things." The servant, cognizant
that this is a preamble to a proposal of marriage, fleshes out that flat statement by speaking of how his master has "grown great" in sheep and cattle
and other livestock, in slaves and silver and gold.

woman will not come after me.' And he said to me, 'The LORD, in 40
whose presence I have walked, shall send His messenger with you,
and he shall grant success to your journey, and you shall take a wife
for my son from my clan and my father's house. Then you shall be 41
clear of my oath; if you come to my clan and they refuse you, you shall
be clear of my oath.' And today I came to the spring and I said, 'O 42
LORD, God of my master Abraham, if You are going to grant success
to the journey on which I come, here, I am poised by the spring of 43
water, and let it be that the young woman who comes out to draw
water to whom I say, 'Let me drink a bit of water from your jug,' and 44
she says to me, 'Drink, and for your camels, too, I shall draw water,'
she is the wife that the LORD has marked for my master's son.' I had 45
barely finished speaking in my heart and, look, Rebekah was coming
out, her jug on her shoulder, and she went down to the spring and
drew water and I said to her, 'Pray, let me drink.' And she hurried and 46
tipped down the jug that she carried and said, 'Drink, and your camels,

---

40. *The* LORD, *in whose presence I have walked.* To "walk before," or live in devoted service to, a particular deity is an idea that would have been perfectly familiar to Abraham's polytheistic kinfolk back in Mesopotamia. What the servant is careful to delete in his repetition of the dialogue with his master are all the monotheistic references to the God of heaven and earth and the covenantal promises to give the land to the seed of Abraham. Similarly excluded is Abraham's allusion to having been taken by God from his father's house and the land of his birth—a notion the family, to whom this God has not deigned to speak, might construe as downright offensive.

from my clan and my father's house. Abraham had actually said, quite simply, "from there," but at this point the servant chooses to elaborate his master's meaning in terms that emphasize to the kinfolk Abraham's admirable sense of family loyalty.

47　too, I shall water,' and the camels, too, she watered. And I asked her,
　　saying, 'Whose daughter are you?' and she said. 'The daughter of
　　Bethuel son of Nahor whom Milcah bore him.' And I put the ring in
48　her nose and the bracelets on her arms, and I did obeisance and
　　bowed to the LORD and blessed the LORD, God of my master Abraham
　　Who guided me on the right way to take the daughter of my master's
49　brother for his son. And so, if you are going to act with steadfast
　　kindness toward my master, tell me, and if not, tell me, that I may
50　turn elsewhere." And Laban [and Bethuel] answered and said, "From
　　the LORD this thing has come; we can speak to you neither good nor
51　evil. Here is Rebekah before you. Take her and go and let her be wife
52　to your master's son as the LORD has spoken." And it happened when

---

47. *And I asked her. . . . and I put the ring in her nose.* The one significant
divergence in the servant's report of the encounter at the well is that he
claims to have asked Rebekah about her lineage before placing the golden
ornaments on her, whereas he actually did this as soon as she had drawn
water for all the camels, and only afterward did he inquire about her family.
This alteration of the order of actions is again dictated by considerations of
audience. The servant, having seen the stipulation of his prayer completely
fulfilled by the beautiful girl at the well, is entirely certain that she is the wife
God has intended for Isaac. But to the family, he does not want to seem to
have done anything so presumptuous as bestowing gifts—implicitly betrothal
gifts—on a young woman without first ascertaining her pedigree. This is a
small but strategic indication of the precision with which social institutions
and values are adumbrated in the dialogue.

49. *turn elsewhere.* The Hebrew says literally, "turn to the right or the left," a
biblical idiom for seeking alternatives to the course on which one is set.

50. *and Bethuel.* The convincing conclusion of many textual critics is that the
appearance of Bethuel is a later scribal or redactorial insertion. The surrounding narrative clearly suggests that Bethuel is deceased when these
events occur. Otherwise, it is hard to explain why the home to which Rebekah goes running is referred to as "her mother's household." It is her brother
who is the male that speaks exclusively on behalf of the family; only her
mother and brother are mentioned, never her father, elsewhere in the report
of the betrothal transaction, and even in this verse, "answered" is in the singular, with an odd switch to the plural occurring only for "said."
　　neither good nor evil. The sense of this idiom is "nothing whatsoever."

Abraham's servant heard their words, that he bowed to the ground to the LORD. And the servant took out ornaments of silver and ornaments 53 of gold and garments and he gave them to Rebekah and he gave presents to her brother and her mother. And they ate and drank, he and 54 the men who were with him, and they spent the night and rose in the morning, and he said, "Send me off, that I may go to my master." And 55 her brother and her mother said, "Let the young woman stay with us ten days or so, then she may go." And he said to them, "Do not hold 56 me back when the LORD has granted success to my journey. Send me off that I may go to my master." And they said, "Let us call the young 57 woman and ask for her answer." And they called Rebekah and said to 58 her, "Will you go with this man?" And she said, "I will." And they sent 59 off Rebekah their sister, and her nurse, and Abraham's servant and his men. And they blessed Rebekah and said to her, 60

---

55. *ten days or so.* The time indication in the Hebrew is not entirely clear, as the phrase—literally "days or ten"—has no parallels. The present translation reflects a modern consensus, but some medieval commentators note, correctly, that "days" (precisely in this plural form) sometimes means "a year," in which case the ten would refer to ten months. The request for such an extended prenuptial period at home might be more plausible than a mere week and a half.

59. *her nurse.* As in other societies, for a young woman to retain her old wet nurse as permanent companion is a sign of social status (one recalls Shakespeare's Juliet). The nurse's name will be given when she is accorded an obituary notice in chapter 35.

"Our sister, become hence myriads teeming.
May your seed take hold of the gate of its foes."

61 And Rebekah rose, with her young women, and they mounted the
camels and went after the man, and the servant took Rebekah and
62 went off. And Isaac had come from the approach to Beer-lahai-roi, as
63 he was dwelling in the Negeb region. And Isaac went out to stroll in
the field toward evening, and he raised his eyes and saw and, look,
64 camels were coming. And Rebekah raised her eyes and saw Isaac, and
65 she alighted from the camel. And she said to the servant, "Who is that
man walking through the field toward us?" And the servant said, "He
66 is my master," and she took her veil and covered her face. And the

---

60. *Our sister.* Rebekah's family sends her off to her destiny in the west with
a poem that incorporates the twofold blessing of being progenitrix to a nation
multifarious in number and mighty in arms. The poem itself may in fact be
authentically archaic: the prosodic form is irregular—the two "lines," approximately parallel in meaning, are too long to scan conventionally and each
invites division into two very short versets—and the diction is elevated and
ceremonial. "Myriads teeming" is literally "thousands of myriads," and the
term for enemy at the end of the poem—literally, "haters"—is one that is
generally reserved for poetry, hence the faintly archaic "foes" of this translation. The virtually identical phrase in the prose blessing bestowed on Abraham in 22:17, uses the ordinary word for "enemy."

63. *to stroll.* The translation reproduces one current guess, but the verb
occurs only here, and no one is sure what it really means.
   and he raised his eyes and saw and, look, camels were coming. The formulaic
chain, he raised his eyes and saw, followed by the "presentative" *look* (rather
like *voici* in French), occurs frequently in these stories as a means of indicating a shift from the narrator's overview to the character's visual perspective.
The visual discrimination here is a nice one: in the distance, Isaac is able to
make out only a line of camels approaching; then we switch to Rebekah's
point of view, with presumably a few minutes of story time elapsed, and she
is able to detect the figure of a man moving across the open country.

65. *covered her face.* This is an indication of social practice, not of individual
psychology: unmarried women did not wear a veil, but there is evidence that
it was customary to keep the bride veiled in the presence of her bridegroom
until the wedding.

servant recounted to Isaac all the things he had done. And Isaac   67
brought her into the tent of Sarah his mother and took Rebekah as
wife. And he loved her, and Isaac was consoled after his mother's
death.

---

67. *into the tent of Sarah his mother.* The proposal of some textual critics to
delete "Sarah his mother" as a scribal error should be resisted. Rebekah fills
the emotional gap left by Sarah's death, as the end of the verse indicates, and
with the first matriarch deceased, Rebekah also takes up the role of matriarch
in the family. It is thus exactly right that Isaac should bring her into his
mother's tent. Interestingly, no mention whatever is made of Abraham at the
end of the story. Many have construed his charging of the servant at the
beginning of the story as a deathbed action: it would not be unreasonable to
surmise that he is already deceased when the servant returns (the genealogical notation concerning Abraham in the next chapter would be out of chronological order—a kind of pluperfect that ends by placing Isaac around Beer-
lahai-roi, where in fact we find him upon Rebekah's arrival). The conclusion
of the betrothal tale in this way creates a curious symmetry between the
household of the bride and the household of the groom. She, evidently, is
fatherless, living in "her mother's household." It is quite likely that he, too, is
fatherless; and though he was bereaved of his mother still earlier, it is to "his
mother's tent" that he brings his bride.

CHAPTER 25

1,2 And Abraham took another wife, and her name was Keturah. And she
bore him Zimran and Jokshan and Medan and Midian and Ishbak and
3 Shuah. And Jokshan begot Sheba and Dedan. And the sons of Dedan
4 were the Ashurim and the Letushim and the Leummim. And the sons
of Midian were Ephah and Epher and Enoch and Abida and Eldaah.
5 All these were the sons of Keturah. And Abraham gave everything he
6 had to Isaac. And to the sons of Abraham's concubines Abraham gave
gifts while he was still alive and sent them away from Isaac his son

---

1. *And Abraham took another wife.* The actual place of this whole genealogical
notice in the chronology of Abraham's life might be somewhere after the
burial of Sarah at the end of chapter 23, or perhaps even considerably earlier.
The genealogy is inserted here as a formal marker of the end of the Abraham
story. Perhaps a certain tension was felt between the repeated promise that
Abraham would father a vast nation and the fact that he had begotten only
two sons. This tension would have been mitigated by inserting this document
at the end of his story with the catalog of his sons by Keturah. In this list,
Abraham figures as the progenitor of the seminomadic peoples of the trans-
Jordan region and the Arabian Peninsula. The second genealogical notice
(verses 12–18), that of the descendents of Ishmael, covers a related group of
tribes—twelve in number, like the Israelite tribes—in the same geographical
region, but also extending up to northern Mesopotamia. Thus, as Ishmael
definitively leaves the scene of narration, the list provides a "documentary"
confirmation of the promise that he, too, will be the father of a great nation.

6. *concubines.* The plural form may imply that Keturah's status, like Hagar's,
was that of a concubine.

eastward, to the land of the East. And these are the days of the years 7
of the life of Abraham which he lived: a hundred and seventy-five
years. And Abraham breathed his last and died at a ripe old age, old 8
and sated with years, and he was gathered to his kinfolk. And Isaac 9
and Ishmael his sons buried him in the Machpelah cave in the field
of Ephron son of Zohar the Hittite which faces Mamre, the field that 10
Abraham had bought from the Hittites, there was Abraham buried,
and Sarah his wife. And it happened after Abraham's death that God 11
blessed Isaac his son, and Isaac settled near Beer-lahai-roi.

And this is the lineage of Ishmael son of Abraham whom Hagar the 12
Egyptian, Sarah's slavegirl, bore to Abraham. And these are the names 13
of the sons of Ishmael, according to their lineage: Nebaioth, the firstborn of Ishmael, and Kedar and Adbeel and Mibsam, and Mishma 14
and Duma and Masa, Hadad and Tema, Jetur, Naphish, and Kedmah. 15
These are the sons of Ishmael and these are their names in their habi- 16
tations and their encampments, twelve chieftains according to their
tribes. And these are the years of the life of Ishmael: a hundred and 17
thirty-seven years. And he breathed his last and died and he was gath-

---

8. *sated with years.* The Masoretic Text has only "sated," but the Syriac,
Samaritan, and Septuagint versions as well as some manuscripts read "sated
with years," which the context clearly requires.

16. *habitations.* The Hebrew term in urban architectural contexts means
"court," but the older meaning is "dwelling place," or perhaps something like
"unfortified village." The cognate in the Ugaritic texts means "house."

18   ered to his kinfolk. And they ranged from Havilah to Shur, which faces
Egypt, and till you come to Asshur. In defiance of all his brothers he
went down.

19   And this is the lineage of Isaac son of Abraham. Abraham begot Isaac.
20   And Isaac was forty years old when he took as wife Rebekah daughter
of Bethuel the Aramaean from Paddan-aram, sister of Laban the Ara-
21   mean. And Isaac pleaded with the LORD on behalf of his wife, for she
was barren, and the LORD granted his plea, and Rebekah his wife
22   conceived. And the children clashed together within her, and she said,

---

18. *And they ranged.* The verb *shakhan* suggests an activity less fixed than "to
settle" or "to dwell," and this translation follows the lead of E. A. Speiser in
using a verb that implies nomadism.

In defiance of all his brothers he went down. The translation reproduces the
enigmatic character of the whole clause in the Hebrew. "In defiance of all
his brothers" repeats exactly the words of Ishmael's blessing in 16:12, and so
the ambiguous "he" here may also be Ishmael, who is mentioned in the previous sentence. But some construe the initial preposition of the clause as
"alongside" or "in the face of." The verb is equally opaque: its most common
meaning is "to fall"; some have imagined it has a military meaning here ("to
attack" or "to raid"); others have construed it as a reference to the "falling" of
the inheritance.

19. *this is the lineage of Isaac.* Modern translations that render "lineage" (or,
"begettings") as "story" are misconceived. The formula is pointedly used to
suggest a false symmetry with "this is the lineage of Ishmael." In this case,
the natural chain of procreation is interrupted, and can proceed only through
divine intervention, as was true for Abraham.

21.–23. In this second instance of the annunciation type-scene, the husband
intercedes on behalf of the wife, and the annunciation to the future mother—
here given the form of an oracle—is uniquely displaced from the period of
barrenness to late pregnancy. The crucial point in this story of the birth of
twins is not the fact of birth itself but the future fate of struggle between the
siblings, which is the burden of the oracular poem.

"Then why me?" and she went to inquire of the LORD. And the LORD   23
said to her:

> "Two nations—in your womb,
>   two peoples from your loins shall issue.
> People over people shall prevail,
>   the elder, the younger's slave."

And when her time was come to give birth, look, there were twins in   24
her womb. And the first one came out ruddy, like a hairy mantle all   25
over, and they called his name Esau. Then his brother came out, his   26

---

22. *Then why me?* Rebekah's cry of perplexity and anguish over this difficult
pregnancy is terse to the point of being elliptical. Her words might even be
construed as a broken-off sentence: Then why am I . . . ?

23. *the elder, the younger's slave.* Richard Elliott Friedman has made the interesting suggestion that the Hebrew oracle here has the ambiguity of its Del-
phic counterpart: the Hebrew syntax leaves unclear which noun is subject
and which is object—"the elder shall serve the younger," or, "the elder, the
younger shall serve."

25. *ruddy, like a hairy mantle . . . Esau.* There is an odd displacement of etymology in the naming sentence, perhaps because the writer was not sure
what "Esau" actually meant. "Ruddy," *'adom,* refers to another name for Esau,
Edom (as in verse 30), and the "hairy" component of the mantle simile, *se'ar,*
refers to Edom's territory, Seir.

hand grasping Esau's heel, and they called his name Jacob. And Isaac
was sixty years old when they were born.

27 And the lads grew up, and Esau was a man skilled in hunting, a man
28 of the field, and Jacob was a simple man, a dweller in tents. And Isaac
loved Esau for the game that he brought him, but Rebekah loved
29 Jacob. And Jacob prepared a stew and Esau came from the field, and

---

26. *they called his name Jacob.* The Masoretic Text has a singular verb, but
some manuscript versions have the plural, as when the same phrase is used
for Esau. In this instance, the etymology is transparent: Ya'*aqob,* "Jacob," and
'*aqeb,* "heel." The grabbing of the heel by the younger twin becomes a kind
of emblem of their future relationship, and the birth, like the oracle, again
invokes the struggle against primogeniture. The original meaning of the name
Jacob was probably something like "God protects" or "God follows after."

And Isaac was sixty years old. With the most deft economy of delayed exposition, the narrator reveals that Rebekah had been childless for twenty
years—an extraordinarily long period for a woman to suffer what in the
ancient setting was an acutely painful predicament.

27. *a simple man.* The Hebrew adjective *tam* suggests integrity or even innocence. In biblical idiom, the heart can be crooked ('*aqob,* the same root as
Jacob's name—cf. Jeremiah 17:9), and the idiomatic antonym is pureness
or innocence—*tom*—"of heart" (as in Genesis 20:5). There may well be a
complicating irony in the use of this epithet for Jacob, since his behavior is
very far from simple or innocent in the scene that is about to unfold.

28. *for the game that he brought him.* The Hebrew says literally, "for the game
in his mouth." It is unclear whether the idiom suggests Esau as a kind of lion
bringing home game in its mouth or rather bringing game to put in his father's
mouth. The almost grotesque concreteness of the idiom may be associated
with the absurdity of the material reason for Isaac's paternal favoritism. Pointedly, no reason is assigned for Rebekah's love of Jacob in the next clause.

29. *And Jacob prepared a stew.* Orah Haim, an eighteenth-century Hebrew
commentary, brilliantly suggests that Jacob, seeing that Esau had won their
father's heart with food, tries to compete by preparing his own (hearty vegetarian) culinary offering.

he was famished. And Esau said to Jacob, "Let me gulp down some   30
of this red red stuff, for I am famished." Therefore is his name called
Edom. And Jacob said, "Sell now your birthright to me." And Esau   31,32
said, "Look, I am at the point of death, so why do I need a birthright?"

---

30. *Let me gulp down some of this red red stuff.* Although the Hebrew of the
dialogues in the Bible reflects the same level of normative literary language
as the surrounding narration, here the writer comes close to assigning sub-
standard Hebrew to the rude Esau. The famished brother cannot even come
up with the ordinary Hebrew word for "stew" *(nazid)* and instead points to
the bubbling pot impatiently as (literally) "this red red." The verb he uses for
gulping down occurs nowhere else in the Bible, but in rabbinic Hebrew it is
reserved for the feeding of animals. This may be evidence for Abba ben
David's contention that rabbinic Hebrew developed from a biblical vernacular
that was excluded from literary usage: in this instance, the writer would have
exceptionally allowed himself to introduce the vernacular term for animal
feeding in order to suggest Esau's coarsely appetitive character. And even if
one allows for semantic evolution of this particular verb over the millennium
between the first articulation of our text and the Mishnah, it is safe to assume
it was always a cruder term for eating than the standard biblical one.

30. *Edom.* The pun, which forever associates crude impatient appetite with
Israel's perennial enemy, is on *'adom-'adom,* "this red red stuff."

31. *Sell now your birthright to me.* Each of Jacob's words, in striking contrast
to Esau's impetuous speech, is carefully weighed and positioned, with "me"
held back until the end of the sentence. If Esau seems too much a creature
of the imperious body to deserve the birthright, the dialogue suggests at the
same time that Jacob is a man of legalistic calculation. Perhaps this is a
quality needed to get and hold onto the birthright, but it hardly makes Jacob
sympathetic, and moral ambiguities will pursue him in the story.

32. *so why do I need.* The words he uses, *lamah zeh li,* are strongly reminiscent
of the words his mother used when she was troubled by the churning in her
womb, *lamah zeh 'anokhi.*

33 And Jacob said, "Swear to me now," and he swore to him, and he sold
34 his birthright to Jacob. Then Jacob gave Esau bread and lentil stew,
and he ate and he drank and he rose and he went off, and Esau
spurned the birthright.

---

34. *and he ate and he drank and he rose and he went off.* This rapid-fire chain
of verbs nicely expresses the precipitous manner in which Esau gulps down
his food and, as the verse concludes, casts away his birthright.

CHAPTER 26

And there was a famine in the land besides the former famine that was   1
in the days of Abraham, and Isaac went to Abimelech king of the
Philistines in Gerar. And the LORD appeared unto him and said,

---

This chapter is the only one in which Isaac figures as an active protagonist.
Before, he was a bound victim; after, he will be seen as a bamboozled blind
old man. His only other initiated act is his brief moment as intercessor on
behalf of his wife in 25:21. Textual critics disagree about whether this chapter
is a "mosaic" of Isaac traditions or an integral literary unit, and about whether
it is early or late. What is clear is that the architectonics of the larger story
require a buffer of material on Isaac between Jacob's purchase of the birthright and his stealing of the blessing—a buffer that focuses attention on
Isaac's right to the land and on his success in flourishing in the land. All of
the actions reported here, however, merely delineate him as a typological heir
to Abraham. Like Abraham he goes through the sister-wife experience, is
vouchsafed a covenantal promise by God, prospers in flock and field, and is
involved in a quarrel over wells. He remains the pale and schematic patriarch
among the three forefathers, preceded by the exemplary founder, followed by
the vivid struggler.

1. *besides the former famine.* The writer (some would say, the editor) signals
at the outset that this story comes after, and explicitly reenacts, what happened before to Abraham.

king of the Philistines. In this version, the anachronistic identification of
Gerar as a Philistine city, not strictly intrinsic to the Abimelech story in chapter 20, is insisted on. There is no obvious literary purpose for this difference;
one suspects it simply reflects the historical context in which this version
was formulated, in which the western Negeb would have been naturally
thought of as Philistine country.

2 "Do not go down to Egypt. Stay in the land that I shall say to you.
3 Sojourn in this land so that I may be with you and bless you, for to
   you and your seed I will give all these lands and I will fulfill the oath
   that I swore to Abraham your father, and I will multiply your seed like
4 the stars in the heavens and I will give to your seed all these lands,
   and all the nations of the earth shall be blessed through your seed
5 because Abraham has listened to my voice and has kept my charge,
   my commandments, my statutes, and my teachings."

6,7 And Isaac dwelled in Gerar. And the men of the place asked of his
   wife and he said, "She is my sister," fearing to say, 'My wife'—"lest the
   men of the place kill me over Rebekah, for she is comely to look at."

---

2. *Do not go down to Egypt.* That is, emulate the pattern of Abraham's second
sister-wife episode, not the first. Following a coastal route, Isaac could well
have used Gerar as a way station to Egypt, and Abraham's pact with Abimelech (chapter 21) would have provided some assurance that the Gerarites
would grant him safe transit.

4. *all these lands.* "lands" occurs in the plural in this version of the promise
because Isaac is in the land of the Philistines.

7. *the men of the place.* The sexual threat against the matriarch is displaced
in this final version from the monarch to the local male populace. The likely
reference of "one of the people" in verse 10 is what it seems to say, any male
Gerarite, despite an exegetical tradition (influenced by the earlier Abimelech
story) that construes it as an epithet for the king.
    she is comely to look at. Isaac's interior monologue uses the identical epi-
thet invoked by the narrator in introducing Rebekah in chapter 24.

And it happened, as his time there drew on, that Abimelech king of   8
the Philistines looked out the window and saw—and there was Isaac
playing with Rebekah his wife. And Abimelech summoned Isaac and   9
he said, "Why, look, she is your wife, and how could you say, 'She is
my sister.'?" And Isaac said to him, "For I thought, lest I die over her."
And Abimelech said, "What is this you have done? One of the people   10
might well have lain with your wife and you would have brought guilt
upon us." And Abimelech commanded all the people saying, "Whoso-   11

---

8. *as his time there drew on*. Rashi, with his characteristic acuteness of
response to nuances of phrasing, construes this as a suggestion that Isaac
became complacent with the passage of time ("From now on I don't have to
worry since they haven't raped her so far.") and so allowed himself to be
publicly demonstrative with Rebekah.

looked out the window. This is the most naturalistic of the three versions
of the story. The matriarch's marital status is conveyed not by divine plagues,
nor by a dream-vision from God, but by ocular evidence.

playing. The meaning of the verb here is clearly sexual, implying either
fondling or actual sexual "play." It immediately follows the name "Isaac," in
which the same verbal root is transparently inscribed. Thus Isaac-the-laugh-
er's birth is preceded by the incredulous laughter of each of his parents; Sarah
laughs after his birth; Ishmael laughs-mocks at the child Isaac; and now Isaac
laughs-plays with the wife he loves. Perhaps there is some suggestion that
the generally passive Isaac is a man of strong physical appetites: he loves
Esau because of his own fondness for venison; here he rather recklessly dis-
ports himself in public with the woman he has proclaimed to be his sister.

10. *One of the people might well have lain with your wife*. Though Abimelech's
words approximately mirror those of the indignant king in chapter 20, this
version is pointedly devised to put the woman first announced as Isaac's
beautiful, strictly virgin bride, in less danger than Sarah was in chapters 12
and 20: Rebekah is never taken into the harem; it is merely a supposition that
one of the local men might seize her for sexual exploitation.

12 ever touches this man or his wife is doomed to die." And Isaac sowed
in that land and he reaped that year a hundredfold, and the LORD
13 blessed him. And the man became ever greater until he was very great.
14 And he had possessions of flocks and of herds and many slaves, and
15 the Philistines envied him. And all the wells that his father's servants
had dug in the days of Abraham his father, the Philistines blocked up,
16 filling them with earth. And Abimelech said to Isaac, "Go away from
17 us, for you have grown far too powerful for us." And Isaac went off
from there and encamped in the wadi of Gerar, and he dwelled there.
18 And Isaac dug anew the wells of water that had been dug in the days
of Abraham his father, which the Philistines had blocked up after
Abraham's death, and he gave them names, like the names his father
19 had called them. And Isaac's servants dug in the wadi and they found
20 there a well of fresh water. And the shepherds of Gerar quarreled with
Isaac's shepherds, saying, "The water is ours." And he called the name
21 of the well Esek, for they had contended with him. And they dug

---

12. *And Isaac sowed.* In keeping with the emphasis of this version on human
action, the bounty that comes to the patriarch after the deflection of the
sexual danger to his wife is not a gift from the monarch but the fruit of his
own industry as agriculturalist and pastoralist. There is a continuity between
his sojourning in the western Negeb near Gerar and his movement somewhat
to the east, to Beersheba, where his father had long encamped. All this creates a direct connection between the sister-wife episode and the theme of
Isaac inheriting and growing prosperous in the land.

and the Philistines envied him. The jealousy over Isaac's spectacular prosperity and the contention over precious water resources that follows lay the
ground for the story of the two brothers struggling over the blessing of land
and inheritance in the next episode. Isaac's being "sent away" by the Philistines adumbrates Jacob's banishment to the east after having procured the
blessing by stealth.

17. *wadi.* The Arabic term, current in modern usage, designates, as does the
biblical *naḥal,* a dry riverbed that would be filled with water only during the
flash floods of the rainy season. But the floor of a wadi might conceal, as
here, an underground source of water.

20. *Esek.* Roughly, "contention," as in the verb that follows in the etiological
explanation of the name.

another well and they quarreled over it, too, and he called its name Sitnah. And he pulled up stakes from there and dug another well, and they did not quarrel over it, and he called its name Rehoboth, and he said, "For now the LORD has given us space that we may be fruitful in the land."

And he went up from there to Beer-sheba. And the LORD appeared unto him on that night and said, "I am the God of Abraham your father. Fear not, for I am with you, and I will bless you and I will multiply your seed for the sake of Abraham My servant." And he built an altar there and he invoked the name of the LORD, and he pitched his tent there, and Isaac's servants began digging a well there. And Abimelech came to him from Gerar, with Ahuzath his councillor and Phicol captain of his troops. And Isaac said to them, "Why have you come to me when you have been hostile toward me and have sent me away from you?" And they said, "We have clearly seen that the LORD is with you, and we thought—Let there be an oath between our two

---

21. *Sitnah.* The transparent meaning is "accusation" or "hostility," though the sentence lacks an etiological clause.

22. *another well.* The struggle over wells, which replays an episode in the Abraham stories but is given more elaborate emphasis, works nicely as part of the preparation for the next round of the Jacob–Esau conflict: a water source is not easily divisible; the spiteful act of the Philistines in blocking up the wells expresses a feeling that if we can't have the water, nobody should; at the end, Isaac's workers discover a new, undisputed well and call it Rehoboth, which means, "open spaces." We are being prepared for the story in which only one of the two brothers can get the real blessing, in which there will be bitter jealousy and resentment; and which in the long run will end with room enough for the two brothers to live peaceably in the same land.

27. *sent me away from you.* It is a mistake to render the verb, as several modern translations do, as "drive away." The verb Isaac chooses is a neutral one, even though the context of the sentence strongly indicates hostile intention. Abimelech in his response (verse 29) uses exactly the same word, adding the qualifier "in peace" in order to put a different face on the action: this was no banishment, we sent you off as a reasonable act of good will. The narrator then uses the same verb and qualifier—which might conceivably be a for-

29 sides, between you and us, and let us seal a pact with you, that you will do no harm to us, just as we have not touched you, and just as we have done toward you only good, sending you away in peace. Be you

30 hence blessed of the LORD!" And he made them a feast and they ate

31 and drank. And they rose early in the morning and swore to each other, and Isaac sent them away, and they went from him in peace.

32 And it happened on that day that Isaac's servants came and told him of the well they had dug and they said to him, "We have found water."

33 And he called it Shibah, therefore the name of the town is Beer-sheba to this day.

34 And Esau was forty years old and he took as wife Judith the daughter of Beeri the Hittite and Basemath the daughter of Elon the Hittite.

35 And they were a provocation to Isaac and to Rebekah.

---

mula for parting after the completion of a treaty—in verse 31, "and Isaac sent them away, and they went from him in peace." (Compare David and Abner in 2 Samuel 3.)

33. *Shibah.* Though the word in this form means "seven," the etiology of the name intimated by the narrative context obviously relates it to *shevu'ah*, "oath," whereas the earlier story about Beer-sheba (chapter 22) appears to link the name with both "seven" and "oath."

34. *And Esau . . . took as wife.* This brief notice about Esau's exogamous unions obviously is distinct from the preceding stories about Isaac. It is probably placed here to remind us of his unworthiness to be the true heir (thus forming a kind of envelope structure with the spurning of the birthright in the last verse of chapter 25), and in this way serves to offer some sort of justification in advance for Jacob's stealing the blessing in the next episode. It also lays the ground for the end of the next episode in which Rebekah will invoke the need for Jacob to find a wife from his own kin as an excuse for his hasty departure for Mesopotamia.

35. *provocation.* Some commentators construe the first component of the compound noun *morat-ruaḥ* as a derivative of the root *m-r-r*, "bitter"—hence the term "bitterness" favored by many translations. But the morphology of the word points to a more likely derivation from *m-r-h*, "to rebel" or "to defy," and thus an equivalent such as "provocation" is more precise.

CHAPTER 27

And it happened when Isaac was old, that his eyes grew too bleary to   1
see, and he called to Esau his elder son and said to him, "My son!"
and he said, "Here I am." And he said, "Look, I have grown old; I   2
know not how soon I shall die. So now, take up, pray, your gear, your   3
quiver and your bow, and go out to the field, and hunt me some game,
and make me a dish of the kind that I love and bring it to me that I   4
may eat, so that I may solemnly bless you before I die." And Rebekah   5

---

1. *his eyes grew too bleary to see.* Isaac the man of taste (25:28) and of touch
(26:8), is deprived of sight in his infirm old age. In the central episode of this
story, he will rely in sequence on taste, touch, and smell, ignoring the evidence of sound, to identify his supposed firstborn.

4. *I may solemnly bless you.* The Hebrew says literally, "my life-breath [*nafshi*]
may bless you." *Nafshi* here is an intensive synonym for "I," and hence something like "solemnly bless" or "absolutely bless" is suggested.

5. *And Rebekah was listening as Isaac spoke to Esau.* According to the convention of biblical narrative, there can be only two interlocutors in a dialogue (as
in Aeschylean tragedy), though one of them may be a collective presence—
e.g., a person addressing a crowd and receiving its collective response. Within
the limits of this convention, the writer has woven an artful chain. The story,
preponderantly in dialogue, is made up of seven interlocking scenes: Isaac-
Esau, Rebekah-Jacob, Jacob-Isaac, Isaac-Esau, Rebekah-Jacob, Rebekah-
Isaac, Isaac-Jacob. (The last of these occupies the first four verses of chapter
28). The first two pairs set out the father and his favorite son, then the mother
and her favorite son, in opposing tracks. Husband and wife are kept apart
until the penultimate scene; there is no dialogue at all between the two
brothers—sundered by the formal mechanics of the narrative—or between
Rebekah and Esau. Although one must always guard against the excesses of

was listening as Isaac spoke to Esau his son, and Esau went off to the field to hunt game to bring.

6 And Rebekah said to Jacob her son, "Look, I have heard your father
7 speaking to Esau your brother, saying, 'Bring me some game and make me a dish that I may eat, and I shall bless you in the LORD's presence
8 before I die.' So now, my son, listen to my voice, to what I command
9 you. Go, pray, to the flock, and fetch me from there two choice kids that I may make them into a dish for your father of the kind he loves.
10 And you shall bring it to your father and he shall eat, so that he may
11 bless you before he dies." And Jacob said to Rebekah his mother,

---

numerological exegesis, it is surely not accidental that there are just seven scenes, and that the key word "blessing" (berakhah) is repeated seven times.

to bring. The Septuagint reads instead "for his father," which is phonetically akin to the word in the Masoretic Text (either variant is a single word in the Hebrew). The Septuagint reading has a slight advantage of syntactic completeness, but subsequent exchanges in the story insist repeatedly on the verb "to bring" as an essential element in the paternal instructions.

7. *and I shall bless you in the LORD's presence.* Rebekah substitutes this for "that I may solemnly bless you" in the actual speech on which she eavesdropped, thus heightening the sense of the sacred and irrevocable character of the blessing she wants Jacob to steal.

8. *So now.* There is a pointed verbal symmetry in Rebekah's use of the same introductory term, *we'atah,* that Isaac used to preface his instructions to Esau.

9. *two choice kids.* Kids will again be an instrument of deception, turned on Jacob, when his sons bring him Joseph's tunic soaked in kid's blood. And in the immediately following episode (chapter 38), Judah, the engineer of the deception, will promise to send kids as payment to the woman he imagines is a roadside whore, and who is actually his daughter-in-law Tamar, using deception to obtain what is rightfully hers.

"Look, Esau my brother is a hairy man and I am a smooth-skinned
man. What if my father feels me and I seem a cheat to him and bring   12
on myself a curse and not a blessing?" And his mother said, "Upon me   13
your curse, my son. Just listen to my voice and go, fetch them for me."
And he went and he fetched and he brought to his mother, and his   14
mother made a dish of the kind his father loved. And Rebekah took   15
the garments of Esau her elder son, the finery that was with her in the
house, and put them on Jacob her younger son, and the skins of the   16
kids she put on his hands and on the smooth part of his neck. And   17
she placed the dish, and the bread she had made, in the hand of Jacob
her son. And he came to his father and said, "Father!" And he said,   18
"Here I am. Who are you, my son?" And Jacob said to his father, "I   19
am Esau your firstborn. I have done as you have spoken to me. Rise,
pray, sit up, and eat of my game so that you may solemnly bless me."
And Isaac said to his son, "How is it you found it this soon, my son?"   20
And he said, "Because the Lord your God gave me good luck." And
Isaac said to Jacob, "Come close, pray, that I may feel you, my son,   21

---

11. *Look, Esau my brother is a hairy man.* It is surely noteworthy that Jacob
expresses no compunction, only fear of getting caught.

15.–16. *the garments of Esau . . . the skins of the kids.* Both elements point
forward to the use of a garment to deceive first Jacob, then Judah, with the
tunic soaked in kid's blood combining the garment-motif and the kid-motif.

18. *Who are you, my son?* The inclination of several modern translations to
sort out the logic of these words by rendering them as "Which of my sons are
you?" can only be deplored. Isaac's stark question, as Tyndale and the King
James version rightly sensed, touches the exposed nerve of identity and moral
fitness that gives this ambiguous tale its profundity.

19. *I am Esau your firstborn.* He reserves the crucial term "firstborn" for the
end of his brief response. As Nahum Sarna notes, the narrator carefully
avoids identifying Esau as firstborn, using instead "elder son." The loaded
term is introduced by Jacob to cinch his false claim, and it will again be used
by Esau (verse 32) when he returns from the hunt.
   Rise, pray, sit up. It is only now that we learn the full extent of Isaac's
infirmity: he is not only blind but also bedridden.

22 whether you are my son Esau or not." And Jacob came close to Isaac
his father and he felt him and he said, "The voice is the voice of Jacob
23 and the hands are Esau's hands." But he did not recognize him for his
24 hands were, like Esau's hands, hairy, and he blessed him. And he said,
25 "Are you my son Esau? "And he said, "I am." And he said, "Serve me,
that I may eat of the game of my son, so that I may solemnly bless
you." And he served him and he ate, and he brought him wine and he
26 drank. And Isaac his father said to him, "Come close, pray, and kiss
27 me, my son." And he came close and kissed him, and he smelled his
garments and he blessed him and he said, "See, the smell of my son
is like the smell of the field that the LORD has blessed.

28   May God grant you
            from the dew of the heavens and the fat of the earth.
29   May peoples serve you,
            and nations bow before you.
      Be overlord to your brothers,
            may your mother's sons bow before you.
      Those who curse you be cursed,
            and those who bless you, blessed."

---

23. *he did not recognize him.* This crucial verb of recognition will return to
haunt Jacob when he is deceived by his sons and then will play through the
story of Judah and Tamar and of Joseph and his brothers.

24. *Are you my son Esau?* Doubt still lingers in Isaac's mind because of the
voice he hears, and so he is driven to ask this question again. His doubt may
seem assuaged when he asks his son to kiss him just before the blessing, but
that, as Gerhard von Rad observes, is evidently one last effort to test the son's
identity, through the sense of smell. The extent of Rebekah's cunning is thus
fully revealed: one might have wondered why Jacob needed his brother's garments to appear before a father incapable of seeing them—now we realize
she has anticipated the possibility that Isaac would try to smell Jacob: it is
Esau's smell that he detects in Esau's clothing.

And it happened as soon as Isaac finished blessing Jacob, and Jacob   30
barely had left the presence of Isaac his father, that Esau his brother
came back from the hunt. And he, too, made a dish and brought it to   31
his father and he said to his father, "Let my father rise and eat of the
game of his son so that you may solemnly bless me." And his father   32
Isaac said, "Who are you?" And he said, "I am your son, your firstborn,
Esau." And Isaac was seized with a very great trembling and he said,   33

---

30. *as soon as Isaac finished.* This entire sentence makes us aware of the
breakneck speed at which events are unfolding. Rebekah and Jacob have
managed to carry out her scheme just in the nick of time, and the physical
"bind" between this scene and the preceding one is deliberately exposed, just
as the bind between the first and second scene was highlighted by Rebekah's
presence as eavesdropper.

31. *Let my father rise and eat of the game of his son . . . bless me.* Jacob's more
nervous and urgent words for his father to arise from his bed were cast in the
imperative (with the particle of entreaty, *n'a,* "pray"). Esau, confident that he
has brought the requisites for the ritual of blessing, addresses his father more
ceremonially, beginning with the deferential third person. (The movement
from third person to second person at the end of the sentence is perfectly
idiomatic in biblical Hebrew when addressing a figure of authority.)

32. *Who are you?* This is the very question Isaac put to Jacob, but, significantly, "my son" is deleted: Isaac is unwilling to imagine that a second "Esau"
stands before him, and so at first he questions the interlocutor as though he
were a stranger.
   I am your son, your firstborn, Esau. The small but crucial divergences from
Jacob's response (verse 18) could scarcely be more eloquent. Esau begins by
identifying himself as Isaac's son—the very term his father had omitted from
his question, and which Jacob did not need to invoke because it was part of
the question. Then he announces himself as firstborn—a condition to which
he has in fact sold off the legal rights—and, finally, he pronounces his own
name. Jacob, on his part, first got out the lie, "Esau," and then declared
himself "firstborn."

"Who is it, then, who caught game and brought it to me and I ate everything before you came and blessed him? Now blessed he stays."
34 When Esau heard his father's words, he cried out with a great and very bitter outcry and he said to his father, "Bless me, too, Father!"
35 And he said, "Your brother has come in deceit and has taken your
36 blessing." And he said,

> "Was his name called Jacob
>   that he should trip me now twice by the heels?
> My birthright he took,
>   and look, now, he's taken my blessing."

And he said, "Have you not kept back a blessing for me?"
37 And Isaac answered and said to Esau, "Look, I made him overlord to you, and all his brothers I gave him as slaves, and with grain and
38 wine I endowed him. For you, then, what can I do, my son?" And Esau said to his father, "Do you have but one blessing, my father?

---

33. *Who is it, then, who caught game.* As a final move in the game of false and mistaken identities, Isaac pretends not to know who it is that has deceived him, finding it easier to let Esau name the culprit himself. Isaac must of course realize at once who it is that has taken the blessing because he already had his doubts when he heard the son speaking with the voice of Jacob.

34. *he cried out . . . "Bless me, too, Father."* Esau, whose first speech in the narrative was a half-articulate grunt of impatient hunger, had achieved a certain stylistic poise when he addressed his father after returning from the hunt, imagining he was about to receive the blessing. Now, however, faced with irreversible defeat, his composure breaks: first he cries out (the Hebrew meaning is close to "scream" or "shout"), then he asks in the pathetic voice of a small child, "Bless me, too, Father." Esau strikes a similar note at the end of verse 36 and in verse 38.

36. *Was his name called Jacob / that he should trip me now twice by the heels?* At birth, Jacob's name, *Yaʿaqob*, was etymologized as "heel-grabber" (playing on ʿaqeb, "heel"). Now Esau adds another layer of etymology by making the name into a verb from ʿaqob, "crooked," with the obvious sense of devious or deceitful dealing.

Bless me, too, Father." And Esau raised his voice and he wept. And   39
Isaac his father answered and said to him,

> "Look, from the fat of the earth be your dwelling
>> and from the dew of the heavens above.
> By your sword shall you live   40
>> and your brother you'll serve.
> And when you rebel
>> you shall break off his yoke from your neck."

---

39. *from the fat of the earth . . . from the dew of the heavens.* The notion put
forth by some commentators that these words mean something quite different from what they mean in the blessing to Jacob is forced. Isaac, having
recapitulated the terms of the blessing in his immediately preceding words
to Esau (verse 37), now reiterates them at the beginning of his blessing to
Esau: the bounty of heaven and earth, after all, can be enjoyed by more than
one son, though overlordship, as he has just made clear to Esau, cannot be
shared. (The reversal of order of heaven and earth is a formal variation, a
kind of chiasm, and it would be imprudent to read into it any symbolic sig-
nificance.)

40. *By your sword shall you live.* Yet Esau's blessing, like Ishmael's, is an
ambiguous one. Deprived by paternal pronouncement of political mastery, he
must make his way through violent struggle.
   And when you rebel. The Hebrew verb is obscure and may reflect a defective text. The present rendering steps up the conventional proposal, "grow
restive," lightly glancing in the direction of an emendation others have suggested, *timrod,* "you shall rebel," instead of *tarid* (meaning uncertain). This
whole verse, however obscurely, alludes to the later political fortunes of
Edom, the trans-Jordanian nation of which Esau is said to be the progenitor.
One of the miracles of the story, and of the story of Joseph and his brothers
that follows, is that the elements that adumbrate future political configurations in no way diminish the complexity of these figures as individual characters. To the extent that there is a kind of political allegory in all these tales,
it remains a secondary feature, however important it might have been for
audiences in the First Commonwealth period.

41 And Esau seethed with resentment against Jacob over the blessing his
father had blessed him, and Esau said in his heart, "As soon as the
time for mourning my father comes round, I will kill Jacob my

42 brother." And Rebekah was told the words of Esau her elder son, and
she sent and summoned Jacob her younger son and said to him, "Look,
Esau your brother is consoling himself with the idea he will kill you.

43 So now, my son, listen to my voice, and rise, flee to my brother Laban

44,45 in Haran, and you may stay with him a while until your brother's wrath
subsides, until your brother's rage against you subsides and he forgets
what you did to him, and I shall send and fetch you from there. Why

---

42. *And Rebekah was told the words of Esau.* This is a shrewd ploy of oblique
characterization of Esau. He had "spoken" these words only to himself, in
what is presented as interior monologue. But one must infer that Esau was
unable to restrain himself and keep counsel with his own heart but instead
blurted out his murderous intention to people in the household.

43. *So now, my son, listen to my voice.* Introducing her counsel of flight, Rebekah uses exactly the same words she spoke at the beginning of her instructions to Jacob about the strategem of deception to get the blessing.

45. *Why should I be bereft of you both on one day?* The verb *shakhal* is used
for a parent's bereavement of a child and so "you both" must refer to Jacob
and Esau: although a physical struggle between the two would scarcely be a
battle between equals, in her maternal fear she imagines the worst-case sce-
nario, the twins killing each other, and in the subsequent narrative, the sedentary Jacob does demonstrate a capacity of unusual physical strength.

should I be bereft of you both on one day? And Rebekah said to Isaac,   46
"I loathe my life because of the Hittite women! If Jacob takes a wife
from Hittite women like these, from the native girls, what good to me
is life?"

---

46. *I loathe my life because of the Hittite women!* Rebekah shows the same
alacrity in this verbal manipulation that she evinced in preparing the kidskin
disguise and the mock-venison dish, and, earlier, in her epic watering of the
camels. Instead of simply registering that Jacob ought not to take a wife from
the daughters of the Canaanite (compare 24:3 and 28:1), she brandishes a
sense of utter revulsion, claiming that her life is scarcely worth living because
of the native daughters-in-law Esau has inflicted on her. This tactic not only
provides a persuasive pretext for Jacob's departure but also allows her—
obliquely, for she does not pronounce his name—to discredit Esau.

what good to me is life? The phrase she uses, *lamah li ḥayim*, contains an
echo of her question during her troubled pregnancy, *lamah zeh 'anokhi*, "why
then me?"

CHAPTER 28

1 And Isaac summoned Jacob and blessed him and commanded him and
said to him, "You shall not take a wife from the daughters of Canaan.
2 Rise, go to Paddan-aram to the house of Bethuel your mother's father,
and take you from there a wife from the daughters of Laban, your
3 mother's brother. And may El Shaddai bless you and make you fruitful

---

1. *and blessed him.* The Hebrew verb *berekh* also has the more everyday sense
of "to greet," but it is quite unnecessary to construe it in that sense here, as
some scholars have proposed. Isaac's clear intention is to give his son a parting blessing: the instructions about taking a wife from Mesopotamia inter-
vene in the last half of this verse and in verse 2 before we reach the actual
words of the blessing in verses 3 and 4, but this sort of proleptic introduction
of a key verb is entirely in accordance with Hebrew literary usage.

and multiply, so you become an assembly of peoples. And may He   4
grant you the blessing of Abraham, to you and your seed as well, that
you may take possession of the land of your sojournings, which God
granted to Abraham." And Isaac sent Jacob off and he went to Paddan-   5
aram to Laban son of Bethuel the Aramean, brother of Rebekah,
mother of Jacob and Esau.

---

4. *And may He grant you the blessing of Abraham, to you and your seed as well.*
Documentary critics assign 27:46–28:9 to the Priestly source and argue that
it contradicts the logic of the story told in chapter 27. Such readings, however,
reflect an unfortunate tendency to construe any sign of tension in a narrative
as an irreconcilable contradiction, and underestimate the resourcefulness of
the Priestly writers in making their own version artfully answer the versions
of antecedent traditions. Sending Jacob off to Paddan-aram to find a wife and
Jacob's flight from his vengeful brother are not alternate explanations for his
departure: the bride search is clearly presented as an *excuse* for what is actually his flight, an excuse ably engineered by Rebekah with her melodramatic
complaint (27:46). Now Isaac, whatever misgivings he may have about Jacob's
act of deception, knows that his younger son has irrevocably received the
blessing, and he has no choice but to reiterate it at the moment of parting.
He does so at this point in the lofty language of procreation and proliferation
and inheritance, harking back to the first creation story, that is characteristic
of the Priestly style, which is in a different register from the earthy and political language of the blessing articulated in the previous chapter. But far from
contradicting or needlessly duplicating the earlier blessing, this scene is a
pointed, low-key replay of the scene in the tent. When Isaac tells Jacob he
will become an assembly of peoples and his seed will take possession of the
land promised to Abraham, he is manifestly conferring on him the blessing
that is the prerogative of the elder son—something he would have no warrant
to do were he not simply confirming the blessing he has already been led to
pronounce, through Jacob's subterfuge, upon his younger son. Esau once
again fails to get things right. Overhearing Isaac's warning to Jacob about
exogamous unions, he behaves as though endogamy were a sufficient condition for obtaining the blessing, and so after the fact of his two marriages with
Hittite women—perhaps even many years after the fact—he, too, takes a
cousin as bride. There is no indication of his father's response to this initiative, but the marriage is an echo in action of his plaintive cry, "Do you have
but one blessing, my Father? Bless me, too, Father."

6   And Esau saw that Isaac had blessed Jacob and had sent him off to
    Paddan-aram to take him a wife from there when he blessed him and
    commanded him, saying, "You shall not take a wife from the daughters
7   of Canaan." And Jacob listened to his father and to his mother and he
8   went to Paddan-aram. And Esau saw that the daughters of Canaan
9   were evil in the eyes of Isaac his father. And Esau went to Ishmael and
    he took Mahalath daughter of Ishmael son of Abraham, in addition to
    his wives, as a wife.

10,11   And Jacob left Beer-sheba and set out for Haran. And he came upon
    a certain place and stopped there for the night, and he took one of the
    stones of the place and put it at his head and he lay down in that

---

11. *a certain place.* Though archeological evidence indicates that Bethel had
been a cultic site for the Canaanites centuries before the patriarchs, this
pagan background, as Nahum Sarna argues, is entirely occluded: the site is
no more than an anonymous "place" where Jacob decides to spend the night.
Repetition of a term is usually a thematic marker in biblical narrative, and it
is noteworthy that "place" *(maqom)* occurs six times in this brief story. In part,
this is the tale of the transformation of an anonymous place through vision
into Bethel, a "house of God."

   one of the stones of the place. There is scant evidence elsewhere of a general (and uncomfortable) ancient Near Eastern practice of using stones as
pillows. Rashi, followed by some modern scholars, proposes that the stone is
not placed under Jacob's head but alongside it, as a kind of protective barrier.
The stone by which Jacob's head rests as he dreams his vision will become
the pillar, the commemorative or cultic marker *(matsevah)* at the end of the
story. J. P. Fokkelman (1975) astutely notes that stones are Jacob's personal
motif: from the stone at his head to the stone marker, then the stone upon
the well he will roll away, and the pile of stones he will set up to mark his
treaty with Laban.

place, and he dreamed, and, look, a ramp was set against the ground   12
with its top reaching the heavens, and, look, messengers of God were
going up and coming down it. And, look, the LORD was poised over   13
him and He said, "I, the LORD, am the God of Abraham your father
and the God of Isaac. The land on which you lie, to you I will give it
and to your seed. And your seed shall be like the dust of the earth and   14
you shall burst forth to the west and the east and the north and the
south, and all the clans of the earth shall be blessed through you, and
through your seed. And, look, I am with you and I will guard you   15
wherever you go, and I will bring you back to this land, for I will not
leave you until I have done that which I have spoken to you." And   16
Jacob awoke from his sleep and he said, "Indeed, the LORD is in this
place, and I did not know." And he was afraid and he said,   17

"How fearsome is this place!
This can be but the house of God,
and this is the gate of the heavens."

---

12. *a ramp.* The Hebrew term occurs only here. Although its etymology is
doubtful, the traditional rendering of "ladder" is unlikely. As has often been
observed, the references to both "its top reaching the heavens" and "the gate
of the heavens" use phrases associated with the Mesopotamian ziggurat, and
so the structure envisioned is probably a vast ramp with terraced landings.
There is a certain appropriateness in the Mesopotamian motif, given the des-
tination of Jacob's journey. Jacob in general is represented as a border crosser,
a man of liminal experiences: here, then in his return trip when he is confronted by Laban, and in the nocturnal encounter at the ford of the Jabbok.

13. *the LORD was poised over him.* The syntactic reference of "over him" is
ambiguous, and the phrase could equally be construed to mean "on it" (i.e.,
on the ramp).

14. *And your seed shall be like the dust of the earth.* God in effect offers divine
confirmation of Isaac's blessing (verses 3 and 4) in language that is more
vivid—indeed, hyperbolic.

18 And Jacob rose early in the morning and took the stone he had put at
19 his head, and he set it as a pillar and poured oil over its top. And he
called the name of that place Bethel, though the name of the town
20 before had been Luz. And Jacob made a vow, saying, "If the LORD God
be with me and guard me on this way that I am going and give me
21 bread to eat and clothing to wear, and I return safely to my father's
22 house, then the LORD will be my God. And this stone that I set as a
pillar will be a house of God, and everything that You give me I will
surely tithe it to You."

---

18. *took the stone . . . and set it as a pillar.* Cultic pillars—Jacob ritually dedi-
cates this one as such by pouring oil over its top—were generally several feet
high. If that is the case here, it would have required, as Gerhard von Rad
notes, Herculean strength to lift the stone. We are then prepared for Jacob's
feat with a massive weight of stone in the next episode.

19. *though the name of the town before had been Luz.* In fact, there is no
indication of any "town" in the story, although Luz-Bethel would have been
familiar to Israelite audiences as a town and cultic center. Perhaps Jacob's
vision is assumed to occur in the open, in the vicinity of Bethel.

20. *If the LORD God be with me.* The conditional form of the vow—if the
other party does such and such, then I on my part will do such and such in
return—is well attested elsewhere in the Bible and in other ancient Near
Eastern texts. But its use by Jacob has a characterizing particularity. God has
already promised him in the dream that He will do all these things for him.
Jacob, however, remains the suspicious bargainer—a "wrestler" with words
and conditions just as he is a physical wrestler, a heel-grabber. He carefully
stipulated conditions of sale to the famished Esau; he was leery that he would
be found out when Rebekah proposed her strategem of deception to him;
now he wants to be sure God will fulfill His side of the bargain before he
commits himself to God's service; and later he will prove to be a sharp dealer
in his transactions with his uncle Laban.
    on this way that I am going. The "way" replicates the mission of Abraham's
servant in chapter 24—to find a bride among his kinfolk in Mesopotamia.
But unlike the servant, who crosses the desert in grand style with a retinue
of camels and underlings, Jacob is fleeing alone on foot—in fact, it is a very
dangerous journey. He will invoke an emblematic image of himself as refugee
and pedestrian border crosser in his reunion with Esau years later: "For with
my staff I crossed this Jordan" (32:11).

CHAPTER 29

And Jacob lifted his feet and went on to the land of the Easterners. And [1,2] he saw and, look, there was a well in the field, and, look, three flocks of sheep were lying beside it, for from that well they would water the flocks, and the stone was big on the mouth of the well. And when all [3] the flocks were gathered there, they would roll the stone from the mouth of the well and would water the sheep and put back the stone in its place on the mouth of the well. And Jacob said to them, "My [4] brothers, where are you from?" And they said, "We are from Haran." And he said to them, "Do you know Laban son of Nahor?" And they [5] said, "We know him." And he said to them, "Is he well?" And they [6] said, "He is well, and, look, Rachel his daughter is coming with the

---

1. *lifted his feet.* Although eyes are frequently lifted or raised in these narratives, the idiom of lifting the feet occurs only here. Rashi suggests that Jacob's elation after the Bethel epiphany imparted a buoyancy to the movement of his feet as he began his long trek to the East. Perhaps this is a general idiom for beginning a particularly arduous journey on foot. In any case, a symmetry of phrasing is created when, at the end of the journey, having discovered Rachel, Jacob "lifted his voice and wept."

2. *And he saw, and, look, . . .* These sentences are an interesting interweave of Jacob's perspective and the narrator's. It is Jacob who sees first the well, then the flocks. It is the narrator who intervenes to explain that from this well the flocks are watered, but it is in all likelihood Jacob who sees the stone, notes its bigness, observes how it covers the mouth of the well (the order of perception is precisely indicated by the word order). Then, in verse 3, the narrator again speaks out to explain the habitual procedures of the Haranites with the stone and the well.

7 sheep." And he said, "Look, the day is still long. It is not time to gather
8 in the herd. Water the sheep and take them to graze." And they said,
   "We cannot until all the flocks have gathered and the stone is rolled
9 from the mouth of the well and we water the sheep." He was still
   speaking with them when Rachel came with her father's sheep, for
10 she was a shepherdess. And it happened when Jacob saw Rachel
   daughter of Laban his mother's brother and the sheep of Laban his
   mother's brother that he stepped forward and rolled the stone from
   the mouth of the well and watered the sheep of Laban his mother's
11,12 brother. And Jacob kissed Rachel and lifted his voice and wept. And

---

7. *Look, the day is still long.* Jacob's scrupulousness about the shepherds' obligation to take full advantage of the daylight for grazing the flocks prefigures
his own dedication to the shepherd's calling and his later self-justification
that he has observed all his responsibilities punctiliously.

10. *he stepped forward and rolled the stone from the mouth of the well and
watered the sheep.* The "Homeric" feat of strength in rolling away the huge
stone single-handed is the counterpart to his mother's feat of carrying up
water for ten thirsty camels. Though Jacob is not a man of the open field,
like Esau, we now see that he is formidably powerful—and so perhaps Rebekah was not unrealistic in fearing the twins would kill each other should they
come to blows. The drawing of water after encountering a maiden at a well
in a foreign land signals to the audience that a betrothal type-scene is
unfolding. But Jacob is the antithesis of his father: instead of a surrogate, the
bridegroom himself is present at the well, and it is he, not the maiden, who
draws the water; in order to do so, he must contend with a stone, the motif
that is his narrative signature. If, as seems entirely likely, the well in the
foreign land is associated with fertility and the otherness of the female body
to the bridegroom, it is especially fitting that this well should be blocked by
a stone, as Rachel's womb will be "shut up" over long years of marriage.

11. *And Jacob kissed Rachel.* As Nahum Sarna notes, there is a pun between
"he watered" (*wayashq*) and "he kissed" (*wayishaq*). The same pun is played
on by the poet of the Song of Songs.

Jacob told Rachel that he was her father's kin, and that he was Rebekah's son, and she ran and told her father. And it happened, when   13
Laban heard the report of Jacob his sister's son, he ran toward him
and embraced him and kissed him and brought him to his house. And
he recounted to Laban all these things. And Laban said to him,   14
"Indeed, you are my bone and my flesh."

And he stayed with him a month's time, and Laban said to Jacob,   15
"Because you are my kin, should you serve me for nothing? Tell me
what your wages should be." And Laban had two daughters. The name   16
of the elder was Leah and the name of the younger Rachel. And Leah's   17
eyes were tender, but Rachel was comely in features and comely to

---

12. *and she ran and told.* The hurrying to bring home the news of the guest's
arrival, generally with the verb *ruts,* ("to run") as here, is another conventional
requirement of the betrothal type-scene.

13. *he ran toward him.* This may be standard hospitality, but Rashi, exercising
his own hermeneutics of suspicion, shrewdly notes that Laban could be
recalling that the last time someone came from the emigrant branch of the
family in Canaan, he brought ten heavily laden camels with him. Rashi pur-
sues this idea by proposing that Laban's embrace was to see if Jacob had gold
secreted on his person.

15. *Because you are my kin, should you serve me for nothing?* In a neat deployment of delayed revelation, a device of which the biblical writers were fond,
we now learn that this "bone and flesh" of Laban's has already been put to
work by his gracious host for a month's time.

17. *Leah's eyes were tender.* The precise meaning in this context of the adjective is uncertain. Generally, the word *rakh* is an antonym of "hard" and means
"soft," "gentle," "tender," or in a few instances "weak." The claim that here it
refers to dullness, or a lusterless quality, is pure translation by immediate
context because *rakh* nowhere else has that meaning. Still, there is no way of
confidently deciding whether the word indicates some sort of impairment
("weak" eyes or perhaps odd-looking eyes) or rather suggests that Leah has
sweet eyes that are her one asset of appearance, in contrast to her beautiful
sister.

18 look at, and Jacob loved Rachel. And he said, "I will serve seven years
19 for Rachel your younger daughter." And Laban said, "Better I should
20 give her to you than give her to another man. Stay with me." And
    Jacob served seven years for Rachel, and they seemed in his eyes but
21 a few days in his love for her. And Jacob said to Laban, "Give me my
22 wife, for my time is done, and let me come to bed with her." And
23 Laban gathered all the men of the place and made a feast. And when
    evening came, he took Leah his daughter and brought her to Jacob,
24 and he came to bed with her. And Laban gave Zilpah his slavegirl to
25 Leah his daughter as her slavegirl. And when morning came, look, she
    was Leah. And he said to Laban, "What is this you have done to me?
    Was it not for Rachel that I served you, and why have you deceived

---

18. *seven years for Rachel your younger daughter.* True to legalistic form, Jacob carefully stipulates the duration of the labor (in lieu of a bride-price that he does not possess), the name of the daughter, and the fact that she is the younger daughter. In the event, none of this avails.

20. *they seemed in his eyes but a few days in his love for her.* The writer's eloquent economy scarcely needs comment, but it should be observed that "a few days" (or, "a little while," *yamim aḥadim*) is exactly the phrase his mother had used in advising him to go off to stay with her brother (27:44).

21. *and let me come to bed with her.* The explicitness of Jacob's statement is sufficiently abrupt to have triggered maneuvers of exegetical justification in the Midrash, but it is clearly meant to express his—understandable—sexual impatience, which is about to be given a quite unexpected outlet.

25. *why have you deceived me?* The verb Jacob uses to upbraid Laban reflects the same root as the key noun Isaac used when he said to Esau, "Your brother has come in deceit and has taken your blessing" (27:35).

me?" And Laban said, "It is not done thus in our place, to give the   26
younger girl before the firstborn. Finish out the bridal week of this   27
one and we shall give you the other as well for the service you render
me for still another seven years." And so Jacob did. And when he   28
finished out the bridal week of the one, he gave him Rachel his daughter as wife. And Laban gave to Rachel his daughter Bilhah his slavegirl   29
as her slavegirl. And he came to bed with Rachel, too, and, indeed,   30
loved Rachel more than Leah, and he served him still another seven
years. And the LORD saw that Leah was despised and He opened her   31

---

26. *It is not done thus in our place, to give the younger girl before the firstborn.*
Laban is an instrument of dramatic irony: his perfectly natural reference to
"our place" has the effect of touching a nerve of guilty consciousness in Jacob,
who in *his* place acted to put the younger before the firstborn. This effect is
reinforced by Laban's referring to Leah not as the elder but as the firstborn
(*bekhirah*). It has been clearly recognized since late antiquity that the whole
story of the switched brides is a meting out of poetic justice to Jacob—the
deceiver deceived, deprived by darkness of the sense of sight as his father is
by blindness, relying, like his father, on the misleading sense of touch. The
Midrash Bereishit Rabba vividly represents the correspondence between the
two episodes: "And all that night he cried out to her, 'Rachel!' and she
answered him. In the morning, 'and, . . . look, she was Leah.' He said to her,
'Why did you deceive me, daughter of a deceiver? Didn't I call out Rachel in
the night, and you answered me!' She said: 'There is never a bad barber who
doesn't have disciples. Isn't this how your father cried out Esau, and you
answered him?' "

31. *Leah was despised and He opened her womb, but Rachel was barren.* The
Hebrew term for "despised" (or "hated") seems to have emotional implications, as Leah's words in verse 33 suggest, but it is also a technical, legal term
for the unfavored co-wife. The pairing of an unloved wife who is fertile with
a barren, beloved co-wife sets the stage for a familiar variant of the annunciation type-scene (as in the story of Peninah and Hannah in 1 Samuel 1). But,
as we shall see, in Rachel's case the annunciation is deflected.

32 womb, but Rachel was barren. And Leah conceived and bore a son
and called his name Reuben, for she said, "Yes, the LORD has seen my
33 suffering, for now my husband will love me." And she conceived again
and bore a son, and she said, "Yes, the LORD has heard I was despised
and He has given me this one, too," and she called his name Simeon.
34 And she conceived again and bore a son, and she said, "This time at

---

32. *Reuben . . . seen my suffering*. All of the etymologies put forth for the
names of the sons are ad hoc improvisations by the mother who does the
naming—essentially, midrashic play on the sounds of the names. Thus "Reuben" is construed as *r'u ben*, "see, a son," but Leah immediately converts the
verb into God's seeing her suffering. The narrative definition of character and
relationship continues through the naming-speeches, as, here, the emotionally neglected Leah sees a kind of vindication in having born a son and des-
perately imagines her husband will now finally love her.

33. *the LORD has heard . . . Simeon*. The naming plays on *sham'a*, "has heard,"
and *Shim'on*. It is noteworthy that Jacob's first two sons are named after sight
and sound, the two senses that might have detected him in his deception of
his father, were not Isaac deprived of sight and had not the evidence of touch
and smell led him to disregard the evidence of sound. Leah's illusion that
bearing a son would bring her Jacob's love has been painfully disabused, for
here she herself proclaims that she is "despised" and that God has given her
another son as compensation.

last my husband will join me, for I have born him three sons." Therefore is his name called Levi. And she conceived again and bore a son,   35
and she said, "This time I sing praise to the LORD," therefore she
called his name Judah. And she ceased bearing children.

---

34. *my husband will join me . . . Levi.* The naming plays on *yilaveh,* "will join,"
and Levi. Once more, Leah voices the desperate hope that her bearing sons
to Jacob will bring him to love her.

35. *Sing praise . . . Judah.* The naming plays on *'odeh,* "sing praise," and *Yehudah,* "Judah." The verb Leah invokes is one that frequently figures in thanksgiving psalms. With the birth of her fourth son, she no longer expresses hope
of winning her husband's affection but instead simply gives thanks to God
for granting her male offspring.

    she ceased bearing children. This may be merely the consequence of natu-
ral process, though one possible reading of the mandrakes episode in the next
chapter is not that the two sisters had their conjugal turns but rather that
Jacob has ceased for a long period to cohabit with Leah.

CHAPTER 30

And Rachel saw that she had born no children to Jacob, and Rachel was jealous of her sister, and she said to Jacob, "Give me sons, for if you don't, I'm a dead woman!" And Jacob was incensed with Rachel, and he said, "Am I instead of God, Who has denied you fruit of the womb?" And she said, "Here is my slavegirl, Bilhah. Come to bed with

---

1. *Give me sons, for if you don't I'm a dead woman!* It is a general principle of biblical narrative that a character's first recorded speech has particular defining force as characterization. Surprisingly, although Rachel has been part of the story for more than a decade of narrated time, this is the first piece of dialogue assigned to her. It is a sudden revelation of her simmering frustration and her impulsivity: in fact, she speaks with an impetuousness reminiscent of her brother-in-law Esau, who also announced to Jacob that he was on the point of death if Jacob did not immediately give him what he wanted.

2. *Am I instead of God.* Through Jacob's words, the writer shrewdly invokes a fateful deflection of the annunciation type-scene. According to the convention of the annunciation story, the barren wife should go to an oracle or be visited by a divine messenger or a man of God to be told that she will give birth to a son. Rachel instead importunes her husband, who properly responds that he cannot play the role of God in the bestowal of fertility, or in the annunciation narrative. Rachel is then forced to fall back on the strategy of surrogate maternity, like Sarai with Hagar. One should note that she demands "sons," not a son. Eventually, she will have two sons, but will die in giving birth to the second one. Perhaps her rash words here, "Give me sons, for if you don't, I'm a dead woman," are meant to foreshadow her premature death.

her, that she may give birth on my knees, so that I, too, shall be built
up through her." And she gave him Bilhah her slavegirl as a wife, and   4
Jacob came to bed with her. And Bilhah conceived and bore Jacob a   5
son. And Rachel said, "God granted my cause, yes, He heard my voice   6
and He gave me a son." Therefore she called his name Dan. And   7
Bilhah, Rachel's slavegirl, conceived again and bore a second son to
Jacob. And Rachel said, "In awesome grapplings I have grappled with   8
my sister and, yes, I won out." And she called his name Naphtali. And   9
Leah saw that she had ceased bearing children, and she took Zilpah,
her slavegirl, and gave her to Jacob as a wife. And Zilpah, Leah's slave-   10
girl, bore Jacob a son. And Leah said, "Good luck has come." And she   11
called his name Gad. And Zilpah, Leah's slavegirl, bore a second son   12
to Jacob. And Leah said, "What good fortune! For the girls have   13
acclaimed me fortunate." And she called his name Asher.

---

3. *give birth on my knees.* Placing the newborn on someone's knees was a
gesture of adoption.

    built up through her. As with Sarai in chapter 16, the verb, *'ibaneh,* puns
on *ben,* "son."

6. *God granted my cause.* The verb *dan* suggests vindication of a legal plea,
and is offered as the etymology of the name Dan.

8. *grapplings.* The Hebrew *naftulim* plays on Naphtali. It is noteworthy that
Rachel chooses an image of wrestling for her relationship with her sister that
marks a correspondence to the relationship of Jacob, the "heel-grabber," with
his older sibling.

11. *Good luck has come.* The translation follows a long-established practice in
separating the enigmatic single word of the Masoretic Text, *bagad,* into *ba'
gad.*

13. *What good fortune! For the girls have acclaimed me fortunate.* Asher's name
is derived from *'osher,* "good fortune," and the entire naming is thus closely
parallel to the naming of Gad. This noun *'osher* produces a common biblical
verb *'isher,* the basic meaning of which is to call out to a lucky person, *'ashrei,*
"happy is he" (or, here, "happy is she").

14   And Reuben went out during the wheat harvest and found mandrakes
     in the field and brought them to Leah his mother. And Rachel said to
15   Leah, "Give me, pray, some of the mandrakes of your son." And she
     said, "Is it not enough that you have taken my husband, and now you
     would take the mandrakes of my son? "And Rachel said, "Then let
16   him lie with you tonight in return for the mandrakes of your son." And
     Jacob came from the field in the evening and Leah went out to meet
     him and said, "With me you will come to bed, for I have clearly hired
     you with the mandrakes of my son." And he lay with her that night.
17   And God heard Leah and she conceived and bore Jacob a fifth son.

---

14. *mandrakes.* As in other, later cultures, these plants with tomato-shaped
fruit were used for medicinal purposes and were thought to be aphrodisiac,
and also to have the virtue of promoting fertility, which seems to be what
Rachel has in mind. The aphrodisiac association is reinforced in the Hebrew
by a similarity of sound (exploited in the Song of Songs) between *duda'im,*
"mandrakes," and *dodim,* "lovemaking."

15. *Is it not enough that you have taken my husband?* The narrator has mentioned Rachel's jealousy of Leah, and Rachel has referred to "grappling" with
her sister, but this is the first actual dialogue between the sisters. It vividly
etches the bitterness between the two, on the part of the unloved Leah as
well as of the barren Rachel. In still another correspondence with the story
of Jacob and Esau, one sibling barters a privilege for a plant product, though
here the one who sells off the privilege is the younger, not the elder.

16. *With me you will come to bed. . . . And he lay with her that night.* In his
transactions with these two imperious, embittered women, Jacob seems
chiefly acquiescent, perhaps resigned. When Rachel instructs him to consort
with her slavegirl, he immediately complies, as he does here when Leah tells
him it is she who is to share his bed this night. In neither instance is there
any report of response on his part in dialogue. The fact that Leah uses this
particular idiom for sexual intercourse (literally, "to me you will come"), ordinarily used for intercourse with a woman the man has not previously enjoyed,
is a strong indication that Jacob has been sexually boycotting Leah. That
could be precisely what she is referring to when she says to Rachel, "You have
taken my husband."

And Leah, said, "God has given my wages because I gave my slavegirl   18
to my husband," and she called his name Issachar. And Leah con-   19
ceived again and bore a sixth son to Jacob. And Leah said, "God has   20
granted me a goodly gift. This time my husband will exalt me, for I
have born him six sons." And she called his name Zebulun. And after-   21
ward she bore a daughter and she called her name Dinah.

---

18. *God has given my wages.* In this case, as again with the birth of Joseph,
there is a double pun in the naming-speech. The word for "wages" (or,
"reward") is *sakhar,* which also means a fee paid for hiring something. Leah
uses this same root when she tells Jacob (verse 16) that she has "clearly hired"
him *(sakhor sekhartikha).* Thus Issachar's name is derived from both the circumstances of his conception and his mother's sense of receiving a reward in
his birth. All this suggests that the naming etymologies may not have figured
so literally in the ancient Hebrew imagination as moderns tend to imagine:
the name is taken as a trigger of sound associations, releasing not absolute
meaning but possible meaning, and in some instances, a cluster of complementary or even contradictory meanings.

20. *a goodly gift. . . . my husband will exalt me.* The naming of Zebulun illustrates how free the phonetic associations can be in the naming-speeches.
Zebulun and *zebed* ("gift") share only the first two consonants. The verb for
"exalt" (this meaning is no more than an educated guess), *zabal,* then exhibits
a fuller phonetic correspondence to Zebulun and evidently represents an
alternative etymology of the name.
   This time my husband will exalt me. Having born Jacob half a dozen sons,
half of the sanctified tribal grouping of twelve, Leah indulges one last time
in the poignant illusion that her husband will now love her.

21. *and she called her name Dinah.* The absence of a naming etymology for
Dinah is by no means an indication, as has often been claimed, that this
verse derives from a different source. There is no naming-speech for Dinah
because she is a daughter and will not be the eponymous founder of a tribe.

22 And God remembered Rachel and God heard her and He opened her
23 womb, and she conceived and bore a son, and she said, "God has
24 taken away my shame." And she called his name Joseph, which is to
say, "May the Lord add me another son."

25 And it happened, when Rachel bore Joseph, that Jacob said to Laban,
26 "Send me off, that I may go to my place and to my land. Give me my
wives and my children, for whom I have served you, that I may go, for

---

22.–23. After the long years of frustrated hopes and prayers (the latter intimated by God's "hearing" Rachel), the gift of fertility is represented in a rapid-
fire chain of uninterrupted verbs: remembered, heard, opened, conceived,
bore.

23. *taken away my shame.* "Taken away," *'asaf,* is proposed as an etymology of
Yosef, Joseph.

24. *May the Lord add me another son.* "Add," *yosef,* Rachel's second etymology, is a perfect homonym in Hebrew for Joseph (and hence the odd name
used among American Puritans, Increase). Leah's double etymology for Issachar had referred in sequence to conception and birth. Rachel's double etymology refers to birth and, prospectively, to a future son. She remains true to
the character of her initial speech to Jacob, where she demanded of him not
a son but sons. She will be granted the second son she seeks, but at the cost
of her life.

26. *for whom I have served you . . . for you know the service that I have done
you.* Jacob's speech repeatedly insists on the service *('avodah)* he has performed for Laban, the same word used in the agreement about the double
bride-price. He has worked seven years before marrying the two sisters and,
given Leah's seven childbirths with a few years' hiatus between the fourth
and fifth sons, several years beyond the second seven he owed Laban as
Rachel's bride-price.

you know the service that I have done you." And Laban said to him,   27
"If, pray, I have found favor in your eyes, I have prospered and the
LORD has blessed me because of you." And he said, "Name me your   28
wages that I may give them." And he said, "You know how I have   29
served you and how your livestock has fared with me. For the little   30
you had before my time has swollen to a multitude and the LORD has
blessed you on my count. And now, when shall I, too, provide for my
household?" And he said, "What shall I give you?" And Jacob said,   31

---

27. *If, pray, I have found favor in your eyes.* This formula of deference is normally followed by a request. If the text is reliable here, Laban begins with
the deferential flourish and then, having mentioned how he has been blessed
through Jacob, lets his voice trail off. A second formula for the introduction
of speech ("and he said") is inserted, and only then does he proceed to his
request: "Name me your wages." Could the thought of the prosperity he has
enjoyed through Jacob's supervision of his flocks lead to this self-interruption,
a kind of hesitation before he asks Jacob to name the separation pay that he
knows he owes his nephew?

   I have prospered. Everywhere else in the Bible, the verb *niḥesh* means "to
divine," but that makes little sense here, and so there is plausibility in the
proposal of comparative semiticists that this particular usage reflects an
Akkadian cognate meaning "to prosper."

30. Once more in a bargaining situation, Jacob does not respond immediately
to the request to name his wages but lays out the general justice of his material claims on Laban, something Laban himself has already conceded.

"You need give me nothing if you will do this thing for me: Let me go

32 back and herd your flocks and watch them. I shall pass through all your flocks today to remove from them every spotted and speckled animal and every dark-colored sheep and the speckled and spotted

33 among the goats, and that will be my wages. Then my honesty will bear witness for me in the days to come when you go over my wages— whatever is not spotted and speckled among the goats and dark-col-

34 ored among the sheep shall be accounted stolen by me." And Laban said, "Let it be just as you say."

35 And he removed on that day the spotted and speckled he-goats and all the brindled and speckled she-goats, every one that had white on it, and every dark-colored one among the sheep, and he gave them

36 over to his sons. And he put three days' journey between himself and

37 Jacob while Jacob herded the remaining flocks of Laban. And Jacob took himself moist rods of poplar and almond and plane-tree, and

---

31. *You need give me nothing.* In a classic bargainer's ploy, Jacob begins by making it sound as though Laban will owe him nothing. As he goes on to name his terms, it seems as though he is asking for next to nothing: most sheep are white, not dark-colored; most goats are black, not speckled; and, Laban, by first removing all the animals with the recessive traits from the flocks, will appear to have reduced to nil Jacob's chances of acquiring any substantial number of livestock. One should note that, as in the stealing of the blessing, Jacob is embarked on a plan of deception that involves goats.

35.–36. *And he removed . . . the spotted and speckled. . . . And he put three days' journey between himself and Jacob.* Laban, taking Jacob at his word, seeks to eliminate any possibility of crossbreeding between the unicolored animals and the others by putting a long distance between the spotted ones and the main herds.

  that had white on it. The Hebrew "white," *lavan,* is identical with the name Laban. As Nahum Sarna puts it, Jacob is beating Laban at his own game— or, with his own name-color.

peeled white strips in them, laying bare the white on the rods. And he   38
stood the rods he had peeled in the troughs, in the water channels
from which the flocks came to drink—opposite the flocks, which went
into heat when they came to drink. And the flocks went into heat at   39
the rods and the flocks bore brindled, spotted, and speckled young.
And the sheep Jacob kept apart: he placed them facing the spotted   40
and all the dark-colored in Laban's flocks, and he set himself herds of
his own and he did not set them with Laban's flocks. And so, whenever   41
the vigorous of the flocks went into heat, Jacob put the rods in full
sight of the flocks in the troughs for them to go in heat by the rods.
And for the weaklings of the flocks he did not put them, and so the   42
feeble ones went to Laban and the vigorous ones to Jacob. And the   43
man swelled up mightily and he had many flocks and female and male
slaves and camels and donkeys.

---

38. *he stood the rods he had peeled in the troughs . . . opposite the flocks, which
went into heat.* The mechanism of Jacob's ingenious scheme has long per-
plexed commentators. At least on the surface, it appears to involve the age-
old belief that sensory impressions at the moment of conception affect the
embryo—here, the peeled rods, with their strips of white against the dark
bark, would impart the trait of spots or brindle markings to the offspring
conceived. (The same effect would then be achieved for the sheep by making
them face the flocks of speckled goats during their own mating time.) Yehuda
Feliks, an authority on biblical flora and fauna, has proposed that the peeled
rods are only a dodge, a gesture to popular belief, while Jacob is actually
practicing sound principles of animal breeding. Using a Mendelian table,
Feliks argues that the recessive traits would have shown up in 25 percent of
the animals born in the first breeding season, 12.5 percent in the second
season, and 6.25 percent in the third season. Jacob is, moreover, careful to
encourage the breeding only of the more vigorous animals, which, according
to Feliks, would be more likely to be heterozygotes, bearing the recessive
genes. It is noteworthy that Jacob makes no mention of the peeled rods when
in the next chapter he tells his wives how he acquired the flocks.

CHAPTER 31

1   And he heard the words of Laban's sons, saying, "Jacob has taken everything of our father's, and from what belonged to our father he has
2   made all this wealth." And Jacob saw Laban's face and, look, it was
3   not disposed toward him as it used to be. And the LORD said to Jacob,
"Return to the land of your fathers and to your birthplace and I will
be with you."

---

1. *the words of Laban's sons.* It is a reflection of the drastic efficiency of biblical
narrative that Laban's sons, who play only a peripheral role in the story, are
not introduced at all until the point where they serve the unfolding of plot
and theme. They are never given names or individual characters, and the first
mention of them is in the previous chapter when Laban places the segregated
particolored flocks in their charge. Here they are used to dramatize in a single
quick stroke the atmosphere of suspicion and jealousy in Laban's household:
they make the extravagant claim that the visibly prospering Jacob "has taken
everything of our father's," thus leaving them nothing. The anonymous sons
would presumably be members of the pursuit party Laban forms to go after
the fleeing Jacob.

2. *Jacob saw Laban's face.* The physical concreteness of the image should not
be obscured, as many modern translators are wont to do, by rendering this as
"manner" or "attitude." Although the Hebrew *panim* does have a variety of
extended or figurative meanings, the point is that Jacob looks at his father-
in-law's face and sees in it a new and disquieting expression of hostility and
suspicion.

3. *and I will be with you.* God's words recall the language of the divine promise to Jacob in the dream-vision at Bethel.

And Jacob sent and called Rachel and Leah out to the field, to his   4
flocks, and he said to them, "I see your father's face, that it is not   5
disposed toward me as it used to be, but the God of my father has
been with me. And you know that with all my strength I have served   6
your father. But your father has tricked me and has switched my wages   7
ten times over, yet God has not let him do me harm. If thus he said,   8
'The spotted ones will be your wages,' all the flocks bore spotted ones.
And if he said, 'The brindled ones will be your wages,' all the flocks
bore brindled ones. And God has reclaimed your father's livestock and   9
given it to me. And so, at the time when the flocks were in heat, I   10
raised my eyes and saw in a dream and, look, the rams mounting the
flocks were brindled, spotted, and speckled. And God's messenger   11
said to me in the dream, 'Jacob!' and I said, 'Here I am.' And he said,   12
'Raise your eyes, pray, and see: all the rams mounting the flocks are
spotted, brindled, and speckled, for I have seen all that Laban has

---

4. *Jacob sent and called Rachel and Leah out to the field.* Jacob proceeds in
this fashion not only because he is busy tending the flocks, as he himself
repeatedly reminds us in the dialogue, but also because he needs to confer
with his wives in a safe location beyond earshot of Laban and his sons.

11. *God's messenger said to me in the dream.* According to the source critics,
divine communication to men through dream-vision is a hallmark of the
Elohist, whereas the direct narrative report of the speckled-flock story in the
previous chapter makes no mention of either a dream or divine instructions
and is to be attributed to the Yahwist. Whatever the validity of such identifications, they tend to scant the narrative integrity of the completed text, the
ability of the biblical Arranger—to borrow a term from the criticism of Joyce's
Ulysses—to orchestrate his sources. Jacob wants to make it vividly clear to
his wives at this tense juncture of imminent flight that God has been with
him and will continue to be with him. It serves this purpose to explain his
spectacular prosperity not as the consequence of his own ingenuity as animal
breeder but as the revelation of an angel of God. It thus makes perfect narrative sense that he should omit all mention of the elaborate strategem of the
peeled rods in the troughs.

13 been doing to you. I am the God who appeared to you at Bethel, where
you anointed a pillar and made me a vow. Now, rise, leave this land,
14 and return to the land of your birthplace.' " And Rachel and Leah
answered and they said to him, "Do we still have any share in the
15 inheritance of our father's house? Why, we have been counted by him
as strangers, for he has sold us, and he has wholly consumed our
16 money. For whatever wealth God has reclaimed from our father is ours
17 and our children's, and so, whatever God has said to you, do." And
18 Jacob rose and bore off his children and his wives on the camels. And
he drove all his livestock and all his substance that he had acquired,
his property in livestock that he had acquired in Paddan-aram, to go
to Isaac his father in the land of Canaan.

---

13. *the God who appeared to you at Bethel.* The Masoretic Text lacks "who
appeared to you at" (which in the Hebrew would be just two words plus a
particle), but both major Aramaic Targums, that of Onkelos and Yonatan ben
Uziel, reflect this phrase, as does the Septuagint. Although the Targums are
often predisposed to explanatory paraphrase, in this instance the Masoretic
Hebrew sounds grammatically off, and it seems likely that they were faithfully representing a phrase that was later lost in transmission. (The Targums,
which translated the Bible into the Aramaic that had become the vernacular
of Palestinian Jewry, were completed in the early centuries of the Christian
Era—Onkelos perhaps in the third century and Targum Yonatan at least a
century later.)

14. *any share in the inheritance.* The Hebrew, literally, "share and inheritance,"
is a hendiadys (two words for one concept, like "part and parcel"), with a
denotative meaning as translated here and a connotation something like "any
part at all."

15. *for he has sold us, and he has wholly consumed our money.* In a socially
decorous marriage, a large part of the bride-price would go to the bride.
Laban, who first appeared in the narrative (chapter 24) eyeing the possible
profit to himself in a betrothal transaction, has evidently pocketed all of the
fruits of Jacob's fourteen years of labor. His daughters thus see themselves
reduced to chattel by their father, not married off but rather sold for profit,
as though they were not his flesh and blood.

And Laban had gone to shear his flocks, and Rachel stole the house-   19
hold gods that were her father's. And Jacob deceived Laban the Ara-   20
mean, in not telling him he was fleeing. And he fled, he and all that   21
was his, and he rose and he crossed the Euphrates, and set his face
toward the high country of Gilead. And it was told to Laban on the   22

---

19. *Laban had gone to shear his flocks.* Rashi reminds us that Laban had earlier
set a precedent of grazing his herds at a distance of three days' journey from
Jacob's herds. In any case, other references to shearing of the flocks in the
Bible indicate it was a very elaborate procedure involving large numbers of
men, and accompanied by feasting, and so would have provided an excellent
cover for Jacob's flight.

Rachel stole the household gods. The household gods, or *terafim* (the etymology of the term is still in doubt), are small figurines representing the
deities responsible for the well-being and prosperity of the household. The
often-cited parallel with the Roman *penates* seems quite pertinent. There is
no reason to assume that Rachel would have become a strict monotheist
through her marriage, and so it is perfectly understandable that she would
want to take with her in her emigration the icons of these tutelary spirits, or
perhaps, symbols of possession.

20. *Jacob deceived Laban.* Rachel makes off with, or steals, the household
gods; Jacob deceives—literally, "steals the heart of Laban" (the heart being
the organ of attentiveness or understanding). This verb, *ganav,* which suggests appropriating someone else's property by deception or stealth, will echo
through the denouement of the story. Jacob, in his response to Laban, will
use a second verb, *gazal,* which suggests taking property by force, "to rob." In
heading for Canaan with his wives, children, and flocks, Jacob is actually
taking what is rightly his (note the emphasis of legitimate possession in verse
18), but he has good reason to fear that the grasping Laban will renege on
their agreement, and so he feels compelled to flee in stealth, making off not
with Laban's property but with his "heart."

Laban the Aramean. For the first time Laban is given this gentilic identification. The stage is being set for the representation of the encounter between
Jacob and Laban as a negotiation between national entities.

21. *the Euphrates.* The Hebrew says "the River," a term which refers specifically to the Euphrates.

the high country of Gilead. The region in question is east of the Jordan, a
little south of Lake Tiberias, and was part of Israelite territory in the First
Commonwealth period. It is thus quite plausible as the setting for a border
encounter between Laban the Aramean and Jacob the Hebrew.

23 third day that Jacob had fled. And he took his kinsmen with him and
pursued him a seven days' journey, and overtook him in the high coun-
24 try of Gilead. And God came to Laban the Aramean in a night-dream
and said to him, "Watch yourself, lest you speak to Jacob either good
or evil!"

25 And Laban caught up with Jacob, and Jacob had pitched his tent on
the height, and Laban had pitched with his kinsmen in the high coun-
26 try of Gilead. And Laban said to Jacob, "What have you done, deceiv-
27 ing me, and driving my daughters like captives of the sword? Why did

---

23. *pursued him a seven days' journey.* Although it would have taken Jacob,
encumbered with his flocks and family, far longer to cross this distance of
nearly three hundred miles, it might have been feasible for a pursuit party
traveling lightly, and so the formulaic seven days actually serves to convey the
terrific speed of the chase. Jacob himself will allude to this speed when
instead of the more usual verb for pursuit, he refers to Laban's "racing" after
him (*dalaq,* a term that also means "to burn" and appears to derive from the
rapid movement of fire).

24. *either good or evil.* As in 24:50, the idiom means "lest you speak . . . anything at all."

26. *driving my daughters.* The common translation "carrying off" fudges the
brutality of Laban's language. The verb *nahag* is most often used for the
driving of animals and is in fact the same term used in verse 18 to report
Jacob's driving his livestock.
    like captives of the sword. The daughters had spoken of their father's treat-
ing them like chattel. Laban on his part chooses a simile with ominous military implications, suggesting that Jacob has behaved like a marauding army
that seizes the young women to serve as sexual and domestic slaves. It is
surely not lost on Jacob that Laban is leading a group of armed men ("My
hand has the might to do you harm.").

you flee in stealth and deceive me and not tell me? I would have sent
you off with festive songs, with timbrel and lyre. And you did not let   28
me kiss my sons and my daughters. O, you have played the fool! My   29
hand has the might to do you harm, but the god of your father said to
me last night, 'Watch yourself, lest you speak to Jacob either good or
evil.' And so, you had to go because you longed so much for your   30
father's house, but why did you steal my gods?" And Jacob answered   31
and said to Laban, "For I was afraid, for I thought, you would rob me
of your daughters. With whomever you find your gods, that person   32
shall not live. Before our kinsmen, make recognition of what is yours
with me, and take it." But Jacob did not know that Rachel had stolen
them. And Laban came into Jacob's tent, and into Leah's tent, and   33
into the tent of the two slavegirls, and he found nothing. And he came

---

27. *deceive me.* At this point, Laban drops the object "heart" from the verb
"to steal" or "make off with," and says instead "me," either because he is using
the idiom elliptically, or because he wants to say more boldly to Jacob, you
have not merely deceived me ("stolen my heart") but despoiled me ("stolen
me").

    with festive songs, with timbrel and lyre. The extravagance of this fantastic
scene conjured up by a past master of fleecing is self-evident. "Festive songs"
is a hendiadys: the Hebrew is literally "with festivity and with songs."

30. *but why did you steal my gods?* Laban once more invokes the crucial verb
ganav at the very end of his speech. Now the object is something that really
has been stolen, though Jacob has no idea this is so. Laban refers to the
missing figurines not as *terafim,* a term that may conceivably have a pejorative
connotation, but as *'elohai,* "my gods," real deities.

32. *that person shall not live.* Jacob does not imagine that anyone in his household could be guilty of the theft. If he is not unwittingly condemning Rachel
to death, his peremptory words at least foreshadow her premature death in
childbirth.

    make recognition. The thematically fraught verb *haker,* which previously
figured in Jacob's deception of Isaac, will return to haunt Jacob, in precisely
the imperative form in which it occurs here.

34 out of Leah's tent and went into Rachel's tent. And Rachel had taken the household gods and put them in the camel cushion and sat on them. And Laban rummaged through the whole tent and found noth-
35 ing. And she said to her father, "Let not my lord be incensed that I am unable to rise before you, for the way of women is upon me." And
36 he searched and he did not find the household gods. And Jacob was incensed and voiced his grievance to Laban, and Jacob spoke out and said to Laban:

> "What is my crime, what is my guilt,
>> that you should race after me?
37 Though you rummaged through all my things,
>> What have you found of all your household things?
> Set it here before my kin and yours
>> and they shall determine between us two.

---

34. *put them in the camel cushion and sat on them.* The camel cushion may be a good hiding place, but Rachel's sitting on the *terafim* is also a kind of satiric glance by the monotheistic writer on the cult of figurines, as necessity compels Rachel to assume this irreverent posture toward them.

35. *for the way of women is upon me.* The impotence of the irate father vis-à-vis his biologically mature daughter is comically caught in the device she hits upon, of pleading her period, in order to stay seated on the concealed figurines. Her invention involves an ironic double take because it invokes all those years of uninterrupted menses before she was at last able to conceive and bear her only son.

36. *voiced his grievance.* The verb here (there is no object noun in the Hebrew) is cognate with *riv,* a grievance brought to a court of law. Jacob's speech is manifestly cast as a rhetorically devised plea of defense against a false accusation. Although previous commentators have noted that his language is "elevated" (Gerhard von Rad), it has not been observed that Jacob's plea is actually formulated as poetry, following the general conventions of parallelism of biblical verse.

   What is my crime, what is my guilt? These cadenced parallel questions signal the beginning of the formal plea of defense.

These twenty years I have been with you,   38
        your ewes and your she-goats did not lose their young,
                the rams of your flock I have not eaten.
What was torn up by beasts I've not brought you,   39
        I bore the loss, from my hand you could seek it—
                what was stolen by day and stolen by night.
Often—by day the parching heat ate me up   40
        and frost in the night,
                and sleep was a stranger to my eyes.

These twenty years in your household I served you, fourteen years for   41
your two daughters and six years for your flocks, and you switched my

---

39. *What was torn up by beasts . . . I bore the loss.* After stating in the previous verse that he took exemplary care of the flocks, Jacob goes on to declare that he assumed a degree of responsibility above and beyond what the law requires of a shepherd. Both biblical and other ancient Near Eastern codes indicate that a shepherd was not obliged to make good losses caused by beasts of prey and thieves, where no negligence was involved.

what was stolen by day and stolen by night. Again, the key verb *ganav* is invoked. The grammatical form of the construct state here—*genuvati*—uses an archaic suffix that is a linguistic marker of poetic diction.

40. *often.* The Hebrew is literally "I was," but, as E. A. Speiser notes, this verb at the beginning of a clause can be used to impart an iterative sense to what follows.

sleep was a stranger to my eyes. The Hebrew says literally, "sleep wandered from my eyes." It is a general idiom for insomnia.

41. *These twenty years in your household.* When Jacob begins to work out the calculation of how many years he has served Laban in return for what, he switches from verse to prose. This enables him to repeat verbatim the words he had used in his (prose) dialogue with his wives, when he said that Laban had "switched my wages ten times over." Understandably, what he deletes from that earlier speech is the blunt accusation that Laban "tricked me."

42 wages ten times over. Were it not that the God of my father, the God of Abraham and the Terror of Isaac, was with me, you would have sent me off empty-handed. My suffering and the toil of my hands God has
43 seen, and last night He determined in my favor." And Laban answered and said to Jacob, "The daughters are my daughters, and the sons are my sons, and the flocks are my flocks, and all that you see is mine. Yet for my daughters what can I do now, or for their sons whom they bore?
44 And so, come, let us make a pact, you and I, and let it be a witness
45 between you and me." And Jacob took a stone and set it up as a pillar.
46 And Jacob said to his kinsmen, "Gather stones." And they fetched
47 stones and made a mound and they ate there on the mound. And
48 Laban called it Yegar-sahudutha but Jacob called it Gal-ed. And Laban said, "This mound is witness between you and me this day." Therefore

---

42. *He determined in my favor.* Jacob uses the same verb of legal vindication that he invoked in his poetic self-defense—"they shall determine between us two."

43. *The daughters are my daughters.* Laban begins his response by refusing to yield an inch in point of legal prerogative. But he concedes that there is nothing he can do about his daughters and all his grandsons—on the face of it, because of their evident attachment to Jacob, and, perhaps, because he fears to use the force he possesses against Jacob after the divine warning in the night-vision.

45. *Jacob took a stone.* Invited to make a pact, Jacob immediately resorts to the language of stones, as after the Bethel epiphany and in his first encounter with Rachel at the well. Thus, in sequence, the stones are associated with religious experience, personal experience, and now politics. Here, there is a doubling in the use of stones: a large stone as a commemorative pillar (and border marker) and a pile of smaller stones as a commemorative mound.

47. *Yegar-sahadutha . . . Gal-ed.* The international character of the transaction is nicely caught in Laban the Aramean's use of an Aramaic term while Jacob uses Hebrew. Both names mean "mound of witness."

its name was called Gal-ed, and Mizpah, for he said, "May the LORD   49
look out between you and me when we are out of each other's sight.
Should you harass my daughters, and should you take wives besides   50
my daughters though no one else is present, see, God is witness
between you and me." And Laban said to Jacob, "Look, this mound,   51
and, look, the pillar that I cast up between you and me, witness be   52
the mound and witness the pillar, that I will not cross over to you past
this mound and you will not cross over to me past this mound, and
past this pillar, for harm. May the god of Abraham and the god of   53

---

49. *and Mizpah.* This is an alternate name for the height of Gilead. The
meaning is "lookout point," as Laban's next words make etymologically clear.

51.–52. *Look, this mound, and, look, the pillar . . . witness be the mound and
witness the pillar.* The studied repetitions and rhetorical flourishes that characterize Laban's speech throughout reflect its function as a performative
speech-act, stipulating the binding terms of the treaty.

I will not cross over to you . . . past this pillar. At this point, the story of
bitter familial struggle is also made an etiology for political history. What
Laban is designating here is clearly an international border.

54 Nahor"—the gods of their fathers—"judge between us." And Jacob swore by the Terror of his father Isaac. And Jacob offered sacrifice on the height and called to his kinsmen to eat bread, and they ate bread and passed the night on the height.

---

53. *the gods of their fathers.* These words, with the pronoun referent "they," could not be part of Laban's dialogue and so must be a gloss, perhaps occasioned by the discomfort of a scribe or editor with the exact grammatical equation between the god of Abraham and the god of Nahor in Laban's oath.

Jacob swore by the Terror of his father Isaac. This denomination of the deity, which occurs only in this episode, is strange enough to have prompted some biblical scholars to argue, unconvincingly, that the name has nothing to do with terror or fear. What is noteworthy is that Jacob resists the universal Semitic term for God, *'elohim,* and the equation between the gods of Nahor and Abraham. He himself does not presume to go back as far as Abraham, but in the God of his father Isaac he senses something numinous, awesome, frightening.

54. *offered sacrifice . . . ate bread.* The treaty-vow is solemnly confirmed by a sacred meal. The term *zevah* refers both to a ceremonial meal of meat and to sacrifice. In effect, the two are combined: the fat of the animal is burnt as an offering, the meat is consumed by those who offer the sacrifice. As frequently elsewhere in biblical usage, "bread" is a synecdoche for the whole meal.

CHAPTER 32

And Laban rose early in the morning and kissed his sons and his daughters and blessed them, and Laban went off and returned to his place. And Jacob had gone on his way, and messengers of God accosted him. And Jacob said when he saw them, "This is God's camp," and he called the name of that place Mahanaim. And Jacob sent messengers before

1
2
3
4

---

1. The verse numbering reflects the conventional division used in Hebrew Bibles. The King James Version, followed by some modern English Bibles, places the first verse here as a fifty-fifth verse in chapter 31, and then has verses 1–32 corresponding to verses 2–33 in the present version.

2. *messengers of God accosted him.* There is a marked narrative symmetry between Jacob's departure from Canaan, when he had his dream of angels at Bethel, and his return, when again he encounters a company of angels. That symmetry will be unsettled when later in the chapter he finds himself in fateful conflict with a single divine being.

God's camp . . . Mahanaim. The Hebrew for "camp" is *maḥaneh.* Mahanaim is the same word with a dual suffix and thus means twin camps, a signification that will be played out in a second narrative etymology when Jacob divides his family and flocks into two camps. The entire episode is notable for its dense exploitation of what Martin Buber and Franz Rosenzweig called *Leitwortstil,* key-word style. J. P. Fokkelman (1975) has provided particularly helpful commentary on this aspect of our text. The crucial repeated terms are *maḥaneh,* "camp," which is played against *minḥah,* "tribute"; *panim,* "face," which recurs not only as a noun but also as a component of the reiterated preposition "before," a word that can be etymologically broken down in the Hebrew as "to the face of"; and *ʿavar,* "cross over" (in one instance here, the translation, yielding to the requirements of context, renders this as "pass").

5   him to Esau his brother in the land of Seir, the steppe of Edom. And he charged them, saying, "Thus shall you say—'To my lord Esau, thus says your servant Jacob: With Laban I have sojourned and I tarried till

6   now. And I have gotten oxen and donkeys and sheep and male and female slaves, and I send ahead to tell my lord, to find favor in your

7   eyes.'" And the messengers returned to Jacob, saying, "We came to your brother, to Esau, and he himself is coming to meet you, and four

8   hundred men are with him." And Jacob was greatly afraid, and he was distressed, and he divided the people that were with him, and the

9   sheep and the cattle and the camels, into two camps. And he thought,

---

4. *Jacob sent messengers before him.* These are of course human messengers, but, in keeping with a common principle of composition in biblical narrative, the repetition of the term effects a linkage with the immediately preceding episode, in which the messengers, *mal'akhim,* are angels.

5. *Thus shall you say.* The syntactic division indicated by the cantillation markings in the Masoretic Text is: "Thus shall you say to my lord Esau." But E. A. Speiser has convincingly demonstrated that "To my lord Esau, thus says your servant Jacob," precisely follows the formula for the salutation or heading in ancient Near Eastern letters and so must be part of the text of the message.

   my lord Esau . . . your servant Jacob. The narrator had referred to Esau as Jacob's "brother," as will the messengers. An elaborate irony of terms underlies the entire reunion of the twins: Jacob, destined by prenatal oracle and paternal blessing to be overlord to his brother, who is to be subject (*'eved*) to him, repeatedly designates himself *'eved* and his brother, lord (*'adon*). The formulas of deferential address of ancient Hebrew usage are thus made to serve a complex thematic end.

7. *he himself is coming . . . and four hundred men are with him.* There is no verbal response from Esau, who has by now established himself as a potentate in the trans-Jordanian region of Edom, but the rapid approach with four hundred men looks ominous, especially since that is a standard number for a regiment or raiding party, as several military episodes in 1 and 2 Samuel indicate.

8. *two camps.* A law of binary division runs through the whole Jacob story: twin brothers struggling over a blessing that cannot be halved, two sisters struggling over a husband's love, flocks divided into unicolored and particolored animals, Jacob's material blessing now divided into two camps.

"Should Esau come to the one camp and strike it, the remaining camp will escape." And Jacob said: "God of my father Abraham and God of   10
my father Isaac! LORD who has said to me, 'Return to your land and your birthplace, and I will deal well with you.' I am unworthy of all   11
the kindness that you have steadfastly done for your servant. For with my staff I crossed this Jordan, and now I have become two camps. O   12
save me from the hand of my brother, from the hand of Esau, for I fear him, lest he come and strike me, mother with sons. And You   13
Yourself said, 'I will surely deal well with you and I will set your seed like the sand of the sea multitudinous beyond all count.'" And he   14
passed that same night there, and he took from what he had in hand a tribute to Esau his brother: two hundred she-goats and twenty he-   15
goats, two hundred ewes and twenty rams; thirty milch camels with   16
their young, forty cows and ten bulls, twenty she-asses and ten he-asses. And he put them in the hands of his servants, each herd by   17
itself, and he said to his servants, "Pass on before me, and put distance between one herd and the next." And he charged the first one, saying,   18
"When Esau my brother meets you and asks you, saying, 'Whose man are you, and where are you going, and whose are these herds before you?', you shall say, 'They are your servant Jacob's, a tribute sent to my   19
lord Esau, and, look, he himself is behind us.'" And he charged the   20

10. *and I will deal well with you.* The first part of the sentence is in fact a direct quotation of God's words to Jacob in 31:3. But for God's general reassurance, "I will be with you," Jacob, in keeping with his stance as bargainer (who at Bethel stipulated that God must provide him food and clothing) substitutes a verb that suggests material bounty.

14. *a tribute.* The Hebrew *minḥah* also means "gift" (and, in cultic contexts, "sacrifice"), but it has the technical sense of a tribute paid by a subject people to its overlord, and everything about the narrative circumstances of this "gift" indicates it is conceived as the payment of a tribute. Note, for instance, the constellation of political terms in verse 19: "They are *your servant* Jacob's, *a tribute sent* to *my lord* Esau."

second one as well, and also the third, indeed, all those who went
after the herds, saying, "In this fashion you shall speak to Esau when
21 you find him. And you shall say, 'Look, your servant Jacob himself is
behind us.' " For he thought, "Let me placate him with the tribute that
goes before me, and after I shall look on his face, perhaps he will show
22 me a kindly face." And the tribute passed on before him, and he spent
that night in the camp.

23 And he rose on that night and took his two wives and his two slavegirls
24 and his eleven boys and he crossed over the Jabbok ford. And he took
them and brought them across the stream, and he brought across all
25 that he had. And Jacob was left alone, and a man wrestled with him

---

21. *Let me placate him with the tribute that goes before me, and after I shall
look on his face, perhaps he will show me a kindly face.* The Hebrew actually
has "face" four times in this brief speech. "Placate" is literally "cover over his
face" (presumably, angry face); and "before me" can be broken down as "to
my face." To "look on his face" is a locution generally used for entering the
presence of royalty; and "show me a kind face," an idiom that denotes forgiveness, is literally "lift up my face" (presumably, my "fallen" or dejected face).

23. *the Jabbok ford.* The word for "ford," *maʿavar,* is a noun derived from the
reiterated verb *ʿavar.* "to cross over." The Jabbok is a tributary of the Jordan
running from east to west. Jacob has been traveling south from the high
country of Gilead, Esau is heading north from Edom to meet him.

25. *a man.* The initial identification of the anonymous adversary is from
Jacob's point of view, and so all he knows of him is what he sees, that he is a
"man."
   wrestled with him. The image of wrestling has been implicit throughout
the Jacob story: in his grabbing Esau's heel as he emerges from the womb, in
his striving with Esau for birthright and blessing, in his rolling away the huge
stone from the mouth of the well, and in his multiple contendings with
Laban. Now, in this culminating moment of his life story, the characterizing
image of wrestling is made explicit and literal.

until the break of dawn. And he saw that he had not won out against   26
him and he touched his hip-socket and Jacob's hip socket was
wrenched as he wrestled with him. And he said, "Let me go, for dawn   27
is breaking." And he said, "I will not let you go unless you bless me."
And he said to him, "What is your name?" And he said, "Jacob." And   28,29
he said, "Not Jacob shall your name hence be said, but Israel, for you
have striven with God and men, and won out." And Jacob asked and   30

---

26. *he touched his hip socket.* The inclination of modern translations to render
the verb here as "struck" is unwarranted, being influenced either by the context or by the cognate noun *neg'a,* which means "plague" or "affliction." But
the verb *nag'a* in the *qal* conjugation always means "to touch," even "barely
touch," and only in the *pi'el* conjugation can it mean "to afflict." The adversary maims Jacob with a magic touch, or, if one prefers, by skillful pressure
on a pressure point.

27. *Let me go, for dawn is breaking.* The folkloric character of this haunting
episode becomes especially clear at this point. The notion of a night spirit
that loses its power or is not permitted to go about in daylight is common to
many folk traditions, as is the troll or guardian figure who blocks access to a
ford or bridge. This temporal limitation of activity suggests that the "man" is
certainly not God Himself and probably not an angel in the ordinary sense.
It has led Claus Westermann to conclude that the nameless wrestler must
be thought of as some sort of demon. Nahum Sarna, following the Midrash,
flatly identifies the wrestler as the tutelary spirit (*sar*) of Esau. But the real
point, as Jacob's adversary himself suggests when he refuses to reveal his
name, is that he resists identification. Appearing to Jacob in the dark of the
night, before the morning when Esau will be reconciled with Jacob, he is the
embodiment of portentous antagonism in Jacob's dark night of the soul. He
is obviously in some sense a doubling of Esau as adversary, but he is also a
doubling of all with whom Jacob has had to contend, and he may equally
well be an externalization of all that Jacob has to wrestle with within himself.
A powerful physical metaphor is intimated by the story of wrestling: Jacob,
whose name can be construed as "he who acts crookedly," is bent, perma-
nently lamed, by his nameless adversary in order to be made straight before
his reunion with Esau.

28. *What is your name?* Whatever the realm from which he comes, the
stranger exercises no divine privilege of omniscience and must ask Jacob to
tell him his name.

29. *Not Jacob . . . but Israel.* Abraham's change of name was a mere rhetorical flourish compared to this one, for of all the patriarchs Jacob is the one whose life is entangled in moral ambiguities. Rashi beautifully catches the resonance of the name change: "It will no longer be said that the blessings came to you through deviousness ['*oqbah*, a word suggested by the radical of "crookedness" in the name Jacob] but instead through lordliness [*serarah*, a root that can be extracted from the name Israel] and openness." It is nevertheless noteworthy—and to my knowledge has not been noted—that the pronouncement about the new name is not completely fulfilled. Whereas Abraham is invariably called "Abraham" once the name is changed from "Abram," the narrative continues to refer to this patriarch in most instances as "Jacob." Thus, "Israel" does not really replace his name but becomes a *synonym* for it—a practice reflected in the parallelism of biblical poetry, where "Jacob" is always used in the first half of the line and "Israel," the poetic variation, in the second half.

striven with God. The Hebrew term *'elohim* is a high concentration point of lexical ambiguity that serves the enigmatic character of the story very well. It is *not* the term that means "divine messenger" but it can refer to divine beings, whether or not it is prefixed by "sons of" (as in Genesis 6). It can also mean simply "God," and in some contexts—could this be one?—it means "gods." In a few cases, it also designates something like "princes" or "judges," but that is precluded here by its being antithetically paired with "men." It is not clear whether the anonymous adversary is referring to himself when he says *'elohim* or to more-than-human agents encountered by Jacob throughout his career. In any case, he etymologizes the name *Yisra'el,* Israel, as "he strives with God." In fact, names with the *el* ending generally make God the subject, not the object, of the verb in the name. This particular verb, *sarah,* is a rare one, and there is some question about its meaning, though an educated guess about the original sense of the name would be: "God will rule," or perhaps, "God will prevail."

and won out. In almost all of his dealings, Jacob the bargainer, trader, wrestler, and heel-grabber *has* managed to win out. His winning out against the mysterious stranger consists in having fought to a kind of tie: the adversary has been unable to best him, and though he has hurt Jacob, he cannot break loose from Jacob's grip.

said, "Tell your name, pray." And he said, "Why should you ask my
name?" and there he blessed him. And Jacob called the name of the   31
place Peniel, meaning, "I have seen God face to face and I came out
alive." And the sun rose upon him as he passed Penuel and he was   32
limping on his hip. Therefore the children of Israel do not eat the   33
sinew of the thigh which is by the hip socket to this day, for he
touched Jacob's hip socket at the sinew of the thigh.

---

31. *Peniel.* The name builds on "face to face" *(panim 'el panim)*, the "face"
component being quite transparent in the Hebrew.

   God. Again the term is *'elohim,* and there is no way of knowing whether it
is singular or plural.

   I came out alive. The Hebrew says literally: "My life [or, life breath] was
saved."

32. *And the sun rose upon him.* There is another antithetical symmetry with
the early part of the Jacob story, which has been nicely observed by Nahum
Sarna: "Jacob's ignominious flight from home was appropriately marked by
the setting of the sun; fittingly, the radiance of the sun greets the patriarch
as he crosses back into his native land."

   he was limping on his hip. The encounter with the unfathomable Other
leaves a lasting mark on Jacob. This physical note resonates with the larger
sense of a man's life powerfully recorded in his story: experience exacts many
prices, and he bears his inward scars as he lives onward—his memory of
fleeing alone across the Jordan, his fear of the brother he has wronged, and,
before long, his grief for the beloved wife he loses, and then, for the beloved
son he thinks he has lost.

33. *Therefore the children of Israel do not eat the sinew.* This concluding etiological notice is more than a mechanical reflex. For the first time, after the
naming-story, the Hebrews are referred to as "the children of Israel," and this
dietary prohibition observed by the audience of the story "to this day" marks
a direct identification with, or reverence for, the eponymous ancestor who
wrestled through the night with a man who was no man.

CHAPTER 33

1   And Jacob raised his eyes and saw and, look, Esau was coming, and
    with him were four hundred men. And he divided the children
2   between Leah and Rachel, and between the two slavegirls. And he
    placed the slavegirls and their children first, and Leah and her chil-
3   dren after them, and Rachel and Joseph last. And he passed before
    them and bowed to the ground seven times until he drew near his
4   brother. And Esau ran to meet him and embraced him and fell upon

---

1. *he divided the children between Leah and Rachel.* Again, the principle of
binary division running through the whole story comes into play. Here, there
is a binary split between the two wives on one side and the two concubines
on the other. The former of these categories is itself split between Rachel
and Leah. Although the division at this point, unlike the previous day's division into two camps, appears to be for purposes of display, not defense, it
looks as though Jacob retains a residual fear of assault, and so he puts the
concubines and their children first, then Leah and her children, and Rachel
and Joseph at the very rear.

2. *Leah and her children after them.* The Masoretic Text reads "last" instead
of "after them" (in the Hebrew merely the difference of a suffix), but the
context requires "after them," a reading that is supported by at least one
ancient version.

3. *bowed to the ground seven times until he drew near.* This practice of bowing
seven times as one approaches a monarch from a distance was common court
ritual, as parallels in the Amarna letters and the Ugaritic documents (both
from the middle of the second millennium B.C.E.) indicate.

4. *Esau ran to meet him and embraced him and fell upon his neck.* This is, of
course, the big surprise in the story of the twins: instead of lethal grappling,

his neck, and they wept. And he raised his eyes and saw the women 5
and the children and he said, "Who are these with you?" And he said,
"The children with whom God has favored your servant." And the 6
slavegirls drew near, they and their children, and they bowed down.
And Leah, too, and her children drew near, and they bowed down, 7
and then Joseph and Rachel drew near and bowed down. And he said, 8
"What do you mean by all this camp I have met?" And he said, "To
find favor in the eyes of my lord." And Esau said, "I have much, my 9
brother. Keep what you have." And Jacob said, "O, no, pray, if I have 10

Esau embraces Jacob in fraternal affection. The Masoretic Text has both
brothers weeping, the verb showing a plural inflection, but some scholars
have conjectured that the plural *waw* at the end of the verb is a scribal error,
duplicated from the first letter of the next word in the text, and that Esau
alone weeps, Jacob remaining impassive.

5. *The children.* Jacob's response makes no mention of the women. It would
have been self-evident that the women were the mothers of the children and
hence his wives, and one senses that he feels impelled to answer his brother
as tersely as possible, not spelling out what can be clearly inferred.

8. *What do you mean by all this camp.* The Hebrew is literally, "Who to you is
all this camp," but both "who to you" (*mi lekha*) and "what to you" (*mah
lekha*) have the idiomatic sense of, what do you mean, or want. "Camp" in
this context means something like "retinue" or "procession of people," but
the continuity with the twin camps of the preceding episode is obviously
important for the writer.

9. *I have much, my brother.* Esau in fact has become a kind of prince, despite
his loss of birthright and blessing, and he can speak to Jacob in princely
generosity. It is striking that he addresses Jacob as "my brother"—the familial
term with the first-person possessive suffix is generally a form of *affectionate*
address in biblical Hebrew—while Jacob continues to call him "my lord,"
never swerving from the deferential terms of court etiquette.

found favor in your eyes, take this tribute from my hand, for have I
not seen your face as one might see God's face, and you received me
11   in kindness? Pray, take my blessing that has been brought you, for
God has favored me and I have everything." And he pressed him, and
12   he took it. And he said, "Let us journey onward and go, and let me go
13   alongside you." And he said, "My lord knows that the children are
tender, and the nursing sheep and cattle are my burden, and if they
14   are whipped onward a single day, all the flocks will die. Pray, let my
lord pass on before his servant, and I shall drive along at my own easy
pace, at the heels of the livestock before me and at the heels of the

---

10. *for have I not seen your face as one might see God's face, and you received me
in kindness?* This most extravagant turn in the rhetoric of deferential address
pointedly carries us back to Jacob's reflection on his nocturnal wrestling with
the nameless stranger: "for I have seen God face to face and I came out
alive." "And you received me in kindness" (just one word in the Hebrew) is
significantly substituted for "I came out alive," the very thing Jacob feared he
might not do when he met his brother.

11. *take my blessing.* The word for "blessing," *berakhah,* obviously has the
meaning in context of "my gift," or, as Rashi interestingly proposes, invoking
as an Old French equivalent, *mon salud,* my gift of greeting. But the term
chosen brilliantly echoes a phrase Jacob could not have actually heard, which
Esau pronounced to their father two decades earlier: "he has taken my blessing" (27:36). In offering the tribute, Jacob is making restitution for his primal
theft, unwittingly using language that confirms the act of restitution.
    I have everything. Jacob of course means "I have everything I need." But
there is a nice discrepancy between his words and the parallel ones of his
brother that is obscured by all English translators (with the exception of Everett Fox), who use some term like "enough" in both instances. Esau says he
has plenty; Jacob says he has everything—on the surface, simply declaring
that he doesn't need the flocks he is offering as a gift, but implicitly "outbid-
ding" his brother, obliquely referring to the comprehensiveness of the blessing he received from their father.

13. *are my burden.* The Hebrew says literally, "are upon me."

14. *at the heels.* Literally "at the foot."

children, till I come to my lord in Seir." And Esau said, "Pray, let me 15
set aside for you some of the people who are with me." And he said,
"Why should I find such favor in the eyes of my lord?" And Esau 16
returned that day on his way to Seir, while Jacob journeyed on to 17
Succoth. And he built himself a house, and for his cattle he made
sheds—therefore is the name of the place called Succoth.

And Jacob came in peace to the town of Shechem, which is in the 18
land of Canaan, when he came from Paddan-aram, and he camped

---

till I come to my lord in Seir. This is a "diplomatic" offer, for in fact Jacob
will head back northward to Succoth, in the opposite direction from Seir.

15. *Why should I find such favor in the eyes of my lord?* In this protestation of
unworthiness, Jacob preserves the perfect decorum of deferential address to
the very end of his dialogue with his brother. Clearly, he is declining the offer
of Esau's retainers because he still doesn't trust Esau and intends to put a
large distance between himself and Esau or any of Esau's men. One should
note that the very last word (one word in the Hebrew) spoken by Jacob to
Esau that is reported in the story is "my lord."

16. *Succoth.* The Hebrew *sukkot* means "sheds."

18. *came in peace.* The adjective *shalem* elsewhere means "whole," and this
has led many interpreters to understand it here as "safe and sound." A tradition going back to the Septuagint, and sustained by Claus Westermann
among modern commentators, construes this word as the name of a town,
Salem, understood to be a synonym for Shechem. (The claim has been made
that a *tell* about two and a half miles from the site of Shechem is the biblical
Salem.) But the Salem where Abraham meets Melchisedek is at an entirely
different location, and if that were also a designation for Shechem, one would
expect here at the very least the explanatory gloss, "Salem, that is, the town
of Shechem" (*Shalem, hi' 'ir Shekhem*). Because these three verses are an
introduction to the story of the rape of Dinah, where in fact Hamor and
Shechem say of the sons of Jacob, "these men come in peace (*sheleimim*) to
us," it is more likely that "came in peace" is the sense here. Ibn Ezra argues
for this meaning, similarly noting the link between the two passages.
when he came from Paddan-aram. Now that Jacob has at last crossed the
Jordan (Succoth is in trans-Jordan) and has taken up residence outside a
Canaanite town, the long trajectory of his journey home is completed.

19   before the town. And he bought the parcel of land where he had
pitched his tent from the sons of Hamor, father of Shechem, for a

20   hundred kesitahs. And he set up an altar there and called it El-elohei-
Israel.

---

19. *a hundred kesitahs.* These are either measures of weight for gold and silver,
or units for the barter of livestock, or a term derived from the latter which
has been transferred to the former. The purchase of real estate, as with Abraham at Hebron, signals making a claim to permanent residence.

20. *El-elohei-Israel.* The name means "El / God, God of Israel." Claus Westermann makes the interesting argument that Jacob marks his taking up residence in Canaan by subsuming the Canaanite sky god in his monotheistic
cult: "El, the creator God, the supreme God in the Canaanite pantheon, now
becomes the God of the people of Israel."

CHAPTER 34

And Dinah, Leah's daughter, whom she had born to Jacob, went out to   1
go seeing among the daughters of the land. And Shechem the son of   2
Hamor the Hivite, prince of the land, saw her and took her and lay

---

1. *to go seeing among the daughters of the land.* The infinitive in the Hebrew is literally "to see," followed not by a direct object, as one might expect, but by a partitive (the particle b^e), which suggests "among" or "some of." Although the sense of the verb in context may be something like "to make the acquaintance of" or "travel around among," the decision of several modern translations to render it as "to visit" is misconceived. Not only does that term convey anachronistic notions of calling cards and tea, but it obliterates an important repetition of terms. This is one of those episodes in which the biblical practice of using the same word over and over with different subjects and objects and a high tension of semantic difference is especially crucial. Two such terms are introduced in the first sentence of the story: "to see" and "daughter." Dinah, Jacob's daughter, goes out among the daughters of the land, an identity of terms that might suggest a symmetry of position, but the fact that she is an immigrant's daughter, not a daughter of the land, makes her a ready target for rape. (In the Hebrew, moreover, "sons" and "daughters," *banim* and *banot,* are differently inflected versions of the same word, so Dinah's filial relation to Jacob is immediately played against Shechem's filial relation to Hamor, and that in turn will be pointedly juxtaposed with the relation between Jacob and *his* sons.) Shechem's lustful "seeing" of Dinah is immediately superimposed on her "seeing" the daughters of the land.

2. *saw . . . took . . . lay with . . . debased.* As elsewhere in Genesis, the chain of uninterrupted verbs conveys the precipitousness of the action. "Took" will become another thematically loaded reiterated term. "Lay with" is more brutal in the Hebrew because instead of being followed by the preposition "with" (as, for example, in Rachel's words to Leah in 30:15), it is followed by a direct object—if the Masoretic vocalization is authentic—and in this form may denote rape.

3   with her and debased her. And his very self clung to Dinah daughter
of Jacob, and he loved the young woman, and he spoke to the young
4   woman's heart. And Shechem said to Hamor his father, saying, "Take
5   me this girl as wife." And Jacob had heard that he had defiled Dinah
his daughter, and his sons were with his livestock in the field, and
6   Jacob held his peace till they came. And Hamor, Shechem's father,
7   came out to Jacob to speak with him. And Jacob's sons had come in
from the field when they heard, and the men were pained and they
were very incensed, for he had done a scurrilous thing in Israel by

---

3. *his very self clung.* The Hebrew *nefesh* (life-breath) is used here as an intensifying synonym of the personal pronoun. ("His very self" in verse 8 represents
the same Hebrew usage.) The psychology of this rapist is precisely the opposite of Amnon's in 2 Samuel 13, who, after having consummated his lust for
his sister by raping her, despises her. Here, the fulfillment of the impulse of
unrestrained desire is followed by love, which complicates the moral balance
of the story.

4. *Take me this girl.* "Take," which indicated violent action in the narrator's
report of the rape, now recurs in a decorous social sense—the action initiated
by the father of the groom in arranging a proper marriage for his son. In verse
17, Jacob's sons will threaten to "take" Dinah away if the townsmen refuse to
be circumcised, and in the report of the massacre, they take first their swords
and then the booty. Shechem refers to Dinah as *yaldah,* "girl" or "child," a
term that equally suggests her vulnerability and the tenderness he now feels
for her.

7. *a scurrilous thing in Israel.* This use of this idiom here is a kind of pun. "A
scurrilous thing in Israel" *(nevalah beYisra'el)* is in later tribal history any
shocking act that the collective "Israel" deems reprehensible (most often a
sexual act). But at this narrative juncture, "Israel" is only the other name of
the father of these twelve children, and so the phrase also means "a scurrilous
thing against Israel."
     *for he had done a scurrilous thing in Israel by lying with Jacob's daughter,
such as ought not be done.* This entire clause is a rare instance in biblical
narrative of free indirect discourse, or narrated monologue. That is, the narrator conveys the tenor of Jacob's sons' anger by reporting in the third person
the kind of language they would have spoken silently, or to each other. It is a
technical means for strongly imprinting the rage of Jacob's sons in the presence of their father who has kept silent and, even now, gives no voice to his
feelings about the violation of his daughter.

lying with Jacob's daughter, such as ought not be done. And Hamor   8
spoke with them, saying, "Shechem my son, his very self longs for your
daughter. Pray, give her to him as wife, and ally with us by marriage—   9
your daughters you will give to us and our daughters, take for yourselves, and among us you will settle, and the land is before you: settle   10
and go about it and take holdings in it." And Shechem said to her   11
father and to her brothers, "Let me find favor in your eyes, and whatever you say to me, I will give. Name me however much bride-price   12
and clan-gift, I will give what you say to me, and give me the young
woman as wife." And the sons of Jacob answered Shechem and Hamor   13
his father deceitfully, and they spoke as they did because he had
defiled Dinah their sister, and they said to them, "We cannot do this   14

---

10. *go about it.* The Hebrew verb *saḥar* has the basic meaning of "to go around
in a circle" and the extended meaning of "to trade." But at this early point of
tribal history, Jacob and his sons are seminomadic herdsmen, not at all merchants, so the commercial denotation of the term seems unlikely in context.

11. *And Shechem said . . . ". . . whatever you say to me, I will give."* The father
had begun the negotiations by asking for Dinah as wife for his son and then
immediately opened up the larger issue of general marriage-alliances with
Jacob's clan and the acquisition of settlement rights by the newcomers.
Shechem now enters the discussion to speak more personally of the marriage
and the bride-price. (According to biblical law, a man who raped an unbe-
trothed girl had to pay a high fine to her father and was obliged to marry her.)
After the two instances of "taking" earlier in the story, he insists here on
"giving": he will give whatever the brothers stipulate in the expectation that
they will give him Dinah as wife.

12. *give me the young woman.* Addressing the brothers, Shechem does not
refer to Dinah now as *yaldah,* "girl," but as *na'arah,* the proper term for a
nubile young woman.

13. *deceitfully.* This is the same term, *mirmah,* that was first attached to
Jacob's action in stealing the blessing, then used by Jacob to upbraid Laban
after the switching of the brides.
  they spoke as they did because he had defiled Dinah their sister. "As they did
because" is merely a syntactically ambiguous "that" in the Hebrew—quite
possibly a means for introducing another small piece of free indirect discourse.

thing, to give our sister to a man who has a foreskin, as that is a
15 disgrace for us. Only in this way may we agree to you—if you will be
16 like us, every male to be circumcised. Then we can give our daughters
to you and your daughters we can take for ourselves, and we can settle
17 among you and become one folk. But if you will not listen to us, to be
18 circumcised, we will take our daughter and go." And their words
seemed good in the eyes of Hamor and in the eyes of Shechem son of
Hamor.

19 And the lad lost no time in doing the thing, for he wanted Jacob's
daughter, and he was most highly regarded of all his father's house.
20 And Hamor, with Shechem his son, came to the gate of their town,
21 and they spoke to their townsmen, saying, "These men come in peace
to us. Let them settle in the land and go about it, for the land, look,
is ample before them. Their daughters we shall take us as wives and
22 our daughters we shall give to them. Only in this way will the men
agree to us, to settle with us to be one folk, if every male of us be

---

14. *We cannot do this thing.* They begin as though their response were a flat
refusal. Then they ignore the offer of generous payment and instead stipulate
circumcision—to be sure, a physical sign of their collective identity, but also
the infliction of pain on what is in this case the offending organ.

16. *become one folk.* This ultimate horizon of ethnic unification was perhaps
implied but certainly not spelled out in Hamor's speech.

19. *the lad.* There was no previous indication of Shekhem's age. The term
na'ar is the masculine counterpart of the term he used for Dinah in verse 12
and suggests that he, too, is probably an adolescent.

circumcised as they are circumcised. Their possessions in livestock   23
and all their cattle, will they not be ours, if only we agree to them and
they settle among us?" And all who sallied forth from the gate of his   24
town listened to Hamor, and to Shechem his son, and every male was
circumcised, all who sallied forth from the gate of his town.

And it happened on the third day, while they were hurting, that Jacob's   25
two sons, Simeon and Levi, Dinah's brothers, took each his sword,
and came upon the city unopposed, and they killed every male. And   26
Hamor and Shechem his son they killed by the edge of the sword, and
they took Dinah from the house of Shechem and went out. Jacob's   27

---

23. *Their possessions in livestock and all their cattle.* Although, in keeping with
the biblical convention of near-verbatim repetition, Hamor's speech repeats
the language used by the sons of Jacob, there had been no mention before of
the Hivites becoming masters of the newcomers' livestock. This may reflect
a tactic of persuasion on the part of Hamor; it may equally reflect the Hivites'
cupidity.

24. *all who sallied forth.* In Abraham's negotiations with the Hittites in chapter 23, the town elders or members of the city council are referred to as "all
the assembled [or, those who come in] in the gates of the town." Here they
are designated as "all who go out from the gate." There are good grounds to
suppose that the latter idiom has a *military* connotation: troops came out of
the gates of walled cities to attack besiegers or to set out on campaigns, and
"to go out and come in" is an idiom that means "to maneuver in battle." The
reference to the Hivites as fighting men makes sense in context because they
are about to render themselves temporarily helpless against attack through
the mass circumcision.

26. *by the edge of the sword.* The Hebrew idiom is literally "the mouth of the
sword"—hence the sword is said to "consume" or "eat" in biblical language.
    and they took Dinah from the house of Shechem. Meir Sternberg (1985),
who provides illuminating commentary on the interplay of opposing moral
claims in this story, shrewdly notes that this is a shocking revelation just
before the end of the story: we might have imagined that Shechem was peti-
tioning in good faith for Dinah's hand; now it emerges that he has been
holding her captive in his house after having raped her.

sons came upon the slain and looted the town, for they had defiled
28   their sister. Their sheep and their cattle and their donkeys, what was
29   in the town and in the field, they took, and all their wealth, and all
their young ones and their wives they took captive, and they looted
30   everything in their houses. And Jacob said to Simeon and Levi, "You
have stirred up trouble for me, making me stink among the land's
inhabitants, among Canaanite and Peruzite, when I am a handful of
men. If they gather against me and strike me, I shall be destroyed, I
31   and my household." And they said, "Like a whore should our sister be
treated?"

---

27. *for they had defiled their sister.* This angry phrase becomes a kind of refrain
in the story. Again, it sounds like the free indirect discourse of Simeon and
Levi, offered as a justification for the massacre they have perpetrated. Precisely in this regard, the element of exaggeration in these words should be
noted: only one man defiled Dinah, but here a plural is used, as though all
the males of the town could in fact be held accountable for the rape.

30. *stirred up trouble.* The root meaning of the verb is "to muddy."

31. *Like a whore should our sister be treated?* The very last words of the story
are still another expression—and the crudest one—of the brothers' anger and
their commitment to exact the most extravagant price in vindication of what
they consider the family's honor. (The Hebrew might also be rendered as
"shall he treat our sister," referring to Shechem, but the third-person singular
does sometimes function in place of a passive.) It is surely significant that
Jacob, who earlier "kept his peace" and was notable for his failure of response,
has nothing to say, or is reported saying nothing, to these last angry words of
his sons. (Only on his deathbed will he answer them.) This moment becomes
the turning point in the story of Jacob. In the next chapter, he will follow
God's injunction to return to Bethel and reconfirm the covenant, but hence-
forth he will lose much of his paternal power and will be seen repeatedly at
the mercy of his sons, more the master of self-dramatizing sorrow than of his
own family. This same pattern will be invoked in the David story: the father
who fails to take action after the rape of his daughter and then becomes
victim of the fratricidal and rebellious impulses of his sons.

CHAPTER 35

And God said to Jacob, "Rise, go up to Bethel and dwell there and make   1
an altar there to the God Who appeared to you when you fled from
Esau your brother." And Jacob said to his household and to all who   2
were with him, "Put away the alien gods that are in your midst and

---

After Jacob's disastrous inaction in response to his daughter's rape in the face
of his vengeful sons, the narrative unit demarcated by this chapter is a collection of miscellaneous notices about Jacob and his household: the consecra-
tion of the altar at Bethel; the death of Rebekah's nurse; a reiteration of
Jacob's name change coupled with a repetition of the covenantal promise
delivered to his father and grandfather; Rachel's death in childbirth; Reuben's
cohabitation with his father's concubine; the death of Isaac. This miscellaneous overview of Jacob's later career—just before his sons entirely preempt
the narrative foreground—bears the earmarks of a literary source different
from that of the immediately preceding material. Nevertheless, thematic
reverberations from the pivotal catastrophe at Shechem sound through it.

1. *Who appeared to you when you fled from Esau your brother.* This clause,
which takes us back to the dream-vision revelation and promise vouchsafed
the young Jacob in chapter 28, signals this injunction to build an altar as a
ritual completion of that early promise. (See the comment on verse 3.)

2. *the alien gods.* Although many interpreters associate these icons or figurines
with the booty taken from Shechem, Rachel's attachment to her father's
household gods suggests that others in this large retinue of emigrating rela-
tives and slaves may have brought cultic figurines with them from Mesopotamia.

3   cleanse yourselves and change your garments. And let us rise and go
up to Bethel, and I shall make an altar there to the God Who answered
me on the day of my distress and was with me on the way that I went."
4   And they gave Jacob all the alien gods that were in their hands and
the rings that were in their ears, and Jacob buried them under the
5   terebinth that is by Shechem. And they journeyed onward, and the
terror of God was upon the towns around them, and they did not
6   pursue the sons of Jacob. And Jacob came to Luz in the land of
Canaan, that is, Bethel, he and all the people who were with him.
7   And he built there an altar and he called the place El-bethel, for there
God was revealed to him when he fled from his brother.

---

cleanse yourselves. Nahum Sarna aptly notes, "chapter 34 is dominated by
the theme of defilement; this chapter opens with the subject of purification."

3. *to the God Who answered me on the day of my distress and was with me.*
When Jacob approximately echoes God's words to him in verse 1, he replaces
God's revelation with God's answering him in his trouble and being with him,
thus confirming that God has fully responded to the terms he stipulated in
28:20, "If the LORD God be with me and guard me on this way that I am
going."

4. *the rings . . . in their ears.* As archeology has abundantly discovered, ear-
rings were often fashioned as figurines of gods and goddesses.
    buried. The verb *taman* is generally used for placing treasure in a hidden
or safe place, and is quite distinct from the term for burial that appears in
verses 8, 19, and 29, which is a verb reserved for burying bodies.

5. *the terror of God.* Perhaps, in the view of this writer, which is more insis-
tently theological than that of the immediately preceding narrative, the
phrase means literally that God casts fear on the Canaanites in order to pro-
tect Jacob and his clan. But the phrase is deliberately ambiguous: it could
also be construed as meaning "an awesome terror," with *'elohim* serving as an
intensifier rather than referring to divinity. In that case, the shambles to
which Simeon and Levi reduced Shechem might be sufficient reason for the
terror.

And Deborah, Rebekah's nurse, died, and she was buried below   8
Bethel under the oak, and its name was called Allon-bakuth.

And God appeared to Jacob again when he came from Paddan-aram,   9
and he blessed him, and God said to him, "Your name Jacob—no   10
longer shall your name be called Jacob, but Israel shall be your name."
And He called his name Israel. And God said to him,   11

> "I am El Shaddai.
> > Be fruitful and multiply.
> A nation, an assembly of nations shall stem from you,
> > and kings shall come forth from your loins.

And the land that I gave to Abraham and to Isaac, to you I will give it,   12
and to your seed after you I will give the land." And God ascended   13

---

8. *Allon-bakuth.* The name means "oak of weeping." Beyond the narrative
etiology of a place-name, there is not enough evidence to explain what this
lonely obituary notice is doing here.

9. *And God appeared to Jacob again when he came from Paddan-aram.* The
adverb "again," as Rashi notes, alludes to God's appearance to Jacob at this
same place, Bethel, when he fled to Paddan-aram. This second version of the
conferring of the name of Israel on Jacob is thus set in the perspective of a
large overview of his career of flight and return, with both his eastward and
westward trajectory marked by divine revelation and promise at the same
spot. The first story of Jacob's name change is folkloric and mysterious, and
the new name is given him as a token of his past victories in his sundry
struggles with human and divine creatures. Here, the report of the name
change is distinctly theological, God's words invoking both the first creation
("be fruitful and multiply") and His promise to Abraham ("kings shall come
forth from your loins"). In this instance, moreover, the new name is a sign of
Jacob's glorious future rather than of the triumphs he has already achieved,
and the crucial element of struggle is not intimated. As elsewhere in biblical
narrative, the sequencing of different versions of the same event proposes
different, perhaps complementary views of the same elusive subject—here,
the central and enigmatic fact of the origins of the theophoric name of the
Hebrew nation.

14 from him in the place where He had spoken with him. And Jacob set
up a pillar in the place where He had spoken with him, a pillar of
15 stone, and he offered libation upon it and poured oil on it. And Jacob
called the name of the place where God had spoken with him Bethel.

16 And they journeyed onward from Bethel, and when they were still
some distance from Ephrath, Rachel gave birth, and she labored hard
17 in the birth. And it happened, when she was laboring hardest in the
birth, that the midwife said to her, "Fear not, for this one, too, is a son

---

14. *And Jacob set up a pillar.* The cultic or commemorative pillar, *matsevah,*
figures equally in the first episode at Bethel, in chapter 28. There, too, Jacob
consecrates the pillar by pouring oil over it, but here, in keeping with the
more pervasively ritualistic character of the story, he also offers a libation,
and he builds an altar before setting up the pillar.

in the place where He had spoken with him. This phrase occurs three times
in close sequence. The underlining of "place" recalls the emphasis on that
key term in the earlier Bethel episode, where an anonymous "place" was
transformed into a "house of God." In the present instance, "place" is strongly
linked through reiteration with the fact of God's having spoken to Jacob:
before the place is consecrated by human ritual acts, it is consecrated by
divine speech.

16. *some distance.* The Hebrew, *kivrat ha'arets,* occurs only three times in the
Bible, and there has been debate over what precisely it indicates. Ibn Ezra,
with his extraordinary philological prescience, suggested that the initial *ki*
was the prefix of comparison *(kaf hadimyon)* and that the noun *barat* was
"the royal measure of distance." In fact, modern Semitic philologists have
discovered an Akkadian cognate, *beru,* which is the ancient mile, the equivalent of about four and a half English miles.

17. *for this one, too, is a son for you.* Rachel, in her naming-speech for Joseph,
had prayed for a second son, just as in her earlier imperious demand to her
husband, she had asked him to give her sons, not a son. The fulfillment of
her uncompromising wish entails her death.

for you." And it happened, as her life ran out, for she was dying, that   18
she called his name Ben-oni, but his father called him Benjamin. And   19
Rachel died and she was buried on the road to Ephrath, that is, Beth-
lehem. And Jacob set up a pillar on her grave, it is the pillar of Rachel's   20
grave to this day.

---

18. *Ben-oni*. The name can be construed to mean either "son of my vigor" or,
on somewhat more tenuous philological grounds, "son of my sorrow." Given
the freedom with which biblical characters play with names and their meanings, there is no reason to exclude the possibility that Rachel is punningly
invoking both meanings, though the former is more likely: in her death agony,
she envisages the continuation of "vigor" after her in the son she has born
(the tribe Benjamin will become famous for its martial prowess).

but his father called him Benjamin. In the reports given in biblical narrative, it is more often the mother who does the naming. This is the sole
instance of competing names assigned respectively by the mother and father.
Jacob's choice of *Bin-yamin* also presents a possibility of double meaning.
The most likely construal would be "son of the right hand," that is, favored
son, the one to whom is imparted special power or "dexterity." But the right
hand also designates the south in biblical idiom, so the name could mean
"dweller in the south." Again, the *yamin* component might be, as some have
proposed, not the word for right hand but a plural of *yom,* day or time, yielding the sense, "son of old age."

21 And Israel journeyed onward and pitched his tent on the far side of
22 Migdal-eder. And it happened, when Israel was encamped in that
land, that Reuben went and lay with Bilhah, his father's concubine,
and Israel heard.

23 And the sons of Jacob were twelve. The sons of Leah: Jacob's firstborn
Reuben and Simeon and Levi and Judah and Issachar and Zebulon.
24,25 The sons of Rachel: Joseph and Benjamin. And the sons of Bilhah,
26 Rachel's slavegirl: Dan and Naphtali. And the sons of Zilpah, Leah's
slavegirl: Gad and Asher. These are the sons of Jacob who were born
27 to him in Paddan-aram. And Jacob came to Isaac his father in Mamre,
at Kiriath-arba, that is, Hebron, where Abraham, and Isaac, had

---

22. *Reuben went and lay with Bilhah.* This enigmatic notice of Reuben's violation of his father's concubine is conveyed with gnomic conciseness. The Talmud saw in the story an intention on the part of Reuben to defile the slavegirl
of his mother's dead rival, Rachel, and so to make her sexually taboo to Jacob.
More recent commentators have observed with justice that in the biblical
world cohabitation with the consort of a ruler is a way of making claim to
his authority (as when the usurper Absalom cohabits with his father David's
concubines), and so Reuben would be attempting to seize in his father's lifetime his firstborn's right to be head of the clan.

and Israel heard. The same verb is used when the report of the rape of
Dinah is brought to Jacob. In both instances, he remains silent. The fact that
he is referred to in this episode as Israel, not Jacob, may be dictated by the
context of sexual outrage, for which the idiom "a scurrilous thing in Israel,"
nevalah beYisra'el, is used, as in the story of Dinah.

And the sons of Jacob were twelve. The genealogical list of the sons of
Jacob, followed by the list of the sons of Ishmael in the next chapter, marks
a major transition in the narrative. When the story picks up again at the
beginning of chapter 37, though old Jacob is very much alive and an
important figure in the background of the narrative, it will become the story
of Joseph and his brothers—a tale that in all its psychological richness and
moral complexity will take up the rest of the Book of Genesis.

sojourned. And Isaac's days were a hundred and eighty years. And   28,29
Isaac breathed his last, and died, and was gathered to his kin, old and
sated with years, and Esau and Jacob his sons buried him.

---

29. *And Isaac breathed his last.* The actual chronological place of this event is
obviously considerably earlier in the narrative. The biblical writers observe
no fixed commitment to linear chronology, a phenomenon recognized by the
rabbis in the dictum, "there is neither early nor late in the Torah."

Esau and Jacob his sons buried him. At this end point, they act in unison,
and despite the reversal of birthright and blessing, the firstborn is mentioned
first.

CHAPTER 36

And this is the lineage of Esau, that is, Edom. Esau took his wives from the daughters of Canaan—Adah daughter of Elon the Hittite and Oholibamah daughter of Anah son of Zibeon the Hittite, and

1,2

3

Chapter 36 offers the last of the major genealogies in Genesis. These lists of generations (*toledot*) and of kings obviously exerted an intrinsic fascination for the ancient audience and served as a way of accounting for historical and political configurations, which were conceived through a metaphor of biological propagation. (In fact, virtually the only evidence we have about the Edomite settlement is the material in this chapter.) As a unit in the literary structure of Genesis, the genealogies here are the marker of the end of a long narrative unit. What follows is the story of Joseph, a continuous sequence that is the last large literary unit of Genesis. The role of Esau's genealogy is clearly analogous to that of Ishmael's genealogy in chapter 25: before the narrative goes on to pursue the national line of Israel, an account is rendered of the posterity of the patriarch's son who is not the bearer of the covenantal promise. But Isaac had given Esau, too, a blessing, however qualified, and these lists demonstrate the implementation of that blessing in Esau's posterity.

The chapter also serves to shore up the narrative geographically, to the east, before turning its attention to the south. Apart from the brief report in chapter 12 of Abraham's sojourn in Egypt, which is meant to foreshadow the end of Genesis and the beginning of Exodus, the significant movement beyond the borders of Canaan has all been eastward, across the Jordan to Mesopotamia and back again. Esau now makes his permanent move from Canaan to Edom—the mountainous region east of Canaan, south of the Dead Sea and stretching down toward the Gulf of Aqabah. Once this report is finished, our attention will be turned first to Canaan and then to Egypt.

1.–8. This is the first of the six different lists—perhaps drawn from different archival sources by the editor—that make up the chapter. Though it does

Basemath daughter of Ishmael, sister of Nebaioth. And Adah bore to   4
Esau Eliphaz while Basemath bore Reuel, and Oholibamah bore Jeush   5
and Jalam and Korah. These are the sons of Esau who were born to
him in the land of Canaan. And Esau took his wives and his sons and   6
his daughters and all the folk of his household and his livestock and
all his cattle and all the goods he had gotten in the land of Canaan
and he went to another land away from Jacob his brother. For their   7
substance was too great for dwelling together and the land of their
sojournings could not support them because of their livestock. And   8
Esau settled in the high country of Seir—Esau, that is, Edom.

And this is the lineage of Esau, father of Edom, in the high country   9
of Seir. These are the names of the sons of Esau: Eliphaz son of Adah,   10

---

record Esau's sons, the stress is on his wives. There are both overlap and
inconsistency among the different lists. These need not detain us here. The
best account of these sundry traditions, complete with charts, is the discussion of this chapter in the Hebrew *Encyclopedia 'Olam haTanakh,* though
Nahum Sarna provides a briefer but helpful exposition of the lists in his
commentary.

2. *Anah son of Zibeon.* The Masoretic Text has "daughter of," but Anah is
clearly a man (cf. verse 24), and several ancient versions read "son."

6. *another land.* The translation follows the explanatory gloss of the ancient
Targums. The received text has only "a land."
    away from. Or, "because of."

7. *the land . . . could not support them.* The language of the entire passage is
reminiscent of the separation between Lot and Abraham in chapter 13. It is
noteworthy that Esau, in keeping with his loss of birthright and blessing,
concedes Canaan to his brother and moves his people to the southeast.

9.–14. The second unit is a genealogical list focusing on sons rather than
wives.

11 Esau's wife, Reuel son of Basemath, Esau's wife. And the sons of
12 Eliphaz were Teman, Omar, Zepho, and Gatam and Kenaz. And Timna
was a concubine of Eliphaz son of Esau, and she bore to Eliphaz
13 Amalek. These are the sons of Adah, Esau's wife. And these are the
sons of Reuel: Nahath and Zerah, Shammah and Mizzah. These were
14 the sons of Basemath, Esau's wife. And these were the sons of Esau's
wife Oholibamah, daughter of Anah son of Zibeon—she bore to Esau
Jeush and Jalam and Korah.

15 These are the chieftains of the sons of Esau. The sons of Eliphaz,
firstborn of Esau: the chieftain Teman, the chieftain Omar, the chieftain Zepho, the chieftain Kenaz, the chieftain Korah, the chieftain
16 Gatam, the chieftain Amalek. These are the chieftains of Eliphaz in
the land of Edom, these are the sons of Adah. And these are the sons
of Reuel son of Esau: the chieftain Nahath, the chieftain Zerah, the
17 chieftain Shammah, the chieftain Mizzah. These are the chieftains of
Reuel in the land of Edom, these are the sons of Basemath, Esau's
wife. And these are the sons of Oholibamah, Esau's wife: the chieftain
18 Jeush, the chieftain Jalam, the chieftain Korah. These are the chieftains of Oholibamah daughter of Anah, Esau's wife. These are the
19 sons of Esau, that is, Edom, and these their chieftains.

---

12. *Timna . . . a concubine . . . bore . . . Amalek.* If Amalek is subtracted, we
have a list of twelve tribes, as with Israel and Ishmael. Perhaps the birth by
a concubine is meant to set Amalek apart, in a status of lesser legitimacy.
Amalek becomes the hereditary enemy of Israel, whereas the other Edomites
had normal dealings with their neighbors to the west.

15.–19. The third unit is a list of chieftains descended from Esau.

15. *chieftains.* It has been proposed that the Hebrew *'aluf* means "clan," but
that seems questionable because most of the occurrences of the term elsewhere in the Bible clearly indicate a person, not a group. The difficulty is
obviated if we assume that an *'aluf* is the head of an *'elef*, a clan. The one
problem with this construal, the fact that in verses 40 and 41 *'aluf* is joined
with a feminine proper noun, may be resolved by seeing a construct form
there ("chieftain of Timna" instead of "chieftain Timna").

These are the sons of Seir the Horite who had settled in the land: 20
Lotan and Shobal and Zibeon and Anah, and Dishon and Ezer and 21
Dishan. These are the Horite chieftains, sons of Esau, in the land of
Edom. And the sons of Lotan were Hori and Hemam, and Lotan's 22
sister was Timna. And these are the sons of Shobal: Alvan and Mana- 23
hoth and Ebal, Shepho and Onam. And these are the sons of Zibeon: 24
Aiah and Anah, he is Anah who found the water in the wilderness
when he took the asses of his father Zibeon to graze. And these are 25
the children of Anah: Dishon and Oholibamah daughter of Anah. And
these are the sons of Dishon: Hemdan and Eshban and Ithran and 26
Cheran. These are the sons of Ezer: Bilhan and Zaavan and Akan. 27
These are the sons of Dishan: Uz and Aran. These are the Horite 28,29
chieftains: the chieftain Lotan, the chieftain Shobal, the chieftain

---

20.–30. The fourth unit of the chapter is a list of Horite inhabitants of Edom.
The Horites—evidently the term was used interchangeably with Hittite (see
the end of verse 2)—were most probably the Hurrians, a people who pene-
trated into this area from Armenia sometime in the first half of the second
millennium B.C.E. They seem to have largely assimilated into the local population, a process reflected in the fact that, like everyone else in these lists,
they have West Semitic names.

20. *who had settled in the land.* "Settlers [or inhabitants] of the land" is closer
to the Hebrew. That is, the "Horites" were the indigenous population by the
time the Edomites invaded from the west, during the thirteenth century
B.C.E.

24. *Aiah.* The Masoretic Text reads "and Aiah."
who found the water in the wilderness. The object of the verb in the
Hebrew, *yemim,* is an anomalous term, and venerable traditions that render
it as "mules" or "hot springs" have no philological basis. This translation follows E. A. Speiser's plausible suggestion that a simple transposition of the
first and second consonants of the word has occurred and that the original
reading was *mayim,* "water." Discovery of any water source in the wilderness
would be enough to make it noteworthy for posterity.

26. *Dishon.* The Masoretic Text reads "Dishan," who is his brother, and whose
offspring are recorded two verses later. There is support for "Dishon" in some
of the ancient versions.

30   Zibeon, the chieftain Anah, the chieftain Dishon, the chieftain Ezer,
the chieftain Dishan. These are the Horite chieftains by their clans in
the land of Seir.

31   These are the kings that reigned in the land of Edom before any king
32   reigned over the Israelites. And Bela son of Beor reigned in Edom
33   and the name of his city was Dinhabah. And Bela died and Jobab son
34   of Zerah from Bozrah, reigned in his stead. And Jobab died, and Hus-
35   ham from the land of the Temanite reigned in his stead. And Husham
died and Hadad son of Bedad reigned in his stead, he who struck
down Midian on the steppe of Moab, and the name of his city was
36   Avith. And Hadad died and Samlah of Masrekah reigned in his stead.
37   And Samlah died and Saul from Rehoboth-on-the-River reigned in his
38   stead. And Saul died and Baal-hanan son of Achbor reigned in his

---

30. *by their clans.* The translation revocalizes the Masoretic *'alufeyhem* as
'alfeyhem (the consonants remain identical) to yield "clans."

31.–39. The fifth unit of the chapter is a list of the kings of Edom. They do
not constitute a dynasty because none of the successors to the throne is a
son of his predecessor.

31. *before any king reigned over the Israelites.* The phrase refers to the estab-
lishment of the monarchy beginning with Saul and not, as some have proposed, to the imposition of Israelite suzerainty over Edom by David, because
of the particle *le* ("to," "for," "over"), rather than *mi* ("from") prefixed to the
Hebrew for "Israelites." This is one of those brief moments when the later
perspective in time of the writer pushes to the surface in the Patriarchal
narrative.

37. *Rehoboth-on-the-River.* Rehoboth means "broad places": in urban contexts, in the singular, it designates the city square; here it might mean something like "meadows." Rehoboth-on-the-River is probably meant to
distinguish this place from some other Rehoboth, differently situated.

stead. And Baal-hanan son of Achbor died and Hadad reigned in his   39
stead, and the name of his city was Pau and the name of his wife was
Mehetabel daughter of Matred daughter of Me-zahab.

And these are the names of the chieftains of Edom by their clans and   40
places name by name: the chieftain of Timna, the chieftain Alvah, the
chieftain Jetheth, the chieftain of Oholibamah, the chieftain Elah, the   41
chieftain Pinon, the chieftain Kenaz, the chieftain Teman, the chief-   42
tain Mibzar, the chieftain Magdiel, the chieftain Iram. These are the   43
chieftains of Edom by their settlements in the land of their holdings—
that is, Esau, father of Edom.

---

39. *Hadad*. The Masoretic Text has "Hadar," but this is almost certainly a
mistake for the well-attested name Hadad, as Chronicles, and some ancient
versions and manuscripts, read. In Hebrew, there is only a small difference
between the graphemes for *r* and for *d*.

40.–43. The sixth and concluding list of the collection is another record of
the chieftains descended from Esau. Most of the names are different, and
the list may reflect a collation of archival materials stemming from disparate
sources. This sort of stitching together of different testimonies would be in
keeping with ancient editorial practices.

CHAPTER 37

₁ And Jacob dwelled in the land of his father's sojournings, in the land of
₂ Canaan. This is the lineage of Jacob—Joseph, seventeen years old,
was tending the flock with his brothers, assisting the sons of Bilhah
and the sons of Zilpah, the wives of his father. And Joseph brought ill

---

1.–2. *And Jacob dwelled in the land of . . . Canaan. This is the lineage of Jacob.*
The aptness of these verses as a transition from the genealogy of Esau to the
story of Joseph is nicely observed by ibn Ezra: "The text reports that the
chieftains of Esau dwelled in the high country of Seir and Jacob dwelled in
the Chosen Land. And the meaning of 'This is the lineage of Jacob' is, 'These
are the events that happened to him and the incidents that befell him.' " Ibn
Ezra's remark demonstrates that there is no need to attach these two verses
to the end of the preceding genealogy, as some modern scholars have argued.
The writer exploits the flexibility of the Hebrew *toledot,* a term that can
equally refer to genealogical list and to story, in order to line up the beginning
of the Joseph story with the *toledot* passage that immediately precedes it.

2. *assisting.* The literal meaning of the Hebrew is "he was a lad with the sons
of Bilhah." But the Hebrew for "lad," *na'ar,* has a secondary meaning, clearly
salient here, of assistant or subaltern. The adolescent Joseph is working as a
kind of apprentice shepherd with his older brothers.
  brought ill report. The first revelation of Joseph's character suggests a
spoiled younger child who is a tattletale. The next revelation, in the dreams,
intimates adolescent narcissism, even if the grandiosity eventually is justified
by events.

report of them to their father. And Israel loved Joseph more than all   3
his sons, for he was the child of his old age, and he made him an
ornamented tunic. And his brothers saw it was he their father loved   4
more than all his brothers, and they hated him and could not speak a
kind word to him. And Joseph dreamed a dream and told it to his   5
brothers and they hated him all the more. And he said to them, "Lis-   6
ten, pray, to this dream that I dreamed. And, look, we were binding   7

---

3. *And Israel loved Joseph . . . for he was the child of his old age.* The explanation is a little odd, both because the fact that Joseph is the son of the beloved
Rachel is unmentioned and because it is the last-born Benjamin who is the
real child of Jacob's old age. It is noteworthy that Jacob's favoritism toward
Joseph is mentioned immediately after the report of questionable behavior
on Joseph's part. One recalls that Jacob was the object of his mother's unex-
plained favoritism.

an ornamented tunic. The only clue about the nature of the garment is
offered by the one other mention of it in the Bible, in the story of the rape of
Tamar (2 Samuel 13), in which, incidentally, there is a whole network of
pointed allusions to the Joseph story. There we are told that the *ketonet pasim*
was worn by virgin princesses. It is thus a unisex garment and a product of
ancient *haute couture*. E. A. Speiser cites a cuneiform text with an apparently
cognate phrase that seems to indicate a tunic with appliqué ornamentation.
Other scholars have pointed to a fourteenth-century Egyptian fresco showing
captive Canaanite noblemen adorned with tunics made of longitudinal panels
sewn together.

5. *And Joseph dreamed.* As has often been noted, the dreams in the Joseph
story reflect its more secular orientation in comparison with the preceding
narratives in Genesis. They are not direct messages from God, like His
appearance in the dream-visions to Abimelech and to Jacob: they may be
literally portentous, but they require human interpretation (here the meaning
is obvious enough), and they may also express the hidden desires and self-
perception of the dreamer.

6. *Listen, pray, to this dream that I dreamed.* In keeping with the rule about
the revelatory force of a character's first words, this whole speech shows us a
young Joseph who is self-absorbed, blithely assuming everyone will be fasci-
nated by the details of his dreams.

sheaves in the field, and, look, my sheaf arose and actually stood up,
8   and, look, your sheaves drew round and bowed to my sheaf." And his
brothers said to him, "Do you mean to reign over us, do you mean to
rule us?" And they hated him all the more, for his dreams and for his
9   words. And he dreamed yet another dream and recounted it to his
brothers, and he said, "Look, I dreamed a dream again, and, look, the
10   sun and the moon and eleven stars were bowing to me." And he

---

7. *And, look.* It is standard technique for the dreamer reporting his dream to
use the presentative *hineh,* "look," to introduce what he has "seen" in the
dream. But Joseph repeats the term three times in a single sentence,
betraying his own wide-eyed amazement, and perhaps his naïveté. The same
attitude is reflected in his exclamatory "arose and actually stood up."

8. *for his dreams and for his words.* It is misguided to construe this as a hendiadys ("for speaking about his dreams") since the sharp point is that they hated
him both for having such dreams and for insisting on talking about them.

9. *And he dreamed yet another dream.* Later (41:32) we shall learn that the
doubling of the dream is a sign that what it portends will really happen, but
it should also be observed that doublets are a recurrent principle of organization in the Joseph story, just as binary divisions are an organizing principle in
the Jacob story. Joseph and Pharaoh have double dreams; the chief butler
and the chief baker dream their pair of seemingly parallel, actually antithetical dreams. Joseph is first flung into a pit and later into the prison-house.
The brothers make two trips down to Egypt, with one of their number seemingly at risk on each occasion. And their descent to Egypt with goods and
silver mirrors the descent of the merchant caravan, bearing the same items,
that first brought Joseph down to Egypt.
    the sun and the moon and eleven stars. Both Hermann Gunkel and Gerhard
von Rad have proposed that the eleven stars are actually the eleven constellations known in the ancient Near East, but these should then be twelve, not
eleven, and at least in the biblical record, knowledge of definite constellations
is reflected only in postexilic literature. The two parallel dreams operate on
different levels of intensity. The agricultural setting of the first one reflects
the actual setting—Freud's "day's residue"—in which Joseph does his dreaming, and so is attached to the first part of the story, even if the brothers detect
in it aspirations to regal grandeur. The second dream shifts the setting
upward to the heavens and in this way is an apt adumbration of the brilliant

recounted it to his father and to his brothers, and his father rebuked him and said to him, "What is this dream that you have dreamed? Shall we really come, I and your mother and your brothers, to bow before you to the ground?" And his brothers were jealous of him, while   11
his father kept the thing in mind.

And his brothers went to graze their father's flock at Shechem. And   12,13
Israel said to Joseph, "You know, your brothers are pasturing at Shechem. Come, let me send you to them," and he said to him, "Here I am." And he said to him, "Go, pray, to see how your brothers fare,   14
and how the flock fares, and bring me back word." And he sent him from the valley of Hebron and he came to Shechem. And a man found   15
him and, look, he was wandering in the field, and the man asked him, saying, "What is it you seek?" And he said, "My brothers I seek. Tell   16

---

sphere of the Egyptian imperial court over which Joseph will one day preside. From a strict monotheistic view, the second dream teeters on the brink of blasphemy.

10. *I and your mother.* This particular episode seems to assume, in flat contradiction of the preceding narrative, that Rachel is still alive, though Benjamin has already been born (there are eleven brothers in the dream bowing to Joseph). Attempts to rescue consistency on the ground that dreams may contain incoherent elements are unconvincing, because it is a perfectly lucid Jacob who assumes here that Rachel is still alive.

12. *Shechem.* As several medieval commentators note, Shechem has already been linked with disaster in these stories.

14. *the valley of Hebron.* The validity of this designation can be defended only through ingenious explanation because Hebron stands on a height.

15. *And a man found him.* The specificity of this exchange with an unnamed stranger is enigmatic. Efforts to see the "man" as an angel or messenger of fate have little textual warrant. What it is safe to say is that the question and answer in a field outside Shechem reinforce the sense that Joseph is being directed, unwitting, to a disastrous encounter.

17   me, pray, where are they pasturing?" And the man said, "They have journeyed on from here, for I heard them say, 'Let us go to Dothan.' "

18   And Joseph went after his brothers and found them at Dothan. And they saw him from afar before he drew near them and they plotted

19   against him to put him to death. And they said to each other, "Here

20   comes that dream-master! And so now, let us kill him and fling him into one of the pits and we can say, a vicious beast has devoured him,

21   and we shall see what will come of his dreams." And Reuben heard

22   and came to his rescue and said, "We must not take his life." And

---

17. *for I heard them.* The Masoretic Text has only "I heard," but several ancient versions supply the *mem* suffix to the verb that would indicate "them" as its object.

19. *that dream-master.* Although time-honored tradition renders this in English simply as "dreamer," the Hebrew term *ba'al hahalomot* is stronger, and thus in context more sarcastic. The *ba'al* component suggests someone who has a special proprietary relation to, or mastery of, the noun that follows it.

20. *let us kill him and fling him into one of the pits.* The flinging after the killing underscores the naked brutality of the brothers' intentions. The denial of proper burial was among the Hebrews as among the Greeks deeply felt as an atrocity.

21.–22. *We must not take his life. . . . Shed no blood.* Reuben eschews the two verbs for killing used respectively by the narrator and the brothers and instead invokes language echoing the primal taboo against taking—literally, "striking down"—life and spilling human blood (compare the powerful prohibition in 9:6). In the event, the substitute blood of the slaughtered kid will figure prominently in the brothers' course of action.

Fling him into this pit. At the same time, Reuben tries not to contradict the violence of his brothers' feelings toward Joseph and uses the same phrase, to fling him into a pit, with the crucial difference that in his proposal it is a live Joseph who will be cast into the pit. This is precisely the verb used for Hagar (21:15) when she flings Ishmael under a bush in the wilderness.

Reuben said to them, "Shed no blood! Fling him into this pit in the
wilderness and do not raise a hand against him"—that he might rescue
him from their hands to bring him back to his father. And it happened   23
when Joseph came to his brothers that they stripped Joseph of his
tunic, the ornamented tunic that he had on him. And they took him   24
and flung him into the pit, and the pit was empty, there was no water
in it. And they sat down to eat bread, and they raised their eyes and   25
saw and, look, a caravan of Ishmaelites was coming from Gilead, their
camels bearing gum and balm and ladanum on their way to take down
to Egypt. And Judah said to his brothers, "What gain is there if we kill 26

---

23. *his tunic, the ornamented tunic that he had on him.* Only now do we learn
that Joseph has the bad judgment to wear on his errand the garment that was
the extravagant token of his father's favoritism. Thus he provokes the brothers' anger, and they strip him—not part of their original plan—and thus take
hold of what will be made into the false evidence of his death as their plan
changes.

24. *they . . . flung him into the pit.* Contrary to the original plan, they do not
kill him straight away. Perhaps they have decided instead to let him perish
trapped in the pit.
    the pit was empty, there was no water in it. Deep cisterns of this sort—too
deep to climb out of—were commonly used for water storage.

25. *Ishmaelites.* This is a generic term for the seminomadic traders of Arab
stock whose homeland was east of the Jordan, but it is also an anachronism,
since at the time of the story, the eponymous Ishmael, the uncle of the twelve
brothers, was still alive, and the only "Ishmaelites" would be their first
cousins.
    gum and balm and ladanum. The precise identity of these plant extracts
used for medicinal purposes and as perfume is in doubt, but it is clear that
they are costly export items.

26. *What gain is there if we kill our brother and cover up his blood?* Judah's
argument for sparing Joseph's life—which most scholars regard as the mani-
festation of an originally different version of the story from the one in which
the firstborn Reuben tries to save Joseph—is based on the consideration of
gain, not on the horror of the taboo against shedding blood that Reuben
invokes. To cover up blood means to conceal bloodguilt.

27   our brother and cover up his blood? Come, let us sell him to the
Ishmaelites and our hand will not be against him, for he is our brother,
28   our own flesh." And his brothers agreed. And Midianite merchantmen
passed by and pulled Joseph up out of the pit and sold Joseph to the
29   Ishmaelites for twenty pieces of silver. And Reuben came back to the
30   pit and, look, Joseph was not in the pit, and he rent his garments, and
he came back to his brothers, and he said, "The boy is gone, and I,
31   where can I turn?" And they took Joseph's tunic and slaughtered a kid

---

27. *for he is our brother, our own flesh.* It is, of course, a dubious expression
of brotherhood to sell someone into the ignominy and perilously uncertain
future of slavery.

28. *And Midianite merchantmen . . . pulled Joseph up out of the pit and sold
Joseph to the Ishmaelites.* This is the one signal moment when the two literary
strands out of which the story is woven seem awkwardly spliced. Up to this
point, no Midianites have been mentioned. Elsewhere, Midianites and Ishmaelites appear to be terms from different periods designating the selfsame
people (compare Judges 8:22 and 24), so the selling of Joseph to the Ishmaelites looks like a strained attempt to blend two versions that respectively used
the two different terms. And the Midianite intervention contradicts the just
stated intention of the brothers to pull Joseph out of the pit themselves and
sell Joseph to the Ishmaelites for profit.

29. *And Reuben came back to the pit.* The contradiction between the two
versions continues, since one is driven to assume that Reuben was not present at the fraternal meal during which the selling of Joseph was discussed,
though there is no textual indication of his absence.

30. *The boy is gone.* The Hebrew says literally, "the boy is not." The phrase
could be a euphemism for death or could merely indicate disappearance. It
is a crucial ambiguity the brothers themselves will exploit much later in the
story.

31. *slaughtered a kid . . . dipped the tunic in blood.* Jacob had used both a
slaughtered kid and a garment in the deception he perpetrated on his own
father.

and dipped the tunic in the blood, and they sent the ornamented tunic   32
and had it brought to their father, and they said, "Recognize, pray, is
it your son's tunic or not?" And he recognized it, and he said, "It is my   33
son's tunic.

> A vicious beast has devoured him,
> Joseph's been torn to shreds!"

And Jacob rent his clothes and put sackcloth round his waist and   34
mourned for his son many days. And all his sons and all his daughters   35

---

32. *they sent . . . and had it brought.* The brothers operate indirectly, through
the agency of a messenger, letting the doctored evidence of the blood-soaked
tunic speak for itself.

   Recognize. When the disguised Jacob deceived his father, we were told,
"he did not recognize him."

33. *And he recognized it, and he said. . . . A vicious beast has devoured him.*
Jacob's paternal anxiety turns him into the puppet of his sons' plotting. Not
only does he at once draw the intended false conclusion, but he uses the very
words of their original plan, "a vicious beast has devoured him." It is noteworthy that his cry of grief takes the form of a line of formal verse, a kind of
compact elegy that jibes with the mourning rituals which follow it.

33–35. All this language of mourning and grieving suggests a certain extrava-
gance, perhaps something histrionic. As the next verse tersely indicates, at
the very moment Jacob is bewailing his purportedly dead son, Joseph is sold
into the household of a high Egyptian official.

rose to console him and he refused to be consoled and he said, "Rather
I will go down to my son in Sheol mourning," and his father bewailed
him.

36   But the Midianites had sold him into Egypt to Potiphar, Pharoah's
courtier, the high chamberlain.

---

36. *Pharoah's courtier, the high chamberlain.* The word for "courtier" in other
contexts can also mean "eunuch," but the evidence suggests that the original
use was as the title of a court official and that the sense of "eunuch" became
associated with the term secondarily because of an occasional Mesopotamian
practice of placing eunuchs in court positions. (The Hebrew *saris* is a loan-
word from the Akkadian *sa resi*, "royal official.") The second title attached to
Potiphar is associated with a root involving slaughter and in consequence
sometimes with cooking (hence the "chief steward" or alternately, "chief exe-
cutioner," of various English versions). The actual responsibilities of this high
imperial post remain unclear.

CHAPTER 38

And it happened at this time that Judah went down from his brothers 1
and pitched his tent by an Adulamite named Hirah. And Judah saw 2
there the daughter of a Canaanite man named Shua, and he took her
and came to bed with her. And she conceived and bore a son and 3
called his name Er. And she conceived again and bore a son and called 4
his name Onan. And she bore still another son and called his name 5
Shelah, and he was at Chezib when she bore him. And Judah took a 6

---

1. *And it happened at this time.* The formulaic indication of time is deliberately vague. The entire story of Judah and the sons he begets spans more
than twenty years. It reads as though it began after the moment Joseph is
sold down to Egypt, but the larger chronology of the Joseph story and the
descent into Egypt suggests that the first phase of this story about Judah may
considerably antedate Joseph's enslavement. Many readers have sensed this
tale of Judah and Tamar as an "interruption" of the Joseph story, or, at best,
as a means of building suspense about Joseph's fate in Egypt. In fact, there
is an intricate network of connections with what precedes and what follows,
as close attention to the details of the text will reveal.

went down. The verb is justified by topography because Judah is coming
down from the hill country to the eastern edge of the coastal plain inhabited
by the Canaanites. But "going down" is also the verb used for travel to Egypt
(compare the end of verse 25 in the preceding chapter), and the next episode,
which returns to the Joseph story, will begin with the words, "And Joseph
was brought down to Egypt."

3. *she . . . called.* The Masoretic Text has "he called," but the more likely
naming of the child by the mother, as in verse 4, is supported by several
manuscript traditions.

7 wife for Er his firstborn, and her name was Tamar. And Er his firstborn
8 was evil in the eyes of the LORD, and the LORD put him to death. And
Judah said to Onan, "Come to bed with your brother's wife and do
your duty as brother-in-law for her and raise up seed for your brother."
9 And Onan knew that the seed would not be his and so when he would
come to bed with his brother's wife, he would waste his seed on the
10 ground, so to give no seed to his brother. And what he did was evil in

---

7. *And Er his firstborn was evil in the eyes of the* LORD. The nature of his moral
failing remains unspecified, but given the insistent pattern of reversal of primogeniture in all these stories, it seems almost sufficient merely to be firstborn in order to incur God's displeasure: though the firstborn is not
necessarily evil, he usually turns out to be obtuse, rash, wild, or otherwise
disqualified from carrying on the heritage. It is noteworthy that Judah, who
invented the lie that triggered his own father's mourning for a dead son, is
bereaved of two sons in rapid sequence. In contrast to Jacob's extravagant
grief, nothing is said about Judah's emotional response to the losses.

8. *do your duty as brother-in-law.* In the Hebrew, this is a single verb, *yabem,*
referring to the so-called levirate marriage. The legal obligation of *yibum,*
which was a widespread practice in the ancient Near East, was incurred
when a man died leaving his wife childless. His closest brother in order of
birth was obliged to become his proxy, "raising up seed" for him by impregnat-
ing his widow. The dead brother would thus be provided a kind of biological
continuity, and the widow would be able to produce progeny, which was a
woman's chief avenue of fulfillment in this culture.

9. *the seed would not be his.* Evidently, Onan is troubled by the role of sexual
proxy, which creates a situation in which the child he begets will be legally
considered his dead brother's offspring.
　he would waste his seed on the ground. Despite the confusion engendered
by the English term "onanism" that derives from this text, the activity referred
to is almost certainly *coitus interruptus*—as Rashi vividly puts it, "threshing
within, winnowing without."

the eyes of the LORD, and He put him as well to death. And Judah 11
said to Tamar his daughter-in-law, "Stay a widow in your father's house
until Shelah my son is grown up," for he thought, Lest he, too, die
like his brothers. And Tamar went and stayed at her father's house.

And a long time passed and the daughter of Shua, Judah's wife, died, 12
and after the mourning period Judah went up to his sheepshearers, he
with Hirah the Adulamite his friend, to Timnah. And Tamar was told, 13
saying, "Look, your father-in-law is going up to Timnah to sheer his

---

11. *Stay a widow in your father's house.* The childless Tamar is not only
neglected but must submit to a form of social disgrace in having to return to
her father's house after having been twice married. Since enough time elapses
for Shelah to grow from prepuberty to at least late adolescence (see verse 14),
this period of enforced return to the status of an unmarried daughter proves
to be a very long one. Amos Funkenstein has observed to me that Tamar
remains silent in the face of her father-in-law's condemnation, saying nothing
of Onan's sexual aberration and leaving Judah to suppose that the death of
both sons is somehow her fault. And though he banishes her to her father's
house, she evidently remains under his legal jurisdiction, as his issuing of a
death sentence against her (verse 24) indicates.

12. *after the mourning period.* The Hebrew says literally, "and Judah was consoled," a verb that may refer to actual feelings or to the simple end of the
prescribed period of mourning. Either way, we pick up the antithetical echo
of Jacob's refusal of consolation at the end of the previous chapter. The death
of Judah's wife and the ensuing mourning set up the condition of sexual
neediness that motivates his encounter with Tamar.
  sheepshearers. As we know from elsewhere in the Bible, sheepshearing was
the occasion for elaborate festivities, with abundant food and drink. In this
way, Judah's going up to join his sheepshearers is itself an indication that he
is done with the rites of mourning and is perhaps in a holiday mood. The
verb twice used for this journey is to "go up," the complementary opposite of
the going down with which the chapter begins.

14   sheep." And she took off her widow's garb and covered herself with a
      veil and wrapped herself and sat by the entrance to Enaim, which is
      on the road to Timnah, for she saw that Shelah had grown up and she
15   had not been given to him as wife. And Judah saw her and he took
16   her for a whore, for she had covered her face. And he turned aside to
      her by the road and said, "Here, pray, let me come to bed with you,"
      for he knew not that she was his daughter-in-law. And she said, "What
17   will you give me for coming to bed with me?" And he said, "I person-
      ally will send a kid from the flock." And she said, "Only if you give a

---

14. *sat by the entrance to Enaim.* If, as is quite likely, this place name means
"Twin Wells," we probably have here a kind of wry allusion to the betrothal
type-scene: the bridegroom encountering his future spouse by a well in a
foreign land. One wonders whether the two wells might resonate with her
two marriages, or with the twins she will bear. In any case, instead of a feast
and the conclusion of a betrothal agreement, here we have a brusque goods-
for-services business dialogue, followed by sex.

16. *Here, pray, let me come to bed with you.* Despite the particle of entreaty
na', "pray," this is brutally direct: there is no preface of polite greeting to the
woman, and the Hebrew idiom, repeatedly used in this story, says literally,
"let me come into you." Judah's sexual importunacy becomes a background
of contrast for Joseph's sexual restraint in the next chapter.

What will you give me for coming to bed with me? Tamar is careful to speak
in character with her role as a roadside whore, but as the events unfold, it
becomes clear that she also has an ulterior consideration in mind.

17. *a kid from the flock.* Though this is plausible enough payment coming
from a prosperous pastoralist in a barter culture, it also picks up the motif of
the slaughtered kid whose blood was used by Judah and his brothers to
deceive Jacob (as Jacob before them used a kid to deceive his father). This
connection was aptly perceived a millennium and a half ago in the Midrash
Bereishit Rabba. The other material element in the brothers' deception of
their father was a garment; Tamar uses a garment—the whore's dress and
veil—to deceive her father-in-law.

Only if you give me a pledge. Tamar is not only bold and enterprising in
getting for herself the justice Judah has denied her but also very shrewd: she
realizes it is crucial for her to retain evidence of the paternity of the child she
may conceive.

pledge till you send it." And he said, "What pledge shall I give you?" 18
And she said, "Your seal-and-cord, and the staff in your hand." And he
gave them to her and he came to bed with her and she conceived by
him. And she rose and went her way and took off the veil she was 19
wearing and put on her widow's garb. And Judah sent the kid by 20
the hand of his friend the Adulamite to take back the pledge from the
woman's hand, and he did not find her. And he asked the men of the 21
place saying, "Where is the cult-harlot, the one at Enaim by the road?"
"And they said, "There has been no cult-harlot here." And he returned 22
to Judah and said, "I could not find her, and the men of the place said

---

18. *Your seal-and-cord, and the staff in your hand.* The seal was a cylinder seal
attached to a cord and usually worn around the neck. Rolled over documents
incised in clay, it would be the means of affixing a kind of self-notarized
signature. It is less clear that the staff had a legal function, though of course
in political contexts it is a symbol of authority. Tamar's stipulated pledge,
then, is an extravagant one: taking the instruments of Judah's legal identity
and social standing is something like taking a person's driver's license and
credit cards in modern society.

he gave them to her and came to bed with her and she conceived by him.
The rapid chain of verbs suggests the pragmatically focused nature of the
transaction for both participants. The last of the three verbs reveals that
Tamar gets exactly what she has aimed for.

20. *by the hand . . . the woman's hand.* As elsewhere, the physical concreteness of the terms of the narrative is salient: Hirah brings in his hand a kid in
order to take back the pledge from the hand of the roadside whore. Since she
remains anonymous for Judah, the narrator is careful to refer to her here as
"the woman" rather than by name.

21. *the place.* The Masoretic Text has "her place," but the more plausible "the
place," as in the next verse, is supported by several of the ancient versions.

22. *the cult-harlot.* Hirah substitutes the more decorous term *qedeshah,* a
woman who practices ritual prostitution in a fertility cult, for the narrator's
frank *zonah,* "whore."

23 as well, "There has been no cult-harlot here." And Judah said, "Let
her take them, lest we be a laughingstock. Look, I sent this kid and
you could not find her."

24 And it happened about three months later that Judah was told, saying,
"Tamar has played the whore and what's more, she's conceived by her
25 whoring." And Judah said, "Take her out to be burned." Out she was
taken, when she sent to her father-in-law, saying, "By the man to
whom these belong I have conceived," and she said, "Recognize, pray,
26 whose are this seal-and-cord and this staff?" And Judah recognized

---

23. *Let her take them, lest we be a laughingstock.* Let her keep the pledge, and
we will keep our mouths shut, lest it become known that I have given such
valuable objects for a fleeting pleasure. Ibn Ezra shrewdly observes: "In his
great lust, he gave three [precious] things for a trivial thing."

24. *played the whore . . . conceived by her whoring.* The very term that Hirah
fastidiously avoided is twice thrust into Judah's attention, *zantah* (played the
whore) and *zenunim* (whoring).
    And Judah said, "Take her out to be burned." The precipitous speed of
Judah's judgment, without the slightest reflection or call for evidence, is
breathtaking. The peremptory character of the death sentence—and burning
was reserved in biblical law only for the most atrocious crimes—is even more
evident in the Hebrew, where Judah's decree consists of only two words,
a verb in the imperative ("take-her-out") followed by "that-she-be-burned,"
hotsi'uha wetisaref.

25. *Out she was taken.* There is no pause between the enunciation of the
death sentence and the beginning of its implementation. This speed is highlighted grammatically in the Hebrew by the unusual use of a passive present
participle (cognate with "take her out")—*hi' mutsei't,* literally, "she is-being-
taken-out."
    when she sent. . . . "Recognize, pray . . ." Like a trap suddenly springing
closed, the connection with the preceding story of the deception of Jacob is
now fully realized. In precise correspondence to Judah and his brothers,
Tamar "sends" evidence—in this case, true evidence—to argue her case. Like
them, she confronts the father figure with the imperative, "Recognize, pray"
(*haker-na'*)—this echo, too, was picked up by the Midrash—and, like his
father, Judah is compelled to acknowledge that he recognizes what has been
brought to him.

them and he said, "She is more in the right than I, for have I not failed to give her to Shelah, my son?" And he knew her again no more.

And it happened at the time she gave birth that, look, there were twins in her womb. And it happened as she gave birth that one put out his hand and the midwife took it and bound a scarlet thread on his hand, to say, this one came out first. And as he was drawing back his hand, look, out came his brother, and she said, "What a breach you have made for yourself!" And she called his name Perez. And afterward out came his brother, on whose hand was the scarlet thread, and she called his name Zerah.

27
28
29
30

---

26. *She is more in the right than I.* The verb used, *tsadaq*, is a legal term: it is she who has presented the convincing evidence. But in the next clause Judah also concedes that he has behaved unjustly toward Tamar, so that in a sense her taking the law into her own hands, however unconventional the act, is vindicated by his words.

27.–30. The twins of course recall Jacob and Esau and the whole chain of paired brothers struggling over the right of the firstborn. Zerah, sticking his hand out first, seems to be the firstborn, but he is overtaken by Perez, who makes a "breach" or "bursts forth" (the meaning of the Hebrew *Perets*). Tamar seems to address the energetic newborn in a tone of wondering affection in the exclamation she pronounces as preface to naming him. Again, the Masoretic Text has "he called his name," but the reading of several of the ancient versions, "she called," makes much better sense. Perez will become the progenitor of the kings of Judea. The name Zerah means "shining," as in the dawning of the sun, and so is linked with the scarlet thread on his hand. The scarlet in turn associates Zerah with Esau-the-Red, another twin displaced from his initial position as firstborn.

CHAPTER 39

And Joseph was brought down to Egypt, and Potiphar, courtier of Pha- 1
raoh, the high chamberlain, an Egyptian man, bought him from the
hands of the Ishmaelites who had brought him down there. And the 2
LORD was with Joseph and he was a successful man, and he was in
the house of his Egyptian master. And his master saw that the LORD 3

This chapter is the most elegantly symmetrical episode in Genesis. It comprises an introductory narrative frame (verses 1–6), a closing frame (20–23)
that elaborately echoes the introductory verses, and the central story of the
failed seduction, which is intricately linked to the framing verses by a network of recurring thematic key words.

1. *an Egyptian man.* This slightly odd designation of the high chamberlain
might perhaps be used here in order to be played off against the derogatory
identification of Joseph as "a Hebrew man" in verse 14. The household staff
are also referred to as "men" (see verse 11), though that plural form can
include both sexes, which it probably does when the mistress calls in the
"people of the house" in verse 14, as she will go on to stress their collective
sexual vulnerability to the Hebrew intruder.

2.–6. The thematic key words, emphatically repeated in phrase after phrase,
are: all, hand, house, blessing, succeed—the last two terms being the mani-
festation of the reiterated "the LORD was with Joseph."

2. *master.* Only in the introductory verse is Potiphar referred to by name.
Afterward he is designated consistently as Joseph's master. Although the
source critics may be right in attributing this difference between verse 1 and
the rest of the chapter to a difference in literary strands, the stylistic peculiar-
ity of referring to Joseph's lord only by role serves the thematic purpose of
constantly highlighting the master-slave relationship and the concomitant
issue of trust and stewardship.

was with him, and all that he did the LORD made succeed in his hand, and Joseph found favor in his eyes and he ministered to him, and he 4 put him in charge of his house, and all that he had he placed in his hands. And it happened from the time he put him in charge of his 5 house that the LORD blessed the Egyptian's house for Joseph's sake and the LORD's blessing was on all that he had in house and field. And 6 he left all that he had in Joseph's hands, and he gave no thought to anything with him there save the bread he ate. And Joseph was comely in features and comely to look at.

And it happened after these things that his master's wife raised her 7 eyes to Joseph and said, "Lie with me." And he refused. And he said 8 to his master's wife, "Look, my master has given no thought with me here to what is in the house, and all that he has he has placed in my hands. He is not greater in this house than I, and he has held back 9 nothing from me except you, as you are his wife, and how could I do this great evil and give offense to God?" And so she spoke to Joseph 10

---

6. *And Joseph was comely in features and comely to look at.* These are exactly the words used to describe Joseph's mother in 29:17. They signal an unsettling of the perfect harmony of Joseph's divinely favored stewardship—that comprehensive management of "all" that is in the "house"—as they provide the motivation for the sexual campaign of his mistress.

7. *Lie with me.* The extraordinary bluntness of this sexual imperative—two words in the Hebrew—makes it one of the most striking instances of revelatory initial dialogue in the Bible. Against her two words, the scandalized (and perhaps nervous) Joseph will issue a breathless response that runs to thirty-five words in the Hebrew. It is a remarkable deployment of the technique of contrastive dialogue repeatedly used by the biblical writers to define the differences between characters in verbal confrontation.

8. *in the house . . . all that he has . . . placed in my hands.* Joseph's protestation invokes the key terms "house," "all," "hand" of the introductory frame, reminding us of the total trust given him as steward.

day after day, and he would not listen to her, to lie by her, to be with

11 her. And it happened, on one such day, that he came into the house
to perform his task, and there was no man of the men of the house

12 there in the house. And she seized him by his garment, saying, "Lie
with me." And he left his garment in her hand and he fled and went

13 out. And so, when she saw that he had left his garment in her hand

14 and fled outside, she called out to the people of the house and said to
them, "See, he has brought us a Hebrew man to play with us. He

15 came into me to lie with me and I called out in a loud voice, and so,

---

10. *to lie by her.* The narrator, by altering the preposition, somewhat softens
the bluntness of the mistress's sexual proposition. This led ibn Ezra to imagine that she adopted the strategem of inviting Joseph merely to lie down in
bed next to her.

12. *she seized him by his garment, saying, "Lie with me."* The two-word sexual
command, which is all she is ever reported saying to Joseph, is now translated
from words into aggressive action. "Garment" (*beged*) is a generic term. It is
certainly not an outside garment or "coat," as E. A. Speiser has it, though
the Revised English Bible's "loincloth" probably goes too far in the opposite
direction. In any case, Joseph would be naked, or nearly naked, when he runs
off leaving the garment behind in her grasping hand.

13. The narrator repeats the terms of the preceding sentence both in order
to build up momentary suspense—what will she do now?—and in order to
review the crucial evidence and sequence of events, which she is about to
change.

14. *he has brought us a Hebrew man to play with us.* Rather contemptuously,
she refers to her husband neither by name nor title. The designation
"Hebrew" is common when the group is referred to in contradistinction to
other peoples, but it may well have had pejorative associations for Egyptians.
"Play" can mean sexual dalliance or mockery, and probably means both here.
"Us" suggests they all could have been game for this lascivious—or, mocking—barbarian from the north and is an obvious attempt on her part to enlist
their sense of Egyptian solidarity. She is probably suggesting that the very
supremacy of this foreigner in the household is an insult to them all.
    He came into me. She plays shrewdly on a double meaning. Though all
she is saying is that he came into the house, or chamber, where she was
alone, the idiom in other contexts can mean to consummate sexual relations.

when he heard me raise my voice and call out, he left his garment by
me and fled and went out." And she laid out his garment by her until   16
his master returned to his house. And she spoke to him things of this   17
sort, saying, "The Hebrew slave came into me, whom you brought us,
to play with me. And so, when I raised my voice and called out, he   18
left his garment by me and fled outside." And it happened, when his   19

(It is the expression that in sexual contexts is rendered in this translation as
"come to bed with.")

15. *when he heard me raise my voice.* We, of course, have been twice informed
that the raising of the voice came after the flight, as a strategy for coping with
it, and not before the flight as its cause.

    he left his garment by me. She substitutes the innocent "by me" for the
narrator's "in her hand." A verbal spotlight is focused on this central eviden-
tiary fact that she alters because of the earlier "left all that he had in Joseph's
hands" (the Hebrew actually uses the singular "hand"), and we are repeatedly
informed that trust was placed in his hand. Now we have a literal leaving of
something in *her* hand, which she changes to by her side.

16. *she laid out his garment by her.* She carefully sets out the evidence for the
frame-up. This is, of course, the second time that Joseph has been stripped
of his garment, and the second time the garment is used as evidence for a
lie.

17. *The Hebrew slave came into me.* Talking to her husband, she refers to
Joseph as "slave," not "man," in order to stress the outrageous presumption
of the slave's alleged assault on his mistress. She avoided the term "slave"
when addressing the household staff because they, too, are slaves. Again,
she uses the ambiguous phrase that momentarily seems to say that Joseph
consummated the sexual act.

    whom you brought us, to play with me. The accusation of her husband in
her words to the people of the house is modulated into a studied ambiguity.
The syntax—there is of course no punctuation in the Hebrew—could be
construed either with a clear pause after "brought us," or as a rebuke, "you
brought us to play with me."

master heard his wife's words which she spoke to him, saying, "Things
20 of this sort your slave has done to me," he became incensed. And
Joseph's master took him and placed him in the prison-house, the
place where the king's prisoners were held.

21 And he was there in the prison-house, and God was with Joseph and
extended kindness to him, and granted him favor in the eyes of the
22 prison-house warden. And the prison-house warden placed in Joseph's
hands all the prisoners who were in the prison-house, and all that they
23 were to do there, it was he who did it. The prison-house warden had
to see to nothing that was in his hands, as the LORD was with him,
and whatever he did, the LORD made succeed.

---

19. *Things of this sort your slave has done to me.* Rashi is no doubt fanciful in
imagining that the first words here are to be explained by the fact that she is
talking to her husband in the midst of lovemaking, but the comment does get
into the spirit of her wifely manipulativeness.

20. *the prison-house.* The reiterated Hebrew term for prison, *beyt sohar,*
occurs only here. It should be noted that the term includes a "house" component which helps establish a link with the opening frame and the tale of
attempted seduction. Joseph, though cast down once more, is again in a
"house" where he will take charge.

    And he was there in the prison-house. The division of the text follows the
proposal of the eighteenth-century Italian Hebrew scholar S. D. Luzatto in
attaching these words to the concluding frame. In this way, the last part of
verse 20 together with verse 21 becomes a perfect mirror image of verse 2.

21.–23. The great rhythm of Joseph's destiny of successful stewardship now
reasserts itself as the language of the introductory frame is echoed here at
the end: "God was with Joseph," "granted him favor in the eyes of," "placed
in Joseph's hands," "all," and, as the summarizing term at the very conclusion
of the narrative unit, "succeed."

CHAPTER 40

And it happened after these things that the cupbearer of the king of Egypt and his baker gave offense to their lord, the king of Egypt. And Pharoah was furious with his two courtiers, the chief cupbearer and the chief baker. And he put them under guard in the house of the high chamberlain, the prison-house, the place where Joseph was held. And the high chamberlain assigned Joseph to them and he ministered to them, and they stayed a good while under guard.

---

4. *And the high chamberlain assigned Joseph to them and he ministered to them.* The source critics take this as a flat contradiction of the end of chapter 39, where Joseph is appointed as general supervisor of the prison, serving as a kind of managing warden. But, in fact, Joseph's "ministering" to the two courtiers need not imply a menial role. These two prisoners had occupied important places in the court, and Pharoah may yet pardon them, so it makes perfect sense that they should be singled out for special treatment in prison, to be attended personally by the warden's right-hand man. There is another seeming discrepancy with the preceding report of Joseph's incarceration: there, the prison was run by a prison warden *(sar beyt hasohar)* whereas here it is governed by the high chamberlain *(sar hatabaḥim),* the title assigned to Potiphar himself at the beginning of chapter 39. But it is easy enough to imagine the high chamberlain as a kind of minister of justice, bureaucratically responsible for the royal prisons, with the warden answering to him.

5   And the two of them dreamed a dream, each his own dream, on a single night, each a dream with its own solution—the cupbearer and

6   the baker to the king of Egypt who were held in the prison-house. And Joseph came to them in the morning and saw them and, look, they

7   were frowning. And he asked Pharaoh's courtiers who were with him under guard in his lord's house, saying, "Why are your faces downcast

8   today?" And they said to him, "We dreamed a dream and there is no one to solve it." And Joseph said to them, "Are not solutions from

9   God? Pray, recount them to me." And the chief cupbearer recounted his dream to Joseph and said to him, "In my dream—and look, a vine

---

5. *solution.* Although a long tradition of translations opts for "interpretation" here, the Hebrew verb *patar* and its cognate noun suggest decipherment (compare the related term *pesher* used in the Dead Sea Scrolls). There is one conclusive decoding for every dream, and a person who is granted insight can break the code.

6. *they were frowning.* The Hebrew *zo'afim* can refer either to a grim mood or to the grim facial expression that it produces. Because both the narrative report in this verse and Joseph's words in the next verse make clear that he sees something is wrong when he looks at their faces, this translation opts for facial expression, against all the previous English versions.

8. *Are not solutions from God?* Joseph in Egyptian captivity remains a good Hebrew monotheist. In Egypt, the interpretation of dreams was regarded as a science, and formal instruction in techniques of dream interpretation was given in schools called "houses of life." Joseph is saying, then, to these two high-ranking Egyptians that no trained hermeneut of the oneiric—no professional *poter*—is required; since God possesses the meanings of dreams, if He chooses, He will simply reveal the meanings to the properly attentive person. But one should note that Joseph immediately proceeds to ask the cupbearer to recount his dream, unhesitantly assuming that he, Joseph, is such a person whom God will favor with insight into the meaning of the dream.

was before me. And on the vine were three tendrils, and as it was   10
budding, its blossom shot up, its clusters ripened to grapes. And Pha-   11
raoh's cup was in my hand. And I took the grapes and crushed them
into Pharaoh's cup and I placed the cup in Pharaoh's palm." And
Joseph said, "This is its solution. The three tendrils are three days.   12
Three days hence Pharaoh will lift up your head and restore you to   13
your place, and you will put Pharaoh's cup in his hand, as you used to
do when you were his cupbearer. But if you remember I was with you   14
once it goes well for you, do me the kindness, pray, to mention me to
Pharaoh and bring me out of this house. For indeed I was stolen from   15

---

10. *and as it was budding, its blossom shot up, its clusters ripened to grapes.* Like
Joseph's pair of dreams, both these dreams are stylized, schematic, and nearly
transparent in regard to meaning. The only item requiring any effort of interpretation is the three tendrils representing three days. (Numbers stand out
in each of the three sets of dreams in the Joseph story—first twelve, here
three, and then seven.) The one manifestly dreamlike element in the cupbearer's dream occurs at this point, when time is speeded up as he looks at
the vine, and in a rapid blur the vine moves from bud to blossom to ripened
grapes to wine.

13. *lift up your head.* As almost any reader of the Hebrew quickly sees, the
biblical idiom, here rendered quite literally, is doubly punned on in the story.
To lift up someone's head, in administrative and royal contexts, means to
single out (as in a census), to invite, to grant favor or extend reconciliation
(as when a monarch lifts up with a gesture the downcast head of a contrite
subject). When Joseph addresses the baker in verse 19, he begins as though
he were using the idiom in the same positive sense as here, but by adding
"from upon you," he turns it into a reference to beheading, the first such
reference in the Bible. In verse 20, when both courtiers are the object of the
idiom, it is used in the neutral sense of "to single out."

the land of the Hebrews, and here, too, I have done nothing that I

16 should have been put in the pit." And the chief baker saw that he had solved well, and he said to Joseph, "I, too, in my dream—and look,

17 there were three openwork baskets on my head, and in the topmost were all sorts of food for Pharaoh, baker's ware, and birds were eating

18 from the basket over my head." And Joseph answered and said, "This

19 is its solution. The three baskets are three days. Three days hence Pharaoh will lift up your head from upon you and impale you on a pole and the birds will eat your flesh from upon you."

20 And it happened on the third day, Pharaoh's birthday, that he made a feast for all his servants, and he lifted up the head of the chief cup-

---

15. *put in the pit.* In the previous verse, Joseph refers to the place of his incarceration as "this house" (invoking elliptically the "house" component of "prison-house"). Now he calls it a pit, perhaps because it is a kind of underground dungeon, but also to make us see the link with the empty cistern into which he was flung by his brothers—twice he has been put in a pit for what he must feel is no good reason.

17. *in the topmost . . . all sorts of food for Pharaoh . . . and birds were eating.* The cupbearer in his dream performs his normal court function, though at fast-forward speed. The baker executes a kind of bizarre parody of his normal function, balancing three baskets of bread one on top of the other. This precarious arrangement may imply, as Amos Funkenstein has proposed to me, a sense that the baker has been negligent in his duties. The pecking of birds at this tower of baked goods is of course an explicitly ominous element. The two dreams parallel Joseph's two dreams in that the first is anchored in an agricultural setting and involves harvesting while the second is oriented toward the sky above. But instead of the glorious celestial bodies, here we have the swooping down of ravenous birds from the sky.

19. *impale.* Despite the fact that the Hebrew verb generally means "to hang," hanging was not a common means of execution anywhere in the ancient Near East, and there is evidence elsewhere that the same verb was used for impalement, which was frequently practiced. The baker's dire fate would seem to be first decapitation and then exposure of the body on a high stake.

bearer and the head of the chief baker in the midst of his servants. And he restored the chief cupbearer to his cupbearing, and he put the cup in Pharaoh's hand; and the chief baker he impaled—just as Joseph had solved it for them. But the chief cupbearer did not remember Joseph, no, he forgot him.

21
22
23

---

23. *did not remember Joseph, no, he forgot him.* The verb for remembering also means "to mention," and Joseph employs both senses of the root in his words to the cupbearer in verse 14. Now, with the emphasis of synonymity (did not remember, forgot), attention is drawn to the cupbearer's failure to respond to the plea of the man who helped him in prison. It will take another pair of dreams—with which the next episode begins—to elicit that mention / remembering. It should also be kept in mind that remembering is central to the larger story of Joseph and his brothers. When he sees them again after more than twenty years of separation, this same crucial verb of memory, *zakhar,* will be invoked for him, and the complicated strategy he adopts for treating his brothers is a device for driving them into a painful process of moral memory.

CHAPTER 41

And it happened at the end of two full years that Pharaoh dreamed,
and, look, he was standing by the Nile. And, look, out of the Nile
came up seven cows, fair to look at and fat in flesh, and they grazed
in the rushes. And, look, another seven cows came up after them out
of the Nile, foul to look at and meager in flesh, and stood by the cows
on the bank of the Nile. And the foul-looking meager-fleshed cows
ate up the seven fair-looking fat cows, and Pharaoh awoke. And he

---

1. *at the end of two full years.* The Hebrew says literally "two years of days."
The expression might simply mean "two years' time," but it is equally plausible, as the King James Version surmised, that the addition of "days" emphasizes that a full period of two years has elapsed before the course of events
compel the chief cupbearer to recall his neglected promise to Joseph.

by the Nile. Given the Nile's importance as the source of Egypt's fertility,
it is appropriate that this dream of plenty and famine should take place on
its banks, a point made as long ago as the thirteenth century in Narbonne by
the Hebrew exegete David Kimhi. As this story set in the pharaonic court
unfolds, its Egyptian local color is brought out by a generous sprinkling of
Egyptian loanwords in the Hebrew narrative: "Nile" (*ye'or*), "soothsayers" (*har-
tumim*), "rushes" (*'ahu*), "ring" (*taba'at*), "fine linen" (*shesh*).

3. *and stood by the cows.* There is a small ominous note in the fact that the
second set of seven cows do not graze in the rushes, as the first seven do,
and as one would expect cows to do. In a moment, they will prove themselves
carnivores.

4. *and Pharaoh awoke.* Although Pharaoh's dreams, like Joseph's, are quite
stylized, the one element of psychological realism is his being shaken out of
sleep by the nightmarish turn of the dream plot.

slept and dreamed a second time, and, look, seven ears of grain came
up on a single stalk, fat and goodly. And, look, seven meager ears,   6
blasted by the east wind, sprouted after them. And the meager ears   7
swallowed the fat and full ears, and Pharaoh awoke, and, look, it was
a dream. And it happened in the morning that his heart pounded, and   8
he sent and called in all the soothsayers of Egypt and all its wise men,
and Pharaoh recounted to them his dreams, but none could solve
them for Pharaoh. And the chief cupbearer spoke to Pharaoh, saying,   9
"My offenses I recall today. Pharaoh had been furious with his servants   10
and he placed me under guard in the house of the high chamberlain—
me and the chief baker. And we dreamed a dream on the same night,   11
he and I, each of us dreamed a dream with its own solution.

---

6. *blasted by the east wind.* The desert lies to the east, and the wind that blows
from there (the *ḥamsin*) is hot and parching.

7. *And the meager ears swallowed the fat and full ears.* The nightmare image
of carnivorous cows is intensified in the second dream by this depiction of
devouring stalks of grain. The imagery of Pharaoh's second dream corresponds to the grain imagery of Joseph's first dream, but an act of depredation
is substituted for the ritual of obeisance.

8. *his heart pounded.* The literal meaning of the Hebrew is "his spirit
pounded."
     none could solve them for Pharaoh. Since it is implausible to imagine that
the soothsayers had no interpretation at all to offer, one must assume that
none could offer a convincing decipherment, as Rashi observes: "they inter-
preted [the dreams] and he was dissatisfied with their interpretation, for they
would say: seven daughters you will beget, seven daughters you will bury."

9. *I recall.* The verb means both to mention and to cause to remember and
so is linked with the theme of remembrance and forgetting that is central
both to this episode and to the larger Joseph story.

12 And there with us was a Hebrew lad, a slave of the high chamberlain, and we recounted to him and he solved our dreams, each of us
13 according to his dream he solved it. And it happened just as he had solved it for us, so it came about—me he restored to my post and him he impaled."

14 And Pharaoh sent and called for Joseph, and they hurried him from the pit, and he shaved and changed his garments and came before
15 Pharaoh. And Pharaoh said to Joseph, "I dreamed a dream and none can solve it, and I have heard about you that you can understand a
16 dream to solve it." And Joseph answered Pharaoh, saying, "Not I! God
17 will answer for Pharaoh's well-being." And Pharaoh spoke to Joseph:
18 "In my dream, here I was standing on the bank of the Nile, and, look, out of the Nile came up seven cows fat in flesh and fair in feature,

---

12. *a slave.* Although the Hebrew *'eved* is the same term the chief cupbearer has just used in the sense of "servant" (and which is used in verses 37 and 38 to refer to Pharaoh's courtiers), it is likely that he invokes it here to highlight Joseph's status as slave.

14. *and he shaved and changed his garments.* It is obvious that an imprisoned slave would have to make himself presentable before appearing in court, but, in keeping with the local color of the story, he does this in a distinctively Egyptian fashion. In the ancient Near East, only the Egyptians were clean-shaven, and the verb used here can equally refer to shaving the head, or close-cropping it, another distinctive Egyptian practice. The putting on of fresh garments is realistically motivated in the same way, but we are probably meant to recall that each of Joseph's descents into a pit was preceded by his being stripped of his garment. When Pharaoh elevates him to viceroy, he will undergo still another change of clothing, from merely presentable dress to aristocratic raiment.

15. *I have heard about you that you can understand a dream.* "Heard" and "understand" are the same verb (*sham'a*), which has both these senses, precisely like the French *entendre*. Though the second clause has often been construed as a kind of hyperbole—you need only hear a dream to reveal its meaning—the straightforward notion of understanding dreams makes better sense.

and they grazed in the rushes. And, look, another seven cows came   19
up after them, gaunt and very foul-featured and meager in flesh, I had
not seen their like in all the land of Egypt for foulness. And the mea-   20
ger, foul cows ate up the first seven fat cows, and they were taken into   21
their bellies and you could not tell that they had come into their bellies, for their looks were as foul as before, and I woke. And I saw in   22
my dream, and, look, seven ears of grain came up on a single stalk,
full and goodly. And, look, seven shriveled, meager ears, blasted by the   23
east wind, sprouted after them. And the meager ears swallowed the   24
seven goodly ears, and I spoke to my soothsayers and none could tell
me the meaning." And Joseph said to Pharaoh, "Pharaoh's dream is   25
one. What God is about to do He has told Pharaoh. The seven goodly   26
cows are seven years, and the seven ears of grain are seven years. The

---

19. *gaunt and very foul-featured and meager in flesh, I had not seen their like in*
all the land of Egypt. In keeping with the biblical convention of near-verbatim
repetition, Pharaoh, in recounting his dreams to Joseph, uses virtually the
same words that the narrator used in first reporting them. The piquant difference, as Meir Sternberg (1985) has noted, is that his language underlines his
own sense of horror at what he has seen in his dream: "foul to look at and
meager in flesh" is elaborated and intensified in Pharaoh's repetition, and he
adds the emphatic exclamation, "I had not seen their like. . . ." (The phrase,
"in all the land of Egypt," will become a verbal motif to indicate the comprehensiveness of the plenty, of the famine, and of the measures that Joseph
adopts.) The comment in verse 21 about the unchanging lean look of the
cows after swallowing their fat predecessors again reflects Pharaoh's horrified
perspective.

    meager in flesh. Here, and again in verses 20 and 27, I read *daqot,* "meager,"
instead of the Masoretic *raqot* ("flat," or perhaps "hollow"). The Hebrew
graphemes for *d* and *r* are similar in form, and several of the ancient versions
reflect *daqot* in these verses.

24. *and none could tell me the meaning.* The Hebrew uses an ellipsis here,
"and none could tell me."

25. *Pharaoh's dream is one.* Joseph, it should be observed, doesn't miss a beat
here. The moment he has heard the dreams, he has everything in hand: the
meaning of all their details, and the explanation for the repetition.

27 dream is one. And the seven meager and foul cows who came up after them are seven years, and the seven meager ears of grain, blasted by
28 the east wind, will be seven years of famine. It is just as I said to
29 Pharaoh: what God is about to do He has shown Pharaoh. Look, seven
30 years are coming of great plenty through all the land of Egypt. And seven years of famine will arise after them and all the plenty will be forgotten in the land of Egypt, and the famine will ravage the land,
31 and you will not be able to tell there was plenty in the land because
32 of that famine afterward, for it will be very grave. And the repeating of the dream to Pharaoh two times, this means that the thing has been
33 fixed by God and God is hastening to do it. And so, let Pharaoh look
34 out for a discerning, wise man and set him over the land of Egypt. Let

---

28. *what God is about to do He has shown Pharaoh.* Although the framework of the Joseph story is "secular" in comparison to the preceding narratives, and though Joseph's exercise of *ḥokhmah* (wisdom) in dream interpretation and economic planning has led scholars to detect a strong imprint of ancient Near Eastern Wisdom literature, he himself is careful to attribute the determination of events as well as his own "wisdom and discernment" to God (compare verse 16). Whatever the considerations of source criticism, moreover, the name he uses for the deity in speaking with Pharaoh is '*elohim*, the term that has general currency among polytheists and monotheists, and not the particularist YHWH.

33. *And so, let Pharaoh look out for a discerning, wise man.* The advice after the interpretation has not been requested. Joseph perhaps runs the risk of seeming presumptuous, but he must have a sense that he has captivated Pharaoh by the persuasive force of his interpretation, and he sees that this is his own great moment of opportunity. One wonders whether Pharaoh's two dreams also make him remember his own two dreams of future grandeur.

Pharaoh do this: appoint overseers for the land and muster the land
of Egypt in the seven years of plenty. And let them collect all the food   35
of these good years that are coming and let them pile up grain under
Pharaoh's hand, food in the cities, to keep under guard. And the food   36
will be a reserve for the land for the seven years of famine which will
be in the land of Egypt, that the land may not perish in the famine."
And the thing seemed good in Pharaoh's eyes and in the eyes of his   37
servants. And Pharaoh said to his servants, "Could we find a man like   38
him, in whom is the spirit of God?" And Pharaoh said to Joseph, "After   39
God has made known to you all this, there is none as discerning and
wise as you. You shall be over my house, and by your lips all my folk   40

---

34. *muster the land of Egypt.* The meaning of the verb ḥimesh is disputed. It
could be derived from *ḥamesh*, "five," and thus refer to a scheme of dividing
the land into fifths or perhaps taking a levy of 20 percent from the crops of
the good years. (In chapter 47, once the great famine is under way, Joseph
institutes a 20 percent tax on the produce of the lands that have been made
over to Pharaoh.) But the same root is also used for the arming or deployment
of troops, and the idea here may be that Joseph is putting the whole country
on a quasimilitary footing in preparation for the extended famine.

35. *under Pharaoh's hand.* Joseph deferentially and diplomatically indicates
that everything will be under Pharaoh's jurisdiction, though it will really be
the "hand"—authority, power, trust—of the "discerning, wise man" that will
run the country.

38. *Could we find a man like him, in whom is the spirit of God?* Pharaoh
produces exactly the response Joseph would have hoped for. Again, the flexibility of 'elohim serves the dialogue well. The Egyptian monarch has not been
turned into a monotheist by Joseph, but he has gone along with Joseph's idea
that human wisdom is a gift of God, or the gods, and the expression he uses
could have the rather general force of "divine spirit."

40. *by your lips all my folk shall be guided.* The Hebrew says literally "by your
mouth." The clear meaning is by your commands, by the directives you issue.
There is some doubt about the verb, *yishaq*. The usual sense of "will kiss" is
extremely unlikely here, unless this is a peculiar idiom for civil obedience not
otherwise attested. It is best to associate it with the noun *mesheq* (15:2),
which appears to refer to economic administration.

41 shall be guided. By the throne alone shall I be greater than you." And
    Pharaoh said to Joseph, "See, I have set you over all the land of Egypt."
42 And Pharaoh took off his ring from his hand and put it on Joseph's
    hand and had him clothed in fine linen clothes and placed the golden
43 collar round his neck. And he had him ride in the chariot of his vice-
    roy, and they called out before him *Abrekh,* setting him over all the
44 land of Egypt. And Pharaoh said to Joseph, "I am Pharaoh! Without

---

41. *And Pharaoh said to Joseph, "See I have set you."* This is a nice deployment
of the convention of a second iteration of the formula for introducing direct
discourse without an intervening response from the interlocutor. Joseph for
the moment has remained silent, uncertain what to say to Pharaoh's astounding proposal, even if eliciting such a proposal may have been his express
intention. So Pharaoh must repeat himself—this time in a performative
speech-act in which he officially confers the high office on Joseph and confirms the act by adorning the Hebrew slave with regal insignia: the signet
ring, the golden collar, and the fine linen dress.

42. *the golden collar.* Although English translators have repeatedly rendered
this as "chain," Egyptian bas-reliefs show a more elaborate ceremonial orna-
ment made out of twisted gold wire that covered part of the shoulders and
upper chest as well as the neck. In fact, the Hebrew word is not the normal
term for "chain," and reflects a root that means "to plait," "to cushion," "to
pad."

43. *Abrekh.* Despite the ingenuity of traditional commentators in construing
this as a Hebrew word, it is evidently Egyptian (in consonance with the loanwords in the surrounding narrative) and may mean something like "make
way." Gerhard von Rad calls attention to this meaning while canvassing other
possibilities and sensibly concluding that the term is not entirely certain.

44. *I am Pharaoh!* Most commentators and translators have construed this as
an implied antithesis: though I am Pharaoh, without you no man shall raise
hand or foot. . . . But this is unnecessary because we know that royal decrees
in the ancient Near East regularly began with the formula: I am King X. The
sense here would thus be: By the authority invested in me as Pharaoh, I
declare that without you, etc.

you no man shall raise hand or foot in all the land of Egypt." And   45
Pharaoh called Joseph's name Zaphenath-paneah, and he gave him
Asenath daughter of Poti-phera, priest of On, as wife, and Joseph went
out over the land of Egypt.

And Joseph was thirty years old when he stood before Pharaoh king   46
of Egypt, and Joseph went out from Pharaoh's presence and passed
through all the land of Egypt. And the land in the seven years of plenty   47
made gatherings. And he collected all the food of the seven years that   48
were in the land of Egypt and he placed food in the cities, the food

---

45. *Zaphenath-paneah*. The change to an Egyptian name is of a piece with
the assumption of Egyptian dress and the insignia of high office. The name
may mean "God speaks, he lives," as Moshe Weinfeld, following the lead of
Egyptologists, surmises.

Poti-phera. This is the full form of the same name born by Joseph's old
master, Potiphar, but evidently refers to a different person, since Potiphar
was identified as courtier and high chamberlain, not as priest. *On* is not a
deity but the name of a city, later designated Heliopolis by the Greeks
because of the sun worship centered there.

Joseph went out over the land. The wording is a little odd. It may be associated with the end of verse 46.

46. *when he stood before Pharaoh*. This could mean, idiomatically, when he
entered Pharaoh's service, though it is equally possible that the verb refers
literally to the scene just reported, when he stood before Pharaoh and made
his way to greatness by interpreting the dreams.

47. *made gatherings*. The Hebrew *qematsim* elsewhere means "handfuls," and
there is scant evidence that it means "abundance," as several modern versions
have it. But *qomets* is a "handful" because it is what the hand gathers in as it
closes, and it is phonetically and semantically cognate with *wayiqbots*, "he
collected," the very next word in the Hebrew text. The likely reference here,
then, is not to small quantities (handfuls) but to the process of systematically
gathering in the grain, as the next sentence spells out.

49   from the fields round each city he placed within it. And Joseph piled
up grain like the sand of the sea, very much, until he ceased counting,
for it was beyond count.

50   And to Joseph two sons were born before the coming of the year of
famine, whom Asenath daughter of Poti-phera priest of On bore him.
51   And Joseph called the name of the firstborn Manasseh, meaning, God
has released me from all the debt of my hardship, and of all my father's
52   house. And the name of the second he called Ephraim, meaning, God
has made me fruitful in the land of my affliction.

53   And the seven years of the plenty that had been in the land of Egypt
54   came to an end. And the seven years of famine began to come, as
Joseph had said, and there was famine in all the lands, but in the land

---

49. *like the sand of the sea, very much, until he ceased counting.* The language
here is strongly reminiscent of the covenantal language in the promise of
progeny to Abraham and thus provides a kind of associative link with the
notice of Joseph's progeny in the next three verses. Upon the birth of
Ephraim, Joseph himself will invoke the verb for making fruitful that is fea-
tured in the repeated promises of offspring to the patriarchs.

51. *Manasseh . . . released me from all the debt.* The naming-pun is on the
verbal stem *n-sh-h*. The virtually universal construal of this term here is
"made me forget," but it must be said that the root in that sense occurs only
five times in the biblical corpus, and at least two or three of those are doubtful. It is also somewhat odd that Joseph should celebrate God for having
made him forget his father's house. But a very common usage of *n-sh-h* is "to
hold in debt," and a natural meaning of that stem in the *pi'el* conjugation, as
here, would be "to relieve from the condition of debt." Such an unambiguously positive verb is a better parallel to "made me fruitful" in the next verse.
I am grateful to Amos Funkenstein for this original suggestion.

52. *Ephraim . . . made me fruitful.* The naming pun is on the verbal stem
p-r-h.

of Egypt there was bread. And all the land of Egypt was hungry and 55
the people cried out to Pharaoh for bread, and Pharaoh said to all of
Egypt, "Go to Joseph. What he says to you, you must do." And the 56
famine was over all the land. And Joseph laid open whatever had grain
within and sold provisions to Egypt. And the famine grew harsh in the
land of Egypt. And all the earth came to Egypt, to Joseph, to get 57
provisions, for the famine had grown harsh in all the earth.

---

55. *all the land of Egypt was hungry.* The contradiction between this report
and the preceding statement that there was bread in Egypt is pointed. There
is food in storage, not to be had from the wasted fields, but Joseph metes it
out to the populace, and at a price.

56. *Joseph laid open whatever had grain within.* The Masoretic Text, which
lacks "whatever had grain," is problematic at this point. The Aramaic Targums
supply these missing words. Other ancient versions presume a phrase like
"stores of grain."

CHAPTER 42

And Jacob saw that there were provisions in Egypt, and Jacob said to
his sons, "Why are you fearful?" And he said, "Look, I have heard that
there are provisions in Egypt. Go down there, and get us provisions

---

1. *fearful.* All English versions construe this as a reflexive of the verb for
seeing (r-ʾ-h) and render it along the lines of "staring at one another." But the
four other occurrences of this root in the reflexive in the Bible invariably link
it with *panim* ("face"), and staring as a gesture of inaction is not characteristically biblical. The Targum of Yonatan derived the verb from the root meaning
"to fear" (y-r-ʾ), a construal feasible without emendation because the *yod* can
be elided. Fearing and the injunction to fear not are recurrent elements in
the story of the brothers' descent to Egypt.

provisions. Most of the biblical occurrences of this noun *shever,* as well as
the transitive verb *shavar* (verse 3, "to buy") and the causative verb *hishbir*
(verse 6) are in this story. The root means "to break," and the sense seems to
be: food provisions that serve to break an imposed fast, that is, a famine
(hence "provisions to stave off the famine," *shever raʿavon,* in verse 19). The
term "rations" adopted by at least three recent translations has a misleading
military connotation.

2. *And he said.* The repetition of the formula introducing speech with no
intervening response from the person or persons addressed accords with the
general biblical convention we have observed elsewhere: such repetition is
an indication of a failure of response by the interlocutors. The brothers here
do not know how to respond to their father's challenge.

from there that we may live and not die." And the ten brothers of   3
Joseph went down to buy grain from Egypt. But Benjamin, Joseph's   4
brother, Jacob did not send with his brothers, for he thought, Lest
harm befall him.

And the sons of Israel came to buy provisions among those who came,   5
for there was famine in the land of Canaan. As for Joseph, he was the   6
regent of the land, he was the provider to all the people of the land.
And Joseph's brothers came and bowed down to him, their faces to
the ground. And Joseph saw his brothers and recognized them, and   7
he played the stranger to them and spoke harshly to them, and said to
them, "Where have you come from?" And they said, "From the land

---

that we may live and not die. The almost excessive spelling out in Jacob's
words may reflect his impatience with his sons, who are acting as though
they did not grasp the urgency of the situation.

3. *the ten brothers.* Biblical narrative is meticulous in its choice of familial
epithets. When the ten go down to Egypt to encounter the man who will
prove to be their supposedly dead brother, they are identified as Joseph's
brothers, not Jacob's sons.

4. *Benjamin, Joseph's brother.* The identification of Benjamin as Joseph's
brother is formally identical to the familial epithet in the previous verse, with
the pointed difference that only Benjamin is Joseph's full brother.

5. *among those who came.* This economical phrase indicates a great crowd of
people, from "all the earth," driven by the famine to Egypt, where there was
food to be bought.

7. *and recognized them, and . . . played the stranger to them.* The verb for "recognize" and the verb for "play the stranger" are derived from the same root
(the latter being a reflexive form of the root). Both uses pick up the thematically prominent repetition of the same root earlier in the story: Jacob was
asked to "recognize" Joseph's blood-soaked tunic and Tamar invited Judah to
"recognize" the tokens he had left with her as security for payment for sexual
services.

8   of Canaan, to buy food." And Joseph recognized his brothers but they
9   did not recognize him. And Joseph remembered the dreams he had
    dreamed about them, and he said to them, "You are spies! To see the
10 land's nakedness you have come." And they said to him, "No, my lord,
11 for your servants have come to buy food. We are all the sons of one
12 man. We are honest. Your servants would never be spies." He said to
13 them, "No! For the land's nakedness you have come to see." And they
    said, "Your twelve servants are brothers, we are the sons of one man

---

8. *And Joseph recognized his brothers but they did not recognize him.* Given the
importance of the recognition theme and the verb to which it is linked, it is
fitting that the fact of Joseph's recognizing his brothers should be repeated,
along with their failure to recognize him (in other words, the success of his
playing the stranger).

9. *And Joseph remembered the dreams.* This brief memory-flashback is a device
rarely used in biblical narrative. Its importance here is that the brothers,
prostrated before Joseph, are unbeknownst to them, literally fulfilling his two
prophetic dreams, the very dreams that enraged them and triggered the violence they perpetrated against him. There is surely an element of sweet triumph for Joseph in seeing his grandiose dreams fulfilled so precisely, though
it would be darkened by his recollection of what the report of his dreams
led his brothers to do. The repetition of Joseph's angry accusation thus has
psychological resonance: he remembers, and he remembers the reason for
his long-standing anger.
    the land's nakedness. The idiom refers to that which should be hidden from
an outsider's eyes, as the pudenda are to be hidden from all but the legitimate
sexual partner. Joseph's language thus casts the alleged spies as *violators* of
the land.

11. *We are all the sons of one man. We are honest. Your servants would never
be spies.* This series of three brief sentences, without connecting "and's," is
uncharacteristic of biblical style, and may well be intended to reflect the
brothers' emphatic, anxious defensiveness in the face of Joseph's wholly
unexpected accusation.

13. *Your twelve servants.* The Hebrew places the number twelve at the very
beginning of the brothers' speech. They use the euphemism "is no more"
(literally, "is not") to indicate that Joseph is dead, not imagining, in the strong
dramatic irony of the scene, that the brother who makes the full complement
of twelve stands before them.

in the land of Canaan, and, look, the youngest is now with our father, and one is no more." And Joseph said to them, "That's just what I told   14
you, you are spies. In this shall you be tested—by Pharaoh! You shall   15
not leave this place unless your youngest brother comes here. Send   16
one of you to bring your brother, and as for the rest of you, you will be detained, and your words will be tested as to whether the truth is with you, and if not, by Pharaoh, you must be spies!" And he put them   17
under guard for three days. And Joseph said to them on the third day,   18
"Do this and live, for I fear God. If you are honest, let one of your   19
brothers be detained in this very guardhouse, and the rest of you go forth and bring back provisions to stave off the famine in your homes. And your youngest brother you shall bring to me, that your words may   20
be confirmed and you need not die." And so they did. And they said   21
each to his brother, "Alas, we are guilty for our brother, whose mortal distress we saw when he pleaded with us and we did not listen. That is why this distress has overtaken us." Then Reuben spoke out to them   22
in these words: "Didn't I say to you, 'Do not sin against the boy,' and

---

15.–16. Joseph's swearing by Pharaoh at first seems merely part of his playing his role as Egyptian. Not until verse 23 do we learn that he is addressing them through an interpreter, so the locution also probably reflects the fact that he is speaking Egyptian.

20. *And your youngest brother you shall bring to me.* The "test" of bringing Benjamin to Egypt is actually a test of fraternal fidelity. Joseph may have some lingering suspicion as to whether the brothers have done away with Benjamin, the other son of Rachel, as they imagine they have gotten rid of him.

21. *Alas, we are guilty.* The psychological success of Joseph's stratagem is confirmed by the fact that the accusation and the hostage-taking immediately trigger feelings of guilt over their behavior toward Joseph. Notably, it is only now, not in the original report, (37:23–24) that we learn that Joseph pleaded with them when they cast him into the pit, a remarkable instance of withheld narrative exposition. Reuben, who tried to save him, now becomes the chief spokesman for their collective guilt.

23   you would not listen? And now, look, his blood is requited." And they did not know that Joseph understood, for there was an interpreter

24   between them. And he turned away from them and wept and returned to them and spoke to them, and he took Simeon from them and placed him in fetters before their eyes.

25   And Joseph gave orders to fill their baggage with grain and to put back their silver into each one's pack and to give them supplies for the way,

26   and so he did for them. And they loaded their provisions on their

27   donkeys and they set out. Then one of them opened his pack to give provender to his donkey at the encampment, and he saw his silver

28   and, look, it was in the mouth of his bag. And he said to his brothers, "My silver has been put back and, look, it's actually in my bag." And

---

23. *And they did not know that Joseph understood.* The verb for understanding, which also means to hear or listen, plays ironically against its use in the immediately preceding verse, "and you would not *listen*."

24. *And he turned away from them and wept.* This is the first of three times, in a clear crescendo pattern, that Joseph is moved to tears by his brothers.

25. *to put back their silver into each one's pack.* The return of the silver is also associated with the brothers' guilt, for it repeats their receiving of silver from the Ishmaelites for the sale of Joseph as a slave. If the story reflects the realia of the Patriarchal period, the silver would be weights of silver, not coins, and the weighing out of silver in Abraham's purchase of the burial site from the Hittites suggests that is what is to be imagined here.

28. *My silver has been put back and, look, it's actually in my bag.* These words of astonishment, with their virtual redundance and their locutions of emphasis—*wegam hineh be'amtaḥti,* "it's actually in my bag"—ironically correspond to the language of amazement used by the young Joseph in reporting his dream (compare 37:7).

they were dumbfounded and trembled each before his brother, saying, "What is this that God has done to us?" And they came to Jacob their 29 father, to the land of Canaan, and they told him all that had befallen them, saying, "The man who is lord of the land spoke harshly to us 30 and made us out to be spies in the land. And we said to him, 'We are 31 honest. We would never be spies. Twelve brothers we are, the sons of 32 our father. One is no more and the youngest is now with our father in the land of Canaan.' And the man who is lord of the land said to us, 33 'By this shall I know if you are honest: one of your brothers leave with me and provisions against the famine in your homes take, and go. And 34 bring your youngest brother to me that I may know you are not spies but are honest. I shall give you back your brother and you can trade in the land.'" And just as they were emptying their packs, look, each 35

---

dumbfounded. The Hebrew says literally. "their heart went out."

What is this that God has done to us? This is a kind of double dramatic irony. It is of course Joseph who has done this to them, but we are also invited to think of him as God's instrument—an idea he himself will emphasize after he reveals himself to his brothers. Thus a double system of causation, human and divine, is brought to the fore.

31.–34. The near-verbatim repetition of reported speech, as we have seen elsewhere, is standard biblical practice, though more commonly there are subtly significant variations in the repetition. Here, the one notable change is that in addressing Jacob directly, they substitute "our father" for "one man."

33. *provisions against the famine.* The Hebrew here uses an ellipsis, simply, "famine."

34. *trade.* The primary meaning of the verb is "to go around," and by extension, "to engage in commerce." Given the situation of going back and forth to Egypt to buy grain, the sense of trading seems more likely here.

35. *look, each one's bundle of silver was in his bag.* The second discovery of the silver in the baggage of course contradicts the first discovery at the encampment and probably reflects the splicing together of two variant traditions—unless one assumes that the brothers deliberately act out a discovery in the presence of their father in order to impress upon him how they are all at the mercy of a superior power.

one's bundle of silver was in his pack. And they saw their bundles,
36 both they and their father, and were afraid. And Jacob their father said
to them, "Me you have bereaved. Joseph is no more and Simeon is no
37 more, and Benjamin you would take! It is I who bear it all." And
Reuben spoke to his father, saying, "My two sons you may put to death
if I do not bring him back to you. Place him in my hands and I will

---

36. *Me you have bereaved.* As earlier in the story, Jacob speaks as a prima
donna of paternal grief: hence the "me" at the beginning of his discourse (the
Hebrew has an accusative pronoun before the verb instead of the normal
accusative suffix appended to the verb), and hence the emphatic rhythmic
arrangement of his speech in a formal symmetry that verges on poetry:
"Joseph is no more and Simeon is no more, and Benjamin you would take!"
In a small envelope structure, the "me" at the beginning is balanced by the
"It is I" at the end (the last sentence is literally: "Upon me they all were.").
Jacob's equation of Joseph and Simeon with the verb "is no more" teeters
ambiguously between two possibilities: either he gloomily assumes that
Simeon is already as good as dead, or, despite his protestations of grief, he
clings to the hope that Joseph, like Simeon, is absent, not dead.

37. *My two sons you may put to death.* Reuben, as usual, means well but
stumbles in the execution: to a father obsessed with the loss of sons, he offers
the prospect of killing two grandsons. Kimhi catches this nicely: "[Jacob]
said: 'Stupid firstborn! Are they your sons and not my sons?' " This is not the
only moment in the story when we sense that Reuben's claim to preeminence
among the brothers as firstborn is dubious, and he will be displaced by Judah,
the fourth-born.

return him to you." And he said, "My son shall not go down with you,   38
for his brother is dead, and he alone remains, and should harm befall
him on the way you are going, you would bring down my gray head in
sorrow to Sheol."

---

38. *My son shall not go down with you.* The extravagant insensitivity of Jacob's
paternal favoritism continues to be breathtaking. He speaks of Benjamin as
"my son" almost as though the ones he is addressing were not his sons. This
unconscious disavowal of the ten sons is sharpened when Jacob says, "he
alone remains," failing to add "from his mother." The histrionic refrain of
descending in sorrow to Sheol, the underworld, is one Jacob first recited
when he was handed Joseph's blood-soaked tunic. "Should harm befall him"
is a formula first spoken by Jacob in an interior monologue (verse 4) and now
repeated in actual speech to the sons. Jacob is of course fearful of another
dreadful accident like the one in which he believes Joseph was torn to pieces
by a wild beast. There is, then, an ironic disparity between Jacob's sense of a
world of unpredictable dangers threatening his beloved son and Joseph's
providential manipulation of events, unguessed by his father and his brothers.

CHAPTER 43

^{1,2} And the famine grew grave in the land. And it happened when they had eaten up the provisions they had brought from Egypt, that their father ³ said to them, "Go back, buy us some food." And Judah said to him, saying, "The man firmly warned us, saying, 'You shall not see my face ⁴ unless your brother is with you.' If you are going to send our brother ⁵ with us, we may go down and buy you food, but if you are not going to send him, we will not go down, for the man said to us, 'You shall ⁶ not see my face unless your brother is with you.'" And Israel said, "Why have you done me this harm to tell the man you had another ⁷ brother?" And they said, "The man firmly asked us about ourselves

---

3. *The man firmly warned us.* "The man" refers elliptically to the phrase the brothers previously used in their report to their father, "the man who is lord of the land" (42:30). Their repeated use of this designation aptly dramatizes their ignorance of Joseph's identity. In the second half of this chapter, there is pointed interplay between the references to the brothers as "the men"— almost as though they were represented from an Egyptian point of view— and to Joseph's majordomo as "the man."

You shall not see my face. The Hebrew idiom has distinct regal overtones: you shall not come into my presence.

5. *You shall not see my face unless your brother is with you.* Judah reiterates this sentence word for word, at the end of his first speech to Jacob as at the beginning. The effect is to spell out the inexorable condition with heavy emphasis for the reluctant Jacob: it is only by bringing Benjamin along that we can return to Egypt.

6. *Why have you done me this harm.* Consistent with his character from chapter 37 onward, Jacob flaunts his sense of personal injury.

and our kindred, saying, 'Is your father still living? Do you have a
brother?' And we told him, in response to these words. Could we know
he would say, 'Bring down your brother?'" And Judah said to Israel his   8
father, "Send the lad with me, and let us rise and go, that we may live
and not die, neither we, nor you, nor our little ones. I will be his   9
pledge, from my hand you may seek him: if I do not bring him to you
and set him before you, I will bear the blame to you for all time. For   10
had we not tarried, by now we could have come back twice." And   11
Israel their father said to them, "If it must be so, do this: take of the
best yield of the land in your baggage and bring down to the man as
tribute, some balm and some honey, gum and ladanum, pistachio nuts

---

8. *that we may live and not die, neither we, nor you, nor our little ones.* The
phrase "live and not die" was used by Jacob to his sons before their first
journey to Egypt (42:2), and Judah now throws it back in his face. By adding
to it, "neither we, nor you, nor our little ones," Judah makes a vividly persuasive point: as Rashi sees, the implicit argument is that if we risk taking Benjamin, he may or may not be seized, but if we stay here, every one of us will
perish from hunger.

9. *I will be his pledge, from my hand you may seek him.* The repetition through
synonymity signals a performative speech-act, a legally binding vow. Judah,
who conceived the scheme of selling Joseph into slavery, now takes personal
responsibility for Benjamin's safety. But befitting the son who will displace
Reuben as the progenitor of the kings of Israel, he asserts solemn responsibility without Reuben's rash offer to put two of his own sons to death if harm
befalls Benjamin.

11. *the best yield of the land.* The Hebrew *zimrat ha'arets* occurs only here.
The most plausible construal of the first term links it with a root that means
"strength" or "power," though it could be related to *zemorah,* "branch" or
"sprout."
    some balm and some honey, gum and ladanum. The tribute or gift (*minḥah*)
to Joseph includes three of the same items as those in the briefer list of
luxury export goods carried by the Ishmaelite traders (37:25) who bought
Joseph from the brothers and sold him as a slave in Egypt. As with the silver
sent back and forth, the brothers are thus drawn unwittingly into a process
of repetition of and restitution for their fraternal crime.

12 and almonds. And double the silver take in your hand, and the silver
that was put back in the mouths of your bags bring back in your hand.
13 Perhaps it was a mistake. And your brother take, and rise and go back
14 to the man. And may El Shaddai grant you mercy before the man, that
he discharge to you your other brother, and Benjamin. As for me, if I
must be bereaved, I will be bereaved."

---

12. *and double the silver take.* Now they are to go to Egypt with three times
the original amount of silver: the amount they intend to return to Joseph, and
double that amount besides. Nahum Sarna construes the second clause, "and
the silver that was put back . . . ," as an explanation of the first, concluding
that only double the amount in sum was taken, but his reading dismisses the
clear additive sense of "and" in "and the silver." Rashi, with characteristic
shrewdness, suggests that extra silver was taken because the brothers were
fearful that the price of grain might have gone up steeply—a plausible possibility, given Egypt's monopoly of food supplies and the persisting famine.

take in your hand. The addition of "in your hand," which is not strictly
required by Hebrew idiom, is repeated several times in the story. One suspects it is linked with the theme of restitution: the very hands that were
"raised against" Joseph (37:22 and 27) now bear tribute to him.

13. *And your brother take.* Jacob holds back the detail that is most painful to
him, the sending down of Benjamin, until the very end of his instructions.
Pointedly, he does not refer to Benjamin by name but instead calls him "your
brother," stressing the fraternal responsibility his nine older sons have for
their half brother.

14. *he discharge to you your other brother, and Benjamin.* Jacob's fearful formulation virtually presupposes that Benjamin will be seized by the Egyptians,
just as Simeon was.

as for me, if I must be bereaved, I will be bereaved. Jacob is of course remembering his grief over the loss of Joseph and perhaps as well his concern over
Simeon's imprisonment. But he is also once more playing his role as histrion
of paternal sorrow, echoing his dirgelike words to his sons (42:36), "Me you
have bereaved," using the same verb that refers specifically in Hebrew to the
loss of children and again placing the first-person singular pronoun at the
beginning of his statement.

And the men took this tribute and double the silver they took in their   15
hand, and Benjamin, and they rose and went down to Egypt and stood
in Joseph's presence. And Joseph saw Benjamin with them and he   16
said to the one who was over his house, "Bring the men into the house,
and slaughter an animal and prepare it, for with me the men shall eat
at noon." And the man did as Joseph had said, and the man brought   17
the men to Joseph's house. And the men were afraid at being brought   18

---

16. *the one who was over his house.* Virtually all the English versions represent
this as "steward," but the Hebrew opts for this more circumlocutionary
phrase (which does occur, in a clear administrative sense, in notices about
the later Israelite royal bureaucracy) instead of one of the available biblical
terms for steward or majordomo. This roundabout designation reflects an
Egyptian title and may at the same time intimate the perspective of the
Hebrew brothers toward this Egyptian "man who was over the house" with
whom they have to deal. It also enables the writer to play "man" against "men"
in his narrative report.

17. *Joseph's house.* The phrase is repeated three times in rapid sequence, and
amplified by the secondary references to "the man who was over his house."
For the ten Hebrew men to go into Joseph's house is a momentous thing,
politically and thematically. Since they are aware that it is not customary for
foreigners who have come to buy grain to be introduced into the residence
of the viceroy, they are afraid it may be a trap (verse 18). Their last encounter
with Joseph in Canaan, more than two decades earlier, was in an open field,
where he was entirely in their power. Now, crossing the threshold of his
house, they will be entirely in his power—whether for evil or for good they
cannot say. Pointedly, their actual sitting down at Joseph's table is prefaced
by a literally liminal moment: they stand at the entrance, expressing their
anxiety to Joseph's steward.

to Joseph's house, and they said, "Because of the silver put back in
our bags the first time we've been brought, in order to fall upon us, to
19   attack us, and to take us as slaves, and our donkeys." And they
approached the man who was over Joseph's house, and they spoke to
20   him by the entrance of the house. And they said, "Please, my lord, we
21   indeed came down the first time to buy food, and it happened when
we came to the encampment that we opened our bags and, look, each
man's silver was in the mouth of his bag, our silver in full weight, and
22   we have brought it back in our hand, and we have brought down more
silver to buy food. We do not know who put our silver in our bags."
23   And he said, "All is well with you, do not fear. Your God and the God
of your father has placed treasure for you in your bags. Your silver has
24   come to me." And he brought Simeon out to them. And the man
brought the men into Joseph's house, and he gave them water and
25   they bathed their feet, and he gave provender to their donkeys. And
they prepared the tribute against Joseph's arrival at noon, for they had
26   heard that there they would eat bread. And Joseph came into the
house, and they brought him the tribute that was in their hand, into
27   the house, and they bowed down to him to the ground. And he asked
how they were, and he said, "Is all well with your aged father of whom

---

18. *to fall upon us.* The Hebrew verb might well have the sense of "to find a
pretext against us," as many English versions render it, but it is at least as
plausible to construe it as a verb of physical assault, in apposition to the term
that follows it.

 and our donkeys. This odd addendum at the very end of the sentence looks
suspiciously like a comic inadvertency.

23. *has placed treasure for you in your bags.* The majordomo dismisses their
fears by introducing a kind of fairytale explanation for the silver they found
in their bags.

 Your silver has come to me. These words take the form of a legal declaration
meaning "I have duly received payment."

25. *they would eat bread.* "Bread," as in the English expression, "to eat the
king's bread," is obviously a synecdoche for food, but it diminishes the literary
dignity of the narrative to render this, as many modern translations have
done, simply as "dine."

you spoke? Is he still alive?" And they said, "All is well with your   28
servant, our father. He is still alive." And they did obeisance and
bowed down. And he raised his eyes and saw Benjamin his brother,   29
his mother's son, and he said, "Is this your youngest brother of whom
you spoke to me?" And he said, "God be gracious to you, my son." And   30
Joseph hurried out, for his feelings for his brother overwhelmed him
and he wanted to weep, and he went into the chamber and wept there.
And he bathed his face and came out and held himself in check and   31
said, "Serve bread." And they served him and them separately and the   32

---

29. *God be gracious to you, my son.* Benjamin, though considerably younger
than Joseph, would be at least in his late twenties at this point. In addressing
him as "my son," Joseph faithfully maintains his role as Egyptian viceroy,
though "my brother" is hiding in the word he uses. The great medieval
Hebrew poet Shmuel Hanagid (eleventh-century Granada) would brilliantly
catch this doubleness in a moving elegy to his brother by altering the end of
the phrase: "God be gracious to you, my brother."

30. *And Joseph hurried out . . . and he wanted to weep, and he went into the
chamber and wept there.* In the pattern of incremental repetition, this second
weeping of Joseph's is much more elaborately reported than the first (42:24),
including as it does the flight to a private chamber and (in the next verse),
his bathing his face to remove evidence of the tears and his effort of self-
restraint when he returns to the brothers.

   his feelings . . . overwhelmed him. The literal meaning of the Hebrew is
"his mercy [the same term used by Jacob in verse 14] burned hot."

Egyptians that were eating with him separately, for the Egyptians
would not eat bread with the Hebrews, as it was abhorrent to Egypt.
33 And they were seated before him, the firstborn according to his birthright, the youngest according to his youth, and the men marvelled to
34 each other. And he had portions passed to them from before him, and
Benjamin's portion was five times more than the portion of all the rest,
and they drank, and they got drunk with him.

---

32. *for the Egyptians would not eat bread with the Hebrews.* The dietary exclu-
sionism of the Egyptians is also attested by Herodotus. Both medieval and
modern commentators have linked this taboo with an Egyptian prohibition
against eating lamb, a staple of Hebrew diet.

as it was abhorrent to Egypt. The consensus of English translations treats
this as "to the Egyptians," but the Masoretic vocalization of the final noun—
mitsrayim and not *mitsrim*—construes it as "to Egypt," which makes perfectly
good sense.

33. *And they were seated before him.* The seating in order of age of course has
been done at Joseph's direction: it constitutes a kind of dramatization of the
contrast between knowledge and ignorance—"and he recognized them but
they did not recognize him"—that has been paramount from the moment the
brothers first set foot in Egypt.

34. *they drank, and they got drunk with him.* In the Hebrew, these are two
entirely distinct verbs. The meeting between the eleven brothers and the man
who is lord of the land of Egypt appears to end on a note of conviviality,
which will quickly be reversed in the next scene of the drama Joseph has
carefully devised for his brothers. It should be noted that the drinking at the
conclusion of this scene anticipates the mechanism of what is to follow, for
it is the alleged theft of Joseph's silver goblet that will bring the brothers back
to his house under strict arrest.

CHAPTER 44

And he commanded the one who was over his house, saying, "Fill the   1
men's bags with as much food as they can carry, and put each man's
silver in the mouth of his bag. And my goblet, the silver goblet, put in   2
the mouth of the bag of the youngest, with the silver for his provis-

---

1. *put each man's silver in the mouth of his bag.* This detail is a small puzzle
because nothing is made of the discovery of silver when the majordomo
searches through the bags. This seeming indiscrepancy has led critics to write
off the return of the silver as a later addition made to harmonize this episode
with the one in chapter 42, but that is by no means a necessary conclusion.
Joseph's scheme, after all, is to make the brothers feel they are trapped in a
network of uncanny circumstances they can neither control nor explain. A
repetition of the device of returning the silver would nicely serve this purpose. The majordomo, however, is exclusively focused on the retrieval of a
particular silver object, the divining goblet, and so does not even deign to
mention the weights of silver in the bags, as though their appearance there
were a matter of course, whatever consternation it might cause the brothers.
Meanwhile, as in dream logic—or perhaps one should say, guilt logic—the
brothers, who once took silver when they sold Joseph down into Egypt, seem
helpless to "return" the silver to Egypt, as much as they try. The returned
silver, moreover, makes the purported stealing of the silver goblet look all the
more heinous.

2. *And my goblet, the silver goblet.* The double formulation highlights both the
fact that the goblet is Joseph's special possession and that it is made of silver.

3 ions." And he did as Joseph had spoken. The morning had just bright-
4 ened when the men were sent off, they and their donkeys. They had
come out of the city, they were not far off, when Joseph said to the
one who was over his house, "Rise, pursue the men, and when you
5 overtake them, say to them, 'Why have you paid back evil for good? Is
not this the one from which my lord drinks, and in which he always
6 divines? You have wrought evil in what you did.'" And he overtook
7 them and spoke to them these words. And they said to him, "Why
should our lord speak words like these? Far be it from your servants
8 to do such a thing! Why, the silver we found in the mouth of our bags
we brought back to you from the land of Canaan. How then could we

---

3. *they and their donkeys.* Again the donkeys are tacked onto the end of the
sentence, perhaps because the donkeys are carrying the packs, which will
have to be set down on the ground and then reloaded (verses 11 and 12), in
which the goblet has been secreted.

5. *Is not this the one from which my lord drinks, and in which he always divines.*
The fact that the goblet is referred to only by a demonstrative pronoun ("the
one from which") may reflect a flaunting of the assumption that, as all concerned should recognize, the only thing at issue here is the goblet. The brothers may well have seen Joseph drinking from the goblet at the dinner the day
before, whereas its use for divination would have been news to them. The
probable mechanism of divination in a goblet would be to interpret patterns
on the surface of the liquid it contained or in drops running down its sides.
Divination would have been a plausible activity on the part of a member of
the high Egyptian bureaucracy, with its technology of soothsaying, but the
emphasis it is given here is also linked with Joseph's demonstrated ability to
predict the future and his superiority of knowledge in relation to his brothers.

steal from your master's house silver or gold? He of your servants with   9
whom it be found shall die, and, what's more, we shall become slaves
to our lord." And he said, "Even so, as by your words, let it be: he with   10
whom it be found shall become a slave to me, and you shall be clear."
And they hurried and each man set down his bag on the ground and   11
each opened his bag. And he searched, beginning with the oldest and   12
ending with the youngest, and he found the goblet in Benjamin's bag.
And they rent their garments, and each loaded his donkey and they   13
returned to the city.

---

9. *He of your servants with whom it be found shall die.* This pronouncement of
a death sentence for stealing may be excessive in relation to the standards of
ancient Near Eastern law, though Gerhard von Rad has proposed that stealing a sacred object would have been deemed a capital crime. The brothers'
words are quite similar to those spoken by their father to Laban (31:32) before
he rummaged through the belongings of Jacob's wives in search of his missing
household gods. It is a teasing parallel with crucial differences: Laban does
not find what he is looking for, but the death sentence pronounced on the
actually guilty party—Benjamin's mother, Rachel—appears to be carried out
later when she dies bearing him.

    and . . . we shall become slaves to our lord. This gratuitous additional condi-
tion, a reflex of their perfect confidence in their innocence of the theft, carries forward the great theme of moral restitution: the brothers who sold
Joseph into slavery now offer themselves as slaves. The term *'eved* means
both servant and slave, and the speeches in this episode pointedly play the
two meanings against each other. When the brothers refer to themselves as
"your servants," they are clearly using courtly language of self-abasement;
when they, or Judah, offer to be slaves, they are proposing to surrender their
freedom and enter into a condition of actual servitude.

10. *Even so, as by your words, let it be.* These first words of response by the
majordomo may constitute a kind of bureaucratic, or legal, flourish. He
begins by seeming to concur in the stern sentence the brothers have pronounced on themselves should the goblet be found among them; but, having
accepted the principle they enunciated that the guilty party should be pun-
ished and a distinction made between him and his brothers, the majordomo
modifies the sentence to make it more reasonable—the guilty brother will be
made a slave and the others allowed to go free.

14 And Judah with his brothers came into Joseph's house, for he was still
15 there, and they threw themselves before him to the ground. And
Joseph said to them, "What is this deed you have done? Did you not
16 know that a man like me would surely divine?" And Judah said, "What
shall we say to my lord? What shall we speak and how shall we prove
ourselves right? God has found out your servants' crime. Here we are,

---

14. *And Judah with his brothers came.* The Hebrew says, "Judah and his brothers" but uses a characteristic grammatical device, a verb conjugated in the
singular instead of the plural, to indicate that the first-stated noun (Judah) is
the principal agent, the thematically focused subject of the verb. In a
moment, Judah will step forward and become the spokesman for all the
brothers, the ringing voice of their collective conscience.

15. *Did you not know that a man like me would surely divine?* Like much else
in this story, Joseph's words are contrived to yield a double meaning. He is
saying they should have known that a person of his standing would practice
divination and so the goblet they purloined was no mere silver cup but a
dedicated instrument of divination. But, in keeping with the sustained theme
of his knowledge and his brothers' ignorance, he is also suggesting that a man
of his powers would be able to divine such a theft, and its perpetrator.

16. *God has found out your servants' crime.* In this case, the double meaning
expresses a buried psychological dimension in Judah's plea to Joseph. On the
surface, he is simply conceding guilt as his only recourse because one of his
brothers had been caught with the evidence and he has no counterarguments
to offer. But he speaks out of the consciousness of a real guilt incurred by
him and his brothers more than two decades earlier—compare their response
at their first detention, 42:21—and thus expresses a real sense that God has
at last exacted retribution for that act of fraternal betrayal. He of course
cannot guess that the man whom he is addressing perfectly understands both
references. One should note that guilt is assumed by Judah in the first-person
plural and is not restricted to "the one in whose hand the goblet was found."

slaves to my lord, both we and the one in whose hand the goblet was
found." And he said, "Far be it from me to do this! The man in whose   17
hand the goblet was found, he shall become my slave, and you, go up
in peace to your father." And Judah approached him and said, "Please,   18
my lord, let your servant speak a word in my lord's hearing and let your
wrath not kindle against your servant, for you are like Pharaoh. My   19
lord had asked his servants, saying, 'Do you have a father or brother?'
And we said to my lord, 'We have an aged father and a young child of   20
his old age, and his brother being dead, he alone is left of his mother,
and his father loves him.' And you said to your servants, 'Bring him   21

Here we are, slaves to my lord. Again, an unconscious principle of retribution asserts itself: the ten who condemned Joseph to slavery offer themselves
as slaves to him, together with Benjamin.

in whose hand the goblet was found. In fact, it was found in the mouth of
his bag. But the reiterated image of the hand holding the goblet links up with
all the previous focusing on hands in the story and stresses the idea of agency
and responsibility.

17. *he shall become my slave.* This is, of course, the last turn of the screw in
Joseph's testing of his brothers: will they allow Rachel's other son to be
enslaved, as they did with her elder son?

20. *an aged father and a young child of his old age.* The phrase suggests the
intimate connection between father and child ("aged," "old age") as well as
Benjamin's vulnerability as youngest (the Hebrew for "young" also means
"little").

his brother being dead, he alone is left of his mother, and his father loves him.
Judah either assumes that after more than twenty years of slavery in a foreign
land Joseph is likely to be dead or he states Joseph's absence as death for the
sake of rhetorical simplicity, to make clear that the son is irrevocably lost to
his doting father. What is remarkable is that now Judah can bring himself,
out of concern for his old father, to accept the painful fact of paternal favoritism ("and his father loves him") that was the root of the brothers' hostility to
Joseph.

22 down to me, that I may set my eyes on him.' And we said to my lord,
'The lad cannot leave his father. Should he leave his father, he would
23 die.' And you said to your servants, 'If your youngest brother does not
24 come down with you, you shall not see my face again.' And it happened when we went up to your servant, my father, that we told him
25 the words of my lord. And our father said, 'Go back, buy us some
26 food.' And we said, 'We cannot go down. If our youngest brother is
with us, we shall go down. For we cannot see the face of the man if
27 our youngest brother is not with us.' And your servant, our father, said
28 to us, 'You know that two did my wife bear me. And one went out

---

21. *that I may set my eyes on him.* This phrase, which in other contexts can
mean something like showing royal favor toward someone, and which for
Joseph has the personal meaning of wanting to behold his full brother,
momentarily seems to have been given a sinister twist by the course of events.

22. *The lad cannot leave his father.* Although Benjamin is considerably beyond
adolescence, "lad" (*na'ar*), as in a number of other notable occurrences, is a
designation that suggests tenderness, and perhaps the vulnerability of the
person so designated, and Judah also uses it here because Benjamin is the
youngest. Joseph, it should be noted, had coldly referred to the purportedly
guilty Benjamin as "the man" (verse 17).

    Should he leave his father, he would die. The translation reflects the ambi-
guity of the Hebrew, and one may be skeptical of the often-made claim that
the second "he" must refer to Jacob. It seems more likely that this is a studied
ambiguity on Judah's part: he leaves it to Joseph to decide whether the old
man would die if he were separated from Benjamin, or whether Benjamin
could not survive without his father, or whether both dire possibilities might
be probable.

25. *Go back, buy us some food.* Judah quotes Jacob's words to his sons (43:2)
verbatim. The report of their response in the next verse is a more approximate
quotation.

27. *two did my wife bear me.* In Judah's report, Jacob speaks characteristically
as though Rachel were his only wife. Judah appears now to accept this outrageous favoritism as part of what his father is, part of the father he must still
love.

from me and I thought, O, he's been torn to shreds, and I have not
seen him since. And should you take this one, too, from my presence   29
and harm befall him, you would bring down my gray head in evil to
Sheol.' And so, should I come to your servant, my father, and the lad   30
be not with us, for his life is bound to the lad's, when he saw the lad   31
was not with us, he would die, and your servants would bring down
the gray head of your servant, our father, in sorrow to Sheol. For your   32
servant became pledge for the lad to my father, saying, 'If I do not
bring him to you, I will bear the blame to my father for all time.' And   33
so, let your servant, pray, stay instead of the lad as a slave to my lord,
and let the lad go up with his brothers. For how shall I go up to my   34
father, if the lad be not with us? Let me see not the evil that would
find out my father!"

---

28. *he's been torn to shreds, and I have not seen him since.* In the first clause,
Jacob is represented as quoting verbatim his actual response to Joseph's sup-
posed death, yet the second clause has the look of clinging to the hope that
Joseph has merely disappeared but has not been killed.

31. *when he saw the lad was not with us.* The Masoretic Text lacks "with us,"
though it is reflected in the Septuagint and in one version of the Samaritan
Bible.

32. *For your servant became pledge.* Judah then proceeds to quote the actual
formula of his pledge of surety to Jacob. As many commentators have noted,
his invocation of his pledge is a way of explaining why he should have put
himself forward as spokesman for the brothers.

33. *let your servant, pray, stay instead of the lad as a slave.* Judah, who conceived the plan of selling Joseph into slavery, now comes around 180 degrees
by offering himself as a slave in place of Benjamin.

34. *Let me see not the evil that would find out my father.* This of course stands
in stark contrast to his willingness years before to watch his father writhe in
anguish over Joseph's supposed death. The entire speech, as these concluding words suggest, is at once a moving piece of rhetoric and the expression
of a profound inner change. Joseph's "testing" of his brothers is thus also
a process that induces the recognition of guilt and leads to psychological
transformation.

CHAPTER 45

¹ And Joseph could no longer hold himself in check before all who stood attendance upon him, and he cried, "Clear out everyone around me!" And no man stood with him when Joseph made himself known to his ² brothers. And he wept aloud and the Egyptians heard and the house ³ of Pharaoh heard. And Joseph said to his brothers, "I am Joseph. Is my father still alive?" But his brothers could not answer him, for they

---

2. *And he wept aloud.* The Hebrew says literally, "and he gave his voice in weeping." This is the third, climactic weeping of Joseph: now he no longer turns aside to weep in secret but sobs uncontrollably in the presence of his brothers, so audibly that he is heard by the Egyptians outside and heard all the way to the palace of Pharaoh. As in English, "house" may refer either to the physical structure or to the people associated with it.

3. *I am Joseph. Is my father still alive?* His very first utterance, after his sobs have subsided, is the essential revelation of identity, a two-word (in the Hebrew) bombshell tossed at his brothers. He follows this by asking whether his father is alive, as though he could not altogether trust the assurances they had given him about this when he questioned them in his guise of Egyptian viceroy. His repeated reference to "my father" serves double duty: the first-person singular possessive expresses his sense of personal connection with old Jacob (he is, after all, *my* father, he is saying to his brothers); but it is also idiomatic usage for the familiar "Father" in biblical Hebrew (rather like 'abba in Aramaic and later Hebrew).

were dismayed before him. And Joseph said to his brothers, "Come   4
close to me, pray," and they came close, and he said, "I am Joseph
your brother whom you sold into Egypt. And now, do not be pained   5
and do not be incensed with yourselves that you sold me down here,
because for sustenance God has sent me before you. Two years now   6
there has been famine in the heart of the land, and there are yet five
years without plowing and harvest. And God has sent me before you   7
to make you a remnant on earth and to preserve life, for you to be a

---

4. *And Joseph said to his brothers, "Come close to me, pray."* The purblindness
to which a mechanical focus on source criticism can lead is nowhere more
vividly illustrated than in the contention of some critics that this verse
reflects a different source from the preceding verse because it is a "doublet"
of it. What should be obvious is that this repeated speech is a brilliant realization of the dramatic moment. When Joseph first reveals himself to his brothers, they are, quite understandably, "dismayed." And so he must speak again,
first asking them to draw close. (The proposal of the Midrash Bereishit Rabba
that he invites them to come close in order to show them that he is circumcised is of course fanciful, but the closing of physical space does reflect his
sense that he must somehow bridge the enormous distance he has main-
tained between himself and them in his Egyptian persona.)

I am Joseph your brother whom you sold into Egypt. The qualifying clause
Joseph now adds to his initial "I am Joseph" is surely a heart-stopper for the
brothers, and could be construed as the last—inadvertent?—gesture of his
test of them. Their most dire imaginings of retribution could easily follow
from these words, but instead, Joseph immediately proceeds in the next sentence to reassure them.

5. *do not be incensed with yourselves.* The literal Hebrew wording is "let it not
be incensed in your eyes."

for sustenance God has sent me before you. Joseph's speech is a luminous
illustration of the Bible's double system of causation, human and divine.
Commentators have tended to tilt the balance to one side, making Joseph a
mouthpiece of piety here. His recognition of a providential plan may well be
admirable from the viewpoint of monotheistic faith, but there is no reason to
assume that Joseph has lost the sense of his own brilliant initiative in all that
he has accomplished, and so when he says "God" (*'elohim,* which could also
suggest something more general like "providence" or "fate"), he also means
Joseph. "Before you" is the first intimation that he intends the whole clan to
come down to Egypt after him.

8   great surviving group. And so, it is not you who sent me here but God,
     and he has made me father to Pharaoh and lord to all his house and
9   ruler over all the land of Egypt. Hurry and go up to my father and say
     to him, 'Thus says your son Joseph: God has made me lord to all
10   Egypt. Come down to me, do not delay. And you shall dwell in the
     land of Goshen and shall be close to me, you and your sons and the
     sons of your sons and your flocks and your cattle and all that is yours.
11   And I will sustain you there, for yet five years of famine remain—lest
12   you lose all, you and your household and all that is yours.' And, look,

---

8. *father to Pharaoh.* The obvious meaning of "father" is "authority," and there
are biblical parallels for this sense of the term. It is a matter of debate among
specialists whether the term also reflects an actual Egyptian administrative
title. Joseph's characterization of his political power moves outward through
concentric circles from Pharaoh to the court ("all his house") to the whole
land of Egypt.

9. *Thus says your son Joseph.* This is the so-called messenger formula that is
regularly used in biblical Hebrew as a kind of salutation to introduce letters
or orally conveyed messages.

10. *the land of Goshen.* "Land" here obviously means a region, not a country.
The area referred to is the rich pastureland of the Nile Delta, which would
also be close to the border of the Sinai. In historical fact, Semitic nomads
from the Sinai were granted permission by the Egyptian government to graze
their flocks in this region.

11. *lest you lose all.* The Hebrew verb here has often been confused with
another one, with which it shares two consonants, meaning "to become poor."
The literal meaning of the verb used by Joseph is "to be inherited," that is, to
lose all of one's possessions, either through bankruptcy or by being conquered
by an enemy.

your own eyes can see, and the eyes of my brother Benjamin, that it
is my very mouth that speaks to you. And you must tell my father all   13
my glory in Egypt and all that you have seen, and hurry and bring
down my father here." And he fell upon the neck of his brother Benja-   14
min and he wept, and Benjamin wept on his neck. And he kissed all   15
his brothers and wept over them. And after that, his brothers spoke
with him.

And the news was heard in the house of Pharaoh, saying, "Joseph's   16
brothers have come." And it was good in Pharaoh's eyes and in his
servants' eyes. And Pharaoh said to Joseph, "Say to your brothers: 'This   17
now do. Load up your beasts and go, return to the land of Canaan.
And take your father and your households and come back to me, that   18

---

12. *it is my very mouth that speaks to you.* As ibn Ezra nicely observed, until
the crucial moment when Joseph said, "Clear out everyone around me" all
his communications with the brothers would have been through an interpreter, as we were reminded in 42:23. Now he has been speaking to them
directly in their native Hebrew, a fact they may have barely assimilated in
their dumbfounded condition, and of which he reminds them now at the end
of his speech as confirmation of his identity.

14. *and he wept, and Benjamin wept.* After the three times Joseph wept apart
from his brothers, there is at last a mutual weeping in the reunion of the two
sons of Rachel.

15. *And after that, his brothers spoke with him.* The brothers' silence through
Joseph's long speech is an eloquent expression of how overwhelmed they are
by this amazing revelation. Only now, after he embraces them and weeps over
them, are they able to speak, but the writer preserves the dramatic asymmetry
between Joseph and his brothers by merely referring to their speaking without
assigning actual dialogue to them.

18. *the best of the land of Egypt.* The source critics have noted an apparent
contradiction with Joseph's instructions, which are to settle specifically in the
region of Goshen—unless one construes "the best of the land" as a reference
to that fertile area, something supported by 47:11.

I may give you the best of the land of Egypt, and you shall live off the

19   fat of the land.' And you, command them: 'This now do. Take you

from the land of Egypt wagons for your little ones and for your wives,

20   and convey your father, and come. And regret not your belongings, for

the best of all the land of Egypt is yours.' "

21   And so the sons of Israel did, and Joseph gave them wagons, as Pha-

22   raoh had ordered, and he gave them supplies for the journey. To all of

them, each one, he gave changes of garments, and to Benjamin he

23   gave three hundred pieces of silver and five changes of garments. And

to his father he sent as follows: ten donkeys conveying from the best

of Egypt, and ten she-asses conveying grain and bread and food for

---

live off the fat of the land. The Hebrew says literally "eat the fat of the land."

19. *And you, command them.* The Masoretic Text has "And you [singular] are commanded," which is a little incoherent in light of what follows. Both the Septuagint and the Vulgate read "command them." Evidently, Joseph is enjoined by Pharaoh to transmit this royal directive to his brothers conferring special status on their clan (Nahum Sarna).

20. *regret not your belongings.* The literal meaning of the Hebrew idiom used is "let not your eye spare."

21. *as Pharaoh had ordered.* This reflects the Hebrew locution that means literally "according to Pharaoh's mouth."

22. *he gave changes of garments, and to Benjamin he gave three hundred pieces of silver.* The bestowal of garments, as Nahum Sarna notes, is a kind of antithetical response to Joseph's having been stripped of his garment. The regal amount of silver given to Benjamin is the final gesture of "restitution" for the twenty pieces of silver the brothers took for the sale of Joseph.

23. *as follows.* Because a whole list of items is being introduced, the narrator announces it with *kezo't,* a term prefaced to catalogs or inventories.

his father for the journey. And he sent off his brothers and they went, 24
and he said to them, "Do not be perturbed on the journey."

And they went up from Egypt and they came to the land of Canaan 25
to Jacob their father. And they told him, saying, "Joseph is still alive," 26
and that he was ruler in all the land of Egypt. And his heart stopped,

---

24. *Do not be perturbed on the journey.* There has been some dispute about
the meaning of the verb here. It is occasionally used in contexts that associate
it with anger, and so many interpreters have imagined that Joseph is warning
his brothers not to yield to mutual recrimination and perhaps fall to blows on
the way home. But the primary meaning of the verb is to quake or to shake,
either physically (as a mountain in an earthquake) or emotionally (as a person
trembling with fear), and it is the antonym of being tranquil or at peace. In
all likelihood, Joseph is reassuring his brothers that they need not fear any
lurking residue of vengefulness on his part that would turn the journey home-
ward into a trap.

26. *his heart stopped.* Translations like "his heart fainted" (King James Version), "his heart was numb" (Speiser and New Jewish Publication Society),
"he was stunned" (Revised English Bible), blunt the force of the original. The
Hebrew verb plainly means to stop, or more precisely, to intermit. Judah had
warned that the loss of Benjamin would kill the old man. Now the tremen-
dous shock of this news about Joseph, which at first he cannot believe—does
he imagine his less-than-trustworthy sons are perpetrating a cruel hoax?—
induces a physical syncope.

27   for he did not believe them. And they spoke to him all the words of
Joseph that he had spoken to them, and he saw the wagons that
Joseph had sent to convey him, and the spirit of Jacob their father
28   revived. And Israel said, "Enough! Joseph my son is still alive. Let me
go see him before I die."

---

27. *And they spoke to him all the words of Joseph . . . and he saw the wagons.*
Jacob's incredulity begins to yield to the circumstantial account of Joseph's
own story that his sons give him. Then he fully registers the presence of the
wagons, which would have been oxen-drawn vehicles of a distinctive Egyptian design that would not normally be seen in Canaan and that mere foreign
buyers of grain would surely not be able to obtain. At this point his "spirit.
. . . revived," that is, came back to life: he emerges from the state of temporary heart failure, or heart pause, triggered by the astounding report. One
should note that the only hint of direct discourse given to the brothers in this
scene is "Joseph is still alive" (just three words, four syllables, in the Hebrew).
The effect is to keep them in the background, even though they are actually
speaking to Jacob. Joseph looms in the foreground in the first half of the
chapter, as does Jacob—the father from whom he has been so long separated—in the second half.

28. *Joseph my son is still alive. Let me go see him before I die.* The wonderful
poignancy of these words should not deflect us from noting that Jacob is
again invoking a kind of self-defining motif. Ever since Joseph's disappearance twenty-two years earlier in narrated time, he has been talking about
going down to the grave. By now, he has in fact attained advanced old age
(see 47:9), and so the idea that he has little time left is quite reasonable. The
brief seizure he has just undergone is of course evidence of his physical
frailty. Jacob's story, like David's, is virtually unique in ancient literature in its
searching representation of the radical transformations a person undergoes
in the slow course of time. The powerful young man who made his way across
the Jordan to Mesopotamia with only his walking staff, who wrestled with
stones and men and divine beings, is now an old man tottering on the brink
of the grave, bearing the deep wounds of his long life.

CHAPTER 46

And Israel journeyed onward, with all that was his, and he came to ₁
Beer-sheba, and he offered sacrifices to the God of his father Isaac.
And God said to Israel through visions of the night, "Jacob, Jacob," ₂
and he said, "Here I am." And He said, "I am the god, God of your ₃
father. Fear not to go down to Egypt, for a great nation I will make you

---

1. *And Israel journeyed onward.* The choice of the verb is a little surprising, as
one might have expected something like "he arose and set out" or "he went
forth." It seems likely that this particular verb, with its etymological background of pulling up tent pegs and moving from one encampment to another,
is intended to signal that the beginning of the sojourn in Egypt is to be construed as a resumption of the nomadic existence that characterized the lives
of Abraham and Isaac. Thus the clan of Jacob does not head down to Egypt
as a permanent place of emigration but as a way station in its continued
wanderings.

2. *Jacob, Jacob . . . Here I am.* This is an exact verbal parallel, as Amos Funkenstein has observed to me, to the exchange between God and Abraham at
the beginning of the story of the binding of Isaac. Perhaps there is a suggestion that the sojourn in Egypt is also an ordeal, with an ultimately happy
ending.

3. *Fear not . . . for a great nation I will make you.* Both the language and the
action of this whole scene are framed as an emphatic recapitulation of
the earlier Patriarchal Tales now that they are coming to an end as the last of
the patriarchs with his offspring leaves Canaan for the long stay in Egypt.
Jacob, traveling south from Hebron, stops at Beer-sheba, where his father
built an altar, and offers sacrifice just as both Isaac and Abraham did. God
appears to him and speaks to him, as He did to Abraham and Isaac. The
language of the dream-vision strongly echoes the language of the covenantal
promises to Jacob's father and grandfather.

4   there. I Myself will go down with you to Egypt and I Myself will surely bring you back up as well, and Joseph shall lay his hand on your eyes."

5   And Jacob arose from Beer-sheba, and the sons of Israel conveyed Jacob their father and their little ones and their wives in the wagons

6   Pharaoh had sent to convey him. And they took their cattle and their substance that they had got in the land of Canaan and they came to

7   Egypt, Jacob and all his seed with him. His sons, and the sons of his sons with him, his daughters and the daughters of his sons, and all his seed, he brought with him to Egypt.

---

4. *I Myself will go down with you.* The first-person pronoun is emphatic because God uses the pronoun *'anokhi,* which is not strictly necessary, followed as it is by the imperfect tense of the verb conjugated in the first-person singular. The reassurance God offers—which is already the kernel of a theological concept that will play an important role in national consciousness both in the Babylonian exile and after the defeat by the Romans in 70 C.E.—is necessary because in the polytheistic view the theater of activity of a deity was typically imagined to be limited to the territorial borders of the deity's worshippers. By contrast, this God solemnly promises to go down with His people to Egypt and to bring them back up.

   Joseph shall lay his hand on your eyes. The reference is to closing the eyes at the moment of death.

5. *and the sons of Israel conveyed Jacob their father.* The repeated stress, in the previous chapter and in this one, on "conveying" or carrying Jacob, together with the women and children, reminds us that he is very old and infirm, no longer an active participant in the journey.

7. *His sons, and the sons of his sons.* This last verse of the narrative report of the departure for Egypt becomes an apt transition to the genealogy, purposefully inserted at this point from what scholarly consensus deems a different literary source.

And these are the names of the children of Israel who came to Egypt, 8
Jacob and his sons: Jacob's firstborn, Reuben, and the sons of Reuben, 9
Enoch and Pallu and Hezron and Carmi. And the sons of Simeon, 10
Jemuel and Jamin and Ohad and Jachin and Zohar and Saul the son
of the Canaanite woman. And the sons of Levi, Gershon, Kohath, and 11
Merari. And the sons of Judah, Er and Onan and Shelah and Perez 12
and Zerah—and Er and Onan died in the land of Canaan—and the
sons of Perez were Hezron and Hamul. And the sons of Issachar, Tola 13
and Puvah and Iob and Shimron. And the sons of Zebulun, Sered and 14,15
Elon and Jahleel. These are the sons of Leah whom she bore to Jacob
in Paddan-aram, and also Dinah his daughter, every person of his sons
and daughters, thirty-three. And the sons of Gad, Ziphion and Haggi, 16
Shuni and Ezbon, Eri and Arodi and Areli. And the sons of Asher, 17
Imnah and Ishvah and Ishvi and Beriah and Serah their sister, and the
sons of Beriah, Heber and Malkiel. These are the sons of Zilpah whom 18
Laban gave to Leah his daughter, and she bore these to Jacob, sixteen
persons. The sons of Rachel, Jacob's wife, Joseph and Benjamin. And 19
to Joseph were born in the land of Egypt, whom Asenath daughter of 20
Poti-phera priest of On bore to him, Manasseh and Ephraim. And the 21
sons of Benjamin, Bela and Becher and Ashbel, Gera and Naaman,
Ehi and Rosh, Muppim and Huppim and Ard. These are the sons of 22
Rachel who were born to Jacob, fourteen persons in all. The sons of 23
Dan, Hushim. And the sons of Naphtali, Jahzeel and Guni and Jezer 24

8.–27. Once again, the genealogical list is used to effect closure at the end of a large narrative unit. The tales of the patriarchs in the land of Canaan are now concluded, and as Jacob and his clan journey southward for the sojourn in Egypt, we are given an inventory of his offspring, a large family already exhibiting in embryo the configuration of the future tribes of Israel.

23. *The sons of Dan, Hushim.* Only one son is mentioned, but this need not reflect a contradiction in the text, as "the sons of" may be a fixed formula for each new item in the list.

25 and Shillem. These are the sons of Bilhah whom Laban gave to Rachel
26 his daughter, and she bore these to Jacob, seven persons in all. All the
    persons who came with Jacob to Egypt, issue of his loins, aside from
27 the wives of Jacob's sons, sixty-six persons in all. And the sons of
    Joseph who were born to him in Egypt, were two persons. All the
    persons of the household of Jacob coming to Egypt were seventy.

28 And Judah he had sent before him to show him the way to Goshen,
29 and they came to the land of Goshen. And Joseph harnassed his char-

---

27. *All the persons of the household of Jacob coming to Egypt were seventy.* The
traditional commentators resort to interpretive acrobatics in order to make
the list come out to exactly seventy—debating as to whether Jacob himself
should be included in the count, whether Joseph and his two sons are part
of the sum, and so forth. In fact, the insistence on seventy at the end of the
list vividly illustrates the biblical use of numbers as symbolic approximations
rather than as arithmetically precise measures. Seventy is a fullness, a large
round number, ten times sacred seven, and its use here indicates that Jacob,
once a solitary fugitive, has grown to a grand family, the nucleus of a nation.

28. *And Judah he had sent before him to show him the way.* Judah, who pledged
to guarantee Benjamin's safety (and from whose descendents the royal line
will spring) is now Jacob's choice as guide for the rest. The phrase "to show
him the way" is a little odd in the Hebrew (there are two variant readings
reflected in the ancient versions), and its meaning is not entirely certain.

29. *And Joseph harnassed his chariot.* The specification of the vehicle is

iot and went up to meet Israel his father in Goshen, and appeared
before him and fell on his neck, and he wept on his neck a long while.   30
And Israel said, "I may die now, after seeing your face, for you are still   31
alive." And Joseph said to his brothers and to his father's household,
"Let me go up and tell Pharaoh and let me say to him, 'My brothers
and my father's household that was in the land of Canaan have come   32
to me. And the men are shepherds, for they have always been handlers

---

another strategic reminder of the Egyptian accoutrements Joseph employs as
a matter of course, even as he hurries to meet his father, who comes from a
world where there are neither chariots nor wagons. Realistically, "harnassed,"
as ibn Ezra and many others have noted, would mean, he gave orders to
harnass. Nevertheless, there is thematic point in the sense of immediacy
conveyed by the transitive verb with Joseph as subject, and Rashi registers
this point, even if his construal is too literal, when he says: "He himself
harnassed the horses to the chariot in order to make haste in honor of his
father."

and appeared before him. This is a slightly odd phrase, since it is more
typically used for the appearance of God before a human. Perhaps the sight
of the long-lost Joseph, in Egyptian royal raiment, riding in his chariot, is a
kind of epiphany for Jacob. In any case, "appearing before" accords with
Jacob's own emphasis on seeing Joseph's face.

and fell on his neck, and he wept on his neck a long while. The absence of
reciprocal weeping on the part of Jacob can scarcely be attributed to ellipsis
or inadvertent narrative omission, for in the identically worded report of
Joseph's falling on Benjamin's neck and weeping, we are told, "and Benjamin
wept on his neck" (45:14). We are invited to imagine, then, a sobbing Joseph
who embraces his father while the old man stands dry-eyed, perhaps even
rigid, too overcome with feeling to know how to respond, or to be able to
respond spontaneously, until finally he speaks, once more invoking his own
death, but now with a sense of contentment: "I may die now, after seeing
your face, for you are still alive."

32. handlers of livestock. The Hebrew phrase, 'anshei miqneh, which occurs
only here and in verse 34, literally means "men of livestock." It is perhaps
influenced by the designation of the brothers as "the men" at the beginning
of this verse.

of livestock, and their sheep and their cattle and all that is theirs they have brought. And so, when Pharaoh calls for you and says, 'What is it you do?' you should say, 'Your servants have been handlers of livestock from our youth until now, we and our fathers as well,' that you may dwell in the land of Goshen. For every shepherd is abhorrent to Egypt.

33,34

---

34. *that you may dwell in the land of Goshen. For every shepherd is abhorrent to Egypt.* This claim is puzzling because there is an indication in the next chapter that Pharaoh had his own flocks (see 47:6), and there is no extrabiblical evidence that shepherding was a taboo profession among the Egyptians, as the categorical language of the last sentence here appears to suggest. The least convoluted explanation is that the Egyptians, who were by and large sedentary agriculturalists and who had large urban centers, considered the seminomadic herdsmen from the north as inferiors (an attitude actually reflected in Egyptian sources) and so preferred to keep them segregated in the pasture region of the Nile Delta not far from the Sinai border.

CHAPTER 47

And Joseph came and told Pharaoh and said, "My father and my broth- 1
ers and their flocks and their cattle and all that is theirs have come
from the land of Canaan and here they are in the land of Goshen."
And from the pick of his brothers he took five men and presented 2
them to Pharaoh. And Pharaoh said to his brothers, "What is it you 3
do?" And they said to Pharaoh, "Your servants are shepherds, we, and

---

2. *And from the pick of his brothers.* The Hebrew prepositional phrase, *miqts-eh 'eḥaw,* has elicited puzzlement, or evasion, from most translators. The common meaning of *miqtseh* is "at the end of," but it is also occasionally used in the sense of "from the best of" or "from the pick of," which would be appropriate here, since Joseph wants to introduce the most presentable of his brothers to Pharaoh. The use of *miqtseh* in Judges 18:2 in reference to elite soldiers nicely illustrates the likely meaning in our own text: "and the Danites sent from their clan five men of their pick [*miqtsotam*], capable men . . . to spy out the land." It might be noted that this term in Judges is associated with "capable men" (*benei ḥayil*)—a phrase that in a military context might also be rendered "valiant men"—just as an equivalent phrase, *'anshei ḥayil,* is associated with Joseph's brothers at this point. There are, however, other occurrences of *miqtseh* or *miqtsot* that suggest it might also have the sense of "a representative sample."

five men. The insistence of various modern commentators that "five" both here and earlier in the story really means "several" is not especially convincing. One should note that the whole Joseph story exhibits a fondness for playing with recurrent numbers: the fraternal twelve, first signaled in Joseph's dreams, then subtracted from by his disappearance, with the full sum made up at the end; the triple pairs of dreams; the two pairs of seven. Five is one half the number of the brothers who enslaved Joseph; Benjamin was given a fivefold portion at Joseph's feast and five changes of garments; and the Egyptians are obliged to pay a tax of one-fifth of their harvest.

4 our fathers as well." And they said to Pharaoh, "We have come to
sojourn in the land, for there is no pasture for your servants' flocks
because the famine is grave in the land of Canaan. And so, let your
[5a–6b] servants, pray, dwell in the land of Goshen." *And Pharaoh said to
Joseph, saying,* "Let them dwell in the land of Goshen, and if you know
there are able men among them, make them masters of the livestock,
over what is mine." *And Jacob and his sons had come to Egypt, to Joseph,*
5 *and Pharaoh king of Egypt heard.* And Pharaoh said to Joseph, saying,
[6a] "Your father and your brothers have come to you. The land of Egypt is
before you. In the best of the land settle your father and your brothers.
7 Let them dwell in the land of Goshen." And Joseph brought Jacob his
8 father and stood him before Pharaoh, and Jacob blessed Pharaoh. And
Pharaoh said to Jacob, "How many are the days of the years of your

---

4. *to sojourn in the land . . . dwell in the land.* First they use a verb of temporary residence, then one of fixed settlement.

[5a–6b.] The Masoretic Text is clearly problematic at this point because it
has Pharaoh speaking to Joseph, appearing to ignore the brothers who have
just addressed a petition to him, and also announcing, quite superfluously in
light of verse 1, "Your father and your brothers have come to you." Coherence
in the sequence of dialogues is improved by inserting the clauses italicized
here, which are reflected in the Septuagint.

7. *and Jacob blessed Pharaoh.* The Hebrew verb here also has the simple
meaning of "to greet," but it seems likely that in this context it straddles both
senses. Jacob of course accords Pharaoh the deferential greeting owed to a
monarch, but it would be entirely in keeping with his own highly developed
sense of his patriarchal role that he—a mere Semitic herdsman chief
addressing the head of the mighty Egyptian empire—should pronounce a
blessing on Pharaoh.

life?" And Jacob said to Pharaoh, "The days of the years of my 9
sojournings are a hundred and thirty years. Few and evil have been
the days of the years of my life, and they have not attained the days
of the years of my fathers in their days of sojourning." And Jacob 10
blessed Pharaoh and went out from Pharaoh's presence.

---

9. *The days of the years of my sojournings.* The last noun here probably has a
double connotation: Jacob's life has been a series of wanderings or
"sojournings," not a sedentary existence in one place, and human existence
is by nature a sojourning, a temporary dwelling between non-being and
extinction.

Few and evil have been the days of the years of my life. Jacob's somber
summary of his own life echoes with a kind of complex solemnity against all
that we have seen him undergo. He has, after all, achieved everything he
aspired to achieve: the birthright, the blessing, marriage with his beloved
Rachel, progeny, and wealth. But one measure of the profound moral realism
of the story is that although he gets everything he wanted, it is not in the way
he would have wanted, and the consequence is far more pain than contentment. From his "clashing" (25:20) with his twin in the womb, everything has
been a struggle. He displaces Esau, but only at the price of fear and lingering
guilt and long exile. He gets Rachel, but only by having Leah imposed on
him, with all the domestic strife that entails, and he loses Rachel early in
childbirth. He is given a new name by his divine adversary, but comes away
with a permanent wound. He gets the full solar-year number of twelve sons,
but there is enmity among them (for which he bears some responsibility),
and he spends twenty-two years continually grieving over his favorite son,
who he believes is dead. This is, in sum, a story with a happy ending that
withholds any simple feeling of happiness at the end.

and they have not attained the days of the years of my fathers. In fact, Jacob,
long-lived as he is, will not attain the prodigious life spans of Abraham and
Isaac. At this point, however, he can scarcely know how much longer he has
to live (seventeen years, as it turns out), and so his words must reflect that
feeling of having one foot in the grave that he has repeatedly expressed
before. One should not exclude the possibility that Jacob is playing up the
sense of contradiction, making a calculated impression on Pharaoh, in dis-
missing his own 130 years as "few." The ideal life span for the Egyptians was
110.

11   And Joseph settled his father and his brothers and gave them a holding in the land of Egypt in the best of the land, in the land of Rameses,

12   as Pharaoh had commanded. And Joseph sustained his father and his brothers and all his father's household with bread, down to the mouths

13   of the little ones. And there was no bread in all the earth, for the famine was very grave, and the land of Egypt and the land of Canaan

14   languished because of the famine. And Joseph collected all the silver to be found in the land of Egypt and in the land of Canaan in return for the provisions they were buying, and Joseph brought the silver to

15   the house of Pharaoh. And the silver of the land of Egypt and of the land of Canaan ran out, and all Egypt came to Joseph, saying, "Let us have bread, for why should we die before your eyes? For the silver is

16   gone." And Joseph said, "Let me have your livestock, that I may give

17   you in return for your livestock if the silver is gone." And they brought their livestock to Joseph, and he gave them bread in return for the horses and the stocks of sheep and the stocks of cattle and the donkeys, and he carried them forward with bread in return for all their

---

11. *the land of Rameses.* Medieval and modern commentators agree that this designation is a synonym for Goshen. The term looks like an anachronism because Rameses is the city later built with Israelite slave labor. Perhaps its use here is intended to foreshadow the future oppression.

13. *And there was no bread in all the earth.* The tension with the preceding verse, in which Joseph is reported sustaining his whole clan, down to the little ones, with bread, is of course pointed, and recalls a similar surface contradiction between verses 54 and 55 in chapter 41. The writer shuttles here between the two common meanings of *'erets,* "earth" and "land," as in his previous accounts of the famine.

15. *why should we die before your eyes?* The last term in the Hebrew is literally "opposite you." In the parallel speech in verse 19, the Egyptians actually say "before your eyes."

17. *he carried them forward with bread.* The usual meaning of the verb is "to lead"; the context here suggests it may also mean something like "to sustain."

livestock that year. And that year ran out and they came to him the   18
next year and said to him, "We shall not conceal from my lord that the
silver has run out and the animal stocks are my lord's. Nothing is left
for our lord but our carcasses and our farmland. Why should we die   19
before your eyes? Both we and our farmland—take possession of us
and our farmland in return for bread, and we with our farmland will
be slaves to Pharaoh, and give us seed, that we may live and not die,
and that the farmland not turn to desert." And Joseph took possession   20
of all the farmland of Egypt for Pharaoh, for each Egyptian sold his
field, as the famine was harsh upon them, and the land became Pha-

---

18. *our carcasses and our farmland.* Previous translations have rendered the
first of these terms blandly as "our bodies" or "our persons." But the Hebrew
gewiyah refers specifically to a dead body and is often used in quite negative
contexts. The Egyptians here are speaking sardonically of their own miserable
condition: they have nothing left but their carcasses, they have been reduced
to walking corpses. The present translation uses "farmland" for the Hebrew
'adamah. That term usually means arable land—it is the reiterated "soil" of
the Garden story—but "soil" would be a little off in these sentences. It cannot
be rendered throughout simply as "land" because that would create a confusion with "land" (*'erets),* which is also used here several times to refer to
Egypt as a country. The fact that the farmland referred to by the Egyptians is
not yielding much produce suggests that in their eyes it is scarcely worth
more than the "carcasses" with which it is bracketed.

19. *slaves to Pharaoh.* The reduction of the entire population to a condition of
virtual serfdom to the crown in all likelihood was meant to be construed not
as an act of ruthlessness by Joseph but as an instance of his administrative
brilliance. The subordination of the Egyptian peasantry to the central government, with the 20 percent tax on agriculture, was a known fact, and our story
provides an explanation (however unhistorical) for its origins.

   that the farmland not turn to desert. As the famine continues, without seed-
corn to replant the soil, the land will turn to desert.

21   raoh's. And the people he moved town by town, from one end of the
22   border of Egypt to the other. Only the farmland of the priests he did
not take in possession, for the priests had a fixed allotment from Pharaoh and they ate from their allotment that Pharaoh had given them.
23   Therefore they did not sell their farmland. And Joseph said to the
people, "Look, I have taken possession of you this day, with your farm-
24   land, for Pharaoh. Here is seed for you, and sow the land. And when
the harvests come, you shall give a fifth to Pharaoh and four parts
shall be yours for seeding the field and for your food, for those in your
25   households and for your little ones to eat." And they said, "You have
kept us alive! May we find favor in the eyes of our lord, in being
26   Pharaoh's slaves." And Joseph made it a fixed law, to this very day, over
the farmland of Egypt, that Pharaoh should have a fifth. Only the
farmland of the priests, it alone did not become Pharaoh's.

---

21. *And the people he moved town by town.* Despite many English versions, it
is problematic to construe the last term as "into the towns," for it would make
no sense to move all the farmers into the cities if there are to be crops in the
future, unless one imagines a temporary gathering of the rural population in
the towns for the distribution of food. But the Hebrew particle *le* in *le'arim*
can also have the sense of "according to"—that is, Joseph rounded up rural
populations in groups according to their distribution around the principal
towns and resettled them elsewhere. The purpose would be to sever them
from their hereditary lands and locate them on other lands that they knew
were theirs to till only by the grace of Pharaoh, to whom the land now
belonged.

25. *in being Pharaoh's slaves.* Most translations construe this as a future verb,
"we shall be." But the introductory clause of obeisance, "May we find favor
. . .", does not necessarily preface a declaration about a future action, and the
Egyptians are already Pharaoh's slaves, both by their own declaration (verse
19) and Joseph's (verse 23). In point of historical fact, Egypt's centralization
of power, so unlike tribal Israel and Canaan with its city-states, must have
astounded and perhaps also troubled the Hebrew writer.

And Israel dwelled in the land of Egypt, in the land of Goshen, and 27
they took holdings in it, and were fruitful and multiplied greatly. And 28
Jacob lived in the land of Egypt seventeen years, and Jacob's days, the
years of his life, were one hundred and forty-seven years. And Israel's 29
time to die drew near, and he called for his son, for Joseph, and he
said to him, "If, pray, I have found favor in your eyes, put your hand,
pray, under my thigh and act toward me with steadfast kindness—
pray, do not bury me in Egypt. When I lie down with my fathers, carry 30
me from Egypt and bury me in their burial place." And he said, "I will
do as you have spoken." And he said, "Swear to me." And Israel bowed 31
at the head of the bed.

---

27. *And Jacob lived in the land of Egypt seventeen years.* The symmetry with
Joseph's seventeen years until he was sold into Egypt was aptly observed in
the Middle Ages by Kimhi: "Just as Joseph was in the lap of Jacob seventeen
years, Jacob was in the lap of Joseph seventeen years."

CHAPTER 48

¹ And it happened after these things that someone said to Joseph, "Look, your father is ill." And he took his two sons with him, Manasseh and ² Ephraim. And someone told Jacob and said, "Look, your son Joseph is coming to you." And Israel summoned his strength and sat up in bed. ³ And Jacob said to Joseph, "El Shaddai appeared to me at Luz in the ⁴ land of Canaan and blessed me, and said to me, 'I am about to make you fruitful and multiply you and make you an assembly of peoples, and I will give this land to your seed after you as an everlasting hold-

---

1. *And he took his two sons with him.* Joseph, even before he receives any word from his father in this regard, anticipates that Jacob will confer some sort of special eminence on his own two sons in a deathbed blessing, and so he brings them with him.

3. *Luz.* This is the older name for Beth-el, where Jacob was vouchsafed his dream-vision of divine messengers ascending and descending the ramp to heaven.

ing.' And so now, your two sons who were born to you in the land of   5
Egypt before I came to you in Egypt, shall be mine—Ephraim and
Manasseh, like Reuben and Simeon, shall be mine. And those you   6
begot after them shall be yours; by their brothers' names they shall be

---

5. *your two sons . . . shall be mine—Ephraim and Manasseh, like Reuben and
Simeon, shall be mine.* These words are equally fraught with thematic and
legal implications. Jacob explicitly equates Joseph's two sons with his own
firstborn and second-born, intimating that the former are to have as good an
inheritance, or better, as the latter, and thus once more invokes the great
Genesis theme of the reversal of primogeniture. (Note that he already places
Ephraim, the younger, before Manasseh when he names Joseph's sons.) The
fact that Reuben has violated Jacob's concubine and Simeon (with Levi) has
initiated the massacre at Shechem may suggest that they are deemed unworthy to be undisputed first and second in line among Jacob's inheritors. The
language Jacob uses, moreover, is a formula of legal adoption, just as the
gesture of placing the boys on the old man's knees (see verse 12) is a ritual
gesture of adoption. The adoption is dictated by the fact that Ephraim and
Manasseh will become tribes, just as if they were sons of Jacob.

6. *And those you begot after them.* It is difficult to square this phrase with the
narrative as we have it, which indicates that Joseph has only two sons. The
efforts of some commentators to make the verb a future is not at all warranted
by the Hebrew grammar, and, in any case, Joseph has been married more
than twenty-five years.

by their brothers' names they shall be called in their inheritance. Although
the idiom is familiar, the meaning is not entirely transparent. What Jacob
probably is saying is that it is Ephraim and Manasseh who will have tribal
status in the future nation, and thus any other sons of Joseph would be
"called by their name," would have claim to land that was part of the tribal
inheritance of Ephraim and Manasseh and so designated.

7   called in their inheritance. As for me, when I was coming from Pad-
    dan, Rachel died to my grief in the land of Canaan on the way, still
8   some distance from Ephrath." And Israel saw Joseph's sons and he
9   said, "Who are these?" And Joseph said to his father, "They are my
    sons whom God has given me here." And he said, "Fetch them, pray,
10 to me, that I may bless them." And Israel's eyes had grown heavy with
    age, he could not see. And he brought them near him, and he kissed
11 them and embraced them. And Israel said, "I had not thought to see
12 your face, and, look, God has also let me see your seed!" And Joseph

---

7. *As for me, when I was coming from Paddan, Rachel died.* This verse is one
of several elements in this chapter that have been seized on by textual critics
as evidence of its highly composite nature and of what is claimed to be a
concomitant incoherence in its articulations. But such conclusions seriously
underestimate the degree of integrative narrative logic that the writer—or
perhaps one must say, the redactor—exhibits. At first glance, Jacob's comment about the death of his beloved Rachel in the midst of blessing his
grandsons seems a non sequitur. It is, however, a loss to which he has never
been reconciled (witness his extravagant favoritism toward Rachel's firstborn). His vivid sense of anguish, after all these decades, is registered in the
single word 'alai ("to my grief," but literally, "on me," the same word he uses
in 42:36, when he says that all the burden of bereavement is on him), and
this loss is surely uppermost in his mind when he tells Pharaoh that his days
have been few and evil. On his deathbed, then, Jacob reverts obsessively to
the loss of Rachel, who perished in childbirth leaving behind only two sons,
and his impulse to adopt Rachel's two grandsons by her firstborn expresses a
desire to compensate, symbolically and legally, for the additional sons she did
not live to bear.

8. *Who are these?* Perhaps, as several commentators have proposed, he could
barely make out their features because he was virtually blind (see verse 10).
"And Israel saw," then, would mean something like, he dimly perceived, and
it need not be an out-and-out contradiction of the indication of blindness in
verse 10. But the question he asks might also be the opening formula in the
ceremony of adoption.

drew them out from his knees, and he bowed, his face to the ground. And Joseph took the two of them, Ephraim with his right hand to Israel's left and Manasseh with his left hand to Israel's right, and brought them near him. And Israel stretched out his right hand and placed it on Ephraim's head, yet he was the younger, and his left hand on Manasseh's head—he crossed his hands—though Manasseh was the firstborn. And he blessed them and said,

13

14

15

> "The God in whose presence my fathers walked,
>   Abraham and Isaac,
> the God who has looked after me
>   as long as I've been till this day,
> the messenger rescuing me from all evil,
>   may He bless the lads,
> let my name be called in them
>   and the name of my fathers, Abraham and Isaac,
> let them teem multitudinous in the midst of the earth."

16

---

14. *he crossed his hands.* This image, extended in the exchange with Joseph in which the old man says he knows what he is doing, is a kind of summarizing thematic ideogram of the Book of Genesis: the right hand of the father conferring the blessing reaches across to embrace the head of the younger brother, and the elder, his head covered by the old man's left hand, receives a lesser blessing.

15. *he blessed them.* The Masoretic Text has, illogically, "he blessed Joseph," but "them" as object of the verb is reflected in the Septuagint, the Syriac, and the Vulgate.

16. *the name of my fathers, Abraham and Isaac, / let them teem multitudinous.* Jacob, after recapitulating the story of his personal providence in the first line of the blessing-poem, invokes the benediction of the patriarchal line, and then, going back still further in the biblical history, the promise, or injunction, of fertility from the Creation story.

17 And Joseph saw that his father had placed his right hand on Ephraim's head, and it was wrong in his eyes, and he took hold of his father's
18 hand to remove it from Ephraim's head to Manasseh's head. And Joseph said to his father, "Not so, my father, for this one is the first-
19 born. Put your right hand on his head." And his father refused and he said, "I know, my son. I know. He, too, shall become a people, and he, too, shall be great. But his younger brother shall be greater than he,
20 and his seed shall be a fullness of nations." And he blessed them that day, saying,

> "By you shall Israel bless, saying,
>   'May God set you as Ephraim and Manasseh,' "

and he set Ephraim before Manasseh.

---

20. *And he blessed them that day.* The introduction of a second blessing is hardly evidence of a glitch in textual transmission. After the exchange with Joseph, which follows the full-scale blessing and also explains its implications, Jacob reaffirms his giving precedence to Ephraim over Manasseh (a real datum of later tribal history) by stating a kind of summary blessing in which the name of the younger precedes the name of the elder. "By you shall Israel bless" is meant quite literally: when the future people of Israel want to invoke a blessing, they will do it by reciting the words, "May God set you as Ephraim and Manasseh."

And Israel said to Joseph, "Look, I am about to die, but God shall be   21
with you and bring you back to the land of your fathers. As for me, I   22
have given you with single intent over your brothers what I took from
the hand of the Emorite with my sword and my bow."

---

22. *I have given you with single intent over your brothers what I took from the
hand of the Emorite.* The phrase represented here by "with single intent" is a
notorious crux, but previous interpreters may have been misled by assuming
it must be the object of the verb "have given." The Hebrew *shekhem 'aḥad*
means literally "one shoulder." Many commentators and translators, with an
eye to the immediate context of inheritance, have construed this as "one
portion," but the evidence elsewhere in the Bible that *shekhem* means "portion" is weak. Others have proposed, without much more warrant than the
shape of the shoulder, that the word here means "mountain slope." A substantial number of scholars, medieval and modern, read this as a proper noun,
the city of Shechem, encouraged by the fact that the Joseph tribes settled in
the vicinity of Shechem. That construal, however, entails two difficulties: if
the city were referred to, a feminine form of the word for "one" (not *'aḥad*
but *'aḥat*) would be required; and at least according to the preceding narrative, Jacob, far from having conquered Shechem with his own sword, was
horrified by the massacre his sons perpetrated there. But the very phrase
used here, *shekhem 'aḥad,* occurs at one other place in the Bible, Zephaniah
3:9, where it is used *adverbially* in an idiomatic sense made clear by the
immediate context: "for all of them to invoke the name of the LORD, / to serve
Him *shekhem 'eḥad* [King James Version, with one consent; Revised English
Bible and New Jewish Publication Society Bible, with one accord]." This
is, then, an expression that indicates concerted, unswerving intention and
execution, and as such is perfectly appropriate to the legal pronouncement
of legacy by Jacob in which it appears. Once the phrase is seen as adverbial,
the relative clause, "what I took. . . ," falls into place with grammatical pre-
ciseness as the object of the verb "have given," and in this reading, no particular city or region need be specified.

CHAPTER 49

And Jacob called his sons and said, "Gather round, that I may tell you what shall befall you in the days to come.

1

As with the life-histories of Moses and David, the extended narrative of Jacob and his sons (with the entire Patriarchal Tale behind it) is given literary closure by the introduction of a long poem. Although the poem chiefly looks forward to the future tribal history of Jacob's twelve sons, it begins by harking back to incidents in the preceding narrative and so preserves some sense of the sons as individual characters, not merely eponymous founders of the tribes. There is debate among scholars as to whether the poem is a single composition or rather a kind of cento of poetic fragments about the fate of the various tribes that were in circulation in the early phase of Israelite history. It is generally agreed, however, that this is one of the oldest extended texts in the Bible. The representation of Levi as a tribe deprived of inheritance, with no hint of its sacerdotal function and the concomitant privileges, suggests a very early date—conceivably even before the completion of the conquest and settlement, as Nahum Sarna has proposed. The royal imagery, on the other hand, associated with Judah seems to reflect a moment after David's founding of his dynasty shortly before 1000 B.C.E. In any case, the antiquity of the poem, as well as the fact that it may be a collage of fragments, means that there are words, phrases, and occasionally whole clauses that are not very well understood. Sometimes this is because of the use of a rare, presumably archaic, term, though there are also at least a few points where the received text looks defective. Differences of interpretive opinion are such that in two instances there is no agreement about whether the language refers to animal, vegetable, or mineral! At such junctures, a translator can do no more than make an educated guess. In any event, the poetic beauty and power of Jacob's Testament cannot be separated from its lofty antique style—its archaic grammatical forms and strange turns of syntax, its rare poetic terms, its animal and vegetal imagery, at some points recalling the old Ugaritic poems—and an English version should seek at least to intimate these qualities.

Assemble and hearken, O Jacob's sons,   2
   and hearken to Israel your father.
Reuben, my firstborn are you—   3
   my strength and first yield of my manhood,
      prevailing in rank and prevailing in might.
Unsteady as water, you'll no more prevail!   4
   for you mounted the place where your father lay,
      you profaned my couch, you mounted!
Simeon and Levi, the brothers—   5
   weapons of outrage their trade.

---

2. *Assemble and hearken . . . hearken.* It is a common convention of biblical poetry to begin with a formal exhortation for those addressed to listen closely. What is slightly odd about the opening line here is that "hearken" is repeated in the second half of the line instead of introducing a synonym like "give ear" (compare the beginning of Lamech's poem, Genesis 4:23).

3. *first yield of my manhood.* The word for "manhood," *'on,* means "vigor," but it is particularly associated with male potency. "First yield," *re'shit,* is a word also used for crops. The biological image of Reuben as the product of Jacob's first inseminating seed sharpens the evocation in the next line of his violation of his father's concubine.

4. *the place where your father lay.* The plural form used, *mishkevei 'avikha,* has an explicitly sexual connotation, whereas the singular *mishkav* can also mean simply a place where one sleeps.
   you'll no more prevail. The verb here may rather mean "you'll not remain" (or pun on that meaning)—a reference to the early disappearance of the tribe of Reuben, perhaps before the period of the monarchy.
   you profaned my couch, you mounted! The translation here emends *'alah* ("he mounted") to *'alita* ("you mounted"), though there is some possibility that the archaic poetic style permitted this sort of abrupt switch in pronominal reference.

5. *their trade.* The meaning of *mekheroteyhem* is highly uncertain. The translation here conjecturally links the term with the root *m-kh-r,* "to sell."

6   In their council let me never set foot,
            their assembly my presence shun.
        For in their fury they slaughtered men,
            at their pleasure they tore down ramparts.

7   Cursed be their fury so fierce,
            and their wrath so remorseless!
        I will divide them in Jacob,
            disperse them in Israel.

8   Judah, you, shall your brothers acclaim—
            your hand on your enemies' nape—
                your fathers' sons shall bow to you.

---

6. *let me never set foot.* Literally, "let my person not come."

their assembly my presence shun. The Hebrew says literally, "in their assembly let my presence not join," but this is clumsy as English, and in any case the point is that Jacob is ostracizing the two brothers.

they tore down ramparts. With many critics, the translation here reads *shur,* a poetic term for "wall," instead of *shor,* "ox," as the Masoretic Text has it. The verb, if it refers to oxen, would mean to maim or hamstring. It was sometimes the ancient practice to hamstring the captured warhorses of an enemy, but it would have been foolish to hamstring captured oxen, which could be put to peaceful use. Moreover, since Jacob is speaking of the massacre at Shechem, the narrative there explicitly noted that the cattle and other livestock were carried off, not maimed.

8. *Judah, you, shall your brothers acclaim.* This line in the Hebrew is a fanfare of sound-play, including a pun on Judah's name, *Yehudah, 'atah yodukha 'ahekha.* Up to this point, Jacob's testament to his first three sons has actually been nothing but curses. Rashi neatly catches the transitional force of "Judah, you . . ." when he notes, "Inasmuch as he had heaped condemnations on the previous ones, Judah began to back away and his father called to him with words of encouragement, 'Judah, you are not like them.'" Judah now displaces the three brothers born before him, and his claim to preeminence ("your brothers acclaim") is founded on his military prowess ("your hand on your enemies' nape"). All this has a distinctly Davidic coloration. "Acclaim" is a more precise equivalent for the verb in context than the usual "praise" because what is involved is recognition of Judah's royal status.

A lion's whelp is Judah,   9
    from the prey, O my son, you mount.
He crouched, he lay down like a lion,
    like the king of beasts, and who dare arouse him?
The scepter shall not pass from Judah,   10
    nor the mace from between his legs,
that tribute to him may come
    and to him the submission of peoples.

---

9. *from the prey, O my son, you mount.* Amos Funkenstein has astutely suggested to me that there is an ingenious double meaning here. The Hebrew could also be construed as "from the prey of my son you mounted," introducing a shadow reference to Judah's leading part in the plan to pass off Joseph as dead. When the bloodied tunic was brought to Jacob, he cried out, "Joseph is torn to shreds" *(tarof toraf)*, and the term for "prey" here is *teref.*

you mount. This is the same verb that is used above for Reuben's act of sexual violation, but here it refers to the lion springing up from the prey it has slain. The proposal that the verb means "to grow" is forced, with little warrant elsewhere in the Bible.

the king of beasts. This English kenning is necessary in the poetic parallelism because there are no English synonyms for "lion," whereas biblical Hebrew has four different terms for the same beast.

10. *mace.* The Hebrew *meḥoqeq* refers to a ruler's long staff, a clear parallel to "scepter." There is no reason to construe it, as some have done, as a euphemism for the phallus, though the image of the mace between the legs surely suggests virile power in political leadership.

that tribute to him may come. This is a notorious crux. The Masoretic Text seems to read "until he comes to Shiloh," a dark phrase that has inspired much messianic interpretation. The present translation follows an exegetical tradition that goes back to the Middle Ages, which breaks up the word "Shiloh" and vocalizes it differently as *shai lo.*

11   He binds to the vine his ass,
        to the grape-bough his ass's foal.
     He washes in wine his garment,
        in the blood of the grape his cloak.

12   O eyes that are darker than wine
        and teeth that are whiter than milk!

13   Zebulun near the shore of the sea shall dwell,
        he'll be near to the haven of ships,
           his flank upon Sidon.

14   Issachar, a big-boned donkey,
        crouched amidst hearths.

15   He saw that the homestead was goodly,
        that the land was delightful,
     and he put his shoulder to the load,
        became a toiling serf.

---

11. *He binds to the vine his ass.* The hyperbole has been explained most plausibly by ibn Ezra, "The yield of his vineyards will be so abundant that his ass
can turn aside to the vine and he won't care if it eats the grapes." This explanation jibes nicely with the next image of washing garments in wine—the
wine will be so plentiful that it can be treated as water.

    the blood of the grape. This vivid poetic epithet for wine, with its intensi-
fying effect, is reminiscent of the Ugaritic kenning for wine, "blood of the
tree," and hence a token of the stylistic antiquity of the poem.

12. *O eyes that are darker than wine.* The Hebrew, like this English version,
gives no pronoun references for these striking images, though they presumably refer to Judah, whose descendants will flourish in beauty in the midst of
their viticultural abundance. The word for "darker," *ḥakhili,* is still another
rare poetic term, cognate with the Akkadian *elelu,* "to be dark."

14. *hearths.* The term occurs only here and in Judges 5:16. Because of the
pastoral setting of the latter text, it is frequently construed as "sheepfolds,"
but the verbal stem from which it appears to derive means "to set a pot on
the fire."

Dan, his folk will judge   16
   as one of Israel's tribes.
Let Dan be a snake on the road,   17
   an asp on the path,
that bites the horse's heels
   and its rider topples backward.
Your deliverance I await, O LORD!   18
Gad shall be goaded by raiders   19
   yet he shall goad their heel.
Asher's bread shall be rich   20
   and he shall bring forth kingly dishes.

---

16. *Dan, his folk will judge.* Dan has always been construed as the subject of the verb "judge" (or "govern"), not its object. But Hebrew grammar makes it equally possible to read "Dan" as object of the verb, and that would explain the otherwise obscure second clause: in historical fact, the tribe of Dan, far from assuming a role of leadership, was obliged to migrate from south to north. Despite its marginal existence, the Israelite people will judge or govern it as one of Israel's tribes.

17. *Let Dan be a snake on the road.* The sudden lethal attack from below on the roadside is an image of the tactic of ambush in guerilla warfare adopted against invaders by the Danite fighters. Again, the image suggests that this tribe, unlike the others, did not enjoy the security of fortified settlement.

19. *Gad shall be goaded by raiders.* The sound-play in the Hebrew is *gad gedud yegudenu*.

   yet he shall goad their heel. The phrase may be a reminiscence of "and you shall bite his heel," which is addressed to the serpent in the Garden. There would be a carryover, then, from the snake imagery of the preceding lines. The snake, one should keep in mind, is not "demonic" but an image of darting, agile, lethal assault.

20. *Asher's bread.* The Masoretic Text reads "from Asher, his bread," but several ancient versions, quite plausibly, attach the initial consonant *mem* ("from") to the end of the preceding word *'aqev* ("heel"), turning it into "their heel."

21 Naphtali, a hind let loose
who brings forth lovely fawns.

22 A fruitful son is Joseph,
a fruitful son by a spring,
daughters strode by a rampart.

23 They savaged him, shot arrows
and harassed him, the archers did.

---

21. *lovely fawns*. The Hebrew *'imrei shafer* is in doubt. The translation follows one prevalent conjecture in deriving the first word from the Aramaic *'imeir*, which usually means "lamb."

22. *A fruitful son*. The morphology of the reiterated noun in this line is so peculiar that some scholars have imagined a reference to branches, others to a wild ass. There is little philological warrant for the former, and the connection between the term used here, *porat*, and *per'e*, "wild ass," seems strained. (The main argument for the wild ass is that it preserves the animal imagery, but there are several other tribes in the poem that have no animal icons.) A link between *porat* and the root *p-r-h*, to be fruitful, is less of a grammatical stretch, and is encouraged by Joseph's play on that same root in naming his son Ephraim. Joseph and Judah, as the dominant tribes of the north and the south respectively, get far more elaborate attention in the poem than do any of their brothers.

daughters strode. This is another crux because the verb "strode" appears to be in the feminine singular. But there are good grounds to assume that the verbal suffix *ah*, which in normative grammar signals third-person feminine singular perfect tense, was also an archaic third-person plural feminine form. There are a number of instances in which the consonantal text *(ketiv)* shows this form with a plural subject and the Masoretes correct it in the *qeri* (the indicated pronunciation) to normative grammar: e.g., Deuteronomy 21:7, "Our hands have not spilled *[ketiv: shafkhah]* this blood." Without emendation, then, the text suggests that Joseph has the twin blessing of fruitfulness and military security. The young women of the tribe can walk in safety alongside the rampart because they will be protected by Joseph's valorous skill in battle (verses 23–24).

by a rampart. This is the same word as the one at the end of verse 6. There is scant warrant for extending it metonymically to "hillside," as some translators have done.

But taut was his bow,   24
    his arms ever-moving,
through the hands of the Champion of Jacob,
    through the name of the Shepherd, and Israel's Rock.
From the God of your fathers, may He aid you,   25
    Shaddai, may He bless you—
blessings of the heavens above,
    blessings of the deep that lies below,
      blessings of breasts and womb.

---

24. *taut was his bow, / his arms ever-moving*. There is some doubt about "taut," though the context makes this a reasonable educated guess. There is also some dispute over the verb represented here as "ever-moving," but its likely literal meaning is "to move about rapidly," "to be nimble."

through the hands. This picks up the previous phrase, referring to Joseph, which is literally, "the arms of his hands" (unless "of his hands" is a scribal slip, a dittography of the next word in the text). In any case, the idea is that the hands of the human warrior are given strength by God's hands.

through the name. Along with some of the ancient versions, the translation here reads *mishem* for the Masoretic *misham*, "from there," which is obscure.

25. *blessings of breasts and womb*. The fertility of the female body is aligned with the fertility of creation, the heavens above and the deep below—a correspondence not lost on the bawdy fourteenth-century Hebrew poet, Emanuel of Rome, who exploited this verse in an erotic poem.

26   Your father's blessings surpassed
            the blessings of timeless heights,
                the bounty of hills everlasting.
        May they rest on the head of Joseph,
            on the brow of the one set apart from his brothers.
27   Benjamin, ravening wolf,
            in the morn he consumes the spoils,
                at evening shares out plunder."

---

26. *the blessings of timeless heights, / the bounty of hills everlasting.* The Masoretic Text is not really intelligible at this point, and this English version follows the Septuagint for the first part of the verse, which has the double virtue of coherence and of resembling several similar parallel locutions elsewhere in biblical poetry. Instead of the Masoretic Text's *horai 'ad* ("my forebears [?] "until "[?]), the Septuagint has the equivalent in Greek of the idiomatic *harerei 'ad* ("timeless heights"). The noun *ta'awat* that immediately follows may also reflect a defective text, but it could mean "that which is desired," hence, "bounty" or "riches." The apparent sense of the whole line is: the blessings granted Joseph and his fathers will be even greater than the blessings manifested throughout time in the natural world, as seen in the verdant, fruit-bearing hillsides.

   the brow. The Hebrew is actually a poetic synonym for "head" (something like "pate"), but "brow" is used here for the sake of the English idiom of blessings, or honors, resting on that part of the anatomy.

27. *Benjamin, ravening wolf.* The last brief vignette of the poem, for the youngest of the twelve sons, is one of its sharpest images of death-dealing animals, and later biblical accounts, especially in Judges, indicate that the tribe of Benjamin was renowned for its martial prowess.

   the spoils. The rare noun *'ad* has been variously construed as "prey" (because of the wolf image) and "enemy," and the compactness of the line even leaves doubt as to whether it is a noun and not an adverb (revocalizing *'ad* as *'od,* "still"). But both its sole other occurrence in the Bible (Isaiah 33:23) and the poetic parallelism argue for the sense of spoils.

These are the tribes of Israel, twelve in all, and this is what their   28
father spoke to them, blessing them, each according to his blessing,
he blessed them. And he charged them and said to them, "I am about   29
to be gathered to my kinfolk. Bury me with my fathers in the cave that
is in the field of Ephron the Hittite, in the cave that is in the field of   30
Machpelah, which faces Mamre, in the land of Canaan, the field that
Abraham bought from Ephron the Hittite as a burial holding. There   31
they buried Abraham and Sarah his wife, there they buried Isaac and
Rebekah his wife, and there I buried Leah—the field and the cave   32
within it, bought from the Hittites." And Jacob finished charging his   33
sons, and he gathered his feet up into the bed, and he breathed his
last, and was gathered to his kinfolk.

---

29. *in the in the cave that is in the field of Ephron the Hittite.* Jacob in his last
words to his sons exhibits an elaborate consciousness of the legal transaction
between his grandfather and Ephron the Hittite. Like the account of the
purchase in chapter 25, he emphasizes the previous owner, the exact location
of the property, and the fact that it was acquired as a permanent holding.
Thus, at the end of Genesis, legal language is used to resume a great theme—
that Abraham's offspring are legitimately bound to the land God promised
them, and that the descent into Egypt is no more than a sojourn.

CHAPTER 50

A nd Joseph flung himself on his father's face and wept over him and
kissed him. And Joseph charged his servants the physicians to embalm
his father, and the physicians embalmed Israel. And forty full days
were taken for him, as such is the full time of embalming, and the
Egyptians keened for him seventy days. And the days for keening him

---

1. *And Joseph flung himself on his father's face and wept over him and kissed him.* These three gestures by now are strongly associated with Joseph's character. In the great recognition scene in chapter 45, he flings himself on Benjamin's neck, embraces and kisses him, and then does the same with his ten half brothers, and before this he has wept three times over the encounter with his brothers. Joseph is at once the intellectual, dispassionate interpreter of dreams and central economic planner, and the man of powerful spontaneous feeling. At his father's deathbed, he only weeps, he does not speak.

2. *his servants the physicians.* Although the Hebrew term means "healer," these are obviously experts in the intricate process of mummification, and the wording indicates that Joseph had such specialists on his personal staff. Mummification would be dictated by Jacob's status as father of the viceroy of Egypt and also by the practical necessity of carrying the body on the long trek to central Canaan.

3. *forty full days.* A Hebrew formulaic number is used rather than the number of days prescribed by Egyptian practice.
   seventy days. Evidently, the Egyptian period of mourning for a royal personage, seventy-two days, has been rounded off to the Hebrew formulaic seventy.

passed, and Joseph spoke to the household of Pharaoh, saying, "If, pray, I have found favor in your eyes, speak, pray, in Pharaoh's hearing, as follows: 'My father made me swear, saying, Look, I am about to die.   5 In the grave I readied me in the land of Canaan, there you must bury me.' And so, let me go up, pray, and bury my father and come back." And Pharaoh said, "Go up and bury your father as he made you swear."   6 And Joseph went up to bury his father, and all Pharaoh's servants, the   7

---

4. *Joseph spoke to the household of Pharaoh.* It is a little puzzling that Joseph, as Pharaoh's right-hand man, is compelled to approach him through intermediaries. Some commentators have explained this by invoking Joseph's condition as mourner, which, it is claimed, would prohibit him from coming directly into Pharaoh's presence. A more reliable key to his recourse to go-betweens may be provided by the language of imploring deference with which he introduces his message to Pharaoh—"If, pray, I have found favor in your eyes, speak, pray . . ." Joseph is aware that he is requesting something extraordinary in asking permission to go up to Canaan with his entire clan, for Pharaoh might be apprehensive that the real aim was repatriation, which would cost him his indispensable viceroy and a whole guild of valued shepherds. Joseph consequently decides to send his petition through the channel of Pharaoh's trusted courtiers, to whom he turns in deferential court language.

5. *In the grave I readied me.* The usual meaning of the Hebrew verb *karah* is "to dig," though it can also mean "to purchase." The latter sense is unlikely here because it would be confusing to use *karah* for buying a grave, when it is so naturally applied to digging the grave. But since the burial site in question is actually a cave, one must assume an extrapolation from the primary meaning of the verb to any preparation of a place for burial.

  and come back. This final verb is of course a crucial consideration for Pharaoh.

7. *and all Pharaoh's servants, the elders of his household, and all the elders of the land of Egypt, went up with him.* This vast entourage of Egyptian dignitaries betokens Pharaoh's desire to accord royal honors to Jacob. The presence of chariots and horsemen (verse 9) might also serve as protection against hostile Canaanites, but the whole grand Egyptian procession is surely an effective means for ensuring that Joseph and his father's clan will return to Egypt.

elders of his household, and all the elders of the land of Egypt, went

8 up with him, and all the household of Joseph, and his brothers, and
his father's household. Only their little ones and their flocks and their

9 cattle they left in the land of Goshen. And chariots and horsemen as

10 well went up with him, and the procession was very great. And they
came as far as Goren ha-Atad, which is across the Jordan, and there
they keened a great and heavy keening, and performed mourning rites

11 for his father seven days. And the Canaanite natives of the land saw
the mourning in Goren ha-Atad and they said, "This heavy mourning
is Egypt's." Therefore is its name called Abel-mizraim, which is across

12,13 the Jordan. And his sons did for him just as he charged them. And his
sons conveyed him to the land of Canaan and buried him in the cave
of the Machpelah field, the field Abraham had bought as a burial

14 holding from Ephron the Hittite, facing Mamre. And Joseph went
back to Egypt, he and his brothers and all who had gone up with him
to bury his father, after he had buried his father.

---

8. *Only the little ones.* The children and flocks are left behind as a guarantee
of the adults' return.

10. *Goren ha-Atad.* The place name means "threshing-floor of the bramble."
across the Jordan. The logical route from Egypt would be along the Medi-
terranean coast, which would necessitate construing this phrase from the
perspective of someone standing to the east of the Jordan. That, however, is
implausible because "across the Jordan" in biblical usage generally means just
what we mean by trans-Jordan in modern usage—the territory east of the
Jordan. Perhaps a circuitous route through the Sinai to the east and then
back across the Jordan is intended to prefigure the itinerary of the future
exodus and return to Canaan. Perhaps local traditions for the etiology of a
place name Abel-mizraim in trans-Jordan led to the intimation of this unlikely
route.

11. *Abel-mizraim.* This is construed in the folk etymology as "mourning of
Egypt," though '*abel* is actually a watercourse.

And Joseph's brothers saw that their father was dead, and they said, 15
"If Joseph bears resentment against us, he will surely pay us back for
all the evil we caused him." And they charged Joseph, saying, "Your 16
father left a charge before his death, saying, 'Thus shall you say to 17
Joseph, We beseech you, forgive, pray, the crime and the offense of
your brothers, for evil they have caused you. And so now, forgive, pray,
the crime of the servants of your father's God." And Joseph wept when
they spoke to him. And his brothers then came and flung themselves 18
before him and said, "Here we are, your slaves." And Joseph said, 19
"Fear not, for am I instead of God? While you meant evil toward me, 20

---

16. *And they charged Joseph.* The verb, which most commonly refers either to
giving instructions or delivering the terms of a last will and testament, is a
little peculiar. If the received text is reliable here, the choice of verb would
be influenced by the fact that the brothers are conveying to Joseph the terms
of what they claim (perhaps dubiously) is their father's "charge" before his
death. In any case, they send this message through an intermediary, for only
in verse 18 are they represented as coming before Joseph—"And his brothers
then *[gam]* came"—so perhaps the odd use of the verb indicates indirection
here.

17. *the servants of your father's God.* In the imploring language of their plea for
forgiveness, they conclude by calling themselves not his brothers but the
faithful servants of the God of Jacob. Rashi nicely observes, "If your father is
dead, his God exists, and they are his servants."

20. *While you meant evil toward me, God meant it for good.* This whole final
scene between Joseph and his brothers is a recapitulation, after Jacob's death,
of the recognition scene in Egypt. Once more the brothers feel guilt and fear.
Once more Joseph weeps because of them. Once more they offer to become
his slaves. (The physical act of prostration, as the early twentieth-century
German scholar Hermann Gunkel observes, carries us back full circle to
Joseph's two dreams at the beginning of the story.) And once more Joseph
assures them that it has been God's purpose all along to turn evil into good,
for the end of "keeping many people alive," with Joseph continuing in his role
as sustainer of the entire clan.

God meant it for good, so as to bring about at this very time keeping
21 many people alive. And so fear not. I will sustain you and your little
ones." And he comforted them and spoke to their hearts.

22 And Joseph dwelled in Egypt, he and his father's household, and
23 Joseph lived a hundred and ten years. And Joseph saw the third generation of sons from Ephraim, and the sons, as well, of Machir son of
24 Manasseh were born on Joseph's knees. And Joseph said to his brothers, "I am about to die, and God will surely single you out and take
you up from this land to the land He promised to Isaac and to Jacob."
25 And Joseph made the sons of Israel swear, saying, "When God indeed
26 singles you out, you shall take up my bones from this place." And
Joseph died, a hundred and ten years old, and they embalmed him
and he was put in a coffin in Egypt.

---

23. *were born on Joseph's knees.* This gesture serves either as a ritual of adoption or of legitimation.

24. *God will surely single you out and take you up from this land.* The ground
is laid at the end of Genesis for the great movement out of Egypt in Exodus.

25. *take up my bones.* Although Joseph knows that Egyptian science will turn
his body into a mummy, he still thinks of his remains in Hebrew terms as he
invokes his eventual restoration to the land of the Hebrews.

26. *a hundred and ten years.* This is a last Egyptian touch, since this is the
ideal Egyptian life span, as against 120 in the Hebrew tradition.
    and he was put in a coffin in Egypt. The book that began with an image of
God's breath moving across the vast expanses of the primordial deep to bring
the world and all life into being ends with this image of a body in a box, a
mummy in a coffin. (The Hebrews in Canaan appear not to have used coffins,
and the term occurs only here.) Out of the contraction of this moment of
mortuary enclosure, a new expansion, and new births, will follow. Exodus
begins with a proliferation of births, a pointed repetition of the primeval
blessing to be fruitful and multiply, and just as the survival of the flood was
represented as a second creation, the leader who is to forge the creation of
the nation will be borne on the water in a little box—not the *'aron,* "the
coffin," of the end of Genesis but the *tevah,* "the ark," that keeps Noah and
his seed alive.

REFERENCES

The following list is limited to modern authors referred to in the commentary or introduction. Comments cited from medieval and late-antique exegetes can be located at the relevant verse and chapter in their commentaries, most of which in any case are available only in Hebrew. Page references to the modern texts seemed superfluous because most are commentaries, where turning to the relevant verse and chapter will suffice. In the case of the occasionally cited book, a consultation of its index should quickly lead the reader to the comment on the verse in question.

Alvarez, A. *Night: Night Life, Night Language, Sleep, and Dreams.* New York: Norton, 1995.

Auerbach, Erich. *Mimesis: The Representation of Reality in Western Literature.* Princeton, N.J.: Princeton University Press, 1953.

Ben-David, Abba. *The Language of the Bible and the Language of the Sages* [Hebrew]. Tel Aviv: Dvir, 1967.

Cassuto, Umberto. *A Commentary on the Book of Genesis. Part One: From Adam to Noah.* Jerusalem: Magnes, 1972. *Part Two: From Noah to Abraham.* Jerusalem: Magnes, 1974.

Feliks, Yehuda. In *The World of the Bible Encyclopedia: Genesis* [Hebrew]. Tel Aviv: Revivim, 1982.

Fokkelman, J. P.:

"Genesis and Exodus." In *The Literary Guide to the Bible,* edited by Robert Alter and Frank Kermode, pp. 36–65. Cambridge, Mass.: Harvard University Press, 1987.

Narrative Art in Genesis. Assen and Amsterdam: Van Gorcum, 1975.

Fox, Everett. *The Five Books of Moses: A New Translation with Introductions, Commentary, and Notes.* New York: Schocken, 1995.

Friedman, Richard Elliott. *The Disappearance of God.* Boston: Little, Brown, 1995.

Funkenstein, Amos. *The Disenchantment of Knowledge.* (Forthcoming.)

Gunkel, Hermann. *Genesis.* Göttingen: Vanderhoek and Ruprecht, 1902.

Hammond, Gerald. "English Translations of the Bible." In *The Literary Guide to the Bible,* edited by Robert Alter and Frank Kermode, pp. 647–666. Cambridge, Mass.: Harvard University Press, 1987.

Marks, Herbert. "Biblical Naming and Poetic Etymology." *JBL* 114 / 1 (1995): 29–50.

Muffs, Yochanan. "Abraham the Noble Warrior." In *Love and Joy* by Yochanan Muffs. New York: Jewish Theological Seminary, 1992.

Sáenz-Badillos, Angel. *A History of the Hebrew Language.* Cambridge, Eng.: Cambridge University Press, 1993.

Sarna, Nahum. *The JPS Torah Commentary: Genesis.* Philadelphia: Jewish Publication Society, 1989.

Speiser, E. A. *The Anchor Bible: Genesis.* Garden City, N.Y.: Doubleday, 1964.

Sternberg, Meir:

"Double Cave, Double Talk: The Indirections of Biblical Dialogue." In *"Not in Heaven": Coherence and Complexity in Biblical Narrative,* edited by Jason C. Rosenblatt and Joseph C. Sitterson, Jr., pp. 28–57. Bloomington, Ind.: Indiana University Press, 1991.

The Poetics of Biblical Narrative. Bloomington, Ind.: Indiana University Press, 1985.

Von Rad, Gerhard. *Genesis.* London: S.C.M., 1972.

Weinfeld, Moshe. In *The World of the Bible Encyclopedia: Genesis* [Hebrew]. Tel Aviv: Revivim, 1982.

Westermann, Claus. *Genesis 1–38: A Commentary.* Minneapolis: Augsberg, 1984–1986.

INDEX

ambiguity *(continued)*
  in Lot's story, 55, 90
  in rape of Dinah, 191
  syntactic, 191, 227
Amnon, 90, 190
anachronism, 102, 114, 131, 189, 213, 282
"and" *(waw)*, xvii–xxi
angels, messengers of God:
  in binding of Isaac, 106
  of destruction, 77, 80
  Hagar addressed by, 100
  in Hager's flight, 69
  in Jacob's dreams, 167, 177, 178
  Jacob's nocturnal wrestling with, 181, 182
  Joseph's enslavement and, 211
  in Sodom story, 77, 80
animals:
  in Creation story, 4, 5
  in Flood story, 30, 35
annalistic narrative, 58
annunciation type-scenes, 155, 158
  of Abraham and Sarah, 78
  of Isaac and Rebekah, 126
anthropomorphism, 33, 36, 65, 69
antitheses, 47, 182, 183, 219
  between Abraham and Lot, 84, 87, 89
  in dreams, 210
  between Jacob and Isaac, 152
  in Joseph's story, 240, 270
aphrodisiacs, 160
Apocrypha, 24
Aramaic, 12, 15, 174, 266, 298
  Hebrew influenced by, xxiii
Aramaic Targums, 12, 17, 109, 168, 203, 243, 244
archaeology, x, 42, 55, 114, 148, 196
Armenia, 205
'arubot ("casements"), xxxvi
Asher, 159
  in Jacob's deathbed poem, 297
Auerbach, Erich, 103
'ayin, xiiin

Babel, Tower of, 42, 44, 45, 46–47, 81
baker, 229–33
Balaam story, 37
bargaining, 111, 112, 150

between Jacob and God, 179
between Jacob and Laban, 163–64
Beer-lahai-roi, 71, 123
Beer-sheba, 102, 134, 136, 273
Ben-ammi, 90
Ben-David, Abba, xxiii, 129
Benjamin, xxxii, 199, 209, 211, 276, 302
  and brothers' first journey to Egypt, 245, 247, 250, 251
  and brothers' second journey to Egypt, 252, 253, 254, 257, 263, 264, 265, 269, 271, 277
  in Jacob's deathbed poem, 300
  at Joseph's feast, 279
Bethel (Luz), 148, 150, 151, 166, 179, 194, 197, 198, 286
Bethuel, 120
betrothal type-scenes, 220
  conventions of, 153
  of Isaac and Rebekah, 114–23
  of Jacob and Rachel, 151–53
Bible:
  division of, 177
  fixing of text of, xxxvii
biblical Hebrew, *see* Hebrew, biblical
Bilhah, 200
birthright, 129, 136, 141
"blessing," 224
bowing, 184
brazier, 66
bread, unleavened, 85
brickmaking, 117
bride-price, 168, 191
Buber, Martin, xii, 177
burial caves, 109–12, 114

Cain, 16, 17, 18, 23
  etymology of, 16
  mark of, 18
camels, 116
  anachronism of, 114
"camp," 177, 185
Canaan (son of Ham), 40
Canaanites, 40, 46, 54, 84, 209
  cultic site of, 148
  myths of, 13, 15, 61, 188
"casements" *('arubot)*, xxxvi
Cassuto, Umberto, 32
characterization, 143

Philistines, 102, 131, 134, 135
philology x–xi, xviii, 198, 199, 205, 298
pillars, commemorative, 148, 150, 174–75, 198
"place," 148, 198
place-names, glossing of, 58
plagues, Abraham and, 52, 53
poetry, xxii, 17, 20, 97
  archaic nature of, xxxv
  diction of, xxxiv–xxxvi, 173
  insets of, xxxiv–xxxv, 20, 32, 34, 37, 98, 122, 215
  inversions in, xxxv
  Jacob's deathbed poem, xxxiv, xliv, 292–301
  naming, 9
  oracular, 126
  parallelism in, 17, 20, 35, 97, 172, 182, 295, 300
  rhythm of, xxxv–xxxvi
  vocabulary of, xxxv
point of view, 55, 89, 122, 151
political allegory, 143
postbiblical Hebrew, 12
Potiphar, 216, 224, 229, 241
  first words of, 228
Poti-phera, 241
prices, 111
Priestly (P) source, xxvii, xli, 72, 147
Primeval History, xliii–xlv
primogeniture, reversal of, 218, 287, 289
prison, 228–33
prolepsis (foreshadowing), 92, 100, 115, 134, 143, 146, 158, 171, 210–11, 282
pronunciation, xxxvii
property:
  purchase of, 188
  transfer rituals for, 57, 110–12
prophecy, 63, 80
Prophets, 80, 81
prostitution, 220–23
Psalms, 9, 12, 15, 80
P (Priestly) source, xxvii, xli, 72, 147
psychology:
  of Joseph and his brothers, 200, 246, 247, 262, 265
  of Lot, 87
  of Pharaoh, 234
  of Shechem, 190

puns, word play:
  "and he laughed," 75
  "And Jacob kissed Rachel," 152
  "built up through her," 67, 159
  "cunning," 11
  "did not remember Joseph," 233
  "Did you not know that a man like me would surely divine?," 262
  "from the prey, O my son, you mount," 295
  "Gad shall be goaded by raiders," 297
  "He who sheds human blood / by humans his blood shall be shed," 38
  "the human, humus," 8
  "Judah, you, shall your brothers acclaim," 294
  "laughing," 98
  "lift up your head," 231
  "a scurrilous thing in Israel," 190
  "steward," 63
  "that had white on it," 164
  "you'll no more prevail," 293
  see also etymologies

rabbinic Hebrew, xxiii–xxiv, 129
Rachel, 67, 200, 209, 247, 263, 264, 269, 281, 288
  barrenness of, 155
  death of, 199, 288
  first reported speech of, 158
  flight of Jacob with, 167, 170, 171–72
  household gods stolen by, 169, 171–72, 195, 261
  Jacob's meeting of, 151–53
  and Jacob's reunion with Esau, 184
  Joseph's dreams and, 211
  Leah's first dialogue with, 160, 189
  Leah substituted for, 154–55
  sons born to, 160–62, 198, 199
  sons born to slave of, 158–59
Rad, Gerhard von:
  on Abraham's story, 51
  on binding of Isaac, 103, 104
  on Hagar's story, 69
  on Jacob's blessing, 140
  on Jacob's negotiations with Laban, 172